MUSIC IN ANCIENT JUDAISM

To my wife Kate and our children
Andrew, Anthony, Richard, Helen, Julia and David

Music in Ancient Judaism and Early Christianity

JOHN ARTHUR SMITH

Routledge
Taylor & Francis Group

LONDON AND NEW YORK

First published 2011 by Ashgate Publishing

Published 2016 by Taylor & Francis
2 Park Square, Milton Park, Abingdon, Oxfordshire OX14 4RN
711 Third Avenue, New York, NY 10017, USA

First issued in paperback 2016

Routledge is an imprint of the Taylor & Francis Group, an informa business

British Library Cataloguing in Publication Data
Smith, John Arthur.
  Music in ancient Judaism and early Christianity.
  1. Jews–Music–History and criticism. 2. Church music–
  Mediterranean Region. 3. Music–Religious aspects–
  Judaism. 4. Music–Religious aspects–Christianity.
  5. Judaism–Mediterranean Region–History–To 70 A.D.
  6. Judaism–Mediterranean Region–History–Talmudic
  period, 10-425. 7. Christian life–Mediterranean Region–
  History–Early church, ca. 30-600. 8. Judaism–
  Relations–Christianity–History. 9. Christianity and
  other religions–Judaism–History.
  I. Title
  781.7'1'0091822-dc22

Library of Congress Cataloging-in-Publication Data
Smith, John Arthur, 1946-
  Music in ancient Judaism and early Christianity / John Arthur Smith.
     p. cm.
  Includes bibliographical references and index.
  ISBN 978-1-4094-0907-6 (hardcover)
  1. Music–Religious aspects–Judaism–History–To 500. 2. Music–Religious aspects–
Christianity–History–To 500. 3. Music in the Bible. I. Title.
  ML164.S65 2010
  781.7'600901–dc22

                                                                              2010032123

ISBN 13: 978-1-138-27393-1 (pbk)
ISBN 13: 978-1-4094-0907-6 (hbk)

Contents

List of Tables

List of Music Examples

List of Abbreviations and Short Titles

ABD	*The Anchor Bible Dictionary*, ed. Freedman et al.
ANET	*Ancient Near Eastern Texts Relating to the Old Testament*, ed. Pritchard.
b.	Talmud Bavli [the Babylonian Talmud].
BHS	*Biblia Hebraica Stuttgartensia*, eds Elliger, Rudolph et al. (see under 'Primary Sources: Bible')
Blackman, *Mishnayoth*	*Mishnayoth*, trans. and ed. Blackman (see under 'Primary Sources: Mishnah').
BS	*Biblia Sacra iuxta Vulgatam Versionem*, ed. Fischer et al. (see under 'Primary Sources: Bible')
CCSL	*Corpus Christianorum, Series Latina*.
CDSSE	*The Complete Dead Sea Scrolls in English*, trans. and ed. Vermes.
CSEL	*Corpus Scriptorum Ecclesiasticorum Latinorum*.
Danby, *Mishnah*	*The Mishnah Translated from the Hebrew with Introduction and Brief Explanatory Notes*, trans. and ed. Danby.
DANE	*Dictionary of the Ancient Near East*, ed. Bienkowski and Millard.
DSSE	*The Dead Sea Scrolls in English*, trans. and ed. Vermes.
Egeria, *Travels*	*Egeria's Travels*, trans. and ed. Wilkinson.
EJ	*Encyclopaedia Judaica*.
EMH	*Early Music History*, ed. Fenlon.
HCSB	*The HarperCollins Study Bible*, ed. Meeks et al.
IB	*The Interpreter's Bible*, ed. Butterick et al.
ISBE	*The International Standard Bible Encyclopedia*, ed. Bromiley et al.
JB	Jerusalem Bible.
JPS	Jewish Publication Society.
KJV	King James Version [of the Bible].
LCL	Loeb Classical Library.
LXX	Septuagint (see under 'Primary Sources: Bible').
m.	mishnah/mishnayoth (individual paragraphs of teaching in tractates of the Mishnah); where the names of tractates are abbreviated, the full versions are as follows: ʿArak. = ʿArakin

B. Bat. = Baba Batra
B. Meṣ. = Baba Meṣiʿa
Ber. = Berakot
Bik. = Bikkurim
Giṭ. = Giṭṭin
Ḥag. = Ḥagigah
Ketub. = Ketubbot
Maʿaś. Š. = Maʿaśer Šeni
Meg. = Megillah
Menaḥ. = Menaḥot
Mid. = Middot
Moʿed Qaṭ. = Moʿed Qaṭan
ʾOhal. = ʾOhalot
Pesaḥ. = Pesaḥim
Roš Haš. = Roš Haššanah
Šabb. = Šabbat
Sanh. = Sanhedrin
Šeqal. = Šeqalim
Taʿan. = Taʿanit
Ter. = Terumot

MAI	Sendrey, *Music in Ancient Israel*.
MAI/P	Braun, *Music in Ancient Israel/Palestine*.
MECL	*Music in Early Christian Literature*, ed. McKinnon.
MGG	*Die Musik in Geschichte und Gegenwart*, ed. Finscher et al.
M&L	*Music & Letters*.
MT	Masoretic Text.
NEAHL	*The New Encyclopedia of Archaeological Excavations in the Holy Land*, ed. Stern et al.
NEB	New English Bible with the Apocrypha.
Nestle–Aland	Nestle, Aland et al. (eds), *Novum testamentum graece* (see under 'Primary Sources: Bible').
Neusner, Mishnah	*The Mishnah: A New Translation*, ed. (and joint trans.) Neusner.
New Grove/1/2	*The New Grove Dictionary of Music and Musicians*, 1st/2nd edn, ed. Sadie.
NHLE/3	*The Nag Hammadi Library in English*, ed. Robinson, 3rd edn.
NHS	*The Nag Hammadi Scriptures*, ed. Meyer.
NIV	New International Version [of the Bible].
NJB	New Jerusalem Bible.
NPNF/1/2	*Nicene and Post-Nicene Fathers*, Series 1, ed. Schaff / Series 2, ed. Schaff and Wace.
NRSV	New Revised Standard Version [of the Bible].
NT	New Testament.

NTA	*New Testament Apocrypha* (rev. edn), ed. Schneemelcher.
OEANE	*The Oxford Encyclopedia of Archaeology in the Near East*, ed. Meyers.
OTP	*The Old Testament Pseudepigrapha*, ed. Charlesworth.
PG	*Patrologiae cursus completus, series graeca*, ed. Migne.
PL	*Patrologiae cursus completus, series latina*, ed. Migne.
PRMA	*Proceedings of the Royal Musical Association.*
PsIW	Mowinckel, *The Psalms in Israel's Worship.*
REB	Revised English Bible.
RSV	Revised Standard Version [of the Bible].
SC	*Sources chrétiennes.*
Schürer/Vermes et al., *History*	Schürer, *The History of the Jewish People in the Age of Jesus Christ*, trans., rev. and ed. Vermes et al.
t.	Tosefta.
Taft, *Hours*	Taft, *The Liturgy of the Hours in East and West.*
Tanakh	Torah, Nevi'im, Ketuvim [the Jewish Scriptures].
y.	Talmud Yerushalmi [the Jerusalem (*or* Palestinian) Talmud].

Foreword

Everyone who looks into the earliest history of Christian music, notably in its relation to ancient-Jewish and Second-Temple antecedents, soon encounters John Arthur Smith's unrivalled series of articles, beginning in the early 1980s. Models of intricate and exact scholarship, they also reflect the humane values of the great James McKinnon, the first scholar to recognize how much John could contribute to this field and a source of encouragement in the early days when he first began to publish.

The question of how the Jewish people used music in ancient times to worship their one God, and of what they bequeathed to Christianity in a rich context of Mediterranean cultic song, requires the most delicate judgement if any attempt at an answer is to carry conviction. The matter also demands imagination tempered by caution. The author of this book must often have prayed, with the psalmist: 'Hold up my goings in thy paths, that my footsteps slip not'. If so, it was well done, for this is indeed a fine and sure-footed study by an experienced traveller, acute in all things and yet kindly. So, 'to the chief musician', now at the end of a work that has occupied him for many years, and which has so much to offer so many, I wish satisfaction and contentment with what he has achieved.

Christopher Page
Cambridge

Preface

It will be evident from the title of this book and its list of contents that a considerable portion of the present work is devoted to music in ancient Judaism. Ancient Judaism is the period of Jewish history extending from the time of the return of the Jews from captivity in Babylonia (the exile) in 539/8 BCE to the close of antiquity. Nevertheless, many aspects of ancient Jewish music have antecedents in ancient Israelite traditions prior to the exile. In order to take account of these, the music of ancient Judaism is viewed here in an extended perspective reaching back to approximately 1,000 BCE. This is most clearly reflected in Chapter 2, which deals with music at the First Temple, and in Chapters 5 and 6, which consider musical traditions of both pre- and postexilic times.

The ancient Israelites, ancient Jews and early Christians had no concept of music as a liberal art. The concept was of course prevalent in ancient Greek culture and eventually became widespread in the eastern Mediterranean lands with the active Hellenization of the region from the mid-third century BCE onwards. However, ancient Hebrew has no word for 'music', and in the Greek used by ancient Jewish and early Christian writers the word *mousikē* (from which the modern word 'music' derives) always implies a combination of musical sound and one or more non-musical elements such as dance, drama or choral recitation. In the title of this book and in the following pages, 'music' is a term of convenience for all vocal and instrumental delivery at fixed pitches, ranging from semi-melodic chant to melodic song, from trumpet calls to plucked-string heterophony. The sound of percussion instruments is also included. Individual contexts make clear the nature of the music under discussion as the book progresses.

Christianity grew initially from within Judaism and thereafter developed alongside it. These historical circumstances, and the questions they inevitably raise about possible relationships between early Christian and ancient Jewish music, are the motivation for presenting surveys of the music of early Christianity and ancient Judaism alongside each other.

Given the historical circumstances of early Christianity in relation to ancient Judaism, there would seem to be a strong likelihood that the music of the earliest Christians owed something to the traditions of the parent culture. The extent to which this can be substantiated is examined in Chapter 9, after the surveys of music in ancient Judaism and early Christianity are complete.

The subject matter in the body of the book is divided into broad topics presented mostly chronologically. But the book is not a historical work in the sense that it traces lines of development. Its sources are discontinuous (especially those from the earliest periods), and the data they supply are often insufficient as grounds for firm conclusions about historical relationships. Nor is the book a musicological work in the conventional sense, since apart from a small amount of musical notation and technical musical information from ancient Syria and Mesopotamia, and a fragment of a Christian hymn preserved from third-century CE Egypt, there is no extant Semitic or Christian music to discuss. The main sources are therefore literary and archaeological. In many instances these are complementary.

The sole precursor of the present book is Eric Werner's two-volume *The Sacred Bridge*.[1] In its day it was a pioneering work exploring for the first time in extended format the common ground between Judaism and Christianity in late antiquity and the early Middle Ages. The first volume was soon superseded, however, and Werner's intention that the second should bring the research up to date was not fulfilled as far as the musical aspects were concerned. Thus both volumes are now seriously out of date.

There are several partial precursors, by which are meant writings that treat aspects of either ancient Jewish or early Christian liturgy and music, but not both together in the same context. Notable recent books include Edward Foley's *Foundations of Christian Music*, and Joachim Braun's *Music in Ancient Israel/Palestine* which, despite its title, is not about music generally, but about instruments and instrumental music, being based primarily on archaeological sources.[2] Braun is sceptical about the ability of written sources – especially biblical ones – to provide concrete information about music.[3] It is true that in written sources the musical information is sometimes difficult to interpret with certainty. But since a large amount of the music of Mediterranean antiquity with which the present book deals was vocal, and only written sources can inform us about vocal music, it is important to make the effort to understand what those sources say.

The last thirty to forty years have seen the publication of a large number of studies on limited topics both within the present field and in related areas such as biblical studies, ethnomusicology, history, language studies and liturgiology. Most have appeared as articles in academic journals, or as chapters in books

---

[1]   Eric Werner, *The Sacred Bridge*, 2 vols (New York, 1959, 1984).

[2]   Edward Foley, *Foundations of Christian Music: The Music of Pre-Constantinian Christianity* (Collegeville MN, 1996); Joachim Braun, *Music in Ancient Israel/Palestine: Archaeological, Written, and Comparative Sources*, trans. Douglas W. Stott (Grand Rapids MI, 2002). See also: William S. Smith, *Musical Aspects of the New Testament* (Amsterdam, 1962); Hans Seidel, *Musik in Altisrael: Untersuchungen zur Musikgeschichte und Musikpraxis Altisraels anhand biblischer und ausserbiblischer Texte* (Frankfurt, 1989); Suzanne Haïk-Vantoura, *The Music of the Bible Revealed: The Deciphering of a Millenary Notation*, ed. John Wheeler, trans. Dennis Weber, 2nd rev. edn (N. Richland Hills TX, 1991); Jeremy Montagu, *Musical Instruments of the Bible* (Lanham MD, 2002); Calvin R. Stapert, *A New Song for an Old World: Musical Thought in the Early Church* (Grand Rapids MI and Cambridge UK, 2007).

[3]   See my review in *M&L*, 85 (2004): 95–9.

with broader overall coverage. There have been some significant scholarly contributions, details of which are presented in the following chapters and in the Bibliography. Interesting and important though these studies and the partial precursors may be, they are limited to either ancient Judaism or early Christianity. Even though Edward Foley's book on music in Christianity before Constantine begins by considering music at the Jewish Temple and the synagogue, it does so in order to provide background to its main topic, and is selective in its choice of Jewish material. The time is therefore ripe for a fresh look at the music of ancient Judaism and early Christianity in a broad context embracing both religious cultures.

This book is not directly concerned with theology. Nevertheless it is written in full awareness that it has as its subject a significant element of the outward expression of religious belief. Respect for the religious traditions that underlie the topics selected for discussion is fundamental throughout. Readers unfamiliar with the ramifications of the basic religious attitudes and doctrines of Judaism and Christianity may find it helpful to consult Theodor Karp's article 'Interpreting Silence' which draws attention to the importance of taking due account of the underlying religious beliefs when discussing Jewish sacred music,[4] and Alister E. McGrath's book *Christian Theology: An Introduction* which provides authoritative summaries of Christian theology, doctrine and practice.[5]

It is sometimes the case that the traditional view of a given sacred concept, event or ritual, handed down to believers over many centuries, is at variance with the view presented by the bald evidence of the sources. There are examples in the present book. But such disparity does not have to mean that one view must exclude the other. Both the ability to believe what cannot be scientifically proved and the ability to reason purely by logic are part of the balance of opposites that go to make up human nature. If this be accepted, it should also be possible to accept that two different views of a concept, event or ritual – one a product of traditional belief, the other a product of scientific enquiry – can exist side by side in equilibrium. It is not part of the aim of this book either to de-mythologize traditional beliefs for which there is no scientific proof, or to preach.

Two books published in the 1990s argue that the biblical material dealing with the pre-exilic history of Israel and Judah is mostly propaganda from exilic and postexilic times, and has little factual or historical value for the times it purports to represent.[6] So extreme a position is not adopted here; but the fact that it can be entertained as a serious possibility by biblical scholars working independently

---

[4] Theodor Karp, 'Interpreting Silence: Liturgy, Singing, and Psalmody in the Early Synagogue', *Rivista internazionale di musica sacra*, 20/1 (1999): 47–109.

[5] Alister E. McGrath, *Christian Theology: An Introduction* (Oxford UK and Cambridge MA, 1994), pp. 14–23 (for the patristic period), pp. 205–477 (for Christian doctrine generally).

[6] Philip Davies, *In Search of 'Ancient Israel'* (Sheffield, 1992); Keith Whitelam, *The Invention of Ancient Israel: The Silencing of Palestinian History* (London, 1996).

is a warning to the rest of us that early texts cannot necessarily be taken at face value. Indeed, the written sources adduced in the present book are such that they do not always admit of concrete conclusions; in many cases likelihoods and probabilities are the closest we can come to certainties. Sometimes we can say only how things 'seem' to have been, or that it is 'possible' that matters were so and so. Nevertheless it is important to be true to the evidence, guarding against being more categorical than it permits, as well as against building unwarranted constructions out of too little of it. Any inconclusiveness there may be is then not a weakness, but rather a dual strength: on the one hand it bears witness to a sober respect for what the sources say, and on the other it is an open invitation to investigate the subject further.

Acknowledgements

The author and publisher are grateful for permission to reproduce the following copyright material in this book.

Quotations on pages 94, 128, 129, and 130 from *The Complete Dead Sea Scrolls in English* by Geza Vermes (Allen Lane, The Penguin Press, 1997), Copyright © G. Vermes, 1962, 1965, 1968, 1975, 1995, 1997. Reproduced by permission of Penguin Books Ltd.

Quotations from the works of Philo of Alexandria on pages 123, 124, 126 and 146: reprinted by permission of the publishers and Trustees of the Loeb Classical Library from *Philo: Volume IX*, Loeb Classical Library Volume 363, translated by F.H. Colson, Cambridge MA: Harvard University Press, Copyright © 1941, by the President and Fellows of Harvard College. Loeb Classical Library® is a registered trademark of the President and Fellows of Harvard College.

Quotations from the Apostolic Fathers on pages 171 and 176: reprinted by permission of the publishers and Trustees of the Loeb Classical Library from *The Apostolic Fathers: Volume I*, Loeb Classical Library Volume 24, edited and translated by Bart D. Ehrman, Cambridge MA: Harvard University Press, Copyright © 2003, by the President and Fellows of Harvard College. Loeb Classical Library® is a registered trademark of the President and Fellows of Harvard College.

Quotations from James McKinnon, *Music in Early Christian Literature*, 1987, © Cambridge University Press 1987, reproduced with permission.

Quotations from Jacob Neusner, *The Mishnah: A New Translation*, Yale University Press, Copyright © 1988 by Yale University.

Quotations from Robert Taft, *The Liturgy of the Hours in East and West*, Copyright © 1986, 1993 by the Order of Saint Benedict, Inc. Published by Liturgical Press, Collegeville MN 56321. Used with permission.

Thirteen brief quotes on pages 217–21 totalling 587 words from *The Nag Hammadi Scriptures* by Marvin Meyer and James M. Robinson, Copyright © 2007 by Marvin W. Meyer. Reprinted by permission of HarperCollins Publishers.

Quotations from John Wilkinson (trans. and ed.), *Egeria's Travels*, 3rd edn, Aris & Phillips, 1999. Reprinted with corrections 2002, 2006. © John Wilkinson. Used with permission.

Quotations from the Jewish Bible in English:

Reprinted from *Tanakh: The Holy Scriptures: The New JPS Translation According to the Traditional Hebrew Text*, © 1985 by The Jewish Publication Society, with the permission of the publisher. <http://www.jewishpub.org/product.php?terms=Tanakh>

Quotations from the Christian Bible in English:

I, as author, would like to add my personal gratitude to the many people whose help and advice have contributed to the writing and production of this book. I would like to mention in particular my wife Kate and our children whose good-humoured keen interest has been an immense support throughout. Kate in particular, at the same time as following a demanding and highly successful career of her own, has unselfishly seen to it that I have had the necessary time and space for work, has acted as unpaid reader and has fed me with wonderful meals.

During the past twelve years it has been my privilege to work alongside a large number of dedicated colleagues. I single out especially three clergymen, Dag Kaspersen, Jon Jørgensen and Per Auen Sveaas. Their intellectual acumen, spirituality, wisdom and commitment to practical theology have been a constant source of inspiration. These men have influenced my thinking more than they will ever know, and I am deeply grateful to be able to count them not only as colleagues but also as friends.

In 2007 Christopher Page, Vice-Master of Sidney Sussex College in the University of Cambridge, proposed me for a Visiting Fellowship at his College, which I took up in the Michaelmas term of 2008. I was thus able to avail myself of the unique facilities of the University and College libraries, to enjoy the company of other Fellows, and not least to discuss with Christopher Page, seemingly endlessly, topics of common interest. I am deeply indebted to Christopher Page, and I thank the Master and Fellows of Sidney Sussex College for electing me to the Visiting Fellowship. I am also grateful to Ivar Nygård, Chief Administrator of the churches in Drammen Deanery, for granting me three months' leave of absence from my regular work in order to take up that Visiting Fellowship, and to his predecessor, Per Ottar Johansen, for granting me two months' leave of absence in 2003 when this book was in an early stage of preparation.

Finally, I wish to thank the staff of Ashgate Publishing Ltd for publishing this book. My thanks go especially to Heidi Bishop (née May), Senior Commissioning Editor, Music Books, who has seen this project through from proposal to publication. I have greatly valued her encouragement and courteous efficiency at all stages of the process.

Chapter 1

Background

Historical Setting

The chronological span of the present book is marked at each end by a period of significant political and religious development.[1] The period with which the book opens is that of the establishment of Jerusalem as the religious and temporal capital of the Israelite nation. According to historical narratives in the Bible, this was accomplished by David and Solomon who, during their successive reigns as kings of Israel, made Jerusalem the royal seat and military capital of their kingdom and built the First Temple there as the dwelling-place for the Israelites' Deity.

The period with which the book closes is that of the emancipation of religion in the Roman Empire and the division of the Empire into two parts, Eastern and Western. The emancipation of religion was begun by the Emperors Licinius and Constantine when, in 313 CE, in Milan, they issued a joint edict giving their subjects freedom to practise the religion of their choice. As a result, the fourth century was a time of material and spiritual growth for both Judaism and Christianity.

After the catastrophic war between the Jews and the Romans in the first century CE, and its tragic aftermath in the late first and early second centuries, Judaism eventually began to prosper again. Roman emperors of the late second and third centuries adopted a fairly neutral attitude towards Judaism; the subsequent edict of Milan created a political and social climate in which Judaism could flourish, albeit within limits. By the mid-fourth century, Jewish communities in the Roman Empire enjoyed social and economic stability and a settled community life centred on the local synagogues.

Nevertheless, although the Jews were not persecuted, the spread of Judaism was constrained by legislation. Thus, despite freedom to own synagogues, to assemble and to worship, Jews were not allowed, for example, to purchase non-Jewish slaves, to circumcise non-Jewish slaves (on pain of death) or to convert Christian women to Judaism (also on pain of death). By the end of the fourth century, marriage between Jews and Christians was prohibited.

Constantine's policy of religious emancipation was particularly favourable to Christianity. The edict of Milan, in addition to giving religious freedom generally, stipulated that all people who had bought or appropriated places of worship from

---

[1] Cultural, historical and religious background in: Schürer/Vermes et al., *History*; J. Alberto Soggin, *An Introduction to the History of Israel and Judah*, trans. John Bowden (London, 1993); Michael D. Coogan (ed.), *The Oxford History of the Biblical World* (New York, 1999); the historical material in the Hebrew Bible, the LXX and the NT.

Christians (Christians having been forced to relinquish them during persecution earlier) were to return them to the Christians without requiring payment. In further legislation enacted in 313 and subsequent years, Constantine ordered the restitution of church property and made funds available to churches for the repair of material damage and for the copying of sacred books. For the first time since the mid-first century, Christians were free from the ever-present threat – and not infrequent reality – of persecution. From this time onwards Christianity was able to develop openly, unhindered by political censure.

The history that unfolds between these two periods provides the political and social background for the bulk of the present book. Solomon, like his father David before him, and Saul before that, was king of Israel. The kingdom consisted of a union of two parts: Israel itself in the north (embracing ten tribal groups) and Judah in the south (embracing two tribal groups). Already during Solomon's lifetime there was rivalry between Israel and Judah. When Solomon died *c.*926 or *c.*922 BCE,[2] he was succeeded by his son Rehoboam (926–910 or 922–915). Rehoboam was unable to hold the rivalry in check; Israel seceded from the union with Judah, taking a disaffected former official of Solomon, Jeroboam, as its king. This Jeroboam (Jeroboam I, 926–907 or 922–901) built up Shechem as the capital of Israel and set up temples at Bethel and Dan so that his subjects could be independent of Judah and its Temple at Jerusalem.

During the reign of Omri, king of Israel from *c.*873 to 869 (or 878–871), the city of Samaria became the capital of Israel. In 722 the city fell to the Assyrians after two years of siege. Israelite resistance continued, but in *c.*720 it was overwhelmed. Thousands of Israelites were deported into Assyrian exile and thousands of Assyrians were resettled in the territory that had been Israel. From that time Israel became a province of the Assyrian empire. With Israel no longer an entity, the period of the divided monarchy came to an end.

Judah was now in a vulnerable position. The inevitable disaster was held at bay for over a century longer, but even so the Assyrians deported many Judaeans during the reign of Manasseh (king of Judah from *c.*687 to 642). Manasseh's reign came to an end when he too was deported to Assyria.

The rise of the Babylonian empire in the last decade of the seventh century BCE was critical for Judah. In 605, king Jehoiakim of Judah (reigned *c.*609–598) became a vassal of Nebuchadnezzar II of Babylon (605–561) for three years. His revolt against the Babylonians in *c.*602 was unsuccessful and the Babylonians besieged Jerusalem for four years. Jehoiakim's son Jehoiachin succeeded him, but reigned for only three months. At the beginning of 597 he and other Judaeans were deported by

[2]   In matters of chronology I follow Soggin, *An Introduction*, pp. 394–417, supplemented by Coogan, *The Oxford History of the Biblical World*, pp. 597–601, except when stated otherwise. It is difficult to determine the chronology of events in ancient Israelite history. For a detailed discussion see H. Tadmor, 'The Chronology of the First Temple Period', in B. Mazar (ed.), *The World History of the Jewish People*, 4 vols (Jerusalem, 1979), vol. 4/1, pp. 44–60, 318–20 (repr. in Soggin, *An Introduction*, pp. 394–409).

Nebuchadnezzar who then put Zedekiah on the throne of Judah. Zedekiah reigned from 597 until 587/6. In 589 he rebelled against the Babylonians who responded by besieging Jerusalem yet again. On this occasion the siege had a violent outcome when in the summer of 587/6 Nebuchadnezzar's forces attacked and captured the city, reduced it and the Temple to ruins and deported large numbers of Judaeans to Babylonia where they remained exiled until c.539. Even though Judaeans had been deported to exile on earlier occasions, it is this exile from 587/6–539 that is referred to in Jewish history as 'the exile'.

From time to time during the pre-exilic period, apostasy threatened religious and political unity in Israel and Judah. Sometimes it was instigated by the monarchs themselves in order to win popular support. Typically they would build altars and shrines to various deities and set up images to be worshipped – on occasion even in the Temple itself, thereby profaning it. Apostasy was curtailed by religious reforms which aimed at destroying the pagan altars and shrines and purifying the Jerusalem Temple so that worship of the Deity could be resumed. Reforms on these lines were introduced in about 622 by Josiah, king of Judah from c.640/39 to 609 (2 Kgs 22:1–23:25; amplified parallel in 2 Chr. 34:1–35:19).[3] It is possible that Josiah's reforms were preceded a century earlier by similar but less far-reaching reforms introduced by Hezekiah (c.715–686 or c.728–700) at the beginning of his reign (2 Kgs 18:1–4), but the historical reliability of the biblical accounts of Hezekiah's reforms is very much in doubt.[4] Josiah's reforms were only partially successful,[5] but they nevertheless seem to have established (or perhaps re-established) the Jerusalem Temple as the central place for the worship of the Israelites' Deity.

Postexilic Near-Eastern history in antiquity may be subdivided into three main periods known by the names of the successive dominating political and cultural powers: the Persian, Hellenistic and Roman periods respectively.[6] The earliest of these was initiated when the armies of Cyrus, king of Persia, entered Babylon in 539. In 539/8 he issued his famous edict allowing the Judaean exiles to return to their homeland and rebuild their Temple. The foundations of the Second Temple were prepared in c.537; the Second Temple itself was built in the period c.520–516/15, during the reign of Darius I of Persia (522–486). Darius consolidated Cyrus's conquests by organizing the Persian Empire. Within it Syria and Palestine formed the fifth satrapy, Egypt the sixth. The period c.445–443 saw the restoration of the walls of Jerusalem under Nehemiah. In c.350 Judaea became a theocratic state.

In c.400, Egypt was able to free herself from Persian domination, but this freedom was short-lived, for in 332 Alexander the Great entered Egypt, having already captured Tyre and Gaza that year, and having conquered Syria the year before. This event marked the beginning of the Hellenistic period – the period

---

[3] See also Soggin, *An Introduction*, pp. 257–8.

[4] Ibid., pp. 246–9.

[5] Ibid., p. 258.

[6] For extensive background, see *The Cambridge History of Judaism*, various eds, 4 vols (Cambridge, 1984–2006).

of Greek political and cultural domination in the Near East – which lasted for nearly three hundred years. From *c.*250 onwards there was a programme of active Hellenization in the Holy Land. Sometimes this progressed harshly, as with Ptolemy IV Philopator (221–204) who, according to 3 Maccabees 3–5, became so incensed by the Jews' refusal to embrace Hellenism that he had large numbers of them rounded up and deported to Alexandria where they were subjected to extreme brutality and degradation. Chapter 5 of 3 Maccabees relates that on one occasion Ptolemy had a large number of them herded into the hippodrome where, for the delight of the spectators, they were trampled by hoards of elephants he had ordered to be maddened with wine and spices. The details of this story may be apocryphal, but they quite likely reflect the kind of harsh treatment the Jews received at the hands of this particular Ptolemy.[7]

From *c.*197–142 Judaea was subject to the Seleucids of Syria. Perhaps the most notorious of these was Antiochus IV Epiphanes (reigned 174–164). In 170 or 169 he invaded Egypt and had himself crowned king. On his return to the Holy Land in 167 he conducted a systematic persecution of the Jews, which lasted until 164. This 'Great Persecution', in which thousands of Jews were massacred, began with the abolition of Jewish practices, the pillaging of the Jerusalem Temple and the establishment of the cult of the Olympian Zeus at the Temple in place of the cult of the Deity of the Jews. The expected Jewish retaliation came in the form of a revolt begun in 166 by the Hasideans and the Hasmoneans (the priest Mattathias and his five sons, three of whom were Judas, Jonathan and Simon Maccabaeus, and their descendants). In 166 Mattathias died; from then onwards the army of Judas Maccabaeus and his brothers continued the revolt, winning many victories over Hellene forces and Hellenizers.

In 164 an agreement was reached between the Maccabees and Antiochus IV Epiphanes, which ended the hostilities and permitted the purification and rededication of the Temple and the resumption of Jewish sacrifices (this is traditionally regarded as the origin of the Jewish festival of Hanukkah, 'Dedication'). The Hasmoneans, however, continued to engage in skirmishes and guerrilla warfare against the Hellenist forces for many years, even after Judas Maccabaeus himself was killed in 160.

Shortly before his death, Judas Maccabaeus had negotiated an alliance with the Romans. Roman power had been increasing noticeably; the Jews reckoned that the Romans would be useful allies against the forces of Hellenization. The alliance was renewed in around 144 by Judas's successor Jonathan Maccabaeus, but it did not come to have any real importance until after the accession in 142 of Simon, Jonathan's brother and successor, and the fall of the Seleucid and Hellenist fortress in Jerusalem in 141. The Jews were now no longer subject to the Seleucids, and furthermore they had the support of Rome. Simon Maccabaeus and his descendents had religious, political and military control of Judaea, being to all intents and purposes temporal rulers as well as high priests.

---

[7]   *OTP*, vol. 2, p. 513.

In the years 66–62 BCE the Roman military general Pompey conquered the Levant. He occupied Jerusalem in 63. It is from this date that the Roman period in the western Near East is reckoned. Judaea was under Roman domination until 330 CE.

Herod the Great was king of Judaea from 37 BCE–4 CE. In 23/22 or 20/19 BCE he began the project that would bring him, Jerusalem and the Jewish people enormous prestige throughout the Mediterranean lands and the Near East, namely the substantial remodelling of the Second Temple.[8] The most important aspects of the work were completed within a decade, although the project as a whole was not completely finished until about 62 CE, during the reign of Herod Agrippa II (reigned 49–92 CE). The years while the work was in progress saw a string of important historical events, among which were the rise of the Pharisaic and Sadducean parties within Judaism, the transformation of Judaea into a Roman province (from 6 BCE), the life of Jesus of Nazareth (*c.*4 BCE–*c.*30 CE), the reigns of Herod Antipas (4–39 CE) and Herod Agrippa I (39–44 CE), Pontius Pilate's governorship of Judaea (26–36 CE), the rise of Christianity and a substantial portion of the reign of the emperor Nero (54–68 CE).

In 66 CE the uneasy tension which had developed between the Jews and the occupying Roman forces erupted into open revolt. This First Jewish Revolt in Judaea against Rome had tragic consequences. In 70 CE the Roman army, under the command of Titus, destroyed Jerusalem and the remodelled Temple. In the three years that followed, the Romans captured the Jewish rebel fortresses of Herodium (in 71), Machaerus (in 72) and Masada (in 73).

For the Jewish people the destruction of Jerusalem and the Temple was a catastrophe comparable only to that of 587/6 BCE. Now they were again deprived of their spiritual and temporal capital – the central focus of their religious and national identity – in a particularly brutal manner. Yet despite this and the continuing overbearing presence of the Romans in Judaea and Galilee, the Jews hoped for the restoration of Jerusalem, the Temple and the worship of their Deity there. History had shown that calamity even on this scale could be overcome. In 132 CE, a group of Jewish rebels under the leadership of Simeon bar Kokhba (also referred to in literature of the period as Bar Kosba or Bar Kosiba), staged a new revolt against the Roman occupying forces.[9] The revolt was at first successful, but in 135, after three and a half years of bitter fighting, it was suppressed by the Romans.

The Romans then followed up their victory over Bar Kokhba with measures designed to make it impossible for the Jews to regroup. Under the then emperor, Hadrian (117–138), a temple to Jupiter was erected on the site of the former

---

[8]   E.P. Sanders, *Judaism: Practice and Belief 63 BCE–66 CE* (London and Philadelphia PA, 1992), p. 57.

[9]   The details of the revolt of the Jews under Bar Kokhba, against the Romans, and the subsequent activities of the triumphant emperor Hadrian and their consequences for the Jews are related in Schürer/Vermes et al., *History*, vol. 1, pp. 543–57.

Jerusalem Temple of the Jews, Jerusalem was rebuilt as a Roman colony and Judaea was renamed Syria Palaestina. It also seems that Jews were banished from Jerusalem and that the city was resettled with a non-Jewish population. Jews fled from Judaea. Some settled in Galilee, but many fled further afield and settled in Babylonia and in other parts of the Roman Empire.

After harsh treatment at the hands of successive Roman emperors from Nero to Hadrian, the Jews were largely left in peace by subsequent emperors, although their social status was limited by legislation, as has been noted above. While they never gave up hope of the eventual restoration of Jerusalem and the Temple, they channelled their energies into reorganizing their religious, social and commercial life in the light of their new circumstances. Synagogues became increasingly important as local centres, not only for communal religious observance, but also for the education of children, the administration of justice and the practical administration of community affairs. During this time, Jewish society prospered materially and culturally. Many of the synagogues from the period are noteworthy for the richness of their decoration and the impressiveness of their architecture. The two centuries from 200 CE onwards saw the production of three monumental literary works that are landmarks in Jewish scholarship in late antiquity: the Mishnah, the Tosefta and the Jerusalem Talmud.

Against this background Christianity emerged from within Judaism. It spread rapidly from Judaea south and west into Egypt and other parts of North Africa, north and west into other countries round the Mediterranean and its associated seas, and north and east into Armenia and Syria. The earliest Christians were Jews, and Christianity became established first in places where there were settled Jewish communities. But the movement soon acquired adherents also from Greek, Roman and other non-Jewish milieux. As the movement grew it developed the systematized doctrine and organized administration of an independent religion. Christians suffered periodic persecution at the hands of several Roman emperors until, under the Emperor Constantine, Christianity became the official religion of the Roman empire.[10]

Ancient Texts

Transliteration of Greek, Hebrew and Aramaic

Ancient texts are quoted herein in modern English translations. But because translations sometimes do not reflect the nuances of the original languages, especially where terminology to do with music is concerned, salient words

---

[10] For extensive background, see *The Cambridge History of Christianity*, vol. 1, ed. Margaret M. Mitchell and Frances M. Young (Cambridge, 2006); Christopher Page, *The Christian West and its Singers: The First Thousand Years* (New Haven CT and London, 2010), pp. 9–171.

are presented in their original languages in romanized transliteration. Since this applies frequently in texts translated from Greek, Hebrew and Aramaic, transliteration tables are provided for these languages (Tables 1.1 and 1.2). The following points may be noted.

In the transliteration of Greek, the acute, grave and circumflex accents employed in many modern printed editions of ancient Greek texts are not represented, nor is subscript iota. Certain letter pairs have special transliterations.

Prior to the eighth century CE, Greek manuscripts were typically written in uncial script (upper-case letters) without breaks between words and without accents, breathings or punctuation.[11] In uncial texts, the letters that became subscripts in minuscule (lower-case) texts were written as upper-case letters alongside the others.

The system of transliteration used here for Hebrew and Aramaic is the scientific one currently recommended by the Society of Biblical Literature.[12] It is a detailed system in which each character stands uniquely for a Hebrew unit of sound and the Hebrew/Aramaic character, or combination of characters, which produces it. It thus functions as a cipher permitting reversal into the original script, while at the same time it is phonetic to the extent that it allows words to be read and pronounced approximately correctly by English speakers. This system is used primarily in passages that are the subject of close discussion. Common words and proper names which have acquired their own generally accepted simpler forms of transliteration (for example, 'Hallel' and 'shofar') are so rendered outside quotations in the original languages.

Transliteration of biblical and rabbinic texts in Hebrew and Aramaic is made from the best available modern critical editions. These are editions furnished with the pointing developed and refined by medieval Jewish biblical scholars, the Masoretes. Masoretic pointing distinguishes between spirant and stopped pronunciation of the six letters *bêt, gîmel, dālet, kāf, pê* and *tāw*, and between long, short, hurried and reduced pronunciation of vowels. However, there is no consensus among present-day linguists as to how far some of these distinctions operated in pre-Masoretic Hebrew and Aramaic.[13] This state of affairs is reflected

---

[11]   Ernst Würthwein, *The Text of the Old Testament: An Introduction to the Biblia Hebraica*, 2nd edn, trans. Erroll F. Rhodes (Grand Rapids MI, 1995), pp. 72–3.

[12]   As given under the heading 'Academic Style' in *The SBL* [Society of Biblical Literature] *Handbook of Style*, ed. Patrick H. Alexander et al. (Peabody MA, 1999, 5th pr. 2006), pp. 26–7, 29.

[13]   A succinct summary of the history of the Hebrew language is presented in Nahum M. Waldman, *The Recent Study of Hebrew: A Survey of the Literature with Selected Bibliography* (Cincinnati OH, and Winona Lake IN, 1989). For early Hebrew orthography, see David Noel Freedman, 'The Evolution of Hebrew Orthography', in David Noel Freedman, A. Dean Forbes and Francis I. Andersen, *Studies in Hebrew and Aramaic Orthography* (Winona Lake IN, 1992), pp. 3–15.

Table 1.1   Transliteration of Greek

Letter name	Greek script		Transliteration
	Lower case	Upper case	
Single letters			
psili	ʼ	ʼ	(not transliterated)
dasia	ʽ	ʽ	h
alpha	α	A	a
bēta	β	B	b
gamma	γ	Γ	g
delta	δ	Δ	d
epsilon	ε	E	e
zēta	ζ	Z	z
ēta	η	H	ē
thēta	θ	Θ	th
iōta	ι	I	i
kappa	κ	K	k
lambda	λ	Λ	l
mu	μ	M	m
nu	ν	N	n
xi	ξ	Ξ	x
omicron	o	O	o
pi	π	Π	p
rho	ρ	P	r
sigma	σ / ς*	Σ	s
tau	τ	T	t
upsilon	υ	Y	u
phi	φ	Φ	ph
chi	χ	X	ch
psi	ψ	Ψ	ps
ōmega	ω	Ω	ō
Special two-letter forms			
digamma	γγ	ΓΓ	ng
gamma-kappa	γκ	ΓΚ	nk
gamma-xi	γξ	ΓΞ	nx
gamma-chi	γχ	ΓΧ	nch

* Terminal form

Table 1.2   Transliteration of Hebrew and Aramaic

Name	Character	Transliteration	Approximate English pronunciation
Consonants			
ʾālep	א	ʾ	glottal stop
bêt	ב	b	light b
gîmel	ג	g	light g
dālet	ד	d	light d
hê	ה	h	h
wāw	ו	w	light v
zayin	ז	z	z
ḥêt	ח	ḥ	ch as in German *Buch*
ṭêt	ט	ṭ	t
yôd	י	y	y as in 'yes'
kāp	כ / ך	k	light k
lāmed	ל	l	l
mêm	מ / ם	m	m
nûn	נ / ן	n	n
sāmek	ס	s	s
ʿayin	ע	ʿ	guttural at back of throat
pê	פ / ף	p	light p
ṣādê	צ / ץ	ṣ	ts as in 'hats'
qôp	ק	q	k
rêš	ר	r	r as in French *rien*
śîn	שׂ *	ś	s
šîn	שׁ *	š	sh as in 'ship'
tāw	ת	t	light t
Vowels			
pataḥ / furtive pataḥ	ַ	a	a as in 'had'
qāmeṣ	ָ	ā	a as in 'father'
sĕgōl	ֶ	e	e as in 'bed'
ṣērê	ֵ	ē	e as 'ey' in 'they'
ṣērê yôd	ֵי	ê	e as 'ey' in 'they'
sĕgōl yôd	ֶי	ê	e as 'ey' in 'they'
ḥîreq	ִ	i	i as in 'lid'
ḥîreq yôd	ִי	î	long i as in French *sourir*
qāmeṣ ḥāṭûp	ָ	o	o as in 'hot'
ḥōlem	ֹ	ō	o as in 'only'
full ḥōlem	וֹ	ô	o as in 'only'
qibbûṣ	ֻ	u	u as in 'put'
šûreq	וּ	û	u as in 'flute'
ḥāṭēp qāmeṣ	ֳ	ŏ	hurried o as in 'monastic'
ḥāṭēp pataḥ	ֲ	ă	hurried a as in 'machine'
ḥāṭēp sĕgōl	ֱ	ĕ	hurried e as in 'decorum'
vocal šĕwāʾ	ְ	ĕ	short, indistinct vocalization as the second e in 'generate' or the a in 'ago'
Vowels: special combined forms			
final qāmeṣ hê	הָ	â	a as in 'father'
3rd person masc. sing. suffix	יָו	āyw	ah-yow (ow as in 'know')
	ֵי	êy	as ey in 'they'
	ֶי	êy	as ey in 'they'
	ִי	îy	long i as in French *sourir*

* Undotted *śîn* and *šîn* are transliterated *ś*.

in the scientific transliteration: spirant and stopped forms of the six consonants named above are not distinguished; the Masoretic vocalized *šĕwā'* (schwa) is not distinguished from the hurried 'e'.

Unpointed words are transliterated in lower-case letters, except for the name of the Deity, which is conventionally rendered in small capitals.

Most Hebrew and Aramaic words are formed from triliteral (occasionally bi- and quadriliteral) consonantal roots. Root forms of words are transliterated in capital letters.

Etymology, Linguistics and Related Matters

Etymology and linguistics are valuable aids to understanding ancient Semitic texts. They can help to elucidate the meaning of obscure terms and idioms, they can suggest alternative meanings worthy of consideration alongside those given in standard translations, and they can provide additional nuances for meanings already established.

But while etymology and linguistics can help to clarify meanings, they cannot supply the meanings themselves. Linguistics is concerned with the technical aspects of how language functions, rather than with meaning in the concrete sense. Etymology may be able to uncover meanings, but it is by and large a retrospective discipline; any meanings uncovered are likely to be historical and therefore possibly different from the contemporary sense of the terms under investigation. Even appeal to a contemporary related language (ancient Arabic and Aramaic are often used as etymological aids in the interpretation of difficult ancient Hebrew) can be fraught with difficulties where specialized terms and usages are concerned. To obtain contemporary meanings it is essential to examine how the pertinent terms are used in their literary contexts as well as to explore their etymological and linguistic aspects. Sometimes context and usage suggest meanings or senses that are at variance with those implied by etymology. In such instances it would clearly be mistaken to rely on etymology alone for enlightenment.[14]

Particular caution has to be exercised when making etymological or linguistic appeal to a language that is not contemporaneous with that of the text under discussion. Ugaritic, for example, which is frequently called upon for help in elucidating ancient Hebrew, had died out before even the oldest parts of the Bible had reached written form in classical Hebrew. Therefore it is impossible to be sure to what extent Ugaritic can contribute to an understanding of biblical Hebrew, especially in matters of contextual

---

[14]   The dangers inherent in 'etymologising' (the etymological investigation of terms in isolation) were pointed out many years ago by Bathja Bayer in her study, 'The Titles of the Psalms', *Yuval*, 4 (1982): 32–3, 54, 56–7; she wrote with particular reference to establishing the functional meaning of terms in the superscriptions to psalms in the MT of the Hebrew Bible.

meaning, even though Hebrew may ultimately be descended from Ugaritic. Generally speaking, the more recent an ancient Hebrew text, the less likely it is that an already extinct Semitic language can help to illuminate its obscurities. Therefore, in determining the sense of important but obscure terms, it will often be the case here that more attention is paid to usage and context than to linguistic background.[15]

Problems in the interpretation of ancient Greek are usually concerned more with orthography than etymology or linguistics. They arise from the way Greek was written in unbroken, unpunctuated uncial script, as described above. From the Middle Ages onwards, editions of the ancient texts separate the words graphically on the page according to traditions of meaning handed down through the centuries. Nevertheless there is no guarantee that all the separations occur at the originally intended places, and there are some ambiguities.

Sources

A great deal of pertinent source material is extant from the ancient Near East, but extracting meaningful information from it is not always a simple matter. An understanding of the chronology, provenance, genre and individual characteristics of the sources is essential for a proper evaluation of the musical data they contain. In practice, however, it is hardly ever possible to obtain as complete a profile of each source as might be desired.

The sources are of three types: literary, archaeological and musical. By 'musical' is meant not only musical notation but also literary material concerned with technical matters about music. The musical sources are very few. Pertinent archaeological sources, on the other hand are relatively numerous, originate from all over the Near East and cover most periods of antiquity. The most numerous sources are literary; they are also the most substantial. Thus they are the most important type of source for the present study.

General Remarks About the Literary Sources

The value of the literary sources, which are described below, lies not only in the musical information they provide – indeed some contain very little of it – but also in the insights they afford into the circumstances in which the music was performed.

Literary sources from so long ago present particular problems for the evaluation of musical data. One problematical area is dating; another is the meaning of musical and music-related terms. The precise dating of literary

---

[15]   On the use of etymology and linguistics in the interpretation of ancient Jewish and early Christian religious texts, see John F.A. Sawyer, *Sacred Languages and Sacred Texts* (London and New York, 1999), pp. 115–17.

material is often impossible. In antiquity, documents were disseminated through the work of copyists. It stands to reason that the date of an ancient copy may not be the date of the document's composition. It is also quite usual that a document, or portion of a document, can be said with confidence to belong to a certain period, but that its date of origin within that period cannot be established. In some cases dating is a matter of wide disagreement. Such vagaries are the result of factors inherent in the texts themselves and of the vicissitudes of textual transmission. The extant text may not be of homogeneous authorship and may therefore contain material from two or more different periods. A narrative text may have been written long after the period in which its narrative is set. Late texts may deliberately employ archaic words and expressions in order to give them an elderly flavour (archaizing). A text may have undergone several revisions over an extended period before it reached its extant form, assimilating and perhaps shedding material at each revision. It is therefore by no means always easy to decide to which period or periods any musical data contained in the sources relate. The datings given below are those of the present general consensus, but they should not be regarded as final except in the limited number of cases where precise datings are possible.

Musical and music-related terms and expressions are sometimes difficult to interpret clearly. Not only are some of them culturally foreign to many modern readers, but also their nuances and implications, as well as the traditions in which they belonged and which might have thrown some light on their meaning, have been lost during the course of time. In some instances it is clear that their meanings had become lost already at an early date. Corruption of the texts in the course of transmission by frequent copying has also added to the difficulties in some cases.[16]

Translations are by no means always reliable guides to the meaning of musical terminology. It is often the case with biblical literature, for example, that confusion in the original text is further confounded in translations. Some examples are presented at the end of this chapter.

Given that ancient Israel and Judah were culturally part of the ancient Near East generally, evidence in literary sources from areas outside Israel/Palestine, although concerned with peoples of different civilizations and ethnic groups, is not to be dismissed. It enables ancient Jewish and early Near-Eastern Christian culture to be viewed in a wider perspective, and illuminates points of contact between Near-Eastern civilizations of the past as well as features that are unique to ancient Jewish culture.

---

[16]   The main types of textual corruption are outlined in Würthwein, *The Text of the Old Testament*, pp. 107–12. Würthwein's remarks about text transmission are also relevant generally to other categories of ancient texts.

Ancient Israelite and Jewish Literary Sources

As far as ancient Jewish music is concerned, the literary sources consist of scriptural writings, the texts from the Judaean Desert (popularly known as the Dead Sea Scrolls), historical and philosophical works and rabbinic writings. Of these the scriptural writings are of fundamental importance since they span a broad period of time and provide the greatest amount of information. They vary considerably in age, provenance and type. This is an aspect of the scriptural writings to which authors of works on ancient Jewish music have generally paid little attention in the past, therefore some space will be devoted here to placing these sources in their chronological, historical and literary contexts.

Paramount among the Scriptural writings are the books of the Hebrew Bible. These are extant in editions based on those of the early medieval Jewish Masoretes, as explained earlier. The Masoretic Text (MT) is the basis of modern printed editions of the Hebrew Bible. The designation 'Hebrew Bible' is used for convenience to mean the Jewish Bible in its original language, although it also contains four passages in Aramaic (Jer. 10:11; Dan. 2:4–7:28; Ezra 4:8–6:18; Ezra 7:12–26).[17]

The tripartite division of the Hebrew Bible into Torah, Prophets and Writings has been known since at least the middle of the second century BCE and certainly since the first century CE by which time the canon of books as it is known today is likely to have been settled.[18] The dates of composition of individual books, on the other hand, are quite a different matter. Many books are not of homogeneous authorship, and many others are formed from a number of different historical or literary traditions. In addition, many books have undergone redaction at several stages of their literary history so that it is often impossible to come to more than general conclusions about dating. In the present context, dating is perhaps best approached by considering the books in groups.

All the points mentioned in the previous paragraph apply to a greater or lesser extent to the books of the Torah and the Former Prophets. The first four books of the Torah make extensive use of three sources known to biblical criticism as 'J' (Jahwist), dating from the ninth or tenth century BCE, 'E' (Elohist), dating from the eighth century BCE, and 'P' (Priestly), dating from the sixth century BCE after the return of the Jews from exile in Babylonia (587/6–539 BCE). Leviticus relies mostly on two strata of P and two strata of a source known as 'H' (the Holiness code). The books in this group had thus reached something approaching their present form by the sixth century BCE although they inevitably contain a considerable quantity of older material some of which stretches back to the tenth century BCE and beyond.

---

[17] In addition, the place name in Gen. 31:47 is given in Aramaic (the language of Laban) as well as Hebrew.

[18] On the formation of the canon of the Hebrew Bible, see Schürer/Vermes et al., *History*, vol. 2, pp. 316–21.

The group of books known as the Former Prophets (Joshua, Judges, 1 & 2 Samuel and 1 & 2 Kings) consists of works of history rather than of prophecy. These books are generally regarded as the products of a process in which Israel's ancient historical tradition was edited and brought up to date during the period of exile following the destruction of Jerusalem by the Babylonians in 587/6 BCE. The main redactional activity began in the wake of the reforms of Josiah, king of Judah from c.640 to 609 BCE. Since the main purpose of the editing seems to have been to bring the traditions into conformity with the view of history and theology expressed in the book of Deuteronomy, the Former Prophets are also known collectively as the Deuteronomistic History.

As for the book of Deuteronomy itself, it is reckoned to have been composed in the period between the fall of Samaria in 722 BCE and the beginning of the restoration of Judah (c.535 BCE) after the exile in Babylonia. Theologically and literarily it occupies a pivotal position between the Torah and the Deuteronomistic History.

The books that consist of actual prophetic oracles – Isaiah, Jeremiah, Ezekiel (the Latter Prophets) and the twelve Minor Prophets – span a broad period stretching from the eighth to the fifth century BCE. The book of Isaiah is a composite work falling into three distinct divisions known as 'First', 'Second' and 'Third' Isaiah respectively. Chapters 1–39 constitute First Isaiah and date from the last four decades of the eighth century BCE (the oracles in chapters 24–27, however, are probably from the early sixth century or later). Chapters 40–55, Second Isaiah, date from the sixth century BCE and are exilic, probably written in Babylon. The final eleven chapters (56–66, Third Isaiah) are immediately postexilic, from the time before the completion of the rebuilding of the Second Temple in 520–515 BCE.

The books of Jeremiah and Ezekiel cover the period 627–571 BCE (the troubled time leading up to and overlapping with the beginning of the exile). Whereas Jeremiah's prophetic career began in 627 BCE and concluded in 587 as the exile began, Ezekiel's seems to have been spent entirely in exile whither he was deported in 597 BCE.

The 12 books of the Minor Prophets (in Jewish tradition all 12 are reckoned together as one book) are short compared with those of the Latter Prophets. Details may be noted about three of them. With regard to the book of Joel, there seems to be no consensus about a date. Opinions vary from the ninth to the fourth century BCE, although the latter half of this span is the current consensus. The book of Habakkuk is usually dated to the last quarter of the seventh century BCE and the first decade of the sixth, that is during the period prior to the destruction of Jerusalem and the main deportation into exile, but including the first wave of deportations in 597 BCE. The third (last) chapter of Habakkuk, however, has been dated to the eleventh century BCE.[19] The book of Zechariah falls into two sections

---

[19]   Wilfred G.E. Watson, *Classical Hebrew Poetry: A Guide to its Techniques* (Sheffield, 1984), p. 40.

of different date. 'First' Zechariah (chapters 1–8) is thought to date from 520–518 BCE, that is after the Jews' return from exile but before the rebuilding work on the Temple was completed. 'Second' Zechariah (chapters 9–14) is not homogeneous and is difficult to date, but is postexilic, perhaps from the late fifth century BCE.

Bearing these points in mind, the following general chronology emerges for the books of the Latter Prophets and the 12 Minor Prophets:

Pre-exilic (in chronological order as far as can be ascertained):
Amos; First Isaiah; Micah; Hosea; Zephaniah; Nahum; Habakkuk; Jeremiah
Exilic:
Ezekiel; Second Isaiah; Obadiah(?)
Postexilic (in chronological order as far as can be ascertained):
Haggai; Third Isaiah; Jonah(?); Zechariah; Malachi; Joel(?)

In contrast to the Torah and the Prophets, the Writings evince a wide variety of types of literature. There are four basic types: poetry, wisdom literature, narratives with a moral message and historical works. The books of poetry are Psalms, Song of Songs and Lamentations. Psalms is a collection of 150 religious poems from the time of David (*c*.1000 BCE) or earlier to probably as late as the fourth century BCE. If the latter date is correct, Psalms as a book cannot be earlier than *c*.400 BCE. Psalms is an important source of musical information.

Lamentations is possibly exilic, composed by one or more individuals left behind in Judaea at the time of the great deportation of Jews to Babylonia. Its traditional attribution to Jeremiah has no historical basis.

On linguistic grounds the Song of Songs has been dated to the fourth or third century BCE. The linguistic evidence could be the result of editing at that time, however, and is not necessarily a sure pointer to the date of composition. Dates from the time of Solomon (mid-tenth century BCE) to the third or even second century BCE have been proposed. The attribution to Solomon in the opening verse is honorific although the book does contain elements from very ancient times. The Song of Songs is unique in the Hebrew Bible in that it consists entirely of secular love poetry. However, traditional Jewish and Christian interpretations see it as one or other form of religious allegory.

The wisdom literature consists of Job, Proverbs and Ecclesiastes. The book of Job cannot be dated precisely but is probably postexilic from the late sixth or early fifth century BCE, although its literary setting is the time of the patriarchs or earlier.

Proverbs is thought to be immediately postexilic, having received its final redaction in the late sixth century BCE. It is a collection of 'wise' sayings. The traditional ascription to Solomon is honorific; it is highly likely that many of the sayings originated as 'folk wisdom' long before the sixth century BCE; it is possible that some originated with Solomon.

Ecclesiastes is thought by most scholars to be the youngest of the three books of wisdom literature, dating probably from the third century BCE.

The narrative books in the Writings are Ruth, Esther and Daniel. None of these have precise datings, but Ruth is generally regarded as by far the oldest, originating perhaps between 950 and 700 BCE. The book of Ruth contains no musical information.

Esther and Daniel are reckoned to be postexilic. The first six chapters of Daniel stem probably from the fourth or third century BCE; the whole book was completed possibly by about 200 BCE. Daniel is an apocalypse, a book of visionary revelations. The book of Esther may originate from just prior to the middle of the second century BCE. It is a story of intrigue and conflict at a foreign (Persian) court and also an aetiology for the celebration of the Jewish festival of Purim (Lots), which has no mention in the Torah. The book does not contain any material of musical interest.

Finally, the historical books among the Writings are Ezra–Nehemiah and Chronicles. In the original form of the Hebrew Bible, Ezra and Nehemiah are one book and 1 & 2 Chronicles are one book, hence the form in which they are named at the beginning of this paragraph. However, in printed editions of the Hebrew Bible from the fifteenth century CE onwards, it has been customary to present them as four separate books: Ezra, Nehemiah, 1 Chronicles and 2 Chronicles. They are presented thus in the standard translations and will therefore normally be cited thus here, although it will be appropriate to refer to them in the form of their original textual units from time to time. In manuscripts of the LXX (see below), 1 & 2 Chronicles are separate books.

Ezra–Nehemiah and Chronicles originated most probably among the clergy of the Second Temple in the fourth century BCE. They are basically concerned with certain aspects of the two historical periods either side of the exile. Chronicles traces the history of the Davidic monarchy from the time of David to the exile. It is a somewhat selective history that shows David and his lineage in a good light. Ezra–Nehemiah continues with the history of Judah after the exile. Both Chronicles and Ezra–Nehemiah display particular interest in the physical attributes of the Jerusalem Temple (in Chronicles, the First Temple; in Ezra–Nehemiah, the Second Temple) and in the regulation of the worship there, including the appointment of Temple musicians and the assignment of their duties. The wealth of musical references make these books central texts for information about ritual and liturgical music in connection with cultic worship. Exactly how much light Chronicles is able to throw on the music of the First Temple, however, is debatable. The musical references in Chronicles, although ostensibly concerned with the First Temple and its cultic precursor, probably reflect to a large extent Second Temple practice, given that Chronicles was written in the fourth century BCE. This matter will be taken up later.

The edition of the Hebrew Bible cited in the present book is the standard critical edition of the MT published as *BHS*. The frequent quotations from the Hebrew Bible in English in the present book are from the second edition of the English translation published by the Jewish Publication Society (JPS) in 1985, cited as the 'JPS *Tanakh*'. Comparison is frequently made with the translation in the New Revised Standard Version (NRSV) Old Testament.

During the last three centuries BCE, the Hebrew Scriptures were translated into Greek. This Greek Version of the Hebrew Bible came to be known subsequently as the Septuagint (LXX). According to a report in the Letter of Aristeas (*c.*170 BCE),[20] the translation was made in Alexandria on the orders of Ptolemy II of Egypt (285–247 BCE). A Greek translation of the Torah may thus have existed in Alexandria as early as the middle of the third century BCE.

Judging from the Prologue to the LXX book Sirach, it would seem that by about 130 BCE 'the law (Greek: *nomou*), the prophets and the other books of our [the Jews'] fathers' were known in Greek. It is generally assumed that 'the law' here refers to the Torah and that 'the other books of our fathers' refers to the Writings. Probably by the turn of the Common Era the material constituting what in Christendom came to be known as the Apocrypha and Deuterocanonical Books had been added and the LXX was in general use in Greek-speaking Jewish communities in the Diaspora and the land of Israel.

The subsequent history of the LXX text is complex. The earliest substantial manuscripts of the LXX are the Codex Sinaiticus and the Codex Vaticanus, both of which date from the fourth century CE, and the Codex Alexandrinus which dates from between the late fourth and the sixth centuries CE. In the third century CE the church father Origen of Alexandria (185–254 CE) produced his *Hexapla* and *Tetrapla* which include his recension of the LXX.[21] Independent Greek versions of the Jewish Scriptures, or some of them, were made by the church fathers Aquila, Symmachus and Theodotion in the second century CE.[22]

The order of books is different in the LXX compared with the MT; some of the books in the LXX also have different chapter and verse divisions from their MT (Hebrew) versions.[23] Details will be provided where it is necessary to cite parallel passages that have different references in the LXX compared with the MT.

There are several modern critical editions of the LXX available. The one cited in the present book is that of Alfred Rahlfs (1935). Despite its age it is still the

[20]   Letter of Aristeas, verses 46–50. For an introduction to, and annotated English translation (by R.J.H. Shutt) of the Letter of Aristeas, see *OTP*, vol. 2, pp. 7–34.

[21]   For fuller details about the history of the transmission of the LXX text, see: John Arthur Smith, 'Concordances for Singing Terms Common to the Septuagint and the Greek New Testament', *Royal Musical Association Research Chronicle*, 28 (1995 [1996]): 1, and the works listed there on p. 19, n. 6; Würthwein, *The Text of the Old Testament*, pp. 48–78; Gerard J. Norton, 'Ancient Versions and Textual Transmission of the Old Testament', in J.W. Rogerson and Judith M. Lieu (eds), *The Oxford Handbook of Biblical Studies* (New York, 2006), pp. 224–6. The following should be added to the list of recent modern-language LXX translations and commentaries given on p. 226 of the last work cited: Albert Pietersma and Benjamin G. Wright (trans. and eds), *A New English Translation of the Septuagint* (New York, 2007).

[22]   On Theodotion's Greek version of the Jewish Scriptures, with particular reference to its transcription from the Hebrew, see M. Pazzini, 'La trascrizione dell'ebraico nella versione di Teodozione', *Studium biblicum franciscanum*, 41 (1991): 201–22.

[23]   See the table in Alexander et al., *The SBL Handbook of Style*, pp. 173–6.

most widely used and most readily available modern edition. An authoritative English translation of the LXX by Albert Pietersma and Benjamin G. Wright was published in 2007 (see n. 21).

The importance of the LXX in the present context is twofold. First, it represents a version of the books of the canonical Jewish Scriptures which pre-dates the Hebrew MT. Making due allowance for errors that may have occurred during the transmission of the text, the LXX can be a valuable aid in the critical evaluation of the MT, although textual priority by no means always belongs to the LXX.

The LXX is important also because it contains Jewish material that is additional to the books of the canonical Jewish Scriptures, thereby increasing the number of potential sources of contemporary data about music. The additional material falls into two categories: (a) additions to canonical books of the Jewish Scriptures and (b) books and other self-contained literary items. Category (a) consists of an addition to Psalms (Psalm 151), additions to Esther (which contain nothing of musical interest) and additions to Daniel (Susanna; the Prayer of Azariah and the Song of the Three Young Men; Bel and the Dragon). Of the additions to Daniel, the episodes about Susanna and Bel and the Dragon contain nothing of musical interest, in contrast to the introduction to the Prayer of Azariah and the text of the Song of the Three Young Men. The two last-named items were inserted into the book of Daniel probably in the second or first century BCE. Whether they had an independent existence before that time is not known. The additional psalm, Psalm 151, is a translation from a Hebrew original dating perhaps from the Hellenistic period. The translation into Greek was probably in existence by the beginning of the second century CE.

Of the items that comprise category (b), Baruch and the Letter of Jeremiah contain nothing of musical interest. However, nine books and a collection of psalms do contain relevant matter: 1 Esdras; Judith; Tobit; 1, 2, 3 & 4 Maccabees; the Wisdom of Solomon; Sirach; and the *Psalms of Solomon*. The composition of these items as a whole occupied a period from roughly early Hellenistic to early Roman times, with the majority of the items having come into being during the last two centuries BCE. The earliest and latest items are the books of Tobit (reckoned to have been written in the fourth or third century BCE) and 4 Maccabees (written probably during the mid-first and early second century CE) respectively. The majority of the extra-canonical material in the LXX thus forms part of the considerable body of postbiblical Jewish scriptural literature.

A third early translation of the Hebrew Bible which is also an instructive source is the Old Testament of the Vulgate, the late fourth- to early fifth-century CE Latin translation of the Jewish Scriptures (from the Hebrew and Greek) and the Christian Scriptures (from the Greek). Although the Vulgate translation is popularly attributed to the church father Jerome (341–420 CE), it is in fact a collection of translations from different times and traditions. Jerome himself was certainly responsible for translating most of the Jewish Scriptures and for assembling pre-existent Latin translations. The book of Psalms in the Vulgate is an Old-Latin version corrected by Jerome to agree with the Greek version by

Origen. Jerome made a translation of Psalms from the Hebrew, but it did not gain widespread acceptance and was subsequently ousted by his corrected Old-Latin version, which was already familiar from long use. Modern critical editions of the Vulgate generally print Jerome's translation of Psalms from the Hebrew (the *Psalterium iuxta Hebraeos* 'Psalter according to the Hebrews') alongside the standard Vulgate Psalter text (the *Psalterium Gallicanum* 'Gallican Psalter', so called because of its currency in Gaul). The Vulgate is cited herein according to BS.[24]

There is a large body of non-canonical apocryphal and pseudepigraphical literature associated with the Jewish Scriptures.[25] All the relevant apocrypha and some of the pseudepigrapha (the *Psalms of Solomon* and 3 & 4 Maccabees) are included among the extracanonical books in the LXX. The relevant pseudepigrapha which are not will be explained as they are encountered below. English translations of the apocrypha are available as Old Testament Apocrypha in most of the modern Christian English-language editions of the Bible. In the present book, the apocrypha in English will be cited according to the NRSV Apocrypha, which contains all the recognized apocryphal literature. English translations of the pseudepigrapha are conveniently available in the two volumes of *OTP*. There is some overlapping between the NRSV Apocrypha and *OTP*. References to critical editions of individual texts will be provided as the texts are dealt with in the course of subsequent chapters.

To conclude this survey, and for the sake of providing a rounded picture, it is important to mention that the New Testament, though Christian in purpose, is also a relevant source of information about ancient Jewish musical practice. Modern editions will be discussed below in the section dealing with the early Christian primary sources.

A body of source literature closely related to the canonical Hebrew Scriptures and their non-canonical apocrypha and pseudepigrapha is the large quantity of texts from the Judaean Desert, discovered from 1947 onwards at 13 sites in and near Qumran on the north-western shore of the Dead Sea, and popularly known as the Dead Sea Scrolls. The majority of the discoveries have been made in caves in the area where the documents are thought to have been deposited by the members of the religious community that used them (the Qumran community – probably a community of Essenes) which flourished there between c.150 BCE and 68 CE.[26] The extant literature is in several languages (predominantly Hebrew, Aramaic and Greek) and exemplifies a wide variety of types including copies and translations of

---

[24] On the composition of the Vulgate, see BS, pp. xx–xxi.

[25] For the significance and scope of the adjectives 'apocryphal' and 'pseudepigraphical' as applied to the non-canonical literature of the Jewish Scriptures and the deuterocanonical literature associated with the Old Testament, see Artur Weiser, *Introduction to the Old Testament*, trans. Dorothea M. Barton (London, 1961), pp. 331–47; *OTP*, vol. 1, pp. xxi–xxix; Schürer/Vermes et al., *History*, vol. 2, pp. 348–55, vol. 3/1, pp. 177–83.

[26] *CDSSE*, pp. 58–60.

canonical and non-canonical books of Jewish Scripture, Scripture commentaries, apocalyptic works, regulations for the Qumran community and unique hymn and psalm texts. Of particular interest here are the documents which in *CDSSE* are called *The Community Rule* (1QS), *The Thanksgiving Hymns* (1QH), *The Psalms Scroll* (11QPsᵃ), *The Temple Scroll* (11QTS), *Songs for the Holocaust of the Sabbath* (4QShirShabaʰ) and *The War Rule* (1QM).[27] The first work listed is concerned with instruction and with the precepts and statutes of the Qumran community; it concludes with an extended poetic section. The second consists of approximately 25 psalm-like religious poems of thanksgiving, some containing musical references. The *Psalms Scroll* from Cave 11 contains several canonical psalms together with non-canonical psalm-like religious poems. Column XXVII of the Scroll contains an exaggerated account of the number of David's compositions. The *Temple Scroll* deals mostly with the Temple building and its furniture and worship. It often parallels the Torah but also contains regulations that are not biblical. The document called *Songs for the Holocaust of the Sabbath* is concerned with heavenly worship and consists of praises purportedly sung by angels to the Deity.

Of the documents excavated from the ruins of the Zealot fortress of Masada, overrun by the Roman army in 73 CE, the Ben Sira Scroll in Hebrew is perhaps the most significant single find.[28] Several fragments from Masada are translated in *CDSSE*.

Valuable additional sources for the postbiblical period are the writings of the Jewish philosopher Philo of Alexandria (c.15 BCE–c.50 CE)[29] and the Jewish historian Flavius Josephus (37 or 38 CE–c.100 CE).[30] Four works of Philo are important: *That Every Good Person is Free*, *On the Contemplative Life*, *Against Flaccus* and *Hypothetica*. The first two contain descriptions of Jewish religious communities, the Essenes and the Therapeutai respectively. *Against Flaccus* is part of a history of the persecution of Jews in Alexandria; *Hypothetica* is an apologetic work.[31]

Two works of Josephus are of outstanding importance: *Jewish War* and *Jewish Antiquities*. The first, completed c.79 CE, is in seven books and is about Jerusalem in the period 175 BCE–70 CE. The second, in 20 books, completed in 93 or 94 CE, is a history of the Jewish people from earliest times to the outbreak of the war with

---

[27] The sigla identify the site of discovery ('Q' = Qumran), give the number under which the item is catalogued and provide an abbreviated indication of content. Comprehensive lists of the texts from the Judaean Desert catalogued up to 2006, together with details of critical editions and translations, are provided variously in *CDSSE*, pp. 601–19 [Appendix], and Alexander et al., *The SBL Handbook of Style*, pp. 177–234 [Appendix F]. The document names are now standardized (see Alexander et al., *The SBL Handbook of Style*, pp. 76–7) and may in some cases differ slightly from those in *CDSSE*.

[28] Schürer/Vermes et al., *History*, vol. 1, pp. 118–19, 122, 511–12.

[29] On Philo's life, works and philosophical thought, see ibid., vol. 3, pp. 809–89.

[30] On Josephus's life and works, see ibid., vol. 1, pp. 43–63.

[31] Further on these works, see ibid., vol. 3, pp. 856–68. Flaccus (A. Avillius Flaccus) was Roman governor of Egypt from 32 to 38 CE: see ibid., vol. 1, pp. 389–91.

the Romans in 66 CE.[32] These works and others by Philo and Josephus are cited here according to the editions of the Loeb Classical Library (LCL), which provide Greek texts and parallel English translations. Relevant passages from historical works by other authors will be identified in context as they occur.

The last group of sources consists of rabbinic writings. Most weighty among these is the Talmudic literature, basically the reduction to written form of the laws, regulations and teachings that had accumulated in an oral tradition known as the 'oral law'. In addition to the Talmudic literature are the Midrashim, collections of rabbinical biblical exegesis written at various times during the fifth to the twelfth centuries CE.

The oral law received written form in the Talmudic literature of rabbinic teachers working in the early centuries of the Common Era. It consists of four collections, which, in chronological order of completion, are: the Mishnah, the Tosefta, the Jerusalem Talmud and the Babylonian Talmud.[33]

The Mishnah has a systematic arrangement of topics presented in sixty-three tractates collected into six 'orders'. Each tractate is divided into numbered chapters; in printed editions the chapters are further divided into numbered paragraphs (the *mishnayoth* 'teachings' themselves). The Mishnah was compiled in approximately 200 CE. The work is traditionally attributed to Rabbi Judah ha-Nasi (Rabbi Judah 'the Prince') who flourished between c.160 and 210 CE. The Mishnah contains mostly disputations, edifying discussions, observations and opinions attributed to named rabbinic teachers and rabbinic schools in the Holy Land from the second century BCE to the second century CE. It also contains much anonymous material that is often impossible to date. The earliest rabbis cited in the Mishnah lived between about 200 BCE and the early first century CE, but they are very few and cited infrequently. The majority of the named rabbis lived in the period stretching from the early first century CE to the time of the compilation of the work. It is reasonable to assume that when their teachings are viewed chronologically they reflect the course of Jewish religious life and outlook from the early first century CE to the end of the second. Nevertheless, their teachings, or the teachings communicated in their names, may not necessarily have originated with them: such teachings may already have been in existence for many decades. Some scholars regard the anonymous teachings as emanating from Rabbi Judah, the compiler of the Mishnah, others see anonymity as an indication of much greater age.

The particular value of the Mishnah as a source is the picture it gives of orthodox Jewish life in the Holy Land, seen through academic eyes, during the first two centuries CE. Of especial interest are accounts of synagogue worship and first-hand descriptions of the Jerusalem Temple – the building, its inventory and its worship – while it still stood.

---

[32] Further on these works, see ibid., vol. 1, pp. 47–8.

[33] Detailed descriptions of these works and comprehensive bibliographies of editions, translations and other secondary literature are provided in ibid., vol. 1, pp. 70–90.

Probably the best original-language edition of the Mishnah is that of
H. Albeck.[34] There are also editions of the Hebrew text with parallel English
translation, particularly that of Philip Blackman.[35] The Hebrew of the Mishnah
is a particular variety of post-biblical Hebrew which presents its own difficulties
of translation. There are three outstanding English translations: that of Herbert
Danby, dating from 1933,[36] the aforementioned translation by Philip Blackman
(although the edition referred to herein is from 2000, the translation it contains
is from 1958) and that of Jacob Neusner, published in 1988.[37] The Mishnah is
cited and quoted herein according to Neusner's translation, except where stated
otherwise. In citations, items from the Mishnah are identified by the siglum *m.*
(*mishnah/mishnayoth*) followed by the appropriate tractate references.

The Tosefta, compiled *c.*250–300 CE, is a supplement to the Mishnah. It
follows the same structure and has the same order of tractates except for
'*Abot*, *Qinnim*, *Middot* and *Tamid*, which are not included. The Tosefta contains,
as well as most of the material in the Mishnah, some rabbinic opinions that are
older and others that are younger than those in the earlier compilation. The
critical edition of the Tosefta most generally used is that of Zuckermandel,
published in 1880, and the same editor's supplement to that work, published
in 1882. The English translation of the Tosefta cited herein is that of Jacob
Neusner published in 2002.[38] In citations the Tosefta is identified by the siglum
t. (*tosefta*) followed by the appropriate tractate references.

The two Talmuds – the Yerushalmi (the 'Jerusalem' or 'Palestinian' Talmud,
which despite its name was not compiled in the city of Jerusalem itself, but
elsewhere in the land of Israel) and the Bavli (the 'Babylonian' Talmud) – are
collections of rabbinic discussions based on the text of the Mishnah. They
were completed in about 400 CE and 600 CE respectively. Like the Mishnah and
Tosefta, each Talmud consists of a number of tractates grouped in 'orders'.
Within the tractates, Mishnah passages are quoted then followed immediately
by 'gemara' (literally 'completion') – explanations of their meaning. Neither
Talmud treats all the tractates of the Mishnah, and several of the Mishnah's
tractates are treated in one Talmud but not the other.[39] The Babylonian Talmud
is approximately four times as long as the Jerusalem. The principal editions of

---

[34]   H. Albeck, *The Six Orders of the Mishnah* (Tel Aviv and Jerusalem, 1954–58) [in
Hebrew] (see under 'Mishnah' in the Bibliography).

[35]   Philip Blackman, *Mishnayoth*, 6 vols (Gateshead, 2000).

[36]   H. Danby (trans. and ed.), *The Mishnah Translated from the Hebrew with Introduction
and Brief Explanatory Notes* (Oxford, 1933, repr. 1980).

[37]   Jacob Neusner (ed. and joint trans.), *The Mishnah: A New Translation* (New Haven
CT, 1988).

[38]   *The Tosefta Translated from the Hebrew With a New Introduction*, 2 vols (Peabody MA,
2002).

[39]   Comparative lists of the tractates of the Mishnah and Talmuds are given in *EJ*, vol.
15, pp. 751–2.

the Talmuds are listed in *EJ*, s.v. 'Talmud', and Schürer/Vermes et al., *History*, vol. 1, p. 84. The English translations and editions cited in the present book are those of Jacob Neusner for the Talmud Yerushalmi,[40] and that of I. Epstein for the Talmud Bavli.[41] When the Talmud is cited herein it is identified by the sigla *y.* for the Yerushalmi and *b.* for the Bavli, followed by the tractate reference. Seven extracanonical minor tractates are included in editions of the Babylonian Talmud, added after the main text. One of these is *Soferim* (also written *Soferim*), which dates probably from the eighth century CE and which will be referred to occasionally herein.[42]

The last type of rabbinic literature to be considered here is the Midrashim. These are collections of scholastic exegeses of the Hebrew Bible, produced at various times from the sixth to the twelfth century CE. Because of their late date, their value as sources for the present book is limited, although they do contain occasional points of interest as well as many curiosities of interpretation.

There is a large body of literature from the ancient Near East outside Israel and Judah. This comes principally from Anatolia, Assyria, Egypt and Mesopotamia, and dates from *c.*3000 BCE to the mid-Second Temple period. Of particular interest are Akkadian and Hittite temple rituals, Babylonian psalms and Egyptian secular songs and poems. Pertinent texts are available in English translation in *ANET*.

Early Christian Literary Sources

The primary sources of information about music in early Christianity are the canonical and apocryphal books of the New Testament, the writings of the Church Fathers and gnostic literature. In addition, church histories, liturgical prescriptions, items of church legislation and accounts of liturgies are important.

The scriptural material comprises both the 27 books of the canonical New Testament and the considerable number of books of the New Testament Apocrypha. Although the New Testament canon was not settled before the fourth century CE,[43] the books that eventually came to comprise it had probably all been written by the turn of the second century. Opinions sometimes differ widely as

[40] *The Talmud of the Land of Israel* [Talmud Yerushalmi] (Chicago IL, 1982–86); *The Talmud of the Land of Israel: An Academic Commentary to the Second, Third, and Fourth Divisions* (Atlanta GA, 1998).

[41] *The Babylonian Talmud Translated Into English with Notes, Glossary and Indices*, ed. I. Epstein, 35 vols (London, 1935–52).

[42] On the tractate Soferim, see *Dictionary of Judaism in the Biblical Period: 450 BCE to 600 CE*, ed. Jacob Neusner and William Scott Green, 2 vols (New York, 1996), vol. 2, p. 592, s.v. 'Soferim, Messekhet'.

[43] On the formation of the New Testament canon, see *NTA*, vol. 1, pp. 10–50.

to when individual books were written,[44] but the consensus is that the end of the first century is a reasonable terminal date. The manuscript sources are in Greek; the earliest are from about 200 CE.[45] The canonical New Testament consists of the gospels of Matthew, Mark, Luke and John, the Acts of the Apostles, letters and Revelation (an apocalypse). The Gospels are primarily theologically motivated narratives of the ministry of Jesus of Nazareth. But it is unlikely that these were the first Christian books to have been written. There is general agreement that priority belongs to the genuine Letters of Paul. These were written in the 50s CE, pre-dating all other completed New Testament writings except possibly the Gospel of Mark (which may have reached its final form by the late 50s) and the Letter of James (which may have been written as early as the late 40s).[46]

The value of the New Testament as a source lies not only in its being a collection of documents fundamental to Christianity, but also in its having Jewish roots. Not only are the New Testament books the products of Christianized Jews,[47] but also the people with whom they are concerned, and the settings in which those people are placed, are mostly Jewish. The New Testament thus reflects something of Jewish life (admittedly with varying degrees of Christian overlay) in the period immediately before and after the destruction of Jerusalem and its Temple in 70 CE. This is not to imply that the history of Jewish music in antiquity is seen as ceasing with the advent of Christianity, but rather to emphasize that the history of Christian music begins, like Christianity itself, in Jewish culture.

The edition of the New Testament referred to here and throughout is the critical Greek edition of Nestle–Aland. Quotations from the New Testament in English are from the New Revised Standard Version of the Bible (NRSV).

There is a large body of apocryphal literature associated with the New Testament. Known collectively as the New Testament Apocrypha, it consists of writings mainly from the first to the third centuries CE. From the historical point of view it is not inferior to the New Testament, even though it did not come to acquire canonical status as Christian Scripture. Much of it came into being alongside the literature that eventually became included in the New Testament, and enjoyed more or less equal status with it in the first three centuries of the Christian era. As source material, much of the earliest apocryphal literature has the same value as that of the canonical. The literature currently recognized as comprising the New Testament Apocrypha is conveniently collected in translation

---

[44]   See, for example, John A.T. Robinson, *Redating the New Testament* (London, 1976).

[45]   Nestle–Aland, pp. 684–710; but see also Carsten Peter Thiede, *The Earliest Gospel Manuscript? The Qumran Papyrus 7Q5 and its Significance for New Testament Studies* (Exeter, 1992).

[46]   Robinson, *Redating the New Testament*, pp. 31–85, 118–39, 336–53; *HCSB*, pp. 1915, 2113, 2269.

[47]   James D.G. Dunn, *Unity and Diversity in the New Testament*, 2nd edn (London and Philadelphia PA, 1990), pp. 81, 236.

in the two volumes of *NTA*. As with the Old Testament pseudepigrapha, works of the New Testament Apocrypha will be explained as they are cited.

Closely associated with the canonical and apocryphal Christian literature is the considerable body of gnostic literature dating from the first to the fourth centuries CE. The largest extant collection is the Nag Hammadi codices discovered in Upper Egypt in 1945. This is published in facsimile[48] and in English translation (together with other, related codices) in *NHS*.

As well as works of a scriptural nature, the writings of the Church Fathers in Coptic, Greek, Latin, Syriac and other languages current in the Mediterranean lands in the early Christian centuries are important sources of information about early Christian music. These date from the end of the first to about the sixth century CE. The corpus includes apologies, letters, homilies, biblical commentaries and (from the early fourth century onwards) church histories. It has been collected in the original languages in various monumental series.[49] The sheer quantity of literature is enormous, which makes searching for musical references a daunting prospect, given that the majority of such references are short and incidental. Volume 201 of *PL* concludes with an *Index musicae* (columns 625 onwards), but this in itself is extensive and undiscriminating. The indexed items themselves therefore have to be sifted before work can begin on evaluating the references that pertain to music. The musical index to the three volumes of Quasten's *Patrology*, published in 1950–60, is similarly too all-inclusive to be used without preliminary sifting.

Shorter collections of patristic references to, and writings on, music have been compiled during the last four centuries or so, greatly easing the work of research. The three earliest are from the seventeenth and eighteenth centuries and contain non-patristic as well as patristic material, the earliest of all including non-Christian Greek philosophical material. These collections are: *Antiquae musicae auctores septem*, edited by Marcus Meibom and published in Amsterdam in 1652; *De cantu et musica sacra*, edited by Martin Gerbert and published in St Blasien in 1774 (reprinted 1968) and *Scriptores ecclesiastici de musica sacra potissimum*, also edited by Gerbert, published in St Blasien in 1784 (reprinted 1963). The middle of the twentieth century saw the publication of Alfred Sendrey's *Bibliography of Jewish Music* (New York, 1951), which includes, on pages 50–56, a section devoted to the writings of the Church Fathers on music. Most of the 167 bibliographical entries in that section are provided with brief explanatory notes in English. The notes are unsatisfactory, but the collection of references is a useful starting point for independent evaluation. The most generally useful collection of patristic writings on music is James McKinnon's *Music in Early Christian Literature* (1987,

---

[48]   *The Facsimile Edition of the Nag Hammadi Codices*, ed. James M. Robinson (Leiden, 1972) (see under 'Nag Hammadi codices' in the Bibliography).

[49]   Especially *PG*, *PL* and more recent series of critical editions such as *CCSL*, *CSEL* and *SC*.

reprinted 1993). This presents each item in English translation and includes bibliographical and background information.

Standing outside both scriptural and patristic literature are legislative and liturgical prescriptions and accounts of liturgies. Some of these are embedded in patristic writings. A prime example is the church order known as the *Apostolic Constitutions*.[50] This work, in eight books, is a late fourth-century compilation of substantial parts of other church orders: the *Didache* (early second century), the *Didascalia apostolorum* (early third century) and the *Apostolic Tradition*.[51] Until the 1980s, the *Apostolic Tradition* was generally thought to be a work of Hippolytus (*c*.170–*c*.236) who became Bishop of Rome in *c*.220.[52] More recent research has shown that both the Hippolytan authorship and the consequently assumed Roman provenance are in doubt. The *Apostolic Tradition* is now thought to be a composite work compiled from different sources and probably from different regions and historical periods ranging from the mid-second to the mid-fourth century CE; the extent of Hippolytus' contribution remains an open question.[53] In the *Apostolic Constitutions* all these church orders are much re-worked and, in places, expanded, so that the extant Greek document, which is of Syrian provenance, cannot be relied on to reflect the chronology of the originals of its constituent items. As it now stands, the *Apostolic Constitutions* probably reflects the ordering of the Christian church and its liturgy in Syria – and most likely in the East generally – at the beginning of the last quarter of the fourth century. Musical references are present in all the books except the seventh, which contains the *Didache*.

A work unique in its detailed description of the liturgies of Jerusalem in the late fourth century, is the *Itinerarium* (alternatively *Peregrinatio*) *Egeriae*, a diary written in Latin by the Christian lady Egeria recording her travels in Turkey, Israel/Palestine and north-eastern Egypt in 381–384 CE.[54] She visited all the

[50]   *Les constitutions apostoliques*, ed. and trans. Marcel Metzger, in *SC*, nos 320, 329, 336 (1985, 1986, 1987). On the Apostolic Constitutions, see also Paul F. Bradshaw, *The Search for the Origins of Christian Worship: Sources and Methods for the Study of Early Liturgy*, 2nd edn (New York and London, 2002), pp. 73–91, especially pp. 84–6.

[51]   *La Tradition Apostolique*, ed. Bernard Botte, in *SC*, no. 11 bis (1984).

[52]   See, for example, Gregory Dix [trans. and] (ed.), *The Apostolic Tradition of St Hippolytus* (London, 1937), 2nd edn, ed. Henry Chadwick (London, 1968); *La Tradition Apostolique*, ed. Botte; J. Cuming, *Hippolytus: A Text for Students, with Introduction, Translation, Commentary and Notes*, 2nd edn (Bramcote, 1987).

[53]   Bradshaw, *The Search for the Origins of Christian Worship*, pp. 80–83.

[54]   Text: *Itinerarium Egeriae*, ed. Georg Röwekamp and Dietmar Thönnes, Fontes Christiani, vol. 20 (Freiburg, 1995) (see under 'Egeria' in the Bibliography). English translation as Egeria, *Travels*, ed. Wilkinson; to the bibliography given on pp. vii–xii of Wilkinson's edition should be added: Pasquale Smiraglia, 'Problemi di struttura e cronologia interna nel diario epistolare della pellegrina Egeria' (Florence, 2002), at <http://www.florin.ms/beth.html> (accessed 15 March 2010). See also Louis Duchesne, *Origines du culte chrétien* (Paris, 1889) [trans. M.L. McClure as *Christian Worship: Its Origin and*

important Christian shrines and places of worship in the Holy Land, and her descriptions of them are lively and colourful. Her descriptions of the churches, liturgies and liturgical music in Jerusalem and its environs are of especial interest.

Finally in this section, brief mention may be made of the Christian sections of the Sibylline Oracles, especially books 6–8. Book 8, dating probably from the mid- to late-second century CE, contains a number of musical references that contrast Christian and non-Christian musical practices in worship in Rome at that time, thereby illuminating both.

Archaeological Sources

During the last hundred years or so, archaeological exploration in the Near East has uncovered a large quantity of ancient remains directly related to music. Some of these are actual musical instruments, or fragments of instruments, while others are figurines, etched illustrations or mosaics that depict instruments or musicians holding or playing instruments. Some of the remains are extremely old, dating back to the Stone Age. Those that are whole, or reasonably so, give a vivid idea of the relative size, shape and weight of the various instruments, and of how the instruments were played. The vast majority of the instruments known from archaeological excavations can be matched to instruments named in ancient literary sources, even if only typologically, although occasionally the matching is uncertain because of present-day ignorance about the implications of some of the instrument names in the literature. None of the musical-archaeological finds is likely to be directly relevant to early Christian music since this seems to have been entirely vocal.

Most of the finds of the types listed above are exhibited in museum collections in various parts of the world. More convenient means of access are through the Internet and books containing drawings, photographs and descriptions of them. Among books the following may be mentioned: the second edition of Bathja Bayer's *The Material Relics of Music in Ancient Palestine and its Environs: An Archaeological Inventory* (1964), *MAI/P* (2002) and Jeremy Montagu's *Musical Instruments of the Bible* (2002). There are also drawings and photographs in the 'Biblical Instruments' sections of *MGG* and *New Grove/2*. Of all these, the most comprehensive is *MAI/P*. In that work Joachim Braun discusses in detail the main types of instruments of the ancient western Near East from a music-archaeological standpoint; he provides a generous number of drawings and photographs. An interesting, and as yet unexplained phenomenon revealed by Braun's research is the almost complete absence of music-archaeological finds in the western Near East from the first 250 to 300 years of the Second-Temple period. This means that archaeological evidence is lacking for a span of time that was crucial in the

---

Evolution, 5th edn (London, 1919, repr. 1931)], pp. 490–523, for an annotated Latin text of chs 24:1–49:3 of the *Itinerarium*, and pp. 541–71 for an English translation of this portion.

history of Judaism, namely that of the renaissance of Jewish society and culture
in Judah after the exile. Historians of Jewish music of this period must therefore
rely solely on the contemporaneous literary sources the most significant of
which are the books of Psalms, Ezra–Nehemiah and Chronicles.

In addition to remains directly related to music, archaeology has also brought
to light remains of ancient buildings – ordinary houses as well as palaces, temples
and churches – in several places in the Near East and the eastern Mediterranean
lands. These permit an appreciation of the physical setting of the music of
ancient Judaism and early Christianity. Pictures, plans and reconstructions of
some of these buildings are reproduced in various reference works,[55] and as
part of the extensive background material provided in Th.A. Busink's important
two-volume work on the architecture of the Jerusalem temple, *Der Tempel von
Jerusalem* (1970, 1980).

Musical Sources

It was stated at the beginning of this main section that the musical sources are
very few. As far as ancient Jewish music is concerned, there are no remains of
musical notation or technical descriptions of music extant from ancient Israel or
Judah. However, there are two groups of sources from elsewhere in the ancient
Near East that could have some significance for ancient Jewish music. One consists
of a number of documents that reveal a set of seven tuning patterns for the
seven-stringed Babylonian lyre. The documents, which date from the eighteenth
to around the fourth century BCE,[56] come from a broad northerly section of the
fertile crescent stretching from Ugarit on the Mediterranean coast of Syria in
the west to Ur and Ashur in Mesopotamia in the east. The other group consists
of approximately 35 fragments of tablets with primitive musical notation. They
are from Ugarit and date probably from the first half of the thirteenth century
BCE.[57] While it is possible that the material in these two groups could have some
bearing on ancient Jewish music, the fact that it emanates from places and
cultures foreign to ancient Israel and Judah and dates mostly from periods that
pre-date by many centuries the building of the First Temple, means that there
is inevitably a high degree of uncertainty about its relevance to ancient Jewish
musical culture. Fuller details and discussions are presented in Chapter 4.

As far as early Christian music is concerned, there is only one musical source
extant from the early Christian period up to the end of the fourth century,
namely the Oxyrhynchus hymn. This is a notated setting of the end of the
Greek text of an otherwise unknown Christian hymn. It is extant on a mutilated
papyrus fragment from Oxyrhynchus in Middle Egypt, which dates from towards

---

[55] For example, *DANE, OEANE* and *NEAHL*.
[56] M.L. West, 'The Babylonian Musical Notation and the Hurrian Melodic Texts',
M&L, 75 (1994): 161–71.
[57] Ibid., pp. 171–9.

the end of the third century CE. The papyrus (designated Oxyrhynchus Papyrus 1786) was discovered in 1918 and published in 1922[58] since when it has attracted much interest.[59] Interesting though the music of the Oxyrhynchus hymn is in its own right and in comparison with music of non-Christian Greek hymnody in antiquity, as a Christian hymn with music it is an isolated example from the period. There is therefore no way of knowing whether, or to what extent, its music might be typical of that of other contemporaneous Greek Christian hymns.[60] Fuller details are provided in Chapter 8.

Excursus: Concerning Translations of Biblical Texts

Although authoritative translations of biblical texts are used for quotations in English, readers should guard against taking everything in these and other translations at face value where musical terminology and references to music are concerned. Translations of the Bible – ancient ones as well as modern – sometimes render musical terms imprecisely, inconsistently or misleadingly. This is not because the translations are poor, but because the translators have wider concerns than the academically accurate and consistent rendering of terminology in incidental matter, which passages about music usually are. Sometimes translators are not helped by the original authors or compilers of the source texts, who, also having wider concerns, occasionally use musical terms imprecisely. In some cases the significance of the ancient musical terms has been lost with the passage of time, so that translators have to make conjectures as to their meaning. Whereas in the present book ambiguous or obscure terms are discussed and alternative suggestions for their meaning weighed, in translations of the Bible concrete choices have to be made, usually without the translators having the opportunity to explain them. The following examples illustrate some of the points made above.

In Isaiah 12:6a, the NRSV, RSV and NIV have 'and sing for joy'. This is misleading. The pertinent Hebrew and Greek words at this place (*wāronnî* and *kai eurainesthe* respectively) mean 'and rejoice' or 'and shout for joy' (compare the JPS *Tanakh*), they do not mean explicitly '*sing* for joy'. Song may have been envisaged as an element in the way the joy was expressed, but neither the MT nor the LXX says so.

An interesting example of translational gloss occurs in certain English versions of Exodus 15:21a, the introduction to the song of Miriam that follows

---

[58] A.S. Hunt and H.S. Jones, 'Christian Hymn with Musical Notation', in *The Oxyrhynchus Papyri*, ed. B.P. Grenfell et al., vol. 15 (1922), pp. 21–5.

[59] See the bibliography on the Oxyrhynchus hymn in James W. McKinnon, 'The Musical Character of Early Christian Song', *New Grove/2*, vol. 5, p. 807.

[60] John Arthur Smith, 'First-Century Christian Singing and its Relationship to Contemporary Jewish Religious Song', *M&L*, 75 (1994): 2.

almost immediately after Moses and the Israelites' Song of the Sea (Exod. 15:1–19). Some translators evidently regard Miriam's song as a refrain – presumably to the Song of the Sea although this is not explicitly stated. The JB, for example, has 'And Miriam led them in the refrain' and the NJB has 'while Miriam took up from them the refrain'; the NEB and REB have 'and Miriam sang them this refrain'. Nowhere in Exodus 15, however, are the two clauses of Miriam's song identified as a refrain, and neither the Greek of the LXX nor the Hebrew of the MT says anything about Miriam singing a 'refrain'. The NRSV has 'And Miriam sang to them'; most of the remaining English translations have this or something similar. But it must be admitted that the Hebrew and Greek texts do not agree in meaning at this point. The Hebrew, where the NRSV has 'sang', has the word *watta'an*, a conjunctive form of the verb *'ānâ* 'answer, repeat, respond, sing'. The Greek, on the other hand, has *exērchen ... legousa* 'led them ... saying'. Nevertheless, in neither case is there any suggestion that Miriam's song is a refrain.[61]

Even if the sense 'answer' or 'repeat' be preferred to 'sing', it would have to mean either that Miriam's song was an answer (a response) to the 'timbrel' playing and dancing of the women who were with her, or that she repeated the words of her song as the women with her played their percussion instruments and danced, or that 'repeat', with reference to her song, is an acknowledgement that the text she sang was a repetition of one that had been used before, namely the one uttered by 'Moses' and the 'Israelites'. There is no implication that her song was material repeated at intervals in the manner of a refrain during the rendition of the Song of the Sea or some other item. The JPS *Tanakh* translates diplomatically here: 'And Miriam chanted for them'.

Mention may also be made of the inconsistency in the English translations of two words for particular sung expressions of grief: *nĕhî* (also spelled *nehî*) and *qînâ*. These two nouns are perhaps most fittingly translated '[a] wail, [a] wailing' and '[a] lament, [a] lamentation' respectively. Thus the translation of Jeremiah 9:19(20) ought to be something on the lines of 'teach your daughters wailing (*nehî*), and every one her neighbour lamentation (*qînâ*)', as in the KJV, very similarly in the JPS *Tanakh* and paraphrastically in the NIV. The RSV, NEB and REB, however, have 'lament' for *nehî* and 'dirge' for *qînâ*. The NRSV, on the other hand, while elsewhere it has 'lament' and 'dirge' as the respective translations of these two Hebrew words, in this verse swaps the translations so that *nehî* is rendered 'dirge' and *qînâ* 'lament'. The JB and NJB make a verb out of *nehî* ('teach your daughters how to wail') and translate *qînâ* as 'dirge'. More will be said about the words *nĕhî* and *qînâ* later. Here it is sufficient to register some of the inconsistencies in their translation.

In the New Testament, in Revelation 4:8, the NRSV translates the introduction to the heavenly beings' hymn 'Holy, holy, holy' thus: 'Day and night without ceasing they sing'. Most English versions, except the KJV and NIV, conclude their translation of this introductory passage with a form of the verb 'sing'. The two

---

[61]   See Athalya Brenner, *The Israelite Woman* (Sheffield, 1985, repr. 1989), p. 51.

exceptions, on the other hand, have 'saying', which is precisely the meaning of the Greek verb *legō* used at this point. While *legō* does not rule out the possibility of singing (the verb does not mean rigidly 'say', but is used for utterance generally), the literary context of Revelation 4:8 gives no hint that the heavenly beings were singing. In the prototype of this passage, Isaiah 6:3, the Greek of the LXX has 'And one cried [*ekekragen* "shouted, yelled"] to the other, and they said [*elegon*] ...' and the Hebrew of the MT says that the heavenly beings 'call' (*qārā'* 'proclaim, recite') to each other. Under the circumstances, translating *legō* in Revelation 4:8 with 'sing' is unwarranted. It is perhaps legitimate to wonder whether later traditions of worship, in which the hymn 'Holy, holy, holy' is often sung, have influenced the translation 'sing'.

Finally, it may be noted that many of the English translations of the names of ancient musical instruments are inconsistent, or give misleading impressions of what the instruments were. In many instances 'flutes', 'harps', 'lutes', 'tambourines', 'timbrels' and 'trumpets' are not necessarily what they seem. The source texts occasionally name instruments that are no longer identifiable. In such cases translators may leave the names untranslated or make conjectures as to what they mean.

Chapter 2

Music at the Tabernacle
and the First Temple

Historical traditions enshrined in the Hebrew Bible relate that when the Davidic monarchy became established in Israel, with its seat at Jerusalem in the province of Judah, a temple was built in Jerusalem as a permanent dwelling place for the Israelites' Deity[1] and as the centre of the Israelites' religious cult. According to biblical tradition it was built by King Solomon.[2] The ancient traditions about its erection, furnishing and dedication, preserved in the Hebrew Bible in 1 Kings 6–8 and 2 Chronicles 3:1–7:11, imply that this Temple, commonly known as Solomon's Temple or the First Temple, was completed in about 950 BCE. There is no independent literary corroboration of Solomon's building a temple in Jerusalem, although there is evidence that he undertook building projects elsewhere which may have included temples.[3] The First Temple stood until 587/6 BCE when it was destroyed by Nebuchadnezzar II, king of Babylon from 605 to 561 BCE. It seems to have lain in ruins during the Babylonian captivity of the Jews (587/6–539 BCE).

Worship at the Jerusalem Temple was a sacrificial cult in which agricultural produce, cattle and birds were considered appropriate offerings. Human sacrifice, a feature of the cult of the Canaanite gods Molech and Baal, was forbidden (Lev. 18:21; 20:2–5; Jer. 19:5). The sacrificial acts were regulated by traditional prescriptions and accompanied by traditional ceremonies.

The Jerusalem Temple was not the only place of cultic worship in ancient Israel and Judah. The Hebrew Bible witnesses to several other locations where sacrifices were offered to the Deity, among them 'the house of the LORD' at Shiloh (1 Sam. 1:1–9) and, by implication, the shrines at Bethel and Dan (1 Kgs 12:26–30), 'the hill of God' at Gilgal (1 Sam. 10:5–8), the 'cultic places' in the vicinity of

---

[1]   Or at least for the Deity's 'name' (2 Sam. 7:4–13; 1 Kgs 5:17–19; 8:12–21, 27–48; 9:3) and 'eyes and ... heart' (1 Kgs 9:3). The theology of the presence of the Deity in the Temple is complex; for a summary, see W.D. Stacey, *Prophetic Drama in the Old Testament* (London, 1990), pp. 47–8 and the literature cited in nn. 47 and 48 there.

[2]   Conjectural plans and elevations are presented in Th.A. Busink, *Der Tempel von Jerusalem*, 2 vols (Leiden, 1970, 1980), vol. 1, pp. 165–72, and between pp. 174 and 175. Some (taken from ibid. and other sources) are more conveniently available in J. Alberto Soggin, *An Introduction to the History of Israel and Judah*, trans. John Bowden (London, 1993), p. 377 (Plate 10) and in the notes to 1 Kgs 7 in HCSB.

[3]   Soggin, *An Introduction*, pp. 70–74.

Bethel and Dan (1 Kgs 12:31–32)[4] and 'the Tabernacle of the LORD at the shrine'[5] at Gibeon (1 Chr. 16:39–40). Archaeology has uncovered temples at Shechem (*c.*1650–1550 CE), Megiddo (late Canaanite period, *c.*1400–1300 BCE), Beer Sheba, Lachish (pre-exilic, from the monarchic period), Arad (from the time of Solomon) and Mamre in Hebron (probably postexilic).[6] The Deity of the Israelites was probably not the sole object of worship at all these places, especially the oldest. And some of the cult places, for example those at Bethel and Dan, were deliberately set up as rivals to the Jerusalem Temple.

The Israelites' Deity, unlike the deities of other ancient eastern Mediterranean peoples, was by tradition incorporeal, and therefore invisible. The Deity's presence was symbolized by a wooden chest known as the Ark of the Covenant, or the Ark of (the Presence of) God, or simply 'the Ark', which was regarded by the Israelites as the Deity's throne. When Jerusalem became the seat of the Davidic monarchy, the Ark was removed to the city amid rejoicing, sacrifices and music. When the Temple was completed, the Ark was placed there in the shrine constructed for it (the Holy of Holies, the most sacred room) to symbolize that the Deity was now in residence. Early in the sixth century BCE the Ark disappeared from the Temple and was never replaced.[7] Thereafter, the empty Holy of Holies was the symbol of the presence of the Deity.

Traditions in the Hebrew Bible relate that the Ark of the Covenant, before it was given its permanent home in the Temple in Jerusalem, was carried by the Israelites wherever they went (for example, Num. 10:11–36; see also 1 Sam. 4:4–7:2). When the Israelites pitched camp, it was placed inside a tent built specially to house it. This tent is called the Tabernacle in many English translations.

The Tabernacle was surrounded by a courtyard bounded by a tent wall of linen cloths suspended between wooden poles driven vertically into the ground. The Tabernacle and its courtyard had various appurtenances, including a table on which twelve loaves of bread were set out as an offering to God (the Showbread or 'bread of the Presence'), a lampstand with seven lamps, an altar for burnt offerings, an altar for incense and a bronze basin for ritual ablutions. When the Israelites struck camp, all this was dismantled and carried, together with the Ark, to the next place of encampment. The Tabernacle was thus a portable shrine for

---

[4]   'cultic places': the MT has *'et-bêt bāmôt* 'a house on high places'. See *BHS* on this phrase.

[5]   'at the shrine': the MT has *babāmôt* 'at the high places'.

[6]   Plans of temples at Hazar, Shechem, Megiddo and sites outside the Levant, some covering several archaeological periods in early antiquity, are available in Aharon Kempinski, Ronny Reich et al. (eds), *The Architecture of Ancient Israel: From the Prehistoric to the Persian Periods* (Jerusalem, 1992), p. 163. Plans and pictures of the temples of Megiddo, Arad, Shechem and Beer Sheba are available in Soggin, *An Introduction*, p. 364. Further, see Soggin, *An Introduction*, p. 107, §6.7.3. and §6.7.4.

[7]   Jer. 3:16; Soggin, *An Introduction*, p. 75.

the Ark of the Covenant.[8] Responsibility for the disassembly, transportation and reassembly of the Tabernacle and its appurtenances, and for the transportation of the Ark of the Covenant, rested with the Levites, specific tasks being allotted to respective Levite clans and families (Num. 4:2–47). Levites were eligible for these tasks from the age of 30 to 50 years (ibid.), but already from the age of 25 they could undergo ritual cleansing and purification to qualify them to serve at the rituals at the Tabernacle (Num. 8:5–26). The last four books of the Torah contain several sets of prescriptions about the Tabernacle and its appurtenances, and about the Israelites' religious observances. Some of these are extremely detailed, especially where they are concerned with the measurements of the component parts of the shrine and the preparation and offering of animal sacrifices.

Despite the evident antiquity of the Israelites' Tabernacle, it is unlikely that the appurtenances and religious observances the Torah associates with it are equally ancient. Two passages from pre-exilic prophetic texts in the Hebrew Bible (Amos 5:25 and Jer. 7:21–23) deny that sacrifices were practised by the nomadic Israelites prior to their settlement in Canaan. Furthermore, the prescriptions in the Torah referred to above presuppose not only a permanent site for cultic worship[9] but also a settled population[10] and a stable economy.[11] These features are consistent with the idea that the books of the Torah originated during the time of the First Temple. The details in the Torah about the appurtenances and religious observances at the Tabernacle are therefore thought to be retrojections from the First Temple.[12] This being the case, it is appropriate to introduce this survey of music at the First Temple with an examination of what the relevant biblical sources say about music at the Tabernacle and at the removal of the Ark of the Covenant.

Music at the Tabernacle and the Removal of the Ark of the Covenant

The pertinent sources are books from the Torah and the Deuteronomistic History, the earliest groups of biblical literature to contain relevant material.

---

[8]   The biblical tradition of the Tabernacle probably has a historical basis since there is ample evidence for the existence of portable tent shrines in the ancient Near East: see Cyrus H. Gordon and Gary A. Rendsburg, *The Bible and the Ancient Near East* (New York, 1997), p. 166. In archaeological terms the pertinent period corresponds to Late Bronze Age II, Iron Age I and Iron Age IIA. For details of the archaeological periods of the ancient Middle East, see Volkmar Fritz, *An Introduction to Biblical Archaeology*, trans. Birgit Mänz-Davies (Sheffield, 1996), pp. 70–77.

[9]   For example, Exod. 29:38–42; Num. 28:1–8 (twice-daily animal sacrifice in perpetuity).

[10]   For example, Exod. 23:10–13; Num. 35:1–8.

[11]   For example, Exod. 25:1–7; 30:11–16; 35:20–36:7; Num. 7:1–88.

[12]   Gordon and Rendsburg, *The Bible and the Ancient Near East*, pp. 166–7.

While Chronicles contains a quantity of apparently relevant material, the postexilic date of that literature[13] seriously undermines its credibility as a source of information about music in pre-exilic times. Chronicles is therefore not regarded as a pertinent source here.[14]

Music at the Tabernacle

Detailed information about music at the Tabernacle is available only with regard to trumpets, which were purportedly used in connection with and during the cultic rites. Numbers 10:1–10 contains instructions for the use of trumpets. The Hebrew Bible witnesses to the use of two types of trumpet at, or in connection with, the Tabernacle and the First Temple. One is the ḥăṣōṣĕrâ (plural ḥăṣōṣĕrôt; sometimes ḥăṣô- in singular and plural, and -rōt in the plural), a trumpet made of beaten metal. The other is the šôpār (shofar), a trumpet made from the horn of an animal, most usually, though not invariably, a ram. The distinction between ḥăṣōṣĕrâ and šôpār is not always preserved in translations. In the LXX both words are typically rendered by a form of the word *salpinx*, a generic word for 'trumpet', and many English translations (but not those of the JPS *Tanakh* and the NJB) give 'trumpet' indiscriminately for both.[15]

Returning to Numbers 10:1–10, it may be noted that it is concerned with metal trumpets of a special kind, with special functions. In Numbers 10:1–2a, Moses is instructed to make 'two silver [*kesep*] trumpets [*ḥăṣōṣĕrōt*] ... of hammered work'. These were to be used mainly for signalling, as the instructions in the subsequent eight and a half verses show. Blowing the silver trumpets was the prerogative of the Aaronite priests (10:8a), a rule that was valid for all time (10:8b). In verse 10 Moses is told, 'And on your joyous occasions – your fixed festivals and new moon days – you shall sound [*ûtĕqaʿĕtem*] the trumpets [*baḥăṣōṣĕrôt*] over [*ʿal*] your burnt offerings and your sacrifices of well-being.' The priestly blowing of silver trumpets was an integral part of the sacrificial rites.

The purpose of the trumpet calls during the sacrifices is stated to be 'a reminder [*zikkārôn*] of you [the Israelites] before your God' (Num. 10:10). The word *ûtĕqaʿĕtem*, rendered 'and ... you shall sound' in the quotation above, is from the verb *tāqaʿ* 'to sound, to blow' a horn or trumpet, and may be onomatopoeic in origin.[16] In Hebrew the word is used in connection with both ram's-horn trumpets and metal trumpets.

---

[13]   Chronicles was written probably in the fourth century BCE: see *PsIW*, vol. 2, p. 200, and the standard commentaries.

[14]   See below and n. 23.

[15]   Compare, for example, Exod. 19:16 and Num. 10:10 in the MT (šôpār and ḥăṣōṣĕrôt respectively), the LXX (a form of the word *salpinx* in each place) and the NRSV ('trumpets' and 'trumpet' respectively).

[16]   Compare the archaic English word 'tucket', meaning a trumpet flourish.

In ancient Hebrew the word *tĕrû'â* is often used to mean a particular type of trumpet call, probably a call to attention (it is frequently translated 'trumpet blast' or 'alarm'). It also has other meanings, however, among which are 'battle cry', 'shout' and 'loud noise'. The word *tĕrû'â* cannot therefore automatically be taken to mean a trumpet or shofar call. In biblical prescriptions for the rite celebrating the first day of the seventh month, the Hebrew of the last clause of Leviticus 23:24, for example, could legitimately be translated 'a sacred occasion commemorated with loud noise [*tĕrû'â*]'; and the Hebrew of the last clause of Numbers 29:1, 'you shall observe it as a day of noisy merrymaking [*tĕrû'â*]' or, as a marginal note in the JPS *Tanakh* suggests, 'You shall observe it as a day of festivity'.

It is not until the appearance of the LXX translation of the Torah that there is any specific indication of the existence of a tradition associating trumpets with that sacred occasion. The LXX version of the end of Leviticus 23:24 has *salpingōn* ('with trumpets') where the Hebrew has *tĕrû'â*; the LXX version of the end of Numbers 29:1 has *sēmasias* (perhaps 'for signalling', from *sēma* 'sign, signal') where the Hebrew has *tĕrû'â*. The word *sēmasias* seems to carry the implication that the signalling would be made on trumpets. But the LXX evidence does not necessarily clarify the picture as far as the early pre-exilic period is concerned since it is uncertain whether the LXX is referring to a custom which was already ancient when the translation was made, and therefore likely to have existed in early pre-exilic times, or to a custom which was comparatively recent – perhaps one that obtained only in Hellenized Judaism in the north Egyptian Diaspora, the milieu in which the LXX translation is likely to have originated. In connection with this last remark, it is of interest that Philo of Alexandria says that the first day of the seventh month, which became celebrated as the Festival of New Year, also became known as the Festival of Trumpets.[17]

There are nevertheless many places in the Hebrew Scriptures where the word *tĕrû'â* is associated with metal trumpets and horn trumpets. It remains possible therefore that the word *tĕrû'â* in Leviticus 23:24 and Numbers 29:1 is intended to imply trumpet calls, although on which type of trumpet it is impossible to say.

Music at the Removal of the Ark of the Covenant

The pertinent material is to be found in the Deuteronomistic History at 2 Samuel 6:1–19. The narrative there relates that the task was accomplished in two stages:

---

[17]   Philo of Alexandria, *Special Laws*, 1. 35, and 2. 31, in *Philo*, ed. F.H. Colson, 10 vols and 2 supp. vols (London, 1941, repr. 1985), vol. 7, using a form of the word *salpinx* in each place. The occasion is still popularly known as the Festival of Trumpets (see, for example, the editorially supplied titles preceding these passages in *HCSB*). The name is somewhat misleading since trumpet blasts are not the purpose of the occasion but rather concomitants of it. The purpose of the occasion in ancient times seems to have been purely and simply to celebrate the seventh month, since the number seven had special significance for the ancient Israelites.

from the house of Abinadab to the house of Obed-edom, then, three months later, onward to 'the tent which David had pitched for it' (2 Sam. 6:17) in Jerusalem. During the first stage,

> [2 Sam. 6:5] David and all the House of Israel danced [*mĕśaḥăqîm*] before the LORD to [the sound of] all kinds of cypress wood [instruments][18] [*bĕkōl 'ăṣê bĕrôšîm*], with lyres [*ûbĕkinnōrôt*], harps [*ûbinĕbālîm*], timbrels [*ûbĕtupîm* '(and) hand drums'], sistrums[19] [*ûbimĕna'anĕ'îm*][20] and cymbals [*ûbĕṣelṣĕlîm*].[21]

The narrative goes on to say that during the second stage of the removal, David offered sacrifices (2 Sam. 6:13) and 'whirled [*mĕkarkēr*] with all his might before the LORD' (2 Sam. 6:14a). When David and the Israelites finally brought the Ark into Jerusalem, they did so 'with shouts [*bitĕrû'â*] and with blasts of the horn [*šôpār*]' (2 Sam. 6:15). The journey of the Ark of the Covenant to its resting place in the Tabernacle in Jerusalem is thus presented as a procession with dancing, shouts, and the playing of plucked-string instruments, various percussion instruments, and the shofar. Although the narrative says that sacrifices were offered both while the Ark was on its journey and when the Ark came to rest in Jerusalem, it makes no specific mention of music in connection with them.

Music at the First Temple

General Aspects

Contrary to the impression given by many writers in the past, the Hebrew Bible provides relatively little concrete information about music at the First Temple. The relevant sources are 1 Kings 10, First Isaiah, the book of Amos and a dozen or so items from the book of Psalms. These are the earliest biblical documents to contain references to music at the Temple. They originate mostly from before the exile and partly from during it – from periods that are respectively contemporaneous with and immediately subsequent to the First Temple. Their authors can therefore reasonably be assumed to be drawing on direct and remembered experience of the Temple when referring to its music. Surprising though it may seem, these documents contain no connected description of music at the First Temple; and neither the long pre-exilic account of the building,

---

[18]   'cypress wood [instruments]': the NRSV gives 'songs' for this term in order to harmonize with the parallel in 1 Chr. 13:8 which has *šîrîm* '[cultic] songs'.

[19]   'sistrums': alternatively, 'rattles'. For the preference, see below.

[20]   Alfred Sendrey holds that the LXX 'mistranslates' this word as *kai en kumbalois* 'and with cymbals' (MAI, pp. 384–5) . It is more likely that the translator of the LXX has deliberately altered the word: see Chapter 3 in this volume.

[21]   Instead of 'and [with] cymbals', the LXX has *kai en aulois* 'and with pipes'.

furnishing and dedication of Solomon's Temple (1 Kgs 5–8), nor the extended exilic narrative of the exiled Ezekiel's vision of the Jerusalem Temple (Ezek. 40–48), contains anything about Temple music.[22]

While Chronicles contains a large quantity of material purportedly about music at the First Temple, it is not a relevant source in the present context for two reasons. First, Chronicles was written in the postexilic period, in about 350 BCE if not later. The span of some 250 years that separates the end of the First-Temple era from the likely date of the composition of Chronicles (a span of time which includes the exile) calls into question the historical credibility of Chronicles as far as musical practices at the First Temple are concerned. Second, Chronicles contains a large amount of material about the Ark of the Covenant, the Tabernacle and the Temple that is supplementary to the material about them in the pre-exilic and exilic portions of the Bible. The current consensus among scholars is that much of this supplementary material is likely to have been retrojected from the time when Chronicles was written.[23] This is especially so where musical details are concerned: the picture of musical activity and musical organization at the Temple is so comprehensive in Chronicles compared with exilic and pre-exilic biblical texts, that it is difficult to account for them other than as the result of retrojection from the Temple of the Chronicler's own day, the pre-Herodian Second Temple. It is possible that some elements of the musical organization described in Chronicles were in place already before the exile; but if they were they could reasonably be expected to be mentioned in the extant pre-exilic and exilic literature. The fact that they are not strengthens the argument for retrojection. This is not to deny the possibility that Chronicles is historically reliable in other areas, but as far as music at the First Temple is concerned it cannot be considered authoritative where it goes beyond the pre-exilic and exilic sources.

The relevant sources are thus few. In addition, they contain little pertinent material, which often consists of no more than passing references. Moreover, there is no guarantee that all their apparently pertinent material has to do with the Temple in Jerusalem although most of it clearly does so. Under these circumstances the resultant picture of music at the First Temple and how it was organized is bound to be somewhat uneven. Nevertheless it is a picture formed from the earliest material and is therefore of greater historical value, despite its shortcomings, than a picture formed from the material in Chronicles or from a conflation of pre-exilic, exilic and postexilic texts.

---

[22]   Ezek. 40:44a has 'there were chambers for the singers in the inner forecourt'. The phrase 'chambers for the singers' is doubtful and should probably read 'two chambers': see *BHS*; compare the LXX and the JPS *Tanakh*.

[23]   *PsIW*, vol. 2, p. 200; John W. Kleinig, *The Lord's Song: The Basis, Function and Significance of Choral Music in Chronicles* (Sheffield, 1993), p. 16, and the literature cited in n. 2 there. See also the standard commentaries and at nn. 13 and 14 above.

The earliest source is the book of Amos. This was written near the beginning of the eighth century BCE and consists of Divine messages to the Israelites, mediated as oracles delivered in poetic form by the prophet Amos. In Amos 5:21–24 the Deity demands justice and righteousness rather than sacrifices:

> [Amos 5:21] I loathe, I spurn your festivals,
> I am not appeased by your solemn assemblies.
> [22] If you offer Me burnt offerings – or your meal offerings –
> I will not accept them;
> I will pay no heed
> To your gifts of fatlings.
> [23] Spare Me the sound [*hămôn*] of your hymns [*šireykā*],
> And let Me not hear the music [*wĕzimrat*] of your lutes [*nĕbāleykā*].
> [24] But let justice well up like water,
> Righteousness like an unfailing stream.

It may be assumed that the picture of sacrificial worship is drawn from Amos's own day. While the Jerusalem Temple is not specified here, there can be little doubt that this is the location envisaged since the context of the whole book is set in the Deity's dwelling place in Zion in Jerusalem (Amos 1:2a–b). Associated with the sacrifices is song and the music of plucked-string instruments. The text does not quite go so far as to say that the vocal and instrumental music was performed during the sacrifices, but it does seem to be open to this interpretation.

Despite the hostile tone of verses 21–23 in the passage above, the word *hămôn* in verse 23, which the JPS *Tanakh* translates 'sound', but which the NRSV translates 'noise', is not in itself pejorative. Given that in this passage *hămôn* is paralleled with [*wĕ*]*zimrat* '[and] music', a neutral term, it should probably not be regarded as pejorative in the present context.

The word *šireykā*, translated 'your hymns' above, means more precisely 'your songs'. It is formed from the root ŠYR, the basis of all the most usual words for 'sing' and 'song' in Hebrew, including the simple word *šîr* itself which means 'sing' (verb) or 'song' (noun). The word *nĕbāleykā*, translated 'your lutes', is formed from the noun *nēbel* which, as has been noted, is the name of a type of plucked-string instrument.

The word *wĕzimrat* is a conjunctive form of the noun *zimrâ*, which is built on the root ZMR. This root can have two possible senses: on the one hand it may mean 'pick, pluck, pinch out' or 'prune'; on the other it may mean 'music, sound, make music' or 'play' as on a musical instrument. In musical contexts, words built on this root may convey the picking, plucking or strumming of stringed instruments. The musical sense of the root may reflect onomatopoeia from the buzzing sound made by massed plucked-string instruments, particularly when it is borne in mind that such instruments were acoustically much less sophisticated than modern plucked-string instruments, and probably sounded predominantly in what today would be called the alto and tenor registers. It is unlikely that the musical ZMR-words would have implied the sounds of the metal trumpet, the horn or the pipe (see below) since the sounds of these instruments would have been too shrill, precise and, in the case of the trumpet and horn, too intermittent, to give an impression of buzzing. In the Hebrew Bible generally, words which are built on the root ZMR and have a musical meaning appear only in contexts concerned with cultic worship, although not exclusively that of the Israelites.[24] This implies that musical ZMR-words refer to cultic music, and in view of what has just been said above, probably the cultic music of massed plucked-string instruments.

It is possible that much later, musical ZMR-words came to refer to the playing of wind instruments also. In support of this, Joachim Braun points to an archaeological find from the Hellenistic–Roman period which consists of an etching representing a woman playing a double pipe. The etching has a caption beneath it, the relevant part of which Joachim Braun translates, 'the beautiful woman *zmrt* the pipe', or 'the beautiful one plays the pipe (*zmrt*)'.[25] The phrase 'the pipe' does not appear in the caption, but is provided by Braun by inference from the etching. Whether this use of *zmrt* in connection with a double pipe has any relevance to music at the First Temple is debatable. Its manifestation is very late in relation to the First Temple, it is an isolated piece of evidence and its nature implies a secular or profane context outside the cult and outside religious observance in general.

The idea that in biblical passages concerned with the cult, musical ZMR-words are associated with plucked-string instruments to the exclusion of wind instruments is supported by the LXX. In almost every instance where the LXX translates a musical ZMR-word, it does so with a form of the verb *psallō* or the noun *psalmos* (see the Appendix). The verb *psallō* originally meant 'to play a stringed instrument with the fingers', and *psalmos* 'music produced by playing a stringed instrument with the fingers'. Later, these words came to mean 'to sing to a plucked-string instrument' and 'a song sung to a plucked-string instrument' respectively, but the association with the type of instrument remained constant.[26] The later meanings arose most probably with the active Hellenization of Egypt from *c.*330 BCE onwards, and of the eastern Mediterranean lands from *c.*250 BCE onwards. They may be understood as a Greek way of viewing the normal musical practice at the Temple, which was that the cultic music of the plucked-string

---

[24] See the column 'Hebrew Bible Reference' in the Appendix. The references in Dan. are concerned with a non-Jewish cult; the word at Ezra 7:24 is an Aramaic equivalent; at Exod. 15:2, where the MT has *wĕzimrāt*, the LXX has *kai skepastēs* 'and protection', and the Vulgate has *et laus* 'and praise'; at Job 35:10, where the MT has *zĕmirôt*, the LXX has nothing that corresponds to the Hebrew, but the Vulgate has *carmina* 'songs'.

[25] *MAI/P*, pp. 35, 218.

[26] Still later they were often interpreted as simply 'sing' and 'song': see the words from the Vulgate and the *Psalterium iuxta Hebraeos* in the column 'Latin Text' in the Appendix.

instruments did not occur alone, but always had song or some other vocal element with it. When string music was heard in the cult, what was heard was in fact a combination of two elements, one instrumental, the other vocal. It is perhaps the later meanings that are intended in the LXX translation of the Hebrew Scriptures. But it is not necessarily these later Greek meanings that should automatically be read back into the ZMR-words of the Hebrew Bible. The text of the Torah and the Prophets in the Hebrew Bible was settled before the Hellenistic period began and may well preserve ancient traditions of meaning. In the Hebrew Bible, musical ZMR-words should always be regarded as meaning first and foremost 'music, sound' (of plucked-string instruments) or 'to play, to make music' (on plucked-string instruments). In this context it is worth bearing in mind that the ancient Aramaic word *zĕmār*, also built on the root ZMR, means music in general or the music of strings in particular.[27]

In any given instance of the use of a word built on the root ZMR, it is first and foremost the literary and narrative contexts that determine which sense is appropriate. One feature that signals a musical instrumental sense for a ZMR-word is the pairing of it with a word built on the root ŜYR. The use of word pairs is a feature of ancient Hebrew poetry, and the pairing of words built on these particular roots, and meaning 'sing ... make melody' or 'sing ... play', occurs at several places in the Hebrew Bible, including the book of Psalms.[28] There are also places where a ZMR-word is paired with a word signifying some other form of vocal utterance such as raising a shout or shouting for joy; it is natural to regard it as meaning 'make melody' or 'play' at these places also.

The use of ŜYR- and ZMR-words in literary parallelism is also an indication of distinction in their meaning. This is illustrated particularly clearly in verse 9 of the pre-exilic Psalm 144, where *šîr* 'song' and *'āšîrâ* 'I will sing' in the first clause are paralleled by *bĕnēbel* 'with the *nēbel*' and *'ăzammĕrâ* 'I will play, I will make music' in the second. The second clause also contains an example of the association of a word built on the root ZMR with a variety of plucked-string instrument, the *nēbel*.

Where a ZMR-word stands alone, unpaired and unparalleled in a narrative context concerned with religious observance, it should be understood to imply music consisting of the vocal as well as the instrumental element: the music of plucked strings with cultic song. Perhaps this is what should be understood in Psalm 47:7: here 'play and sing!' could be an appropriate translation of the imperative *zammĕrû* (which occurs four times in the verse).[29]

The nuances of meaning of ŜYR- and musical ZMR-words in contexts concerned with religious observance may be understood by saying that both ŜYR- and ZMR-

---

[27]   In J. Hoftijzer and K. Jongeling, *Dictionary of the North-West Semitic Inscriptions* (Leiden, 1995), the meaning of ZMR is given as 'sing', but this is misleading.

[28]   Mitchell Dahood SJ and Tadeusz Penar, 'The Grammar of the Psalter', in Mitchell Dahood SJ, *Psalms III: 101–150* (New York, 1970), p. 456. The authors identify nine instances in the book of Psalms and one similar instance in a Ugaritic text.

[29]   Similarly in Ps. 66:4 (quoted below) where the imperative occurs twice.

words imply cultic music, the former emphasizing its vocal aspect, the latter its instrumental, but neither excluding the aspect emphasized by the other.

Even though in cultic worship stringed instruments were apparently normally played in conjunction with (at the same time as) vocal utterance (song or shouting), their music should not be thought of as an 'accompaniment' to the vocal element. The idea that the instruments 'accompanied' the voices suggests, at least to modern minds, that the instrumental element was subordinate to the vocal. But this is a position not supported by ancient Near Eastern sources. In the cultic music of ancient Israel, instrumental and vocal elements were of equal importance.

Music at the First Temple is further evinced by two passages from First Isaiah. One is Isaiah 30:29, which says:

> [Isa. 30:29] For you [the 'people in Zion, dwellers of Jerusalem' (30:19)], there
> shall be singing [*haššîr*]
> As on a night when a festival is hallowed;
> There shall be rejoicing as when they march
> With flute [*behālîl* 'with pipe']³⁰
> To the Rock of Israel on the Mount of the Lord.

Here, 'Rock of Israel' is an epithet for the Deity, and by association may also refer to the Jerusalem Temple which was built on a rocky hill (the 'Mount of the Lord', the Temple Mount). The music (singing and pipe playing) is placed in non-sacrificial cultic settings that are clearly expected to be familiar to the reader: at night during festivals and during joyful processions to the Temple respectively. The 'pipe' that was played was the *ḥālîl* (plural: *ḥālîlîm*). This was a slender reed pipe, possibly single but more probably double with a mouthpiece for each pipe,³¹ an ancestor of the reed pipes still common today throughout the Near East. The LXX usually translates the word as *aulos*. The JPS *Tanakh*, in common with most English translations of the Bible, renders the word as 'flute', which is misleading.

The other passage, Isaiah 38:20, refers to the cultic use of stringed instruments. It occurs at the end of King Hezekiah's 'song' of thanksgiving for his recovery from illness:

> [Isa. 38:20] [It has pleased] the Lord to deliver us [Hezekiah],
> That is why we offer up music [*ûněginôtay něnagēn* 'And play upon my stringed
> instruments']³²
> All the days of our lives
> At the House of the Lord.

---

³⁰ At this point the JPS *Tanakh* adds 'with timbrels [*bětuppîm*], and with lyres [*ûběkinnōrôt*]' brought forward from verse 32.

³¹ Joachim Braun, 'Biblical Instruments', *New Grove/2*, vol. 3, p. 525 (text), p. 526 (picture).

³² Compare the NRSV: 'And we will sing to stringed instruments'.

The stringed instruments are unspecified here, but since the verb *nāgan* (from which *něnagēn* is formed) is associated with the *kinnôr* at three places in the pre-exilic and exilic literature in the Hebrew Bible,[33] it is a reasonable supposition that *kinnōrôt* should be understood here.

Complementary information which could relate to the First Temple at a fairly early stage of its existence is provided by 1 Kings 10:12. The first half of this verse says that Solomon used the almug wood that was a gift from the Queen of Sheba, 'for decorations in the House of the LORD and in the royal palace, and for harps [*wěkinnōrôt*] and lyres [*ûněbālîm*] for the singers [*laššārîm*]'. The passage shows that the singers to whom it refers not only sang but also played plucked-string instruments of the type already noted as being used in cultic worship. The singers are not identified, but they or their activities were evidently sufficiently important to merit royal attention. The context suggests that both Temple singers and secular singers in the service of the royal household are meant.

By far the most fruitful source is the book of Psalms. Some 38 psalms are reckoned to have been composed during the period of the First Temple, and approximately 30 during the exile.[34] Pertinent material occurs in six of the First-Temple period psalms (Pss 7, 61, 66, 68, 81, 87), in four of the exilic-period psalms (Pss 43, 96, 98 and 137) and in Psalm 95 which could belong to either period. It is possible that Psalms 24 and 118 are also relevant (both are pre-exilic). This selection takes account of only the actual poetic texts of the psalms; superscriptions, subscriptions and rubrics attached to them in the MT and LXX are ignored here since they are likely to be additions from the Second-Temple period.[35]

Only in Psalm 96 is the Temple setting specified: 'in His temple [*běmiqdāšô* 'sanctuary']' is where strength and splendour abide (96:6b). Otherwise, the Temple setting is implied either by indirect references to it or by circumstantial details.

The musical references witness to vocal and instrumental music in both sacrificial and non-sacrificial cultic contexts, although in some of the psalms the type of context cannot be determined. Music in sacrificial contexts is evident in Psalms 43, 61 and 66. Psalm 43:3–4 has:

> [Ps. 43:3] Send forth Your light and Your truth;
> they will lead me;
> they will bring me to Your holy mountain,
> to your dwelling-place,
> [4] that I may come to the altar of God,
> God, my delight, my joy;

---

[33]   1 Sam. 16:16 ('lyre' in the JPS *Tanakh* and the NRSV); 1 Sam. 16:23 ('lyre' in the JPS *Tanakh* and the NRSV); Isa. 23:16 ('lyre' in the JPS *Tanakh*, 'harp' in the NRSV).

[34]   Listed in S.E. Gillingham, *The Poems and Psalms of the Hebrew Bible* (Oxford, 1994), pp. 253–4. Ps. 95 is borderline between the two periods.

[35]   John Arthur Smith, 'Which Psalms Were Sung in the Temple?' *M&L*, 71 (1990): 168.

that I may praise [*wĕʾôdĕkā* 'give thanks to'] You with the lyre [*bĕkinnôr*],
O God, my God.

Here there is a clearly implied association of music – plucked strings (and voice?)
– with sacrifice (the altar). Psalm 61:9(8) has:

[Ps. 61:9(8)] So I will sing hymns [*ʾăzammĕrâ* 'make melody'] to Your name
forever,
as I fulfil my vows day after day.

and Psalm 66:2b(a), 4, 13 has:

[Ps. 66:2b(a) sing [*zammĕrû* 'sound'] the glory of His name

...

[4] all the earth bows to You,
and sings hymns [*wîzammĕrû* 'and makes music'] to You;
all sing hymns [*wĕzammĕrû* 'and (all) make music'] to Your name.

...

[13] I enter Your house with burnt offerings,
I pay my vows to You

In these psalms the music takes place in the context of the offering of sacrifices
alluded to as 'coming to the altar', 'paying vows' and 'entering God's house with
burnt offerings'.

Music in non-sacrificial cultic contexts, especially processions, is evinced by
Psalms 68, 81 and possibly 95 and 118. Psalm 68:25(24)–26(25) has:

[Ps. 68:25(24)] Men see Your processions, O God,
the processions of my God, my king,
into the sanctuary.
[26(25)] First come singers [*šārîm*)], then musicians [*nōgĕnîm*],
amidst maidens [*ʿălāmôt*] playing timbrels [*tôpēpôt* 'hand drums'].

The word *nōgĕnîm* in verse 26(25) is cognate with the verb *nāgan*, which, as has
been noted earlier, is associated with the *kinnôr* in three places in pre-exilic
biblical literature.[36] It is likely therefore that the musicians referred to in this
verse were players on the *kinnôr*. Elsewhere in this psalm there are two instances
of the imperatives *šîrû* and *zammĕrû* being paired parallelistically:

[Ps. 68:5a(4a)] Sing [*šîrû*] to God, chant hymns [(*zammĕrû* 'play'] to His name.

and:

---

[36] See at n. 33.

> [Ps. 68:33(32)] O kingdoms of the earth,
> sing [*šîrû*] to God;
> chant hymns [*zammĕrû* 'play'] to the Lord.

Processions, possibly with musical elements, may be alluded to in Ps. 118:

> [Ps. 118:19] Open the gates of victory for me
> that I may enter them and praise the LORD.
> [20] This is the gateway to the LORD –
> the victorious shall enter through it.
> ...
> [26] May he who enters be blessed in the name of the LORD;
> we bless you from the House of the LORD.

Verse 27b of this Psalm has often been translated as if it referred to a procession. The NRSV at this point, for example, has 'Bind the festal procession with branches, up to the horns of the altar'. This is fairly representative of many translations. However, the meaning of the Hebrew (MT) of this half-verse is uncertain, and there is no guarantee that it has anything to do with a procession. The JPS *Tanakh* has 'bind the festal offering to the horns of the altar with cords' and the NEB has '[the LORD has given light to us,] the ordered line of pilgrims by the horns of the altar'. A radical translation from 1976 has 'Rope the sacrifice to the altar-horns'.[37] The LXX version of this half-verse (LXX Ps. 117:27b) is as opaque as the MT, meaning, perhaps, 'concelebrate the festival with the multitude[?], even to the horns of the altar'. In the light of the uncertainty about the meaning of the Hebrew and the Greek, it would be unwise to insist that Psalm 118:27b has to do with a procession.[38]

Sigmund Mowinckel saw Psalm 24 as a processional psalm. He noted that it falls into three distinct parts (verses 1–2, verses 3–6 and verses 7–10), which he believed could have been used 'during the procession on the way to the Temple, before the gates, and when the procession winds in through the gates' respectively.[39] Whether this psalm was actually sung during processions is not known, but it is possible that processions began outside the Temple precincts and made their way into, or up to, the sanctuary.

Psalm 81:3(2)–4(3) has:

> [Ps. 81:3(2)] Take up the song [*šĕ'û-zimrâ* 'take up the instruments'],
> sound the timbrel [*ûtĕnû-tōp* 'sound the hand drum'],
> the melodious lyre [*kinnôr nā'îm* 'sweet lyre'] and harp ['*im-nābel*].

37　*The Psalms*, trans. Peter Levi (Harmondsworth, 1976), p. 189.
38　Hans-Joachim Kraus, *Psalmen*, 6th edn, 2 vols (Neukirken-Vluyn, 1989), vol. 2, pp. 984–5, thinks that Ps. 118:27b has to do with a sacred dance that circumambulates the altar, and points to Ps. 26:6 by way of illustration. Ps. 26 is reckoned to be postexilic.
39　*PsIW*, vol. 1, p. 6.

[4(3)] Blow [*tiqʻû*] the horn [*šôpār*] on the new moon,
on the full moon for our feast day.

Here the music of percussion, plucked strings and the horn is associated with the New Moon festival, at which sacrifice was offered (Num. 10:10). However, in the present passage there is no reference to the sacrifice itself. The reference to blowing the shofar 'on the new moon ... for our feast day' alludes to the use of this instrument for signalling the beginning of the festival. The inclusion of the *tōp* among the instruments suggests that the psalmist may have had a non-sacrificial ritual in mind – perhaps a procession prior to the sacrifice.
   Psalm 95:2 suggests an entrance, perhaps in procession:

[Ps. 95:2] let us come into His presence with praise;
let us raise a shout for Him in song [*bizmirôt* 'with instruments']!

The psalms that give no clear indication of the context of the music to which they refer are 7, 87, 96, 98 and 137. In Psalm 7:18(17) the psalmist declares:

[Ps. 7:18(17)] ... and [I will] sing a hymn [*waʻăzammĕrâ* 'make music'] to the name of the LORD Most High.

Psalm 87 is a short hymn in praise of Zion. Its last verse (verse 7) says that Zion is the source of inspiration for 'singers and dancers alike' (see below). Psalm 96 opens with an invitation to 'all the earth' to sing to the LORD:

[Ps. 96:1] Sing [*šîrû*] to the LORD a new song [*šîr ḥādāš*],
sing [*šîrû*] to the LORD, all the earth.
[2] Sing [*šîrû*] to the LORD, bless His name.

Psalm 98:1, 4–6 presents a picture of voices and various types of instrument making music in the presence of the Deity:

[Ps. 98:1] Sing [*šîrû*] to the LORD a new song [*šîr ḥādāš*],
...
[4] Raise a shout to the LORD, all the earth,
break into joyous songs of praise![40]
[5] Sing praise [*zammĕrû* 'play' or 'play and sing'] to the LORD with the lyre [*bĕkinnôr*],
with the lyre [*bĕkinnôr*] and melodious song [*wĕqôl zimrâ* 'and the sound of music'].
[6] With trumpets [*baḥăṣōṣĕrôt*] and the blast [*wĕqôl*] of the horn [*šôpār*]
raise a shout before the LORD, the king.

---

[40]   'break into joyous songs of praise': the MT has 'break forth and shout for joy [*wĕrannĕnû*] and make melody [*wĕzammērû*]'.

Psalm 137 is a poignant expression of an exile's nostalgia for Zion. Verses 2–6 have:

> [Ps. 137:2] There [in Babylonia] on the poplars
> we hung up our lyres (*kinnōrôtênû*),
> [3] for our captors asked us there for songs (*dibrê-šîr*),
> our tormentors for amusement,
> 'Sing (*šîrû*) us one of the songs (*miššîr*) of Zion'.
> [4] How can we sing ('*êk nāšîr*) a song of the Lord ('*et-šîr-yhwh*)
> on alien soil?
> [5] If I forget you, O Jerusalem,
> let my right hand wither;
> [6] let my tongue stick to my palate
> if I cease to think of you,
> if I do not keep Jerusalem in memory
> even at my happiest hour.

Verses 2–4 show that the Jewish exiles found it impossible to play their lyres and sing 'songs of Zion' – 'a song of the Lord' – in Babylonia. The phrases 'songs of Zion' and 'a song of the Lord' are synonymously parallel, implying that these were sacred songs specific to the religious cult at Jerusalem. The implication is strengthened by the despairing question in verse 4, 'How can we sing a song of the Lord on alien soil?' Clearly, to do so would have been meaningless (if not sacrilegious) away from Zion, in a land whose people did not worship the Lord. That the exiles 'hung up' (that is to say 'put away') their lyres because of this, means that these instruments were also specific to the Jewish cult. It is possible that the psalmist and his company had been Temple musicians. These three verses confirm that in cultic worship at the Temple the players of plucked-string instruments were also the singers, and that they sang as they played.

In verses 5 and 6, the oaths that disaster could befall the psalmist's right hand and tongue if he should forget Jerusalem probably allude to playing the *kinnôr* and singing the songs of Zion: if his right hand were to wither, he would not be able to play; if his tongue were to cling to the roof of his mouth, he would not be able to sing.[41]

In five psalms instrumental music is associated with non-musical forms of expression. In Psalms 66:1b(1)–2; 81:2(1)–3(2); 95:1–2; and 98:4–5 the non-musical forms are *rûaʿ* 'raising a shout' and *rānan* 'shouting for joy';[42] instrumental music is implied by words built on the root ZMR.

In Psalm 87:7 dancing is associated with song:

---

[41]   Kraus, *Psalmen*, vol. 2, p. 1085.

[42]   Note that in Ps. 81:2 the MT has *harĕnînû* 'shout for joy' but the JPS *Tanakh* has 'sing joyously', and in Ps. 95:1 the MT has *nĕrannĕnâ* 'let us shout for joy' but the JPS *Tanakh* has 'let us sing joyously'.

[Ps. 87:7] Singers [wĕšārîm] and dancers [kĕḥōlĕlîm] alike [will say]:
'All my roots are in You'.

The literary style here is rhetorical, underlining the patriotism of the dwellers in Jerusalem. In common with the vast majority of translations, non-English as well as English, the JPS *Tanakh* translates ḥōlĕlîm as 'dancers'.[43] This presupposes that the Hebrew word is derived from either the noun mĕḥōla 'ring-dance, round-dance', or the gerund māḥôl 'ring-dancing, round-dancing', or a form of the verb ḥûl/ḥîl meaning 'to dance (the ring-dance)'. A small number of translators apparently derive ḥōlĕlîm from the verb ḥālal 'to pipe, to play an instrument'. Thus, for example, the KJV translates the beginning of verse 7a: 'As well the singers as the players on instruments'; the NIV, swapping the groups of performers, renders the same passage: 'As they make music, they will sing'; and an interlineary Hebrew–English edition of Psalms has: 'And the singers as well as the pipers'.[44] From a linguistic point of view both 'pipers' and 'dancers' can be justified; perhaps ambiguity is deliberate in order to suggest both groups. Nevertheless, considering the affinity of 'ḥōlĕlîm' with words for 'ring-dance' and 'ring-dancing', there seems no compelling reason to doubt the view of the majority of translators that the second group of performers listed in Psalm 87:7a is to be understood as 'dancers'. That dancers and singers are mentioned together in this verse does not necessarily mean that they were directly associated with each other, but when this verse is read in the context of the whole of Psalm 87, it becomes evident that they at least belonged together in cultic celebrations.

It is a reasonable assumption that the musicians at the sacrificial rites were men. The sources make no specific mention of women having any function at, or in connection with, sacrifices, and the people whom they do mention in this way – the priests and the Levites in particular – are men. The cult, like the society in which it was embedded, was male-oriented; female participation in the offering of sacrifice to the Deity, the central act of the cult, would have been unlikely. The musicians were therefore probably men. It may be noted that they are referred to in the masculine plural: šārîm 'singers' and nōgĕnîm 'players [of instruments]'; and when imperatives are used of their musical activities, these are also masculine plural: šîrû 'sing!' and zammĕrû 'play!' But since masculine plurals are used in Hebrew for mixed groups as well as all-male ones, masculine plural forms alone are not proof of exclusive male involvement.

The musicians at non-sacrificial rites, on the other hand, were not exclusively male. This is shown, for example, by Psalm 68:26(25), where the psalmist lists the participants in processions as šārîm 'singers', nōgĕnîm 'players' and 'ălāmôt 'maidens, young girls' who played hand drums.

43 Among non-English translations the following may be mentioned: the Vulgate (Ps. 86:7a) has 'choris'; Kraus, *Psalmen*, vol. 2, p. 765, has 'Tänzer'; Henri Meschonnic, *Gloires: Traduction des psaumes* (Paris, 2001), p. 233 (text), p. 484 (commentary), has 'les danseurs'.
44 *The Interlineary Hebrew and English Psalter* (London, n.d.).

The material assembled above gives no certain indication as to whether singers might have performed as soloists. The first-person singular formulations in Psalms 7:18(17); 43:4; 61:9 and 137:6 could refer to the individual's singing within a group. Singers certainly sang in groups, in both sacrificial and non-sacrificial worship at the Temple. Material presented in the next section will show, however, that there are good grounds for believing that women as well as men sang as soloists.

The Repertory of Song

It is impossible to know for certain what was sung at the First Temple, but it is possible to make some suggestions based on the content of the sources. To begin with, sources relevant to the First-Temple period contain a number of poetic passages which may be described as cultic songs. The adjective 'cultic' is used here in the sense that in their literary settings the passages are presented as celebrating events or ideas of religious significance for the Israelites. They are termed 'songs' not only because they are self-contained lyrical items, but also because their texts or the preambles to their texts indicate that traditions of sung performance belonged to them. It is possible that some of these passages are examples of material sung at the First Temple.

The most obvious cultic songs are the Song of the Sea (Exod. 15:1–18), Miriam's Song (Exod. 15:21), the Song of the Well (Num. 21:17–18), the Song of Moses (Deut. 32:1–43), the Song of Deborah (Judg. 5:2–31), David's lament over Saul and Jonathan (2 Sam. 1:19–27), David's song of thanksgiving (2 Sam. 22:2–51) and Isaiah's song of thanksgiving and praise (Isa. 12:1b–6).[45] A superficial reading of these songs in their scriptural setting produces the impression that many of them were sung by specific people in given situations, sometimes apparently with instrumental accompaniment. A closer examination reveals that neither their musical aspects nor their relationship to their literary contexts are always as straightforward as might at first appear.

All the cultic songs listed above are introduced into their literary contexts by preambles that either identify the singers with whom they are traditionally associated, or indicate what is to be sung, or both. The preamble to Miriam's Song relates in addition that she played a hand drum (*tōp*) and was followed by women dancing and playing hand drums (*tuppîm*). The preamble to David's lament over Saul and Jonathan (2 Sam. 1:17–18) begins by identifying David as the singer. Identification of individuals as singers (whether in preambles or texts) may be taken to imply traditions of solo performance.

The poetic texts of all the songs except the Song of Moses (Deut. 32:1–43) contain musical information. In David's song of thanksgiving (2 Sam. 22:2–51)

---

[45]   For detailed discussion of these and subsequent points, see John Arthur Smith, 'Musical Aspects of Old Testament Canticles in their Biblical Setting', *EMH*, 17 (1998): 221–64. In the following discussion some of the points made there are modified.

this is confined to the notice that David will 'hymn' (*'ăzammēr*) the Deity's name (2 Sam. 22:50b).[46] Otherwise the texts of the remaining items refer clearly to song or singing. In the text of David's lament over Saul and Jonathan, a responsive method of performance is suggested by the occurrence of the phrase 'how have the mighty fallen' three times in the manner of a refrain. In the texts of the Song of Deborah, David's song of thanksgiving and Isaiah's song of thanksgiving and praise, musical instruments are implied by the use of verbs built on the Hebrew root *ZMR*.

Whether these songs were actually sung at the First Temple is impossible to determine although there is no immediate reason to doubt that they were. Miriam's Song and the Song of Deborah suggest contexts such as processions with dancing and popular non-sacrificial rites respectively.[47] The second verse of the preamble to David's lament over Saul and Jonathan (2 Sam. 1:18), although its meaning is problematical,[48] seems to point to the dissemination of the lament throughout Judah and its committal to writing in the 'Book of Jashar'[49] so that it became a standard cultic lament.[50] It may have been sung at the First Temple on Yom Kippur (the Day of Atonement). A lament was a formal expression of sorrow in song.

In addition to the cultic songs discussed above, it would seem reasonable to include among the items that might have been sung at the Temple the pre-exilic psalms which refer to or imply music there, namely Psalms 7, 61, 66, 68, 81, 87 and possibly also Psalm 95, as quoted and discussed earlier. All these psalms and the cultic songs discussed above fall comfortably within the categories 'songs of Zion' and 'the Lord's song' used in Psalm 137:3, 4 to characterize the vocal music of cultic worship at the First Temple.

Instruments at the Tabernacle, the Removal of the Ark of the Covenant and the First Temple

The various instruments are of three types: strings, percussion and wind. The wind instruments are the metal trumpet (*ḥăṣōṣĕrâ*), the shofar and the pipe (*ḥālîl*) described earlier. The name 'shofar' is possibly generic for a musical horn since according to a postbiblical source (*m. Roš Haš.* 3:3) it could be used for instruments made from the horns of wild goats (*yā'ēl* 'antelope, chamois, wild

---

[46]   There is no obvious reason why the JPS *Tanakh* begins the first clause of this verse (2 Sam. 22:50a) 'For this I sing Your praise'. According to the MT it should read 'For this I thank [*or* "praise"] you, Lord'.

[47]   Smith, 'Musical Aspects of Old Testament Canticles': 229–31, 258–9.

[48]   J.P. Fokkelman, *Narrative Art and Poetry in the Book of Samuel* (Assen/Maastricht, 1986), pp. 649–51.

[49]   Alternatively 'Book of the Upright' or 'Book of the Song' (as LXX 3 Kingdoms 8:53a).

[50]   See J.L. Mays, 'The David of the Psalms', *Interpretation*, 40 (1986): 148.

goat') as well as for those made from rams' horns.[51] The name *ḥālîl*, on the other hand, is probably specific to the double reed pipe seeing that biblical texts refer to an additional type of pipe, the *'ûgāb*,[52] which was possibly an end-blown flute or a syrinx, and may have had pagan associations.[53]

The stringed instruments are the *kinnôr* (plural: *kinnōrôt*) and the *nēbel* (plural: *nĕbālîm*). Both were of the plucked-string variety. They were small enough to be easily portable and to be played whilst being carried. The *kinnôr* was a lyre, a type of instrument common throughout the ancient Near East. The details of its shape varied, but it consisted basically of a fairly flat, square or rectangular sound box (probably made of wood) and two wooden arms that extended parallel to each other from each end of it. The arms were linked near their open end by a yoke from which the instrument's strings were stretched to the sound box.[54] The *kinnôr* of the First Temple may have had seven strings in common with the Babylonian lyre, which was ubiquitous in the Levant from the eighteenth to about the fourth century BCE.[55] Sources from the postbiblical period show that the *kinnôr* had from six to ten strings made of thin gut, and that it was normally played with a plectrum, but whether this also applied in pre-exilic times is not known. To judge from ancient pictorial representations, the instrument was held by its sound box which was gripped between the player's upper arm and ribs; the rest of the instrument projected forward and was supported beneath the lower arm by the player's left hand, leaving the right hand free to pluck the strings.

The *nēbel* is often mentioned together with the *kinnôr* in the literature, but biblical sources say little or nothing about its physical and musical characteristics. According to postbiblical sources it was similar in appearance to the *kinnôr* but had a bulbous sound box made perhaps from the dried shell of a gourd or from a stiffened skin bag such as the inflated and dried bladder of an animal (the name of the instrument means 'waterskin, wineskin'). The consensus of modern scholarship is that the *nēbel* was probably a variety of lyre, though possibly larger than the *kinnôr*.[56] Postbiblical sources also say that

---

[51]   See further within the sections 'The Musical Instruments: Additional Remarks' in Chapter 4, and 'In War', subsection *During Preparations for Battle*', in Chapter 6.

[52]   Gen. 4:21; Ps. 150:4; Job 21:12; 30:31.

[53]   *MAI/P*, pp. 31–2. The word *'ûgāb* is translated 'pipe' in both the JPS *Tanakh* and the NRSV. In the Hebrew Bible the word occurs only at the four places listed in the previous note. The LXX renders it by three different words: *kitharan* (Gen. 4:21), *organōn* (Ps. 150:4) and *psalmou/psalmos* (Job 21:12; 30:31).

[54]   In *MAI/P*, pp. xxxii–xxxvi, Joachim Braun gives (in his Table 2) a chronologically arranged pictorial catalogue of the outline shapes of Near-Eastern lyres from the early second millennium BCE to the Roman period.

[55]   M.L. West, 'The Babylonian Musical Notation and the Hurrian Melodic Texts', *M&L*, 75/2 (1994): 161–71.

[56]   Bathja Bayer, 'The Biblical Nebel', *Yuval*, 1 (1968): 89–131; *MAI*, pp. 278–89; *MAI/P*, pp. 23–4.

the *nēbel* had twelve strings made of thick gut, and that it was played with the fingers. Whether this was so in earlier periods is not known.

The phrase *bĕnēbel 'āśôr* 'with (*or* "on") a ten-stringed harp' in verse 9 of the pre-exilic Psalm 144 and verse 2 of the postexilic Psalm 33,[57] seems to indicate that the *nēbel* had ten strings in very early times. Most translations of Psalms 144:9 and 33:2 interpret the word *'āśôr* 'ten' in the sense of a material attribute of the *nēbel*, rendering it 'ten-stringed', as in the JPS *Tanakh* and the NRSV. But the word could have an alternative significance. It is noteworthy that the Hebrew of this verse supplies no word for 'stringed'. It is possible that *'āśôr* here does not have to do with the number of strings, but that it is a coded reference to the Deity since the initial letter of the Deity's name in Hebrew, the letter *yôd*, is the tenth letter of the alphabet. The sense of the phrase *nēbel 'āśôr* could therefore be something like 'with the *nēbel* of the Lᴏʀᴅ'. While this might seem far-fetched to modern Western minds, it would not have been so to Near-Eastern ones in antiquity: number symbolism has always been part of Near-Eastern patterns of thought.[58]

The name *nēbel* is frequently translated 'harp', and occasionally 'lute'. Admittedly, present-day knowledge of harps and lutes in the ancient western Near East is limited since there is no archaeological evidence for such instruments in the region prior to the Hellenistic period.[59] Nevertheless, such translations probably give misleading impressions of the instrument.

The percussion instruments are the *'aṣê bĕrôšîm* (cypress wood instruments), the *tōp* (hand drum; plural: *tuppîm*, also sometimes in the form *tôpēpôt*), the *mĕna'anĕ'îm* (rattles), and the *ṣelṣelîm* (cymbals). Recent musical scholarship regards the *'aṣê bĕrôšîm* as cypress wood clappers used in orgiastic cultic festivities.[60]

The *tōp* was a small, round, hand-held frame drum; its name is probably onomatopoeic.[61] In many English translations of the Bible the name *tōp* is translated 'timbrel' or 'tambourine'. These translations are unsatisfactory: the former because it is archaic and therefore liable to be misunderstood, the latter because it could be taken to imply that the ancient *tōp* had jingles, or that it had jingles but no skin, whereas neither was the case. The LXX translation of the name as *tumpanon*, a generic word for 'drum', is not especially enlightening.

[57] Gillingham, *Poems and Psalms*, p. 254.

[58] See, with particular reference to number symbolism (gematria) in Greek and Hebrew texts in late antiquity, John F.A. Sawyer, *Sacred Languages and Sacred Texts* (London and New York, 1999), pp. 126–7. Numerology was also prevalent in the ancient Near East. For its application in ancient Near-Eastern architecture, see *The New Jerusalem Scroll from Qumran*, ed. Michael Chyutin, trans. Richard Fiantz (Sheffield, 1997), pp. 131–6. (See under 'New Jerusalem Scroll' in the Bibliography.)

[59] *MAI/P*, pp. 23, 117.

[60] *New Grove/2*, vol. 3, p. 525; *MAI/P*, p. 12; compare *MAI*, p. 385.

[61] *MAI/P*, pp. 29–31.

The *měnaʿaněʾîm* were shakers of a type that originally belonged to ancient Egyptian culture. Joachim Braun agrees with Bathja Bayer that they were probably hollow clay rattles,[62] whereas other writers regard them as sistrums.[63] Their name is probably best translated 'rattles' rather than 'sistrums' (which the JPS *Tanakh* has) or 'castanets' (which the NRSV has). The name *měnaʿaněʾîm* occurs in the Hebrew Bible only at 2 Samuel 6:5 in the narrative of the removal of the Ark of the Covenant to Jerusalem.

Another kind of shaker, the *šāliš*, probably a sistrum, is named in the plural (*šālišîm*) – again only once – at 1 Samuel 18:6.[64]

The *ṣelṣelîm* were probably small metal cymbals which existed in various sizes from 3 to 12 cm in diameter. The name (also probably onomatopoeic) occurs only in the plural, suggesting that they were not played singly. The *ṣelṣelîm* may originally have been used in the pagan Canaanite cult.[65] Perhaps the smallest of them were played as finger cymbals worn on the thumb and middle finger (or thumb and forefinger) of each hand.

A certain amount may be surmised about the sound of the instruments. The metal trumpet and shofar, being valveless and having conical bore, would probably have been able to produce only the second, third and fourth notes of the harmonic series (the octave, a fifth above it, and a fourth above that). The fundamental would most likely have been impossible to obtain, and any notes higher than the fourth harmonic would have required abnormally strong diaphragm and lip pressure. With regard to the metal trumpets, it may be appropriate to imagine sounds similar to those of modern valveless fanfare trumpets, which the metal trumpets of ancient Israel and Judah resembled in shape. But owing to the thicker walls, wider bore and shorter length of the ancient trumpets (to judge from archaeological remains) they would not have had the brilliance of tone of modern fanfare trumpets. By comparison, the shofars would probably have had a lower pitch, a rougher sound and a duller tone because of the dull resonance of natural horn and the inherent irregularities in the inside surfaces of the walls of the instrument. To what extent the pitch was the same from metal trumpet to metal trumpet, and from shofar to shofar, is not known. The pitch of metal trumpets would have been relatively easy to regulate

---

[62]   Ibid., pp. 19–20, 101–4 (Illustrations III.18–25).

[63]   *MAI*, pp. 381 (pictures), 384; Eric Werner, 'Jewish Music, §I, 4: The Instruments of the Temple', *New Grove*/1, vol. 9, pp. 618–19 (with picture).

[64]   See further, Chapter 6 in this volume, the section 'In War', subsection '*At Victory Celebrations*'.

[65]   Compare *MAI*, pp. 375–81; *MAI/P*, pp. 107–9. Alfred Sendrey's statement that the word *měṣiltayim* '[pair of] cymbals' 'appears for the first time in the Bible at the transfer of the Ark of the Covenant to Jerusalem (2 Sam. 6:5)', is incorrect: the word used in 2 Sam. 6:5 is *ṣelṣelîm*, as given herein in the quotation of that verse at n. 21. The word *měṣiltayim* is used for the first time in the Hebrew Bible at Ezra 3:10; thereafter at Neh. 12:27. Its next occurrence is at 1 Chr. 13:8 in a text that is a modified parallel of 2 Sam. 6:5. It appears subsequently several times in 1 & 2 Chr.

during manufacture; the pitch of shofars would have been determined by their state as ready-made natural products; it probably varied from one instrument to another. It was probably not as important for the shofars to be in tune with each other as it was for the metal trumpets.

Cymbals (*ṣelṣelîm*, 2 Sam. 6:5; Ps. 150:5 twice) are the only type of percussion instrument that would have been capable of being played in more than one way, thereby producing different types of sound. In the Hebrew Bible *ṣelṣelîm* are referred to in the plural, suggesting they were played in pairs. They could have been held vertically and clashed together in the same manner as modern orchestral cymbals (although they were much smaller than the modern specimens) or alternatively they could have been held horizontally, but at slightly different heights, and moved vertically towards each other so that the rim of one made contact with the rim of the other, resulting in a weak clanging sound. Given that *ṣelṣelîm* could have diameters as small as 3–6 cm, it is possible that the name subsumed finger cymbals which produced high-pitched ringing sounds when clashed together.

The *ḥālîl*, if a reed pipe, as suggested earlier in this chapter, would probably have produced a sound similar to that of a modern oboe, but quieter and less round on account of the slender bore. If the instrument had double pipes, one of them may have been used to play a drone or an ostinato, the other a more or less ornamented melodic line.

Turning finally to the plucked-string instruments *nēbel* and *kinnôr*, if the ancient *nĕbālîm* were similar to the postbiblical variety, they would have had thicker strings, a larger overall form, and thus a deeper tone than the *kinnōrôt*. If they were played with the fingers, they would have had a softer tone than the *kinnōrôt* if the *kinnōrôt* were played with a plectrum. The sound of a *nēbel* or *kinnôr* would have been much quieter, and would have had much less carrying power, than that of a shofar, a metal trumpet, a pipe or a percussion instrument. This would have rendered the plucked-string instruments ideally suited to playing with song. Since each Temple singer played his plucked-string instrument, the balance between the sound of the singing and the sound of the strings would have been self-regulating.

The Musicians

The pre-exilic and exilic sources give little direct information about the identity of the First-Temple musicians. They say that Aaronite priests blew metal trumpets over the sacrifices of burnt offering and well-being, and they show that at non-sacrificial cultic rituals men and women sang and played instruments. But it is only by inference one concludes that men alone were responsible for music at sacrifices.

This is in marked contrast to the postexilic books of Chronicles and some of the postbiblical literature, which provide detailed information. These writings probably have little or no direct bearing on the First Temple (despite the apparent focus of the books of Chronicles), but they do show that at the sacrifices at the Second Temple there was a highly organized musical service that was the responsibility of non-priestly groups appointed from among the Levites. Pre-exilic sources, on the other hand, although they have much to say about the Levites' work in connection with the transportation of the Ark of the Covenant and the Tabernacle, and about the Levites' general duties in connection with religious observances, make no mention of any Levitical musical duties at either the Tabernacle or the Temple. It is therefore possible that the music at the First Temple was not the responsibility of Levites, but of some other non-priestly group closely associated with cultic places and the rites performed at them. In the 1950s and 1960s Sigmund Mowinckel and Alfred Sendrey proposed that the First-Temple musicians (other than the trumpet-blowing priests) were drawn from among the prophets.[66] This is not an altogether improbable idea; it is worth reconsidering here, taking into account material not available to Mowinckel and Sendrey.

According to the chronology implied by the narratives in the Hebrew Bible, the prophets may be divided into two groups:[67] 'early' prophets, active from the supposed time of Samuel and Saul (prior to the First Temple) until just over a century or so into the First-Temple period, and 'late' prophets, active during the remainder of the First-Temple period and onwards. Both groups include notable biblical figures: Samuel, Elijah and Elisha among the early prophets and, among the late prophets, the men whose oracles are preserved in the biblical books which bear their names. Prophets were not exclusively men: in Exodus 15:20 Miriam is referred to as a prophet, as are Deborah in Judges 4:4, Hulda in 2 Kings 22:14 and the anonymous woman in Isaiah 8:3.[68]

Prophets communicated Divine messages to the world; they were intermediaries between the Deity and mortals. Their messages were delivered typically as inspired oracles, sometimes in poetic form, as is the case with most of the written examples in the Hebrew Bible. The utterance of sacred oracles was a form of prophetic activity which took place in addition to worship of the Deity. It was not in itself worship, but it was an important aspect of the cult since it witnessed to the belief that the Deity was actively concerned for his people.

Some of the ancient prophets were consulted by monarchs and others of high standing, and had considerable religious and political influence. It seems

---

[66] Sigmund Mowinckel, *Offersang og sangoffer* (Oslo, 1951), pp. 310–13; *PsIW*, vol. 2, pp. 55–8; *MAI*, pp. 488–9, 529.

[67] The summary here and in the following paragraphs is based on: J. Lindblom, *Prophecy in Ancient Israel* (Oxford, 1962); Gerhard von Rad, *Old Testament Theology*, trans. D.M.G. Stalker, 2 vols (Edinburgh, 1965), vol. 1, pp. 6–79; Edmond Jacob, *Theology of the Old Testament* (London, 1971), pp. 239–46; Robert R. Wilson, *Prophecy and Society in Ancient Israel* (Philadelphia PA, 1980); Stacey, *Prophetic Drama*.

[68] The word 'prophetess' in Isa. 8:3 probably signifies Isaiah's wife rather than a female prophet: see the note to this verse in the JPS *Tanakh*.

that it was customary for individuals to give gifts of food or money to prophets in return for private consultation (1 Sam. 9:5-10; 1 Kgs 14:1-3). Nevertheless, prophecy seems not to have been a profession in the sense of a closed, paid occupation.

In addition to these general observations, particular points are significant in the present context. The early prophets were more or less loosely grouped as disciples (*bānîm* 'sons, juniors, followers') round masters (*'ābôt* 'fathers, seniors, leaders'; singular: *'āb*, as at 2 Kings 2:12; no blood relationship is necessarily implied by the Hebrew terminology). The groups have sometimes been referred to as 'guilds', 'brotherhoods' or 'schools' of prophets,[69] but the biblical sources suggest styles of organization more fluid than these terms imply. Nevertheless, the prophet masters (or 'seniors' or 'leaders') were mentors for their disciples, teaching them and looking after their physical welfare (for example, 2 Kgs 2:3-18; 6:1-7). Exactly how much of their time the masters and their disciples spent together is not known. It may not have been normal for disciples to reside with their masters: there were prophets in this period who lived alone or with their families; and the late prophets – the great literary prophets from Amos onwards – seem not to have been associated with groups of disciples.

Prophets were often to be found in or near cultic centres, where pilgrims and periodic festival crowds would ensure audiences. 1 Samuel 10:5 mentions a 'band of prophets coming down from the shrine' of Gibeah; 2 Kings 2:3, 5 mention prophets' disciples (*běnê-hannĕbî'îm*, literally: 'sons of prophets') at Bethel and Jericho respectively. First Isaiah speaks of 'the prophets' (implying a recognized group) at Jerusalem (Isa. 29:10; 30:10). Jeremiah prophesied in the Temple (Jer. 26:2, 7), at certain of the Temple gates (Jer. 7:1-2; 17:19-20; 19:1-2) and in Jerusalem at large (Jer. 2:2; 4:5). Prophets were evidently an institutionalized group in the Jerusalem Temple by Jeremiah's time (immediately prior to the exile) since Jeremiah 26:7-10 reports that it was they (together with the priests) who heard him prophesy in the Temple and recommended (jointly with the priests) that he should be put to death for speaking against the city.[70]

On two occasions musical instruments are associated with prophetic utterance. One is when Saul is told that he will meet a group of prophets 'coming down from the shrine' at Gibeah (1 Sam. 10:5), referred to above. These prophets, he is told, will arrive

> [1 Sam. 10:5] preceded by lyres [*nēbel*], timbrels [*wětōp* '(and) hand drums'], flutes [*wěhālîl* '(and) pipes'], and harps [*wěkinnôr*], and they will be speaking in ecstasy.

---

[69] See the literature cited in n. 67. Alfred Sendrey (*MAI*, pp. 482-9) makes unwarranted and exaggerated claims about what he calls the 'schools of prophets'.

[70] Compare *PsIW*, vol. 2, pp. 55-6.

The other occasion is when the prophet Elisha is consulted by the kings of Israel, Judah and Edom, and he requests the services of a musician (2 Kgs 3:15–19):

> [2 Kgs 3:15] '[15] Now then, get me a musician [*měnaggēn*]'. As the musician [*haměnaggēn*] played [*kěnaggēn*], the hand[71] of the Lᴏʀᴅ came upon him [Elisha], [16] and he said, 'Thus said the Lᴏʀᴅ ...'

These passages suggest that instrumental music was a normal concomitant of prophetic utterance. The music may have been used partly to induce the states of frenzy, ecstasy or trance in which prophecies were uttered, as illustrated by the above passages and their continuations.

The practice of uttering prophecy to the sound of instrumental music probably lies behind the way in which the author of the book of Ezekiel expresses the Deity's warning to Ezekiel about how his prophecies will be received:

> [Ezek. 33:32] To them [the audience of Israelites] you [Ezekiel] are just a singer [*kěšîr* or *kōšār*] of bawdy songs, who has a sweet voice and plays [*naggēn*] skilfully; they hear your words, but will not obey them.

Furthermore, the simile of a singer suggests that prophecy could be uttered as song. If this were the case, it would most likely have applied first and foremost to prophecies formulated as poetry.

There is no clear indication that pre-exilic prophets functioned as cultic musicians, but when they are considered alongside the non-priestly cultic musicians of the Second Temple – the Levite musicians – several points of similarity emerge which together suggest close parallels between the two groups.

First, there are points of outward similarity. As has been pointed out, the early prophets were typically organized in disciple–master groups as 'sons' of their 'fathers'; the Levites were organized in family groups as 'sons' of their forefathers, although in the case of the Levites, blood relationship is implied by the father–son terminology. Most prophets seem to have been based in or near cultic centres; the Levite musicians were settled in towns (Ezra 2:70) and villages near Jerusalem (Neh. 12:28–29; 1 Esd. 5:46). The prophets at the First Temple were closely associated with the priests; this was also the case with the Levites at the Second Temple. The prophets sometimes made their utterances – some of which could have been in the form of song – to the sound of musical instruments. The instruments included the *nēbel* and the *kinnôr*, two of the three types of instrument played by the Levite singers in their musical service at the Temple.

---

[71]   'hand': so the JPS *Tanakh* is following the MT (*yad*). The NRSV has 'power', translating according to the majority of manuscripts and the Targum, which have *rûaḥ* 'power, spirit'. See *BHS*; compare *HCSB*.

Second, there are points of terminological similarity in the respective groups of pertinent biblical texts. Apart from the commonality of the father-son terminology, the prophetic title *ḥōzēh* 'seer' is used for the Levitical singers Heman (1 Chr. 25:5), Asaph (2 Chr. 29:30) and Jeduthun (2 Chr. 35:15), as well as for pre-exilic prophets (2 Sam. 24:11; 2 Kgs 17:13; Isa. 29:10; 30:10).[72] Furthermore, the musical service of the Levitical families is referred to as 'prophesying' (*nābā'* 'to be inspired, to prophesy, to speak or sing as a prophet': 1 Chr. 25:1-6).

Taken together, the points of similarity provide grounds for believing that non-priestly First-Temple musicians were drawn from among the prophets.[73] Yet while this seems highly plausible, the absence of concrete evidence means that it can be no more than a promising hypothesis.

Concluding Remarks

The sources give no precise idea of how the singing and playing was fitted into the rites. Nevertheless it is clear that the music was an intrinsic element of cultic worship, not an accompaniment to it or an ornamentation of it.

Certain instruments had special functions. The ways in which they were used suggest that there existed what might be termed a 'hierarchy of sanctity' among them. Plucked-string instruments and shofars could be employed at sacrifices and at non-sacrificial rituals; percussion instruments and the *ḥālîl* would have ranked below these since they do not seem to have been employed at sacrifices. Metal trumpets would have ranked highest since, apart from their use for signalling, they were blown 'over' the sacrifices as a 'reminder' on the Israelites' behalf before their Deity (Num. 10:10).

The sources say nothing about either the style or the aesthetic qualities of the music. Hurrian notational remains from the second millennium BCE, taken together with evidence supplied by later musical traditions in the Near East and eastern Mediterranean generally, suggest that vocal melody moved mainly by conjunct motion in a pentatonic framework. Plucked-string instruments and pipes probably played heterophonic ornamentation of the vocal lines.[74] Music at the First Temple may have exhibited similar characteristics.

As to the aesthetic qualities of the music, the sources supply no evidence sufficient to provide meaningful insights. To make value judgements about the performance of ancient Israelite and Jewish music on the basis of modern Western musical traditions[75] is unhelpful. The frequently mentioned 'shout' (*rûa'*, *rānan*) seems to have been a loud outburst of sound from voices and instruments

---

[72]   See Wilson, *Prophecy and Society*, pp. 254–5.

[73]   Sigmund Mowinckel (*PsIW*, vol. 2, pp. 56–7) presents a cogent argument for this view. Alfred Sendrey (*MAI*, pp. 488–9, 529), treats it as a foregone conclusion.

[74]   West, 'The Babylonian Musical Notation': 173, 179.

[75]   As, for example, in *MAI*, p. 425.

simultaneously. Processions were probably energetic and noisy, with dancing, singing and the playing of plucked-string and percussion instruments.[76] Psalm 81:3(2) mentions the *kinnôr nā'îm* 'melodious [*or* 'sweet, pleasant'] lyre'. However, *nā'îm* is used there as a poetic and general characterization of the instrument; there is no indication of the feature, or features that inspired the psalmist to use this adjective. In this instance, *nā'îm* conveys no more than that the *kinnôr* was in some way, or ways, agreeable.[77] Furthermore, that *nā'îm* is used to qualify the *kinnôr* cannot be held to carry pejorative implications for the *tōp* and the *nēbel* also named in this verse but without qualifying adjectives.

Yet perhaps it is beside the point to inquire about the aesthetic qualities of the music. The music of the cult was not intended for artistic enjoyment; rather, it was an inseparable part of the worship of the Deity at the Temple in Jerusalem. In non-sacrificial contexts the music was directed primarily towards the assembled worshippers and visitors, to induce in them a state of enthusiasm appropriate to worship. During sacrifices it was directed towards the Deity, to alert Divine attention to the offerings being made by faithful mortals in obedience to Divine commands, and to praise, thank and extol the Deity.

---

[76] Compare *PsIW*, vol. 1, pp. 6, 10.

[77] Compare the use of *n'ym* (the consonantal word on which *nā'îm* is vocalized) at 2 Sam. 1:23 and 23:1.

Chapter 3
Music at the Second Temple, 1

When the Israelites who had been exiled in Babylonia returned to Judah in 539 BCE and 458 or 398 BCE,[1] the ruined Temple in Jerusalem was rebuilt. The traditions about this are contained in Ezra 3:8–6:15. They relate that the work, begun in 537 BCE, took approximately twenty years to complete. This 'Second' Temple was finished and dedicated in 516[2] or 515 BCE.[3]

The Second Temple probably changed little in appearance for almost five hundred years until 23/22 or 20/19 BCE when Herod the Great began a comprehensive remodelling of its architecture. This included enlarging the courts round the Temple building itself and improving the amenities for personnel, worshippers and spectators.[4] The remodelled Temple, known as 'Herod's Temple', was completed in about 62 CE. It was a vast and magnificent edifice famous throughout the Near East. It stood until it was destroyed by Roman soldiers in 70 CE.

General Aspects of Music at the Second Temple

Principle Sources

The principal sources are literary; they originated at various times between about 450 BCE and 200 CE and fall into three chronologically determined groups. The earliest, consisting of the books of Psalms, Ezra–Nehemiah and Chronicles, provides a picture of music at the Second Temple up to around 300 BCE. The Temple with which Chronicles is concerned is ostensibly the First Temple, but since

---

[1] *Israelites* who returned with Ezra (Ezra 7:7–10; 8:1–14) would have done so in either 458 BCE or 398 BCE depending on whether Artaxerxes I or II is meant in Ezra 7:7.

[2] J. Alberto Soggin, *An Introduction to the History of Israel and Judah*, trans. John Bowden (London, 1993), p. 415.

[3] Ezra 6:14–17 and the notes on these verses in *HCSB*.

[4] Detailed description and discussion in E.P. Sanders, *Judaism: Practice and Belief 63 BCE–66 CE* (London and Philadelphia PA, 1992), pp. 57–69; see also ibid., pp. 308–14: elevations and plans reproduced from (on p. 308) Kathleen Ritmeyer and Leen Ritmeyer, 'Reconstructing Herod's Temple Mount in Jerusalem', *Biblical Archaeological Review*, 15/6 (1989): 23–42, and (on pp. 310–14) Th.A. Busink, *Der Tempel von Jerusalem*, 2 vols (Leiden, 1970, 1980), vol. 2. The main primary sources are Josephus, *Jewish War* [c.75 CE], book 5, 5:1–8; Josephus, *Jewish Antiquities* [93 or 94 CE], book 15, 11:1–7; Mishnah, *Middot*.

most of the details Chronicles provides are reckoned to have been retrojected from the pre-Herodian Second Temple (as explained in Chapter 2), Chronicles is a relevant source here. The sources in this group witness to already established and settled forms and patterns of worship.

The next group, consisting of books from the Old Testament Apocrypha in the LXX, provides details from the last two centuries of the Second Temple. Other portions of the LXX are also useful. The LXX is thought to have come into being between about 450 and 150 BCE; contemporary cultic practice probably informed its Greek rendering of the cultic vocabulary of the Hebrew Scriptures. It may be reckoned as a source belonging to both this and the earliest group.

The third group consists of literature written during the time of, and shortly after, Herod's Temple, and includes works by Josephus, small sections of the New Testament Apocrypha and the Mishnah. Of all the sources, the most valuable are the Mishnah and those belonging to the earliest group.

The Evidence of 1 Chronicles 13:6–16:7

One of the passages examined at the beginning of Chapter 2 was the narrative in 2 Samuel 6:1–19 about the removal of the Ark of the Covenant to Jerusalem. A greatly expanded version of that narrative is found in 1 Chronicles 13:6–16:7 where considerable attention is given to the organization of the musical service of the cult. An examination of 1 Chronicles 13:6–16:7 thus affords valuable insights into cultic music at the Second Temple as the Chronicler saw it from his postexilic standpoint.

The text of the narrative in 2 Samuel 6 reappears discontinuously, but otherwise almost verbatim, in the Chronicler's expanded version. However, there are noteworthy differences of musical detail, all of which are confined to one verse: 1 Chronicles 13:8. A comparison of this verse with its pre-exilic version at 2 Samuel 6:5 reveals that where the pre-exilic text has the phrase *'ăṣê bĕrôšîm* 'cypress wood [instruments]', the postexilic parallel has the word *šîrîm* 'songs' (alternatively 'singers, cultic singers'); where the pre-exilic text has the word *mĕna'ănĕ'îm* 'rattles', the postexilic parallel has the word *mĕṣiltayim* 'paired cymbals'; and where the pre-exilic text has the word *ṣelṣelîm* 'cymbals', the postexilic parallel has the word *ḥăṣōṣĕrôt* '[metal] trumpets'. These differences are probably the result of the Chronicler's updating the list of instruments to bring it into line with the instruments used in the cult at the time when he wrote. It is possible that at some stage between the compilation of the Deuteronomistic History and the composition of Chronicles 'cypress wood [instruments]' and 'rattles' had been eliminated from the cult.[5] In this connection it is interesting that in the LXX version of 2 Samuel 6:5 (LXX 2 Kingdoms 6:5) there are also differences similar to those in the MT of 1 Chronicles 13:8: there are no 'cypress wood instruments', but *ōdais* 'songs'

---

5 Compare *MAI/P*, p. 12.

instead;[6] and the last type of instrument listed is *aulois* 'pipes'. In the LXX version of 1 Chronicles 13:8 the first item listed is *psaltōdois*, '[cultic] singers', corresponding to *šîrîm* in the MT.

It is the supplementary material in 1 Chronicles 13:6–16:7, however, that contains the most significant musical details. Of overwhelming importance is the tradition that David organized the music of the cult by making members of Levite clans responsible for the execution of most of it (1 Chr. 15:16–22; 16:4–5). The only exception was the priestly blowing of metal trumpets (15:24; 16:6). According to the tradition, the Levites, acting on David's orders, appointed Heman, Asaph and Ethan to play *mĕṣiltayim* 'cymbals', some of their kinsmen to play *nĕbālîm* 'harps' and others of their kinsmen to play *kinnōrôt* 'lyres' (15:16–21).[7]

Details about the Levites' instruments are provided in 1 Chronicles 15:19–21. Certain of their cymbals were *nĕḥōšet* 'of bronze' (15:19). Their 'harps' were *ʿal-ʿălāmôt* 'on alamoth' (15:20) and their lyres were *ʿal-haššĕmînît* 'on the sheminith' (15:21). The former phrase occurs also in the superscription to Psalm 46, the latter also in the superscriptions to Psalms 6 and 12. Their significance is unclear, and the nature of their relevance to the names of the plucked-string instruments to which they stand adjacent in 1 Chronicles 15:20–21 is uncertain. In most Bible translations from the LXX onwards they are left untranslated. It seems likely that in the present context the word *ʿălāmôt* should be regarded as deriving not from *ʿalmâ* 'girl, young woman', but from *ʿālam* 'to be hidden, to be in secret', and that it should read *ʿēlāmît* 'hidden, secret'.[8] The basic meaning of *haššĕmînît* is 'the eighth'.

Many suggestions as to what *ʿal-ʿălāmôt* and *ʿal-haššĕmînît* might mean have been put forward.[9] In an essay published in 1971, David Wulstan suggested that *ʿălāmôt* and *šĕmînît* might be the names of modes or tuning patterns for the *nĕbālîm* and *kinnōrôt* mentioned with them in 1 Chronicles 15:20–21,[10] so that the phrase *binĕbālîm ʿal-ʿălāmôt* would mean 'with harps according to [*or* "in" *or* "tuned to"] *alamoth*', and the phrase *bĕkinnōrôt ʿal-haššĕmînît* would mean 'with lyres according to [*or* "in" *or* "tuned to"] the *sheminith*'. This has become the standard view. Wulstan also proposed that *haššĕmînît* might at the same time indicate the number of the day on which this particular mode or tuning pattern

---

[6]   A version of 2 Sam. 6:5 from Cave 1 at Qumran also has 'songs' instead of 'cypress wood [instruments]'.

[7]   See also the notice about the Davidic institution of the Levitical musical service in 1 Chr. 6:16(31)–18(33); the subsequent verses serve to establish the Levitical pedigree of Heman, Asaph and Ethan.

[8]   *PsIW*, vol. 2, pp. 215–16, and the note on the word *ʿălāmôt* in *BHS* at 1 Chr. 15:20. In the superscription to LXX Ps. 45 (= MT Ps. 46), *kruphiōn* 'secret things' translates the Hebrew *ʿălāmôt*.

[9]   *MAI*, pp. 120–26, 320–21.

[10]   David Wulstan, 'The Origin of the Modes', in Egon Wellesz and Miloš Velimirović (eds), *Studies in Eastern Chant*, 2 vols (Oxford, 1966, 1971), vol. 2, pp. 8–11.

was employed, namely the eighth day.[11] But what significance this might have had in relation to the religious festivities which according to 1 Chronicles 15:1–16:1 accompanied the removal of the Ark to Jerusalem, is not clear since the Chronicler does not say how long those festivities lasted.[12] Furthermore, Wulstan's ingenious theory that since important festivals tended to last for eight days, if *haššĕmînît* could imply the eighth (last) day, *ʾălāmôt* might imply the first,[13] has no linguistic or narrative support in the sources.

An alternative to Wulstan's theory about *ʿal-ʾălāmôt* is that in its emended form, *ʿal-ʾēlāmît*, it refers to 'secret' knowledge in the sense of truths known to the faithful but withheld from non-believers. The *nĕbālîm ʿal-ʾēlāmît* of 15:20 would be the 'harps' played when texts concerned with such matters were sung, as, for example, in the case of Psalm 46.

A possible alternative understanding of *ʿal-haššĕmînît* is that it refers to a location where the lyres were played: 'on the eighth [gate or step or stone – some specific place or feature familiar to the readers]'. A passage in Ezekiel's description of the First Temple mentions three staircases of eight steps each, which led up to gateways on the south, east and north sides respectively of what Ezekiel calls the inner court of the Temple, the court where the priests and Levites served during sacrificial rites (Ezek. 40:28–37). The word *haššĕmînît* in 1 Chronicles 15:21 and Psalms 6:1 and 12:1 could be an elliptical reference to the eighth (topmost) step of one or more of those staircases.[14]

At the beginning of the second half of verse 16 in 1 Chronicles 15 the phrase -*kĕlê-šîr*, literally 'instruments of song', is used of Levitical instruments, implying that they were associated with the cultic song of the Levite musicians. The phrase is followed immediately by the names of the three types of Levitical instrument 'harps', lyres and cymbals. Modern translations imply by their punctuation that harps, lyres and cymbals were the 'instruments of song', but this may not have been the Chronicler's understanding. At two places in Chronicles cymbals (and trumpets) are excluded from among the 'instruments of song' by being named before them. One is 1 Chronicles 16:42: 'Heman and Jeduthun had with them trumpets [*ḥăṣōṣĕrôt*] and cymbals [*ûmĕṣiltayim*] to sound [*lĕmašmîʿîm*], and instruments for the songs of God [*ûkĕlê šîr hāʾĕlōhîm*]'. The other is 2 Chronicles

---

[11] Ibid., p. 9.

[12] Wulstan's claim (ibid.) that Ps. 12 was used on the eighth day of the Festival of Booths is misleading. There is no evidence that Ps. 12 (or Ps. 6, the superscription to which also contains the phrase *ʿal-haššĕmînît*) was used at the Temple during the Festival of Booths. It may have been used at the Second Temple (see below, also n. 14, and Table 4.1, but see the section 'The Repertory of Song and its Performance' in Chapter 4), but on what occasion or occasions is impossible to say. Although Ps. 12, like Ps. 6, is reckoned to be pre-exilic (S.E. Gillingham, *The Poems and Psalms of the Hebrew Bible* (Oxford, 1994), p. 253), there is no evidence that it was used at the First Temple.

[13] Wulstan, 'The Origin of the Modes', p. 9.

[14] This hypothesis would imply the use of Pss 6 and 12 at the Second Temple.

5:13: '... the sound of the trumpets [*ûbaḥăṣōṣĕrôt*], cymbals [*ûbimĕṣiltayim*], and other musical instruments [*ûbikĕlê haššîr* "and the instruments of song"] ...'. At a third place, 1 Chronicles 16:5, 'instruments' (*kĕlê*) – which the verse specifies as 'harps' and lyres – are mentioned separately from cymbals. These three passages together point to the conclusion that the 'instruments of song' were 'harps' and lyres. The Masoretes evidently understood the second half of 1 Chronicles 15:16 in this way, as is shown by their use of conjunctive and disjunctive punctuation signs.[15] In terms of the Masoretic punctuation of this verse, 'harps and lyres' should be regarded as a parenthetic gloss on 'instruments of song'. The sense of 1 Chronicles 15:16 should probably be: 'David ordered the officers of the Levites to install their kinsmen, the singers, with instruments of song (harps and lyres) and cymbals, joyfully making their voices heard'.

According to the reckoning above, the 'instruments of song' are the same types of instrument, with the same function, as those implied by musical words built on the root ZMR encountered in the pre-exilic and exilic literature of the Hebrew Bible, namely the plucked-string instruments *nēbel* and *kinnôr* associated with cultic song. In the postexilic literature of the Hebrew Bible, ZMR-words that have a cultic musical sense occur only twice outside the Book of Psalms: once in Ezra 7:24 and once in 1 Chronicles 16:9. In the first instance the pertinent word (*zammārayyāʾ*) is not Hebrew, but Aramaic; in the second the pertinent word (*zammĕrû*) is not genuinely postexilic since it falls within a quotation from Psalm 105 which is exilic. Within the book of Psalms, ZMR-words occur in the poetic texts themselves in only five of the 83 postexilic psalms.[16] In other words, ZMR-words are seldom used in a cultic musical sense in Hebrew postexilic biblical literature concerned with worship at the Temple. The preference for *kĕlê šîr* encapsulates the idea that in the cultic rites at the Temple the sound of plucked-string instruments and song was a sacred unity.

The phrase *kĕlê šîr* has nuances of meaning additional to implying the use of plucked-string instruments in association with Levitical song.[17] The first word of

---

[15]　The conjunctive and disjunctive signs relevant to the Hebrew text of the second half of 1 Chr. 15:16 are: the *ṭipḥâ* (disjunctive: a short pause), the *ʾatnāḥ* (disjunctive: a marked pause) and the *mêrĕkāʾ* (conjunctive). The complete Masoretic system of punctuation uses some 28 signs (usually called 'accents' after their Latin designation *accentum*) which have complex interrelationships. Further on the Masoretic accents, see *BHS* (which provides, on an inserted card, tables of the accents giving the name and function of each one); Daniel S. Katz, 'Biblische Kantillation und Musik der Synagoge: Ein Rückblick auf die ältesten Quellen', *Musiktheorie*, 15 (2000): 59–62; Eliyahu Schleifer, 'Biblical Cantillation' (Jewish Music, §III, 2(ii)(b): 'Synagogue Music and its Development'), *New Grove/2*, vol. 13, pp. 41–7.

[16]　Pss 33:2; 57:8, 10; 59:18; 71:22, 23; 101:1. See the Appendix.

[17]　The phrase occurs in contexts to do with the Temple at Neh. 12:36 (*bikĕlê-šîr dāwîd*); 2 Chr. 7:6 (*bikĕlê-šîr YHWH*); 2 Chr. 23:13 (*bikĕlê haššîr*); and 2 Chr. 34:12 (*bikĕlê šîr*) in addition to 1 Chr. 15:16; 16:5, 42; 2 Chr. 5:13, cited above.

the phrase is derived from *kĕlî*, which on its own means 'instrument' in a general sense ('implement, tool, utensil') or 'vessel'. Coupled with *šîr* 'song' (where it occurs idiomatically in the plural construct state: *kĕlê*) it has the specific sense of 'instruments of music'. At the same time, *kĕlê šîr* means more than 'musical' instruments: it implies instruments that can 'sing', melodic instruments. This is consistent with the idea that the 'instruments of song' were plucked-string instruments but not cymbals. The former would have been capable of playing melody with the Levitical song, whereas the latter obviously would not (a limitation also applicable to the *tōp* and to metal trumpets and shofars). In the context of cultic music of the Second Temple, the phrase *kĕlê šîr* implies the melodic musical instruments *nēbel* and *kinnôr* played by Levite musicians in conjunction with their singing.

The Levitical music was presided over by Chenaniah, an 'officer' who was 'in charge' of it (1 Chr. 15:22, 27). He was appointed because he was a 'master' (15:22). The meaning of the crucial Hebrew words in these verses is uncertain. Nevertheless, it is clear that the musical service was developed to the extent that it required some sort of direction or coordination.

The purpose behind the Levitical musical service was 'to invoke, to praise, and to extol the LORD, the God of Israel' (1 Chr. 16:4) – almost identical with that of the music of the First Temple, which was that it should be 'a reminder' of the Israelites before their Deity (Num. 10:10). The difference between 'reminder' and 'invoke' in these instances is more apparent than real: while the English translation uses different words, the Hebrew uses words built on a common root: *ZKR*. This has the sense of 'memorial, remembrance, reminder', when used as a noun, and 'to cause to remember, to remind', when used as a verb. Where the JPS translation of 1 Chronicles 16:4 has 'invoke', the sense could equally well be 'remind', namely to alert the Deity to the worship being offered by the Israelites, as at the First Temple.

The Organization of the Musical Service

The features noted so far about postexilic cultic music have been read out of the 1 Chronicles version of the narrative of the removal of the Ark to Jerusalem. While these features are justifiably reckoned to apply to the Second Temple, material specifically concerned with the musical service there does not appear until the last seven chapters of 1 Chronicles (chapters 23–29). Those chapters deal mainly with the general organization of the cultic service. In terms of the Chronicler's chronology of the events he describes, the Temple is not yet built; the organization of its service is presented as having been prescribed by David ready for when his son Solomon will have built the Temple.

According to the tradition in 1 Chronicles 23:24–32, the Ark of the Covenant would have a permanent home in the Temple; consequently the Levites, whose job it had been to carry the Ark, the Tabernacle and all its appurtenances from place to place, would be redeployed. The Levites' service came to comprise administrative, practical and musical duties, specific numbers of Levites being allotted to various tasks.

According to the traditions in 1 Chronicles 23–25, all Levites were organized into 'divisions' (sometimes referred to by other writers as 'courses') for their service. When Levites attended the Temple for service they did so in their divisions, in rotating tours of duty. Serving Levites were lodged in rooms in the Temple and were exempt from all extraneous duties (9:33). Food and drink were provided for them each day from freewill offerings.[18] Levites could enrol for service from the age of 20.[19] Their retirement age is not mentioned in postexilic sources; it probably remained at 50 years, as given in the book of Numbers.

The Levite musicians were organized into 24 divisions, with 12 participants in each division; they thus numbered 288 individuals. The Levite families from which musicians were drawn were those of Asaph, Heman and Jeduthun (1 Chr. 25:1–7) from the clans of Gershon, Kohath and Merari (23:6b–23). They were apparently under royal command (25:2, 6), the significance of which will become clearer later. Each division was subdivided by lot into 'shifts' for the distribution of daily duties (25:8). At sacrificial rites the Levite musicians served alongside the Aaronite priests, who were similarly organized in 24 divisions (24–26).

The Hebrew Bible does not specify the length of the tour of duty for each division of either priests or Levite musicians. Verse 25 of 1 Chronicles 9 suggests that Levites who were gatekeepers had weekly tours of duty. Verse 8 of 2 Chronicles 23 suggests that this was the case for all Levites, and furthermore that each tour of duty began and ended on the Sabbath.

Since the Levites' service was inextricably bound up with the service of the priests, and both priests and Levites were divided into 24 divisions, it is reasonable to assume that the Levites' tours of duty were organized in the same way as those of the priests. This seems to be implied already in Nehemiah 13:30, 2 Chronicles 8:14 and 31:2 and perhaps also by the phrase '[the heads of the Levites] served opposite them in shifts' in Nehemiah 12:24 where 'them' could be interpreted as meaning 'the priestly divisions'. Josephus confirms this for Herod's Temple when he says in *Jewish Antiquities*, book 7, 14:7, that the priestly divisions ministered to the Deity for eight days, from one Sabbath to the next inclusively, and that the divisions of the Levites were organized in the same manner.[20]

The Levite musicians lived in towns and villages near Jerusalem (Ezra 2:70; Neh. 12:28–29; 1 Esd. 5:46), as did the members of most of the other Levitical groups of Temple servants. They were thus conveniently placed to travel to Jerusalem when it was the turn of their division to serve at the Temple, and when

---

[18] For example, Neh. 11:23; 12:44–47; and by inference from Neh. 13:10 and 2 Chr. 31:4–10).

[19] Ezra 3:8; 1 Chr. 23:24; 2 Chr. 31:17.

[20] Compare 2 Chr. 23:8. This timetable would imply that the act of changing division was regarded as belonging to the Levites' sacred duties in the Temple, and therefore did not infringe the religious law forbidding Jews to work on the Sabbath.

they were summoned for special additional service as was the case, for example, when the rebuilt wall of Jerusalem was dedicated (Neh. 12:27). The leaders of the people, including Levitical leaders, settled in Jerusalem, and a small percentage of the rest of the population (one out of ten according to Neh. 11:1) elected to live there (Neh. 11:1–2; 1 Chr. 9:34). This implies that a small number of ordinary Levites, in addition to the Levitical leaders, would have lived in Jerusalem.

The Levite musicians were to offer praises 'with instruments I [David] devised [or "instituted" or "prescribed"] for singing praise' (1 Chr. 23:5). This is the earliest reference to the tradition that David determined the instruments to be used in cultic worship at the Temple. The Levitical musicians were required to perform their service 'every morning, to praise and extol the LORD, and at evening too, and whenever offerings were made to the LORD, according to the quantities prescribed for them, on Sabbaths, new moons and holidays, regularly [tāmîd], before the LORD' (1 Chr. 23:30–31). The reference at the beginning of this quotation is to the sacrifices of burnt offering offered morning and evening daily in the Temple; the 'holidays' are elucidated in 2 Chronicles 8:13 as the Three Pilgrim Festivals.

Chapter 25 of 1 Chronicles enlarges on the nature of the Levites' musical service. The basic information is set out in the first verse of the chapter: 'David and the officers of the army set apart for service the sons of Asaph, Heman and Jeduthun, who prophesied [hannibĕy'îm] to the accompaniment of[21] lyres [bĕkinnōrôt], harps [binĕbālîm], and cymbals [ûbimĕṣiltāyim]' (1 Chr. 25:1). This is subsequently amplified by the information that the sons of Asaph 'prophesied by order of the king' (25:2), that the sons of Heman uttered 'prophecies of God for His greater glory' (25:5) and that the sons of Jeduthun were 'under the charge of ['al yĕdê] their father Jeduthun, who, accompanied on the harp (bakinnôr),[22] prophesied, praising and extolling the LORD' (25:3).

The remaining sources in the present group add little about the organization of the musical service. In 2 Chronicles 8:14, 29:25 and 35:15 the Chronicler claims that Solomon, Hezekiah and Josiah respectively appointed the Levites to serve in the Temple according to the prescriptions of David. This is endorsed in Ezra–Nehemiah although in Ezra 6:18 the prescriptions are attributed to Moses.

Considerably more information is provided by the Mishnah. Mishnah Tamid 7:3 says that at the daily sacrifices of burnt offering there were always at least two priests with ḥăṣōṣĕrôt 'metal trumpets',[23] but on these occasions, and especially on days of special significance, their number could be increased indefinitely (m. 'Arak. 2:5). However, there was only one ṣilṣēl 'cymbal' (m. 'Arak.

---

[21] 'to the accompaniment of': the MT does not have this phrase; it uses prepositional prefixes meaning 'with' and 'and with'; likewise in the Hebrew in the remainder of the verse.

[22] 'accompanied on': the MT has ba- 'on, with'. See n. 21.

[23] The Hebrew of the Mishnah here and subsequently is given according to Blackman, Mishnayoth.

2:5); Ben Arzah was 'over [*'al*] the cymbal [*haṣṣalṣēl*]' (*m. Šeqal.* 5:1).[24] The word used here for 'cymbal' is singular whereas the biblical words for the cultic cymbals, namely *ṣelṣelîm* and *mĕṣiltayim*, are respectively plural and dual. This implies that the instrument played by Ben Arzah[25] was a single cymbal as opposed to a pair of cymbals. It may have been fairly large and played with a beater.[26] The *ṣilṣēl/ṣalṣēl* may have been used instead of the Levites' cultic cymbals at sacrificial rites in Herod's Temple but, as will be shown later in connection with music at non-sacrificial rites, it did not render the Levites' cymbals redundant.

There were never fewer than two 'harps' (*nĕbālîm*) and never more than six (*m. 'Arak.* 2:3), and there were never fewer than nine lyres (*kinnôrôt*) and their number could be increased indefinitely (*m. 'Arak.* 2:5). Pipes (*ḥălîlîm*) – never fewer than two or more than 12 – were played 'before the Altar' (*lipnê hammizbēaḥ*) on 12 days in the year: at the slaughtering of the sacrificial animals at First Passover (Passover itself), at the slaughtering of the sacrificial animals at Second Passover (a month later than Passover),[27] on the first day of Passover, on the day of the Festival of Weeks and on the eight days of Booths (*m. 'Arak.* 2:3). Mishnah *'Arakin* 2:4 says that the players of these instruments (implying strings and pipes) were Levites.

As for the Levite musicians themselves, there were never fewer than 12, and their number could be increased indefinitely (*m. 'Arak.* 2:6). Male juvenile members of the families of Levite musicians[28] could participate with their elders in the musical service, but only as singers (*bĕpeh* 'with the voice'); they did not play harps or lyres, and they were not reckoned in the number of serving Levites (*m. 'Arak.* 2:6). One Hugros ben Levi, an accomplished singer,[29] was 'in charge of [*'al* "over"] the singing [*haššîr*]' (*m. Šeqal.* 5:1). This may mean that he had administrative as well as musical responsibility for the singers.[30]

---

[24] 'over the cymbal' in Blackman, *Mishnayoth*; Neusner, *Mishnah*, has 'in charge of the cymbals [plural]'.

[25] That Ben Arzah actually played the cymbal, rather than administered others who played it (compare Sanders, *Judaism*, p. 83), is confirmed by *m. Tamid* 7:3 (where his name is given as Ben Arza).

[26] This is likely in view of the fact that *m. Tamid* 3:8 says that the sound of the cymbal (*haṣṣelṣāl*) could be heard in Jericho, some 25 km (about 15.5 miles) away: a deliberate exaggeration in order to make the point that the sound was loud. Further, see Chapter 2.

[27] Israelites who were prevented from celebrating Passover at its appointed time (the fourteenth day of the first month, see Num. 9:3), had a second opportunity to celebrate it a month later (Num. 9:10–11), hence 'Second' Passover (Pesach Sheni), alternatively 'Lesser' Passover.

[28] Those younger than thirteen years and one day (the standard Jewish definition of minority).

[29] *m. Yoma* 3:11.

[30] Compare Sanders, *Judaism*, p. 83.

It is not known what criteria governed decisions about the number of instruments and Levite musicians that were, or could be, deployed. In the case of metal trumpets and *kinnôrôt*, perhaps it was their importance in the cult that allowed their number to be increased without limit.

It is noteworthy that according to the Mishnah pipes were played before the altar on 12 days of the year (*m. 'Arak.* 2:3), and linked with this that the Mishnah, *'Arakin* 2:4, implies that the pipers were Levites. In biblical sources the use of pipes in cultic contexts is mentioned only in connection with non-sacrificial rites such as processions; in Chronicles pipes are not named among the Levitical instruments belonging to the tradition of the Davidic organization of the musical service. The use of pipes as related in the Mishnah tractate *'Arakin* is thus a departure from both earlier practice and Davidic tradition, if only on 12 days in the year. It must be a late custom seeing there is no mention of it in Chronicles or Ezra–Nehemiah.

The Ritual Setting of the Music

Music at Sacrificial Rites

Information about the place of music in the sacrificial rites is provided in all three of the chronologically determined groups of sources. In the first group there are three general descriptions of sacrificial rites at 2 Chronicles 5:12–13; 7:3–6 and 29:26–30. Common to all these descriptions are Levitical song and instrumental music and the priestly blowing of trumpets, which accompany the sacrificial actions. The Levitical instruments are named in the first description as *měṣiltayim* 'cymbals', *něbālim* 'harps' and *kinnōrôt* 'lyres', the instruments which, according to the tradition in Chronicles, David prescribed for use in the cult. In the two remaining descriptions these instruments are not named but are referred to as 'instruments for the Lord's music that King David had made to praise the Lord' (7:6) and *kělê dāwîd* 'instruments of David' (29:26, 27). The priestly trumpets are named as such (*ḥăṣōṣěrôt*) in the first and third descriptions (5:12; 29:26, 27) and referred to in the phrase *wěhakōhănîm maḥěṣěṣrîm* 'and the priests were blowing trumpets' in the second (7:6).

According to the second and third descriptions there was general prostration as the burnt offering began – as the trumpets were blown and immediately before the Levites began to sing and play. These descriptions also say that the Levites' singing consisted of 'the psalms of David that they knew' (7:6) and 'the words of David and Asaph the seer' (29:29), the latter being a circumlocution for psalms. The first description says only that the 'trumpeters and the singers joined in unison [*qôl-'eḥād* "with one voice"][31] to praise and extol the Lord' (5:13).

---

[31]   The JPS *Tanakh* and the NRSV have 'in unison', which is misleading. The metal trumpets at least would have been incapable of playing in unison with the singing

The third description gives the clearest picture of the order of the rite:

1. Offering of the sacrifice, accompanied by
2. Levitical cultic song, and
3. Priestly trumpet blowing.
4. General prostration.
5. The sequence of elements 1–4 is repeated until the burnt offering is finished, then
6. Levitical singing of psalms (or a psalm).
7. General prostration.

In connection with praise of the Deity, the first description quotes the phrase 'For He is good, for His steadfast love is eternal' and the second quotes the phrase both in full (7:3) and in part: 'For His steadfast love is eternal' (7:6). This phrase, either complete or partial or preceded by 'praise the LORD', appears as a more or less freestanding element at 12 places in the Hebrew Bible.[32] Four of those places are the first verses of Psalms 106, 107, 118 and 136.[33] It is possible that the Chronicler's quotation of the phrase, or a part of it, is an allusion to the use of one or other of these psalms at sacrifices. Alternatively, the phrase in itself may have been used as a cultic shout; in Hebrew it is relatively short: *kî ṭôb kî lĕʿôlām hamĕdô*.

The second and third of these rites were royal occasions. At the second, king Solomon was present and offered sacrifice. At the third, king Hezekiah was present and had a presiding role: he issued the command for the burnt offering to begin, and he and his officers commanded the Levites to praise the Deity in the words of psalms. This probably explains what is meant in 1 Chronicles 25:2 and 6 by the statement that the sons of Asaph and Heman performed their musical service 'by order of the king'.

Descriptions of sacrificial rites in the second group of sources are to be found in Sirach 50:11–19 and 1 Maccabees 4:52–56. Most of Sirach 50 is an encomium of the Temple's high priest Simon son of Onias in the context of the performance of his sacred duties at a sacrifice. The rite described in

---

unless this were confined to the three notes of the harmonic series playable on those instruments.

[32]   The phrase may be seen as consisting of three segments of text, which in order are: (i) 'praise the LORD', (ii) 'for He is good', (iii) 'for His steadfast love is eternal'. These appear variously as follows: Ps. 106:1 (i)+(ii)+(iii); Ps. 107:1 (i)+(ii)+(iii); Ps. 118:1 (i)+(ii)+(iii); Ps. 118:29 (i)+(ii)+(iii); Ps. 136:1 (i)+(ii)+(iii) (2b, 3b, etc., have (iii) as a refrain throughout the Psalm); Ezra 3:11 (ii)+(iii)+'for Israel'; 1 Chr. 16:34 (i)+(ii)+(iii); 1 Chr. 16:41 (iii); 2 Chr. 5:13 (ii)+(iii); 2 Chr. 7:3 (ii)+(iii); 2 Chr. 7:6 (iii); 2 Chr. 20:21 (i)+(ii)+(iii) (segment (ii) does not appear at this place in the majority of manuscripts).

[33]   According to Gillingham, *Poems and Psalms*, pp. 253–4, Ps. 118 is pre-exilic, Ps. 107 is exilic, and Pss 106 and 136 are postexilic.

1 Maccabees 4 is that with which the dedication of the rebuilt altar in the Temple and the resumption of normal worship there was celebrated in 164 BCE (following the military victory of Judas Maccabaeus over enemies who had profaned the sanctuary).[34]

The rite described in Sirach 50 has five main elements:

1. The act of sacrifice (burnt offering then drink offering) performed by the high priest.
2. Invocation of the Deity by means of a cultic shout and the blowing of trumpets by Aaronites (presumably priestly Aaronites), which make a loud noise (50:16).
3. Prostration of the people in worship.
4. Song (unspecified) sung by 'the singers' (presumably Levites) in 'sweet and full-toned melody' in praise of the Deity (50:18).
5. Prayers of the people, offered until the ritual is completed.

It is possible that element 5 should be interpreted as meaning that the sequence trumpet blowing–prostration–cultic song (elements 2–4) was repeated until the rite was finished.

In 1 Maccabees 4:52–55 the description is somewhat general and does not specify the relationship of the music to the individual cultic actions. It makes no mention of the cultic shout or the blowing of trumpets. It implies Levitical song and names the Levitical instruments, saying that the rebuilt altar 'was dedicated with songs [*ōdais*] and harps [*kitharais*] and lutes [*kinurais*; compare Hebrew *kinnōrôt*] and cymbals [*kumbalois*]' (4:54). It follows this with the statement, 'All the people fell on their faces and worshipped and blessed Heaven' (4:55). Here the sequence of liturgical elements is Levitical song–prostration.

The most comprehensive descriptions of sacrificial rites at the Temple are to be found in sources from the third group. In the Mishnah, *Tamid* 7:3 presents a description of the twice-daily sacrifice of burnt offering; and *Pesaḥim* 5:5–7, provides details about the music at the sacrificial rite at Passover. *Tamid* 7:3 provides the fullest description extant from antiquity. The essential elements are as follows:

1. The high priest offers the burnt offering.
2. The high priest receives the drink offering.
3. Two priests blow *tāqʿû wĕhērîʿû wĕtāqʿû* 'a long and a wavering (or "quavering")[35] and a long' flourish on metal trumpets.
4. The high priest pours the drink offering.
5. When element 4 begins, the prefect waves 'the flag' (or ' the towel').[36]

---

[34] The dedication came to be celebrated annually as the midwinter festival of Hanukkah.

[35] 'wavering' in Neusner, *Mishnah*; 'quavering' in Danby, *Mishnah*.

[36] 'the flag' in Neusner, *Mishnah*; 'the towel' in Danby, *Mishnah*.

6. Ben Arza strikes (*hiqqîš*) the cymbal.
7. Levites sing a psalm.[37]
8. At breaks in the Levitical song there is a blowing of trumpets by the two priests, and
9. General prostration.

The rite falls into two parts: the rite of burnt offering and the rite of drink offering. The priestly trumpet blowing (element 3 above) occurred while the fire consumed all the members of the sacrificial animal thrown onto the altar (element 1). This marked the end of the first part of the rite. The Levitical music (element 7) was performed while the drink offering was poured (element 4).

The Levites made breaks in their singing. No explanation is given for this, but it may be correct to infer from the passage that the high priest made a drink offering at each horn (corner) of the altar in turn. If this were so, elements 5–7 above would have been repeated with each drink offering. The Prefect's waving of the flag (or towel) seems to have been a signal to Ben Arza to strike the cymbal, and this in turn to have been a signal to the Levites to start singing. It is possible that the Levites could not see clearly what was happening at the altar (either because their view was obscured or because, in the event of repetitions of the sequence of elements 2–4, they were prostrated with their faces to the ground) and were therefore dependent on an audible signal to begin their singing. There is no mention of the Levitical cultic cymbals, and it is possible that by the late postexilic period they had been superseded in the daily sacrificial rites by the one cymbal struck by Ben Arza.

There is a certain amount of diversity in the descriptions of the rites. There are nevertheless several common elements. Levitical singing and playing and the priestly playing of metal trumpets are mentioned in all the descriptions except that in 1 Maccabees 4:52–55. In all the descriptions except those in Sirach 50 and 1 Maccabees 4, it is either stated or implied that the Levites' singing consisted of material from Psalms, or else a text that has parallels in certain psalms is inserted into the narrative. Prostrations are a feature of all the rites except that described in 2 Chronicles 5. In the two latest rites prostrations follow immediately on the priests' trumpet blowing, and it is possible that this was also the case in the rite described in 2 Chronicles 29 although the description is too vague at this point for certainty. The pattern music–prostration (or prostration–praise in 2 Chronicles 7:3) is firmly attested; in at least the two latest rites this is more developed, becoming trumpet blowing–prostration–Levitical music.

The Mishnah also provides details about the music at the sacrificial rite at Passover; specifically, the details concern music at the slaughtering of the Passover offering. *Mishnah Pesaḥim* 5:5–7 relates that the male Israelites

---

[37] Psalms for the daily sacrifice of burnt offering are listed in *m. Tamid* 7:4: see Chapter 4.

presented their sacrificial offerings in three groups successively, each one announced by a shofar call consisting of 'a sustained, a quavering, and a sustained note' (*m. Pesaḥ.* 5:5). After slaughtering his offering, each Israelite took it to an area nearby in the Temple court where he flayed it and removed the sacrificial parts of the animal (the fat pieces) which he gave to a priest to throw onto the altar to be consumed as a burnt offering (this is part of the ritual is briefly described in *mishnah Pesaḥim* 5:9–10). It would seem that slaughtering, flaying and burning of the sacrifices took place for each group in succession. *Mishnah Pesaḥim* 5:7 says that during all this:

> [*m. Pesaḥ.* 5:7] D. [The Levites meanwhile] proclaimed {*qārĕʾû*} the Hallel psalms {*ʾet-hahallēl*}.
> E. If they completed [the recitation], they repeated it, and if they completed the second time, they repeated it for a third –
> F. even though they never in all their days had to repeat it a third time.[38]

It would seem that the repetitions of the Hallel (Pss 113–118) covered the complete ritual from slaughtering by the first group to burning of the last offering.

Finally in this section, consideration may be given to music at the rite for the Day of Atonement (Yom Kippur). This occasion of national confession was kept annually on the tenth day of the seventh month. Neither the Torah passages concerned with the institution of the Day[39] nor the Mishnah tractate *Yoma*, which provides details of the order of its rite for both Temple and synagogue, makes any mention of music or of items that might have been susceptible of being sung. At the Temple, special animal sacrifices belonged to the rite; these took place in addition to the normal daily sacrifices of burnt offering. Levitical song could therefore reasonably be expected to have had a place in the rite. An indication that this was the case is to be found in the Dead Sea Scrolls in a list of David's lyrical compositions.[40] The list, which honorifically exaggerates David's production, includes the item '30 songs [*šîr*] for the New Moons, for Feast days and for the Day of Atonement'.[41] The association of these 'songs' with David suggests they were psalms; given the penitential nature of the Day of Atonement, psalms of lamentation would have been appropriate. While this is speculative, it is worth noting that a passage in the book of Zechariah speaks of priests and people who 'fasted and lamented [*wĕsāpôd*] in the fifth and seventh months' (Zech. 7:5). The Hebrew word translated 'lamented' here is from *sāpad*, meaning 'mourn, beat the breast' (as an expression of grief). The reference to the 'seventh month' could be

---

[38]   Here and in subsequent quotations from Neusner, *Mishnah*, square brackets are Neusner's, braces enclose my interpolations.

[39]   Lev. 16:1–34; 23:26–32; Num. 29:7–11.

[40]   The Psalms Scroll (11QPsᵃ), column 27.

[41]   *CDSSE*, p. 307. Hebrew from J.A. Sanders (ed.), *The Psalms Scroll of Qumran Cave 11 (11QPsᵃ)* (Oxford, 1965, repr. 1998) (see under 'Psalms Scroll' in the Bibliography).

an allusion to cultic expressions of penitence on the Day of Atonement, which fell in that month.[42]

Music at Non-Sacrificial Rites

Popular festivities during major festivals, and cultic processions prior to the sacrifices on festival days, were features of cultic worship at the Temple after the exile. Concrete evidence for the general occurrence of such activities in the early and mid Second-Temple periods is difficult to find. There is, however, evidence of their occurrence – with music – at two unique events. One is the laying of the foundation of the Second Temple, reported in Ezra 3:10–11:

> [Ezra 3:10] When the builders had laid the foundation of the Temple of the LORD, priests in their vestments with trumpets [*baḥăṣōṣĕrôt*], and Levites sons of Asaph with cymbals [*bamĕṣiltayim*] were stationed to give praise to the LORD, as King David of Israel had ordained. [11] They sang songs [*wayya'ănû* 'sang responsively'; see LXX 2 Esd. 3:11: *apekrithēsan*], extolling and praising the LORD,
> 'For He is good,
> His steadfast love for Israel is eternal'.
> All the people raised [*hērî'û* 'shouted'] a great [*gĕdôlâ*] shout [*tĕrû'â*] extolling the LORD because the foundation of the House of the LORD had been laid.

Here there was priestly playing of metal trumpets, Asaphite Levitical playing of cymbals, singing (perhaps of psalmodic material) and the cultic shout. The non-sacrificial character of the rite is emphasized by the absence of any mention of the Levites' plucked-string instruments.[43]

The other unique event is the dedication of the repaired walls of Jerusalem, as related in Nehemiah 12:31–42. This is reported mostly in the first-person singular, creating the impression that Nehemiah himself is giving a first-hand account. The climax of the event was the offering of 'great sacrifices' in the Temple. This was preceded by a procession round the walls of Jerusalem. Two groups of similar size, consisting of Levitical singers ('two large thanksgiving

---

[42]   The reference to fasting and lamenting in the fifth month could be an allusion to the expressions of sorrow that became traditional on the ninth day of the month Av (the fifth month) in memory of the destruction of the Temple; see, however, the note on Zech. 7:5 in *HCSB*.

[43]   In the opening verse of the parallel of this passage in 1 Esdras 5:59 (NRSV; 1 Esd. 5:57b in Rahlfs' edition of the LXX), the text reads: 'And the priests stood arrayed in their vestments, with musical instruments [*meta mousikōn*] and trumpets [*kai salpingōn*]'. 1 Esdras is, however, a somewhat confused text and it is doubtful whether much weight should be attached to the phrase 'with musical instruments' in reference to the priests. In no other ancient source is there any mention of the Jewish priests playing instruments other than metal trumpets or shofars.

[choirs]': Neh. 12:31), officers of Judah, priests playing metal trumpets (12:35) and Levites with 'the musical instruments [*bikĕlê-šîr*] of David, the man of God' (12:36), circumambulated the walls in opposite directions, starting from a point west of the Temple building. The groups processed along the walls as far as the Water Gate and the Gate of the Prison Compound respectively. From there they came together in the Temple's inner court where the sacrifices were offered.

The employment of 'instruments of song' ('harps' and lyres) would have been consistent with the choral groups' task of 'giving thanks' since this was one of the categories of cultic song to which the playing of the instruments of song belonged.[44] The phrase 'instruments of song' is problematical, however, when compared with the LXX text at the same place. The LXX version of Nehemiah 12:36 (LXX 2 Esd. 22:36) says that the task of the Levite musicians was 'to praise with the songs of David [*ainein en ōdais Dauid*] the man of God', in other words, to sing psalms. The possibility exists that the LXX preserves the original text here and that in the MT of this verse '*bikĕlê-*' is a later insertion.

Cymbals are not mentioned in the report. Nevertheless, they should probably be assumed since they are named already at Nehemiah 12:27 (together with 'singing', 'harps' and 'lyres') in the introductory material which sets the scene for the celebration (Neh. 12:27–30).

There is evidence of music at both processions and popular cultic festivities under more usual circumstances during the last century and a half or so of the Second Temple and Herod's Temple. The Second book of Maccabees contains a passage parallel to that in 1 Maccabees 4:52–56 about the festival celebrating the dedication of the rebuilt Temple in 164 BCE (see above). Here, in 2 Maccabees 10:6–7, it is related:

> [2 Macc. 10:6] They celebrated it [the dedication] for eight days with rejoicing, in the manner of the festival of booths [*skēnōmatōn*] ... [7] Therefore, carrying ivy-wreathed wands and beautiful branches and also fronds of palm, they offered hymns [*humnous*] of thanksgiving to him [God] who had given success to the purifying of his own holy place [the Temple].

The comparison with the Festival of Booths suggests that a procession, or processions, may have been part of the festivities since one of the daily customs during the Festival of Booths was for people to go in procession round the altar (see the quotation from *m. Sukkah* 4:5 below).

In 141 BCE the Jews, under the leadership of Simon the High Priest, took back the citadel at Jerusalem from anti-Maccabean factions. The event was marked by an annual celebration which included a procession with music, as is related in 1 Maccabees 13:51–52:

---

[44] 'giving thanks': also rendered 'praise/praising' in the JPS *Tanakh*; see 1 Chr. 23:30; compare NRSV.

[1 Macc. 13:51] On the twenty-third day of the second month, in the one hundred and seventy-first year [141 BCE], the Jews entered it [the citadel] with praise and palm branches, and with harps [*kai en kinurais*: compare Hebrew *kinnôr*] and cymbals [*kai en kumbalois*] and stringed instruments [*kai en nablais*: compare Hebrew *nēbel*], and with hymns [*kai en humnois*] and songs [*kai en ōdais*], because a great enemy had been crushed and removed from Israel. [52] He [Simon the High Priest] decreed that every year they should celebrate this day with rejoicing.

The Mishnah witnesses to music at processions and popular cultic festivities at Herod's Temple. *Mishnah Bikkurim* 3:2–6 describes how the offerings of first fruits were brought to the Temple. This could take place at any time from the Festival of Weeks onwards. Adult male representatives of the people of the outlying towns collected the first fruits and brought them, together with an ox for a peace offering, to the city. The journey to and through the streets of Jerusalem was in the nature of a joyful procession: the horns of the ox were overlaid with gold, and its head adorned with a wreath of olive leaves; the baskets containing the first fruits were decorated and a piper preceded them until they came near to Jerusalem where Temple officials and craftsmen of the city greeted the bearers of the offerings (*m. Bik.* 3:3). The description continues:

[*m. Bik.* 3:4] A. A flutist {*heḥālîl* 'pipe, piper'} plays before them, until they reach the Temple mount.
B. [Once] they reached the Temple mount,
C. Even Agrippa the King puts the basket [of first-fruits] on his shoulder, and enters, [and goes forth] until he reaches the Temple court.
D. [Once] he reached the Temple court, the Levites sang the song {*baššîr*},
E. 'I will extol thee, O Lord, for thou hast drawn me up, and hast not let my foes rejoice over me' (Ps. 30:1).

Mishnah Sukkah 4:5, briefly referred to above, is concerned with processions at the Festival of Booths. It begins with the question, 'How was the rite of the willow branch fulfilled?' and by way of answer continues:

[*m. Sukkah* 4:5] B. There was a place below Jerusalem, called Mosa. [People] go down there and gather young willow branches. They come and throw them along the sides of the altar, with their heads bent over the altar.
C. They blew on the shofar[45] a sustained, a quavering and a sustained note.
D. Every day {for the first six days of the festival} they walk around the altar one time and say, '*Save now, we beseech thee, O Lord! We beseech thee, O Lord, send now prosperity* (Ps. 118:25).'
E. ...

---

45   The Hebrew does not have 'on the shofar'.

F. And on that day [the seventh day of the willow branch] they walk around
the altar seven times.

Trumpet calls (on the shofar or metal trumpet) marked the completion of the
dressing of the altar; perhaps they also signalled the start of the processions,
although the Mishnah is not specific on this point. The processions were
accompanied by verse 25 of Psalm 118, which would most likely have been
repeated as often as necessary to cover the circumambulation. Verse 27b of
the Psalm could perhaps refer to those processions; but, as was pointed out in
Chapter 2, the meaning of both the Hebrew of the MT and the Greek of the LXX
is uncertain at this half-verse.

The Mishnah does not make clear who took part in the rite. Priests and
Levites are the most obvious candidates since non-priests and non-Levites could
not acquire the state of holiness necessary to give them access to the sacred
court where the altar stood.

According to *mishnah Sukkah* 5:1, there was a non-sacrificial ritual of a popular
nature connected with something called the *bêt haššô'ēbâ* – 'the place (or "the
act") of the water-drawing'[46] – during the Festival of Booths. An aside about this
in the Mishnah says, 'Anyone who has not seen the rejoicing of *bet hashshoebah*
in his life has never seen rejoicing' (*m. Sukkah* 5:1). The Mishnah says that the
ritual did not override the Sabbath or a festival day, but gives no details about
its form. It does say, however, that the pipe was played during it on sometimes
five and sometimes six days (ibid.). The alternative of five days allows for the
intervention of a Sabbath.[47]

Probably the most colourful of the popular cultic festivities at the Second
Temple were those which took place in the Court of Women at the close of the
first day of the Festival of Booths. They have often been referred to as if they
were part of the ritual at the *bêt haššô'ēbâ* described briefly immediately above,[48]
and this seems at first glance to be the impression given in the Mishnah. But
since the Mishnah says that the festivities in question took place at the close of
the first day of the festival, they were probably separate from the ritual at the *bêt
haššô'ēbâ*, occurring on this one evening only.

The festivities are described in *mishnah Sukkah* 5:2–4. They began with the
lighting of large oil lamps set on tall stands made of gold, four lamps to a stand
(*m. Sukkah* 5:2–3). The description continues at 5:4:

---

[46]   This is Danby's interpretation of the phrase (Danby, *Mishnah*, p. 179, n. 12). The
meaning and significance of the phrase *bêt haššô'ēbâ* (given as *Beth ha-She'ubah* in Danby,
Mishnah; as *bet hashshoebah* in Neusner, *Mishnah*) are uncertain.

[47]   The Festival of Booths lasted for eight days, but only the first and last days were
regarded as festivals, therefore the rejoicing at the *bêt haššô'ēbâ* would take place on the
six mid-festival days, or on five of them if a Sabbath intervened.

[48]   For example, *MAI*, pp. 177, 219, 424–5, 458–9, 462, 468, 497.

[*m. Sukkah* 5:4] A. The pious men and wonder workers would dance {*mĕraqqdîm*}before them {the lamps?} with flaming torches in their hand,

B. and they would sing {*wĕ'ômĕrîm*, literally: 'and they say'} before them songs {*šîrôt*} and praises {*wĕtišbāḥôt*}.

C. And the Levites beyond counting played on harps {*bĕkinnôrôt*}, lyres {*ûbinĕbālîm*}, cymbals {*ûbimĕṣaltayim*}, trumpets {*ûbaḥăṣôṣĕrôt*}, and [other] musical instruments {*ûbikĕlê šîr*},

D. [standing, as they played] on the fifteen {*ḥămiššâ 'āśār*} steps {*ma'ălôt*} which go down from the Israelites' court to the women's court –

E. corresponding to the fifteen Songs of Ascents {*šîr hamma'ălôt*} which are in the Book of Psalms –

F. on these the Levites stand with their instruments {*bikĕlê šîr* 'with instruments of song'} and sing their song {*šîrâ*}.

G. And two priests stood at the upper gate which goes down from the Israelites' court to the women's court, with two trumpets {*ḥăṣôṣĕrôt*} in their hands.

H. [When] the cock crowed, they sounded a sustained {*tāq'û*}, a quavering {*wĕhērî'û*}, and a sustained note {*wĕtāq'û*} on the shofar.[49]

I. [When] they got to the tenth step, they sounded a sustained, a quavering, and a sustained blast on the *shofar*.

J. [When] they reached the courtyard {of the women}, they sounded a sustained, a quavering, and a sustained blast on the *shofar*.

K. They went on sounding the *shofar* in a sustained blast until they reached the gate which leads out to the east.

L. [When] they reached the gate which goes out toward the east, they turned around toward the west,

M. and they said, 'Our fathers who were in this place *turned with their backs toward the Temple of the Lord and their faces toward the east, and they worshipped the sun toward the east* (Ezek. 8:16).

N. 'But as to us, our eyes are to the Lord'.

The description shows that the occasion included cultic dance performed by men as they sang songs and praises, and music performed by innumerable Levites who played instruments and sang. Their instruments are listed as 'harps', lyres, cymbals and 'instruments of song'. Since the instruments of song were harps and lyres, there must be a reason why 'instruments of song' are named in addition to the others. The clue probably lies in the phrase 'instruments of song' itself. As has been shown above, this phrase designates a group of cultic instruments consisting of harps and lyres. The remaining instruments (harps, lyres and cymbals) also constitute a group, namely that generally referred to in scriptural texts as the 'instruments of David' and consisting of the harps,

---

[49]   'on the shofar': the Hebrew does not have this phrase, and it does not mention the shofar (likewise in sentences I, J and K). The Hebrew text implies that the various calls were played by the two priests on their trumpets.

lyres and cymbals traditionally believed to have been prescribed by David for the cultic use of Levite musicians, as has also been shown above. The groups should be thought of as separate entities, even though they have the two types of plucked-string instrument in common. They are normally clearly differentiated in both postexilic scriptural texts (as has been shown earlier) and the Mishnah.[50] In the scriptural texts this probably reflects a desire to preserve the tradition of the Davidic prescription of harps, lyres and cymbals for Levitical use in cultic worship, alongside the anonymous tradition of the 'instruments of song'. In the Mishnah, however, the differentiation seems to reflect a state of affairs in which instruments of song (harps and lyres) were used at sacrificial and non-sacrificial rites, but 'instruments of David' (harps, lyres, and cymbals – plurals) were used only at non-sacrificial rites.[51]

The association of the Songs of Ascents with the 15 steps that connected the Court of the Israelites and the Court of the Women in the Temple invites speculation about the significance of the mention of the Songs of Ascents in the description of this particular occasion. The Songs of Ascents are the 15 psalms, 120–134, in the book of Psalms in the Hebrew Bible, each of which has as its superscription, or as part of its superscription, the phrase *šîr hamma'ălôt*, often translated 'song of ascents'.[52] The conventional understanding of the phrase is that it designates the psalms sung by pilgrims as they went up – made their 'ascent' – to the Temple.[53] This is an attractive idea. But while Psalms 120–134 may have been sung by pilgrims 'going up' to the Temple (no contemporary source provides information one way or the other on the matter), this does not seem to be the implication of the phrase *šîr hamma'ălôt* in their superscriptions.

The word *hamma'ălôt* is the definite form of the word *ma'ălôt* meaning 'steps', as in *mishnah Sukkah* 5:4, quoted above (also *m. Middot* 2:5, end). It is therefore probable that the sense of the phrase *šîr hamma'ălôt* should be 'song of the steps' rather than 'song of ascents'. Comparison with other ancient versions confirms this: the Greek of the LXX has *ōdē tōn anabathmōn*, and the Latin of the Vulgate *canticum graduum*; in both languages the meaning is 'song of the steps'.[54] In this light, and since there are 15 psalms so superscribed, which *mishnah Sukkah* 5:4 associates with the 15 steps connecting the Court of the Israelites and the Court of the Women, the inference that those psalms were sung on those steps seems unavoidable. Since the Mishnah, in the same paragraph, goes on to say that the

[50] In addition to the present passage, see *m. Mid.* 2:5.

[51] See at n. 50.

[52] The superscription to Ps. 121 has a minor variant: *šîr lamma'ălôt* rendered in the JPS *Tanakh* as 'a song for ascents'.

[53] For example, F. Kirkpatrick, *The Book of Psalms*, 2 vols (Cambridge, 1894), vol. 1, pp. xxv–xxvi; Artur Weiser, *Introduction to the Old Testament*, trans. Dorothea M. Barton (London, 1961), p. 286; *MAI*, p. 85; Eric Werner, *The Sacred Bridge*, 2 vols (New York, 1959, 1984), vol. 2, pp. 8, 15, 53.

[54] See *PsIW*, vol. 2, pp. 208–9.

Levites stood on those steps to sing their song, the inference that it was the Songs of Ascents the Levites sang when they stood there also seems unavoidable.[55] Moreover, since the Songs of Ascents, the 15 steps and the Levites' song are mentioned together in the context of the festivities at the close of the first day of the Festival of Booths, it also seems a reasonable inference that the Levitical singing of those psalms on those steps occurred during that occasion. Indeed, when the Tosefta treats this Mishnah passage, it answers its own anonymous question, 'What did they [the Levites] sing?' by quoting the first two verses of Psalm 134, the last Psalm of the Songs of Ascents (*t. Sukkah* 4:7–8).

However, the extent to which these inferences are valid is open to question. *Mishnah Sukkah* 5:4 says that Levites played instruments and sang on the 15 steps, but it does not say in so many words what they sang; and while it links in thought the 15 steps and the 15 Songs of Ascents, it does not specify what, if anything, these had to do with each other.[56]

Although the Tosefta, *Sukkah* 4:7–8, claims that an element from one of the Songs of Ascents was sung by the Levites on the 15 steps during the festivities at the close of the first day of the Festival of Booths, those paragraphs in the Tosefta may not be historically reliable. By the time the Tosefta was compiled there was already a growing body of folklore about the Temple. Anonymous and uncorroborated claims about the Temple in the Tosefta, such as those at *Sukkah* 4:7–8, may well belong to this folklore. All that can be said with certainty about the Levitical music on this particular occasion is that a large number of Levites stood on the 15 steps and played harps, lyres and cymbals, and sang.

What, then, would have been the point of associating the Songs of Ascents-psalms with the steps within the description of the occasion, if not to imply that those psalms were sung on the steps during it? One possible answer is that the writer wanted to make the number of steps memorable for his readers, and he chose a comparison that would be familiar to them (perhaps he was concerned to give the generations growing up after the Temple's destruction as vivid a picture as possible of what the Temple was like).

Another possible answer lies in the mystical significance of the number '15' in Jewish spirituality in late antiquity. From at least Maccabean times until the Renaissance, the consonantal letters of Hebrew functioned also as numerical symbols. The units were represented by the first nine letters of the alphabet, the tens by the next nine letters, and the hundreds up to 400 by the last four. Compound numbers were represented by placing the appropriate alphabetical symbols in order after each other. Thus the number 11 was expressed by the letters for 10 and 1, the number 12 by the letters for 10 and 2, and so on. According to this system the number 15 would logically have been expressed by the letters for 10 and 5: *yh*. These are also the first two letters of

---

[55]   John Arthur Smith, 'Which Psalms Were Sung in the Temple?' *M&L*, 71 (1990): 175.

[56]   Likewise in the parallel passage at the conclusion of *m. Mid.* 2:5.

the Tetragrammaton, the Divine name, and are a frequently used abbreviation of it. Thus from the time of the late pre-Herodian Second Temple onwards, the concept '15' not only represented a numerical value, but also symbolized the Deity. However, in sacred literature from that time onwards the numeral '15' is never written or printed in the form *yh* because this would lead to confusion with the Divine name; the numeral '15' is therefore expressed as '9+6': *ţw*.[57] In religious contexts, however, the concept 'fifteen', whether expressed by the letter symbols *ţw* or by the words for 'fifteen' (as, for example, in *m. Sukkah* 5:4 and *m. Middot* 2:5), could trigger a mental association with the Deity. It is noteworthy that in *mishnah Sukkah* 5:4, it is the *number* of items comprising the Songs of Ascents that is associated with the *number* of steps in the Temple. By pointing to 15 units of each, the anonymous author of this Mishnah passage is affirming the Deity's presence in both the Temple and its song.

In answer to the question posed above, it may be said that if the point of associating the 15 psalms with the 15 steps were not to imply that those psalms were sung in that location, it could have been on the one hand to make the number of steps memorable and on the other to play on the mystical significance of the concept 'fifteen'. While it is possible that the Mishnah's association of the 15 steps with the Songs of Ascents implies the actual use of these psalms on the Temple steps during the popular festivities in question, it is also possible that the association is a literary device motivated by pedagogical and religious considerations. It is possible too that the pertinent portion of the text of the description is intended to operate on three levels simultaneously: actual, pedagogical, and spiritual.

The description concludes with an account of two priestly trumpeters heralding the dawn. They began at cock-crow, the time in the early morning when the eastern sky began to become light, about half an hour before sunrise. On metal trumpets they blew a threefold call from three different positions: at the gate at the top of the steps, on the tenth step, and then on the floor of the Court of the Women. Number symbolism may have influenced the choice of the topmost step (the fifteenth) and the tenth step for the first and second sets of trumpet calls (the numeral '10' in Hebrew is expressed by the letter *yôd*, which is the initial letter of the Divine name). The priestly trumpeters then proceeded to the gate at the eastern end of the Court of the Women, turned towards the Temple, and recited a pledge of loyalty to the Deity. It is likely that by this time the sun had risen. The point of the inclusion of this account in the description of the ceremony would seem to be to indicate that the festivities lasted throughout the night. The dawn trumpet calls probably signalled the end of the festivities.

---

[57]   Similarly with the number '16', which would logically be '10+6': *yw*. This is also an abbreviation of the Divine name, though occurring less frequently than *yh*, and usually in compounds. In writing and in print, therefore, the number '16' is represented by '9+7': *ţz*. Confusion with the Divine name does not arise when the cardinal numbers are expressed as words: 'fifteen' = *ḥămēš 'eśrēh*, literally 'five ten'; 'sixteen' = *šēš 'eśrēh*, literally 'six ten'.

The Role of Women

There is no evidence that women took part in the performance of music at sacrifices at the Jerusalem Temple. Both Alfred Sendrey and the author of the article 'Women' in the *Encyclopaedia Judaica* think they did, but a close reading of the evidence suggests otherwise. At the outset it may be noted that nowhere in the biblical traditions about David's institution of the Temple service is there any mention that he appointed women to any of the tasks, musical or otherwise.

The mainstay of writers who argue for the inclusion of women is a passage in Ezra 2:65, and its parallel in Nehemiah 7:67, which lists 'male and female singers' (*měšōrěrîm ûměšōrěrôt*, literally: 'male singers and female singers') among the groups who returned to Jerusalem after the exile. It has been supposed that the 'male and female singers' were Temple servants, and hence that these verses imply female participation in the choral song of the sacrificial rites at the Temple.[58] However, this supposition is false, as Roland de Vaux pointed out many years ago.[59] In Ezra 2 and Nehemiah 7 the male and female singers are listed separately from Temple servants (Ezra 2:43–54; Neh. 7:46–56) and separately from Temple singers (Ezra 2:41; Neh. 7:44), the latter being characterized by words of male gender and identified as male descendants of Asaphite Levites: 'The singers [*haměšōrěrîm*, masculine]): the sons [*běnê* "descendants"; LXX: *huioi* "sons"]) of Asaph'. This is also the case in Josephus's version of the return from exile (*Jewish Antiquities*, book 11, 3:10). In 1 Esdras 5:27 in the LXX, which is parallel with Ezra 2:41 and Nehemiah 7:44, the Temple singers are also identified as male: 'The temple singers [*hieropsaltai*, literally: "sacred singers"]: the descendants [*huioi*, literally: "sons"] of Asaph', and listed separately from 'temple servants' (1 Esd. 5:29–32) and 'musicians and singers' (1 Esd. 5:41(42)). Therefore the 'male and female singers' of Ezra 2:65 and Nehemiah 7:67 cannot be regarded as belonging with the Levite musicians in the musical service at the sacrificial rites at the Temple. In biblical times it was customary for wealthy households to have the services of male and female singers for secular entertainment. In 2 Samuel 19:36(35), for example, David's wealthy servant and benefactor, Barzillai, complains that at his advanced age he cannot listen to [hear?] the 'singing of men and women [*šārîm wěšārôt*, literally: "male singers and female singers"]'; and in Ecclesiastes 2:8 the author of the book[60] says that among the luxuries he acquired for himself in his pursuit of pleasure were 'male and female singers [*šārîm wěšārôt*]'. The 'male and female singers' in Ezra 2 and Nehemiah 7 are most likely entertainers of this type.

Another crucial passage is 1 Chronicles 25:5-6:

---

[58]   See *MAI*, pp. 518–519; *EJ*, vol. 16, p. 626.

[59]   Roland de Vaux, *Ancient Israel: Its Life and Institutions*, trans. John McHugh, 2nd edn (London, 1965), p. 383.

[60]   See the note on Eccles. 1:1 in *HCSB*. Ecclesiastes dates probably from between 300 and 200 BCE (see Raymond C. Van Leeuwen's introduction to Ecclesiastes in *HCSB*).

[1 Chr. 25:5] All these [*kol-'ēlleh*] were the sons of Heman, the seer of the king, [who uttered] prophecies of God for His greater glory. God gave Heman fourteen sons and three daughters; [6] all these [*kol-'ēlleh*] were under the charge of their father for the singing in the House of the Lord, to the accompaniment of[61] cymbals, harps and lyres for the service of the House of God ...

Alfred Sendrey accepts Augustin Calmet's view that this passage constitutes evidence that Levites' daughters sang with their male relatives in the musical service at the Temple.[62] However, a close examination of the text and its narrative context shows that the passage cannot support this view. Chapter 25 of 1 Chronicles is concerned with the tradition that David appointed certain families of Levites as the musicians for the sacrificial rites at the Temple. The first verse of the chapter announces that 'David and the officers of the army set apart for service the sons of Asaph, of Heman, and of Jeduthun, who prophesied with lyres, harps and cymbals'. Verses 2 and 3 list the particular clans ('sons') of the families of Asaph and Jeduthun that did this work, and briefly mention their duties; the clans number four and six respectively. Verse 4 lists the pertinent clans (again 'sons') of the family of Heman; these number 14. The first half of verse 5 explains who 'all these' were and states their function. The second half of the verse ('God gave Heman ...') is parenthetic, an aside about Heman's offspring. The beginning of verse 6 ('all these ...') should be understood as taking up the narrative again after the parenthesis. In reiterating the opening words of verse 5 here, the Chronicler makes clear that it is the sons of Heman spoken of earlier who are the subject of the continuation of his narrative. Verses 5 and 6 of 1 Chronicles 25 should not be taken to imply that the tradition promoted the idea that David appointed Heman's daughters as well as his sons to musical service at the Temple.

A major problem with most of the earlier discussions of this topic is their failure to distinguish between sacrificial and non-sacrificial rites where musicians are concerned. While there is no evidence that women sang or played at the sacrificial rites, there is evidence that they did so at non-sacrificial ones. This has already been pointed out in Chapter 2 with reference to the First Temple in the discussions of the traditions incorporated into the texts of, and literary material associated with, Psalm 68, Miriam's Song (Exod. 15:21) and the Song of Deborah (Judg. 5:2–31). There is no reason to believe that the position was any different at the postexilic Jerusalem Temple. Indeed, the likelihood of the continued use of Psalm 68 at the Temple after the exile, together with the existence of a first-century CE reworking of the Song of Deborah (see Chapter 4), point to the continuation of pre-exilic practices at the Second Temple.

---

[61]   'to the accompaniment of' in the JPS *Tanakh*; the MT has 'with'.

[62]   *MAI*, p. 518, citing Augustin Calmet, *Dictionnaire historique, critique, chronologique, géographique et litteral de la Bible*, 5 vols (Geneva, 1780; English edition: Boston, 1832), vol. 3, p. 335.

This is further supported by the context and text of Judith's hymn of praise in Judith 16:1–17. The book of Judith in the LXX is didactic historical fiction written *c.*100 BCE and set in the time just after the Israelites' return from exile and their rededication of the restored Temple in Jerusalem (Judith 4:3). The anonymous author gives the book a pseudo-historical background by conflating historical situations, producing a string of historical impossibilities.[63] The hymn of praise in Judith 16:1–17 is likely to be contemporary with the composition of the book. It celebrates a fictitious victory of the Israelites (led by Judith) over the Assyrians. Its immediate context is a victory procession to the Temple at Jerusalem, as the surrounding narrative shows: Judith 15:13b relates that 'She [Judith] went before all the people in the dance, leading all the women, while all the men of Israel followed, bearing their arms, wearing garlands and singing hymns [*humnoun*]'; then immediately after the hymn of praise the narrative continues, 'When they arrived at Jerusalem, they worshipped God. As soon as the people were purified, they offered their burnt-offerings, their freewill-offerings, and their gifts' (Judith 16:18).

Judith's hymn itself is introduced by a prose preamble which, despite the NRSV translation, does not mention song or singing. The poetic text, however, does contain references to singing. Its opening verse (Judith 16:1) has, 'Begin[64] to my God with tambourines [*en tumpanois* "with hand drums"], sing [*asate*] to my Lord with cymbals [*en kumbalois*]. Raise to him a new psalm [*psalmon kainon*, or *psalmon kai ainon* "a psalm and praise"]'; and Judith 16:13a has, 'I will sing [*humnēsō*] to my God a new song [*humnon kainon*]'. The hymn is a deliberate imitation of processional victory songs of the past and is not likely itself to have been used in the cult.[65] But the fact that it is modelled on ancient material of that type strengthens the likelihood that processional songs sung by women (such as the songs of Miriam and Deborah) were a familiar feature of the cult, not only in pre-exilic times but also at the time when the story of Judith was written. It is possible that the 'male and female singers' listed in Ezra 2:65 and Nehemiah 7:67 among the returnees from exile included female musicians who played and sang at non-sacrificial cultic ceremonies and rituals.

Excursus: Worshippers at the Temple

There is no evidence that individuals or groups other than the Levite musicians had any musical role at the sacrificial rites. But in order to provide as rounded a picture as possible of cultic activity at the Temple, and because worshippers at

---

[63]   These are succinctly summarized in Weiser, *Introduction to the Old Testament*, pp. 400–401.

[64]   After 'begin' the NRSV inserts 'a song'. This has no justification in the LXX.

[65]   John Arthur Smith, 'Musical Aspects of Old Testament Canticles in their Biblical Setting', *EMH*, 17 (1998): 259-60.

the Temple are referred to herein from time to time, it is appropriate to clarify who the worshippers were and what their function was.

Worship at the Jerusalem Temple should not be thought of in terms of modern acts of corporate worship conducted for the benefit of local congregations assembled at appointed times. The worshippers were a distinct group of people with a particular function. Casual visitors to the Temple at times when the rites were performed were not counted as worshippers, even though their purpose might have been devotedly to pray and follow the progress of the rites.

The essential act of worship at the Temple was the perpetual (*tāmîd*) twice-daily sacrifice of whole-burnt offering performed on behalf of the nation of Israel by traditionally prescribed groups of officiants in accordance with Divine commands handed down in the Torah. Each act of sacrifice had two consecutive stages: presentation of the sacrificial offering at the Temple, and offering the sacrifice. Offering the sacrifice – the sacrificial act itself – was carried out by priests assisted by Levites. The presentation of the offering at the Temple was made by lay adult male Israelites (*'et-běnê yiśrā'ēl* 'the sons of Israel') on behalf of the people of Israel, in accordance with the Divine commands in Numbers 28:2–6. The epic style of that passage gives the impression that the whole lay adult male population of Israel was to attend the Temple to present the nation's sacrifices. However, in reality this would have been a practical impossibility; the operation of a system of representation must therefore be assumed. There is evidence for the existence of such a system, but this evidence is not earlier than the Mishnah. The extent to which it reflects the situation prior to the time of Herod's Temple is therefore open to question. According to *mishnah Ta'anit* 4:2, the system of 24 divisions, into which priests and Levites were organized for their service at the Second Temple, applied also to lay adult male Israelites. From each of the 'lay' divisions a delegation (*ma'ămād*) was chosen to attend the Temple in turn for a week at a time, each delegation bringing with it the sacrifices to present to the Deity on behalf of its lay division. Thus the members of the delegations (*ma'ămādôt*)[66] were worshippers at the Temple on behalf of the whole nation of Israel. This system ensured that the commands in Numbers 28:2–6 were observed. Perhaps at some earlier time there had been an interim stage during which the lay adult male Israelites attended the Temple a whole division at a time.

The delegates who represented Israel stood in the Inner Court (at the pre-Herodian Second Temple) or the Court of the Israelites (at the Herodian Second Temple) to present the sacrifices. They then remained in the Court while priests, assisted by Levites, performed the sacrificial rites. Their participation in the rites, apart from being present at them, was probably confined to joining

---

[66]   This plural Hebrew noun is anglicized 'maamads' in Danby, *Mishnah*; in Neusner, *Mishnah*, it is translated 'delegation' (singular).

with the priests and Levites in the periodic prostrations[67] and the cultic shouts of 'Amen!' 'Hallelujah!'[68] and 'Glory!'[69]

The Mishnah says that when a delegation was on duty in Jerusalem, the remaining members of its parent division would assemble in their own towns and read the same passages of Scripture their delegates would hear read at the Temple, and fast on the same four days of the week as their delegates (*m. Ta'an.* 4:2–3). The Mishnah also specifies that the delegations did not attend every sacrifice. They were not present, for example, at the morning sacrifice on a day when the Hallel was appointed (principally the days of the major festivals such as the Three Pilgrim Festivals – each household presented its own sacrifice), or at the afternoon sacrifice on a day when there was an additional sacrifice (New Year's Day, the first day of the month, and the Sabbath – additional sacrifices were supernumerary to the *tāmîd* sacrifices) or at the ceremony of the Closing of the Gates on the nine days each year when a wood offering was brought (*m. Ta'an.* 4:4–5 – wood offerings did not belong among the *tāmîd* sacrifices).

---

[67] 2 Chr. 7:3; 29:28–30; Sir. 50:17, 21; *m. Tamid* 7:3.

[68] 1 Chr. 16:36, end; compare Ps. 106:48b.

[69] Ps. 29:9.

Chapter 4
Music at the Second Temple, 2

The Repertory of Song and its Performance

The Repertory

Sources relevant to the Second Temple show that psalms from the book of Psalms constituted the bulk of the material sung at cultic rites. Sources cited in Chapter 3 show that at sacrificial rites psalm singing was the prerogative of the Levite musicians. More detailed information is given in the Mishnah and some of the psalms themselves. *Mishnah Tamid* 7:4 opens with the announcement: 'The singing which the Levites did sing in the sanctuary' and proceeds to list seven psalms which the Levites sang at the twice-daily sacrifices, one on each day of the week: Psalms 24, 48, 82, 94, 81, 93 and 92 respectively. The assignment of Psalm 92 to the seventh day, the Sabbath, is underlined by its superscription: 'A psalm [*mizmôr*]. A song [*šîr*]; for the sabbath day'. The same daily assignments for Psalms 24, 48, 94, 93 and 92 are given in the superscriptions to their LXX equivalents,[1] a feature which suggests that the Mishnah's weekly cycle of psalms was in use by at least the end of the second century BCE.

Mishnah Bikkurim 3:4, says that during the presentation of the first-fruits at the Temple, the Levites sang Psalm 30. This psalm also receives an assignment in its superscription in the MT and the LXX, but to the dedication of the Temple: 'A song [*šîr*] for the dedication of the house [the Temple]'. Notwithstanding the discrepancy, the superscription implies use of this psalm in a sacrificial context.

Mishnah Pesaḥim 5:7 witnesses to Levitical singing of the Hallel during the sacrifice of the lambs at Passover. The Levites were also required to be present at the remaining two Pilgrim Festivals, at which the Hallel was sung in the Temple, and possibly at the Festival of Dedication.

The Mishnah mentions other psalms employed on other occasions, but does not specify sacrificial contexts or Levitical performance. These psalms may have to do with non-sacrificial rites at the Temple or with religious observance in the home or at the synagogue.

The total number of psalms known to have been sung by Levites at sacrificial rites at the Second Temple is thus 14. So relatively small a repertory for daily and festal use is consistent with the methods by which Levite musicians learned their musical skills, with their singing from memory (on these, see below) and with the infrequency of their tours of duty at the Temple. Concerning the last

---

[1]   LXX Pss 23, 47, 93, 92, 91.

point, Levite musicians would have been more numerous than the 288 individuals implied by the 24 divisions of 12 men each. If each individual were to share in serving at the Temple, and if each division were to consist of 12 individuals, membership of the divisions would have had to rotate. This would mean that no individual could reckon to serve at the Temple even as often as two weeks in each year (52 weeks divided by 24 divisions) plus Pilgrim Festivals.

There is evidence to suggest that in non-sacrificial cultic rituals at the Temple, many psalms in addition to the 14 named above would have been sung, whether exclusively by Levites or not. It has been estimated that a total of between 109 and 126 psalms could have been sung at the Temple.[2] Reconsideration of the available evidence suggests that these numbers may have to be adjusted downwards.

Many psalms are furnished with superscriptions and rubrics of a liturgical or musical nature, which suggests that they were used in the cult. However, it is possible that some psalms not actually used in the cult have had superscriptions and rubrics added in imitation of those attached to psalms which were so used. That such imitation occurred is illustrated by comparing the Greek text of the *Psalms of Solomon* with the Greek (LXX) text of the 14 psalms stated in the Mishnah to have been sung at the Temple.

The *Psalms of Solomon* are 18 pseudepigraphical religious poems, dating probably from the period 63–48 BCE.[3] They were written originally in Hebrew but are extant in Greek and Syriac;[4] their literary style is similar to the psalms in the Hebrew Bible. The rubric *diapsalma* (the Greek equivalent of the Hebrew *selâ*) occurs in two of them[5] and also in four of the 14 'Mishnah' psalms in their LXX version.[6] The phrase (*psalmos*) *tō Salōmōn* '(a psalm) of Solomon' in the superscriptions to seven of the *Psalms of Solomon*[7] is paralleled by expressions such as '(a psalm) of David', or '(a psalm) of Asaph', in the superscriptions to six of the 14 'Mishnah' psalms in their LXX version.[8] But even though the *Psalms of Solomon* were originally written in Hebrew and would have been stylistically similar to the psalms in the Hebrew Bible, it is unlikely that they were sung at the Temple. Their rubrics and superscriptions have been written in imitation of those in the canonical Psalms; they cannot be taken as guides to the *Sitz im Leben* of the individual items from the *Psalms of Solomon* to which they are attached.

The same may be the case with some of the rubrics and superscriptions attached to Hebrew canonical psalms outside the 14 'Mishnah' psalms. Of

---

[2]   John Arthur Smith, 'Which Psalms were Sung in the Temple?' *M&L*, 71 (1990): 181.

[3]   Text in LXX, ed. Rahlfs (see under 'Bible: ancient Versions' in the Bibliography), vol. 2, pp. 471–89. English translation in *OTP*, vol. 2, pp. 639–70. On *Pss Sol.*, see *PsIW*, vol. 2, pp. 118–20; *OTP*, vol. 2, pp. 639–50; Schürer/Vermes et al., *History*, vol. 3, pp. 192–7.

[4]   *OTP*, vol. 2. p. 640.

[5]   *Pss Sol.* 17, between verses 29 and 30; *Pss Sol.* 18, between verses 9 and 10.

[6]   LXX/MT Pss 23/24, 47/48, 80/81, 81/82.

[7]   *Pss Sol.* 2, 3, 5, 13, 15, 17, 18.

[8]   LXX Pss 23, 29, 80, 81, 92, 93.

the 14 psalms which the Mishnah says were sung at the Temple, four have superscriptions designating them as *mizmôr* (the LXX equivalents have *psalmos*),[9] two have superscriptions designating them as *šîr* '[a] song' (for special cultic use)[10] and four contain the word *selâ*.[11] Psalm 92, in addition to its superscription 'A psalm [*mizmôr*], a song [*šîr*]; for the Sabbath day', has the rubric *'ălê higgāyôn běkinnôr* 'upon *higgayon* with [*or* "of"] the lyre' as the second clause of its fourth verse. Several psalms outside the 14 'Mishnah' psalms exhibit one or more of these features, perhaps in some cases as the result of additions made in imitation of one or other of the 14. The rubrics and superscriptions attached to Hebrew canonical psalms outside the 'Mishnah' psalms are thus, by themselves, untrustworthy indications of cultic use. To establish cultic use with a reasonable degree of certainty, additional information is necessary, such as is provided for the 'Mishnah' psalms.

Two groups of psalms over and above the 14 already referred to can be considered likely to have been sung by the Levite musicians at the Temple. One is the 15 Songs of Ascents (Psalms 120–134) each of which has as its superscription, or part of its superscription, the phrase *šîr hamma'ălôt* (*šîr lamma'ălôt* in the superscription to Ps. 121) 'song of the steps'. While there is uncertainty about the significance of the superscription (see Chapter 3), the texts of these psalms suggest that they might have been sung by the Levite musicians during the changeover of the priestly and Levitical divisions after their tours of duty in the Temple. This is hinted at in the last verse of Psalm 121, where the affirmation that the Deity will guard 'your going and coming' ('your going out and your coming in' in the NRSV translation, following the Hebrew phraseology) can be understood as being addressed by people at the Temple either to a group that is departing and will return at some later date or to two groups, one departing, the other arriving. The ideas expressed in the remainder of these psalms well suit a situation in which priests and Levites are assembled at the Temple to serve in joyful collegiality.

The other pertinent group comprises the 57 psalms the superscriptions to which include the word *mizmôr*. In each one *mizmôr* seems to refer in some way to the religious poem that follows the superscription. In the LXX this word is translated *psalmos*, the basic meaning of which is a song sung with the music of plucked-string instruments.[12] The precise meaning of *mizmôr* is unknown. Some

---

[9]   Pss 30, 48, 82 and 92.

[10]   Pss 30 and 92.

[11]   Pss 24, 48, 81, 82. Ps. 48 is also designated *šîr* 'song' in its superscription. While the MT of Ps. 94 does not have *selâ*, the LXX version (Ps. 93) has the equivalent Greek word *diapsalma*.

[12]   There is a high degree of correlation between *mizmôr* in the superscriptions to psalms in the MT and *psalmos* in the superscriptions to psalms in the LXX: details in J.A. Smith, 'First-Century Christian Singing and its Relationship to Contemporary Jewish Religious Song', *M&L*, 75 (1994): 5, n. 26.

earlier writers have thought it means 'song', the same as *šîr*.[13] But this is unlikely to be correct since *mizmôr* and *šîr* often occur together in psalm superscriptions, and there would be little point in there being two words of identical meaning to designate the ensuing poem. Other writers have thought it signifies a particular type of literary composition.[14] Still others, noting its likely derivation from the root ZMR, and its translation *psalmos* in the LXX, have regarded it as a generic term for cultic poetic texts sung to the accompaniment of plucked-string instruments.[15] This meaning is the current consensus.

An alternative possibility is that *mizmôr* indicates the source of the psalm. Assuming that the root of the word is ZMR, its first syllable, *mi-*, may be taken to be a prefixal form of the preposition *min* which most usually means 'from'. The basic meaning of *mizmôr* would consequently be 'from ZMR', which, glossed so as to make it comprehensible, would conjecturally mean '[an item] from [the repertory (or 'the collection') of] cultic music for plucked-string instruments and voices'. To see the psalms superscribed *mizmôr* as being taken from a pre-existent repertory is in keeping with the generally accepted view that the extant book of Psalms is a compilation of items drawn from various sources. Interestingly in this connection, the superscription to Psalm 4 in the LXX announces that the Psalm is not only 'for the end' and 'a song [*ōdē*] of David', but also *en psalmois* 'among the psalms' (perhaps more aptly 'from among the psalms').

There is less certainty about the value of the term *mizmôr* as a pointer to cultic use than there is about the phrase 'song of the steps'. Five of the psalms with *mizmôr* in their superscriptions also occur among the 14 'Mishnah' psalms.[16] The possibility that the word was imitated in some of the canonical psalms outside those specified for cultic use in the Mishnah, must be taken into account. Table 4.1 summarizes the foregoing discussion.

Additional factors could have some bearing on the question of which psalms were sung in the Temple, although these carry even less weight than the presence of *mizmôr*. Thirteen psalms, aside from the 14 'Mishnah' psalms and Psalms 120–134, have the word *šîr* 'song' in their superscriptions as a designation of the ensuing poetic material.[17] Nine of these 13 carry the additional designation *mizmôr* 'psalm',[18] one of them (Ps. 45) carries the additional designation *maśkîl* 'a

---

[13]   For example, *IB*, vol. 4, p. 9; Otto Eissfeldt, *Einleitung in das Alte Testament*, 3rd (rev.) edn (Tübingen, 1964), p. 611; Ernst Sellin, *Einleitung in das Alte Testament*, rev. George Fohrer (Heidelberg, 1969), p. 305.

[14]   For example, *ISBE*, vol. 3, p. 1031; *ABD*, vol. 5, pp. 527–8. This is the position adopted in Smith, 'Which Psalms?'.

[15]   For example, Artur Weiser, *Introduction to the Old Testament*, trans. Dorothea M. Barton (London, 1961), p. 22; *PsIW*, vol. 2, p. 208; *MAI*, p. 276; Bathja Bayer, 'The Titles of the Psalms', *Yuval*, 4 (1982): 97.

[16]   Pss 24, 30, 48, 82, 92.

[17]   Pss 18, 45, 46, 65–68, 75, 76, 83, 87, 88, 108.

[18]   Pss 65, 66, 67, 68, 75, 76, 83, 87,108.

Table 4.1   Psalms Sung at the Second Temple

Col. A: psalms listed in the Mishnah as having been sung by Levites at the Temple.
Col. B: psalms designated *šîr* in their superscriptions in the MT.
Col. C: psalms designated *mizmôr* in their superscriptions in the MT.

Psalm	A	B	C		Psalm	A	B	C		Psalm	A	B	C
3			•		67		•	•		125		•	
4			•		68		•	•		126		•	
5			•		73			•		127		•	
6			•		75		•	•		128		•	
8			•		76		•	•		129		•	
9			•		77			•		130		•	
12			•		79			•		131		•	
13			•		80			•		132		•	
15			•		81	•				133		•	
18		•			82	•		•		134		•	
19			•		83		•	•		139			•
20			•		84			•		140			•
21			•		85			•		141			•
22			•		87		•	•		143			•
23			•		88		•	•		**Total**			
24	•		•		92	•	•	•		**84**	**14**	**31***	**57†**
29			•		93	•							
30	•	•	•		94	•							
31			•		98			•					
38			•		100			•					
39			•		101			•					
40			•		108		•	•					
41			•		109			•					
45		•			110			•					
46		•			113	•							
47			•		114	•							
48	•	•	•		115	•							
49			•		116	•							
50			•		117	•							
51			•		118	•							
62			•		120		•						
63			•		121		•						
64			•		122		•						
65		•	•		123		•						
66		•	•		124		•						

* Three of these psalms are also marked in col. A; the same three are also marked in col. C.
† Two of these psalms are also marked in col. A, but not col. B; ten are also marked in col. B, but not col. A; three are also marked in both cols. A and B.

maskil' and one (Ps. 88) is designated 'song', 'psalm' and 'maskil'. The presence of more than one term of designation in any one superscription implies that each had its special significance. The term *šîr* in the superscription to a psalm probably signifies a song to be sung in connection with the Temple cult. The likelihood of this is supported by a passage in the Psalms Scroll from Qumran cave 11 (11QPsᵃ),[19] column XXVII, lines 1–13. This purports to be an account of David's poetic achievements. Lines 2–11 state:

> YHWH gave him [King David] an intelligent and brilliant spirit, and he wrote 3,600 psalms [*těhillîm*] and 364 songs [*šîr*] to sing before the altar for the daily perpetual [*tāmîd*] sacrifice, for all the days of the year; and 52 songs [*šîr*] for the Sabbath offerings; and 30 songs [*šîr*] for the New Moons, for Feast days and the Day of Atonement ... and 4 songs [*šîr*] to make music on behalf of those stricken (by evil spirits). (*CDSSE*, p. 307)[20]

Aside from the obviously exaggerated claims made for David, the salient point here is that 'songs' are listed separately and that they (with the possible exception of the four songs for the 'stricken') were for singing at sacrificial rites, hence at the Temple.

To what extent the presence of the word *šîr* 'song' in the superscriptions to the 13 psalms that are not among either the 14 from the Mishnah or the 15 Songs of Ascents is a genuine indication of cultic use, is an open question. The texts of five of them[21] contain more or less direct references to singing in connection with the Temple, its worship and ritual,[22] which supports the possibility of cultic use. Nevertheless the fact that the superscriptions to *Psalms of Solomon* 15 and 17 also contain the word 'song' (in the phrase *meta ōdēs* 'with a song') is a reminder of the possibility that imitation might also have occurred in Hebrew texts.

Another additional factor that might identify psalms sung in the Temple is the presence in the superscriptions to 19 psalms of terms which have been regarded as prescribing the melodies or modes to which those psalms were sung,[23] thereby implying Levitical performance at the Temple. The meaning

---

[19]   Critical edition: J.A. Sanders (ed.), *The Psalms Scroll of Qumran Cave 11 (11QPsᵃ)* (Oxford, 1965, repr. 1998) (see under 'Psalms Scroll' in the Bibliography). Sanders assigns this scroll to 'the first half of the first century AD' (ibid., p. 9).

[20]   Square brackets enclose my interpolations; rounded brackets enclose material supplied by the translator. Hebrew from Sanders, *The Psalms Scroll of Qumran Cave 11.*

[21]   Pss 18, 66, 68, 87, 108.

[22]   See Smith, 'Which Psalms?': 169–72.

[23]   David Wulstan, 'The Origin of the Modes', in Egon Wellesz and Miloš Velimirović (eds), *Studies in Eastern Chant*, 2 vols (Oxford, 1966, 1971), vol. 2, pp. 5–20; David Wulstan in a review of Bayer, 'The Titles of the Psalms', in *M&L*, 66 (1985): 378–81, especially pp. 379, 381. The terms as given in the JPS *Tanakh* are: 'on the *sheminith*' (Pss 6, 12); 'on the *gittith*'

and significance of those terms are, however, uncertain,[24] and doubts have been expressed as to whether they have anything to do with musical performance.[25] It is nevertheless likely that the phrases 'on the *sheminith*' (Pss 6:1; 12:1), and 'on *alamoth*' (Ps. 46:1) imply cultic use of the psalms they superscribe in view of the Chronicler's use of them to qualify the Levitical plucked-string instruments named in 1 Chr. 15:20–21.[26]

A third additional factor is that the superscriptions to several psalms contain what appear to be prescriptions for the use of cultic instruments in conjunction with the utterance of those psalms, thereby suggesting that the psalms in question were used in the cult. The superscription to Psalm 5 contains the expression 'el-hannĕḥîlôt. This is translated 'for the flutes' in NRSV, while Sigmund Mowinckel prefers 'to the flute-playing' or 'to the flutes'.[27] The JPS *Tanakh* leaves the expression untranslated: 'on nehiloth'. If Mowinckel and the NRSV are right about it having to do with 'flutes' (pipes), it may point to the cultic use of Psalm 5.

The expression 'al-māḥălat 'on *mahalath*' in the superscriptions to Psalms 53 and 88 may imply cultic use. Sigmund Mowinckel would translate the expression 'to the flute',[28] suggesting that the psalms might have been sung at the Temple on an occasions when the pipe was played there.[29] However, the MT probably embodies an error of pointing here since several early versions (Aquila, Theodotion, Symmachus and certain manuscripts of Jerome) understand the pertinent Hebrew word to be *mĕḥōlôt* 'dancing, choral dance' (Greek: *choreia*; Latin: *choro*). This interpretation suggests a non-sacrificial cultic context for those psalms.

The expression *binĕgînôt* in the superscriptions to Psalms 4, 6, 54, 55, 67 and 76, and the expression 'al-nĕgînat in the superscription to Psalm 61, might also imply the use of cultic instruments in conjunction with the psalms to

---

(Pss 8, 81, 84); "*almuth labben*' (Ps. 9; NRSV: 'according to Muth-labben'); 'on *ayyeleth ha-shahar*' (Ps. 22; NRSV: 'according to The Deer of the Dawn'); 'on *shoshannim*' (Pss 45, 69, 80; NRSV: 'according to Lilies'); 'on *alamoth*' (Ps. 46); 'on *mahalath*' (Pss 53, 88); 'on *yonath elem rehokim*' (Ps. 56; NRSV: 'according to The Dove on Far-off Terebinths'); 'al tashheth' (Pss 57, 58, 59, 75; NRSV: 'Do Not Destroy'); and 'on *shushan eduth*' (Ps. 60; NRSV: 'according to The Lily of the Covenant').

[24]   The JPS *Tanakh* leaves the salient words untranslated and notes that the meaning of the Hebrew is uncertain.

[25]   *PsIW*, vol. 2, pp. 213–17.

[26]   See below and Chapter 3.

[27]   *PsIW*, vol. 2, pp. 213–17.

[28]   *PsIW*, vol. 2, pp. 210–11.

[29]   In the superscriptions to the LXX equivalents of these psalms (LXX Pss 52 and 87) the corresponding Greek is '*huper maeleth*'; '*maeleth*' is a Greek phonetic approximation of the Hebrew, and of unknown meaning.

which they are attached.[30] These expressions are sometimes translated 'with stringed instruments' (so, for example, in the REB and NRSV) although the JPS *Tanakh* gives 'with instrumental music' and notes that the meaning of the Hebrew is uncertain. The superscriptions to the LXX equivalents of those psalms contain nothing that corresponds to the Hebrew terms. In view of what was said earlier about the association of the verb *nāgan* (with which *nĕgînôt* and *nĕgînat* above are cognate) with the *kinnôr* in pre- and postexilic biblical literature,[31] it is likely that the instruments envisaged were *kinnōrôt*. There seems to be no reason to deny the most obvious implication of the presence of the expressions *binĕgînôt* and *'al-nĕgînat* in the superscriptions to psalms, namely that *kinnōrôt* (or at any rate plucked-string instruments) were to be played as those psalms were sung.

The fourth and final additional factor is that the rare expression *higgāyôn*, which occurs in the texts of Psalm 9 and the 'Mishnah' Psalm 92, may have had cultic musical significance. According to Sigmund Mowinckel, it could mean 'pealing'.[32] It seems to be used as a musical rubric since in Psalm 9:17 it is followed immediately by *selâ* (LXX: *ōdē diapsalmatos*), and in Psalm 92:4 it is preceded by *'ălê* 'upon'(?) and followed immediately by *bĕkinnôr* 'with [*or* "of"] the lyre' (LXX Ps. 91:4: *ōdēs en kithara*). The word *higgāyôn* seems to have had some cultic musical significance, but exactly what this was is unknown.

To conclude this discussion, it is first necessary to recall material presented earlier. In Chapter 3 it was noted that the phrase 'For He is good, for His steadfast love is eternal', or a shortened form of it, is inserted into two of the Chronicler's descriptions of sacrificial rites (2 Chr. 5:13; 7:3, 6). It was noted too that this phrase also occurs in the first verses of Psalms 106, 107, 118 and 136. One of the explanations offered for the Chronicler's use of the phrase in those contexts was that it alludes to the use of one or other of these psalms. This explanation could also apply in other instances where the phrase appears as a freestanding element.

On the other hand, there is no reason why the presence outside the book of Psalms of a text that has parallels in four psalms, has to imply the use of one or other of those psalms. As far as the passages in 2 Chronicles are concerned, it would have been in keeping with the Chronicler's propagandist approach to history for the phrase to be inserted as a rhetorical device – a rallying motto – rather than as historical information. It is also possible to see its use elsewhere, for example in Ezra 3:11, in the same light.[33] Two observations support this view. One is that there is no explicit statement in the narratives of any of these three occasions that the phrase was actually uttered – it is simply placed in the text, perhaps as a stock response to the mention of the Deity. This

---

[30]   Compare Smith, 'Which Psalms?': 175–6.

[31]   Chapter 2, n. 33, and at n. 36; compare Ps. 68:25.

[32]   *PsIW*, vol. 2, p. 211.

[33]   Compare Smith, 'Which Psalms?': 178–9.

is particularly clear in 2 Chronicles 7:6: 'The priests stood at their watches; the Levites with the instruments for the LORD's music that King David had made to praise the LORD, "For His steadfast love is eternal," by means of the psalms of David that they knew'. The use of '[For] His steadfast love is eternal' as a stock response is also demonstrated in the opening four verses of Psalm 118.

The other observation is that whereas in Psalms 106, 107, 118 and 136 the phrase is preceded immediately by the acclamation 'Praise[34] the LORD', in the pertinent places in Ezra 3 and 2 Chronicles 5 and 7 the acclamation is absent, and in 2 Chronicles 7:6 the segment 'for He is good' is also absent. Deprived of the elements of text that would identify it specifically with one or other of the four psalms, the phrase is simply a slogan. That it was also used in certain psalms does not mean that every instance of its appearance outside the book of Psalms must refer to the psalms in which it appears. It may be regarded as belonging to a common stock of cultic slogans, along with 'Amen!', 'Hallelujah!' and 'Glory!'[35]

Under the circumstances there can be no absolute certainty about which psalms, over and above the 14 specified in the Mishnah, were sung by the Levite musicians at the Second Temple, although there must be little doubt that the Songs of Ascents were sung there. Hypothetically, the Levites' repertory could have included some 84 psalms (Table 4.1).

Important though psalms were in the cult, they were not the only constituents of the repertory of cultic song. A late source, Babylonian Talmud, *Roš Haššanah* 31a, states that the Levites performed the Song of the Sea (Exod. 15:1–18) and the Song of the Well (Num. 21:17–18) at the afternoon sacrifice on the Sabbath – presumably at the occasions of New Year since New Year is the subject of the tractate. It is difficult to know how much reliance to place on so late a source, but in the absence of any hard evidence against it, there is no reason not to take it at face value. The Song of the Sea and the Song of the Well are two of the oldest cultic poems outside Psalms in the Hebrew Bible.

Several more of the cultic poems in the Hebrew Bible and non-canonical sacred texts would have been appropriate for use at the Temple, and there is contextual and internal evidence to suggest that many of them were sung in cultic worship. In Chapter 2, eight such items from pre-exilic biblical literature were noted. For the Second Temple period the following may be added: Ezekiel's lament for the princes of Israel (Ezek. 19:2–14), Habakkuk's prayer (Hab. 3:2–19), the psalm of praise in 1 Chronicles 16:8–36 and the Song of the Three Young Men

---

[34] 'Praise': some translations have '(O) give thanks to' (for example, KJV, NJB, NRSV) or a similar formulation (for example, REB).

[35] If there is anything in the literary context of this phrase in Ezra 3:11; 2 Chr. 5:13 and 2 Chr. 7:3, 6, that might suggest its association with one or other of the four psalms, it is the presence of references to 'praising the LORD' that are written into the narratives leading into the phrase. These could be seen as allusions to the prefatory acclamation 'Praise the LORD' in Pss 107, 107, 118, 136. See the pertinent quotations in Chapter 3.

in the non-canonical additions to the book of Daniel in the LXX (Dan. 3:52–90; NRSV Apocrypha, The Prayer of Azariah and the Song of the Three Jews, verses 29–68). All these additional items appear in either an exilic document (Ezekiel) or in postexilic ones (Habakkuk 3; 1 Chronicles; LXX Daniel).[36]

Performance of the Repertory

The Levites' music consisted of choral song with the music of plucked-string instruments. On occasion the Levite musicians also played cymbals. Collective and responsive methods of performance were probably the norm for Levitical cultic song. Responsive performance is suggested by the form of several song texts, especially the Hallel. Some biblical texts use the first person singular when referring to playing and singing; this should be regarded as referring to the individual's playing and singing within a group, but would not preclude the possibility of an individual taking on the role of leader in responsive performance.

It is unlikely that soloistic song was cultivated in cultic worship at the Temple. The attention which demonstrative solo performance would focus on an individual other than the Deity, the high priest or the king, would have been considered improper. It is said of one Levite singer, Hygras (also Hugras) ben Levi, who was 'in charge of the singing' (*m. Šeqal.* 5:1), that he 'knew a lesson of singing but did not want to teach it to anyone else' (*m. Yoma* 3:11). The context of *mishnah Yoma* 3:11 shows that Hygras ben Levi's unwillingness to teach his skill was disapproved of by his peers. This implies that the norm, or the ideal, among the Levite singers was that vocal skills should be shared by being taught to each other, an implication which argues against individualism in Levitical song. Although *mishnah Yoma* 3:11 says that Hygras ben Levi had unique ability as a singer, this does not in itself permit the inference that he used his skill individualistically during the Temple ritual, or that singing of an individualistic, soloistic type was a feature of Levitical cultic song. Hygras/Hugras ben Levi's unwillingness to teach his special skill has been interpreted as professional jealousy,[37] but that is conjecture.

A group of late sources shows that methods of responsive performance could also be envisaged as applying to material that exists as plain poetic text.[38] The sources in question are rabbinic opinions, preserved in the Mishnah, the Tosefta, the Jerusalem Talmud and the Midrash Rabbah, as to how Moses and the Israelites sang the Song of the Sea (Exod. 15:1–18) at the Red Sea (see Exod. 14:10–15:19). Five responsive methods are identified:

---

[36] Detailed discussions in John Arthur Smith, 'Musical Aspects of Old Testament Canticles in their Biblical Setting', *EMH*, 17 (1998): 244, 246–59.

[37] For example, *MAI*, p. 257.

[38] What follows is based on Smith, 'Musical Aspects of Old Testament Canticles', pp. 232–6, but reaches different conclusions.

1. The leader sang the first clause of the first unit of text (for example the first clause of the first verse), then the company repeated this after him and completed the unit of text, and so on with each successive unit of text.[39]
2. The leader sang the first unit of text, then the company repeated it, and so on with each successive unit of text.[40]
3. The company sang the opening words of the first unit of text as a refrain after each unit of text sung by the leader.[41]
4. The leader sang the opening of the first unit of text, then the company completed the unit.[42]
5. The leader sang the complete text, then the company sang it.[43]

In the sources the first four methods listed above are illustrated with references to contemporary examples of recitation in school and synagogue, three of them specifically naming the Hallel and the Shema. The fifth method is arrived at by means of a theoretical abstraction: a literal reading of the beginning of the preamble to the Song of the Sea ('then sang Moses and the sons of Israel ...') where the verb is singular and may therefore be taken to imply that Moses sang the Song, and then so did the Israelites. None of the rabbinic opinions is drawn from contemporary use of the Song of the Sea itself – not even the first one listed above, which was uttered in the name of Rabbi Yosé ben Rabbi Haninah who was active in the period c.80–120 CE and probably experienced worship at the Temple in the early years of his life.[44] The rabbinic opinions are clearly unreliable witnesses as to how the Song of the Sea might have been performed at the Second Temple. Nevertheless they provide useful illustrations of the possibilities that existed for methods of responsive performance of a plain text in late antiquity.

Collective singing of a plain text could also take various forms. There are grounds for believing that the so-called Song of Deborah in Judges 5:2–31[45] was

---

[39] *y. Soṭah* 5:4; English translation in *The Talmud of the Land of Israel*, trans. and ed. Jacob Neusner (Chicago, 1982–86), vol. 27, p. 154; Jacob Neusner (trans. and ed.), *The Talmud of the Land of Israel: An Academic Commentary to the Second, Third, and Fourth Divisions* (Atlanta GA, 1998), vol. 19, p. 112. The units of text used in the sources to exemplify the points they make do not necessarily coincide with the verse divisions in modern printed editions and translations of the Bible.

[40] *m. Soṭah* 5:4; *t. Soṭah* 6:2–3, English translation in Jacob Neusner (trans. and ed.), *The Tosefta Translated from the Hebrew With a New Introduction*, 2 vols (Peabody MA, 2002), pp. 854–5.

[41] *t. Soṭah* 6:3; Neusner, *Tosefta*, p. 855.

[42] Ibid.

[43] Exodus Rabbah 23:9 on Exod. 15:1. English in Midrash Rabbah, p. 288.

[44] Blackman, *Mishnayoth*, vol. 1, p. 509.

[45] Compare Smith, 'Musical Aspects of Old Testament Canticles': 239–41.

performed in three different ways in antiquity. As the text stands, the song is about Deborah and her military commander Barak who was instrumental in helping her to win victory over the Canaanites, as recounted in the song. It could have been sung by a soloist or a group. The first-person singular formulations in Judges 5:3 ('to the Lᴏʀᴅ I will sing, I will make melody to the Lᴏʀᴅ') and 5:9 ('my heart goes out to the commanders of Israel') may be understood as remarks made by the poet, whose role as narrator the singer or singers would assume when they sang the song. The song may have been sung in this way before it was incorporated into the biblical narrative (which probably happened during the compilation of the Deuteronomistic History).

In the book of Judges the song is introduced into its literary context by means of a preamble (Judg. 5:1) which, translated literally, states, 'Then sang [*watāšar*, singular; LXX, Codex Alexandrinus: *kai ēsen*, singular; LXX, Codex Vaticanus: *kai ēsan*, plural] Deborah and Barak son of Abinoam on the day itself, saying [*lē'mōr*; LXX, Codex Alexandrinus: *kai eipen* "and said," singular; Codex Vaticanus: *legontes* "saying"]'. The form of words here is very similar to that in the preamble to the Song of the Sea; it suggests there was a tradition of performance by two singers, or groups of singers, the ritual substitutes for Deborah and Barak.

However, some of these passages would be more appropriately sung by a narrator. They could of course be sung by 'Deborah' and 'Barak' combined, thereby satisfying the preambular prescription of these two singers while in practice admitting a third element ('Deborah with Barak') as narrator. It would seem more natural, nevertheless, for the song to be distributed among three completely different singers or groups. This is what may lie behind the version of the preamble given by Pseudo-Philo (first century ᴄᴇ) in the *Liber antiquitatum biblicarum*: 'Then Deborah and Barak the son of Abino [*sic*] and all the people together [*et omnis populus unanimiter*] sang a hymn [*hymnum dixerunt*, plural] to the Lᴏʀᴅ on that day, saying ...'[46] It is thus possible that the Song of Deborah may have been performed variously by one, two or three singers, or groups of singers, at various early stages of its existence.

Although the sources frequently refer to the playing of instruments in conjunction with singing, and although they frequently mention instruments in, or in connection with, texts that can be reckoned to have been sung at the Temple, they are uninformative about how the playing and singing were combined. Whether they began and ended simultaneously, whether the playing was heterophonic, and what the rhythmic and tonal relationships between instruments and voices may have been, are not known. It is probably safe to assume monophonic or heterophonic performance by analogy with the sacred music of other ancient Near-Eastern and Mediterranean cultures, but certainty on this matter is elusive.

---

[46]   Pseudo-Philo, *Liber antiquitatum biblicarum* 32:1; English from D.J. Harrington's introduction to, and annotated translation of, this work in *OTP*, vol. 2, p. 345. Latin from D.J. Harrington et al., *Pseudo-Philon: Les antiquités bibliques*, in *SC*, no. 229 (1976), p. 244.

Acquiring the Tradition and Learning the Repertory

Ralph W. Klein, in his note on 1 Chronicles 25:8 in *HCSB*, speculates on the possibility that there was some kind of programme of tuition for the Levitical singers. This is not idle speculation in view of the complexity of the organization of the musical service at the Temple and the strong likelihood that systematic instruction in cultic ritual and music was given to the staff of the larger temples of other ancient Near-Eastern peoples such as the Babylonians, Egyptians and Hittites. Alfred Sendrey enthusiastically champions the idea that there existed an institutionalized system of training in ritual and music, which, like that provided by a modern music conservatory, produced 'professional' (Sendrey's word) musicians – conductors as well as instrumentalists and singers – for the Jerusalem Temple. On the other hand there is no conclusive evidence for this, and some of the source passages regarded as key texts are ambiguous or equivocal or linguistically problematical. This being the case, it is worth taking a fresh look at the matter to see whether any reasonable conclusions can be drawn about how the Levite musicians acquired their ritual knowledge and musical skill.

There was a significant difference in organization between the Jerusalem Temple and many of the temples of the gods of Israel's neighbours. It was normal for temples in neighbouring nations to be staffed by permanently resident personnel. These were coenobites who, in addition to pursuing spiritual exercises, had duties in the temple in connection with the rituals. Some of the larger temples had their own schools for training neophytes in reading and writing (so that they could read and copy sacred texts), in doctrine, ritual and ritual music (so that they could serve in the temple).

At the Jerusalem Temple there were no resident coenobites. Instead, most of the Temple's cultic personnel lived in towns and villages outside Jerusalem, except for some of their leaders who lived in the city (1 Chr. 9:34). As has been noted in Chapter 3, these were organized in divisions, each division serving at the Temple for one week in every 24 and at the three annual Pilgrim Festivals of Passover, Weeks and Booths. Only during their tours of duty at the Temple – which occupied no more than five weeks of the year for each division, fewer if a tour of duty coincided with any of the Three Pilgrim Festivals – did they live there. Otherwise they lived in their homes working at their professions and tending their land and livestock. It is likely that the Levites received instruction about their service when they were on duty at the Temple, but in no source is this mentioned, nor is there any mention of a Temple school for either Levites or priests.

The view that the Levite musicians were 'professional' musicians has no support in the sources. Levites did not choose to be cultic musicians. Performance of their cultic service was a sacred obligation on all males born into particular families of Levites, and was therefore not something they could undertake for reward: it was not 'work' in the sense of gainful employment. The free board and lodging they received at the Temple when they were on duty there were not wages in kind, but simply provision for their bodily needs when they were away from home. The food and drink they received at the Temple was nevertheless special: it had to be ritually pure and therefore had to come from food and drink offerings presented at the Temple itself; there was no question of their bringing with them, or being sent, 'ordinary' food and drink from outside. On one occasion the Levitical musicians withdrew their service when this provision was not forthcoming (Neh. 13:10–11), but this was not a strike: they could not stay at the Temple for a week without sustenance, so they had no alternative but to remain at home.

The Levites and their families were distributed in their towns and villages according to their functions in the cult:

> [Ezra 2:70] The priests, the Levites and some of the people, and the singers, gatekeepers, and the temple servants took up residence in their towns and all Israel in their towns.

Thus Levite musicians lived alongside each other, thereby creating milieux steeped in Levitical musical traditions. There is evidence that there were schools in the towns and villages, but these were for children; there is no evidence that there were institutions for training Levite musicians in conducting, playing instruments and singing.

It is nevertheless natural that young Levites would learn about the traditions of cultic music from their elders. By means of more or less continuous informal teaching, the traditions would be handed down from one generation to the next. The home would inevitably have been of prime importance in this process. It is known that even from earliest times the religious instruction of children was customarily a parental duty, and that it took place in the home.[47] In the LXX, 4 Maccabees 18:10–19 shows that on such occasions a father might sing psalms to his children:

> [4 Macc. 18:10] While he [the father of seven sons] was still with you [his seven sons], he taught you the law and the prophets. [11] He read to you about Abel slain by Cain, and Isaac who was offered as a burnt-offering, and about Joseph in prison. [12] He told you of the zeal of Phinehas, and he taught you about Hananiah, Azariah, and Mishael in the fire. [13] He praised Daniel in the den of the lions and blessed him. [14] He reminded you of the scripture of Isaiah, which says, 'Even though you go through the fire, the flame shall not consume you'. [15] He sang [*emelōdei*] to you songs of the psalmist [*humnographon*] David, who said, 'Many are the afflictions of the righteous'.[48] [16] He recounted to you Solomon's proverb, 'There is a tree of life for those who do his will'.[49] [17] He

---

[47]　For example, Gen. 18:19; Exod. 13:8; Deut. 4:10; 6:6–7; 11:18–19; Pss 44:1; 78:3–6; Prov. 1:8; 4 Macc. 18:10–19.

[48]　LXX Ps. 33:20a; MT Ps. 34:20a(19).

[49]　Prov. 3:18 modified.

confirmed the query of Ezekiel, 'Shall these dry bones live?'[50] [18] For he did not forget to teach you the song [*ōdēn*] that Moses taught, which says, [19] 'I kill and I make alive: this is your life and the length of your days.'[51]

According to *mishnah 'Arakin* 2:6, when the Levite musicians served at the Temple it was customary for their juvenile male relatives to stand with them and join in the singing. The Mishnah makes several points about these juvenile Levites. They sang but did not play instruments; they stood down on the ground, not up on the platform with their elders; and they were not counted in the official number of Levites on duty. Their presence was thus extraneous to the ritual requirements, and they bore no responsibility for the performance of the musical service. This is significant because it implies that the Levite juveniles were present in order to learn from first-hand experience what they would eventually be required to do when they became fully fledged Temple musicians at the age of 20. It may be supposed that mundane but necessary practical details (the route to take when walking into the Temple Court, when to sing, when to make prostrations) would also be learned on such occasions.

Serving Levite musicians played and sang from memory. E.P. Sanders infers from a passage in Josephus's *Jewish Antiquities*, book 20, 9:6, that up to the time of Agrippa II in *c*.65 CE the Levites had to hold scrolls while they sang, and therefore that up to this time at least they had not sung from memory.[52] These inferences are mistaken. In *c*.65 CE Rome allowed Agrippa II to regulate matters concerned with the Temple. The Levites petitioned him to be allowed to wear linen garments instead of the traditionally prescribed woollen ones when on duty, and to be allowed to learn certain hymns. Agrippa II granted the petitions. As far as the learning of hymns is concerned, the context of the passage in *Jewish Antiquities*, book 20, suggests that it was the enlargement of the repertory that was the point of the petition, not the learning in itself. The passage cannot be held to support the idea that the Levites' petition was for a new method of performance, singing from memory. In any case, it seems unlikely that the Levites would have held scrolls while they sang. To hold a scroll open so that it can be read requires the use of both hands; if the Levites had sung from scrolls they would have been unable to hold and play their instruments at the same time.

In the light of the foregoing background material, the biblical passages that could be considered to be key texts may now be examined. According to the translation of 1 Chronicles 15:22 in the JPS *Tanakh*, there was an officer in charge of the Levitical music, Chenaniah, appointed apparently because he was a 'master':

---

[50]   Compare Ezek. 37:2–3.

[51]   Deut. 32:39.

[52]   E.P. Sanders, *Judaism: Practice and Belief 63 BCE–66 CE* (London, UK, and Philadelphia PA, 1992), p. 81.

> [1 Chr. 15:22] ... Chenaniah, officer [*śar*] of the Levites in song [*bĕmaśśā' '*in music'; LXX omits], he was in charge of [*yāsōr*] the song [*bammaśśā'* 'the music'] because he was a master [*mēbîn*].

The sense of the Hebrew, however, is slightly different in places. The word *yāsōr* 'was in charge' should possibly read *yāśar* 'was to lead', which some LXX, Targum and Vulgate manuscripts understand here. It could mean that Chenaniah was to take the lead in responsive performance; it does not imply musical conducting in the modern sense. The NRSV translation of *yāsōr* as 'to direct' is open to misunderstanding in a context that deals with the performance of music. The word *mēbîn* means 'skilful'; a person who is skilled at what he does is by implication a master of it, but this is not what the Hebrew says. The LXX version of this passage probably conveys the sense more reasonably:

> [LXX 1 Chr. 15:22] And Chenaniah, leader [*archōn*] of the Levites, [was] leader [*archōn*] of the song [or 'the music' *tōn ōdōn*] because he was skilful [*sunetos*].

At 1 Chronicles 25:2, 3, 6a and elsewhere, the Levite musicians are described as being *'al[-]yĕdê* (*'al yad*, a related form, is used in 25:2) 'under the charge of' their fathers or named heads of clans.[53] The phrase means more precisely 'responsible to', which indicates a line of authority. The expression does not necessarily have any musical or pedagogical connotations, as is demonstrated in 1 Chronicles 25:2 and 6b where it is used to show that Asaph, Jeduthun and Heman were responsible to (*'al yĕdê*) the king. The LXX has no equivalent in its version of 1 Chronicles 25:2; it uses *meta* ('after' or 'with') in 25:3 and 6a, and *echomena* ('near, beside') in 25:6b.

Last among the pertinent texts is 1 Chronicles 25:7–8. This does seem to give the impression that the Levitical singers had undergone organized, systematic tuition:

> [1 Chr. 25:6(7)] ... Asaph, Jeduthun, and Heman – [7(7)] their total number with their kinsmen, trained singers [*mĕlummĕdê-šîr*] of the LORD – all the masters [*kol-hammēbîn*], 288. [8] They cast lots for shifts on the principle of 'small and great alike, like master [*mēbîn*] like apprentice ['*im-talmîd*]'.

How formal the system might have been, however, is another matter. In the Hebrew, the phrase translated 'trained singers' has more the sense of 'who were accomplished in singing', or 'who had been taught to sing', which is precisely the formulation in the LXX: *dedidagmenoi adein*. This does not seem quite as redolent of institutionalized education as the English 'trained'. The nouns in the phrase translated 'like teacher like pupil' mean rather 'the skilled' and 'the aspiring' respectively or, as the LXX translates, *teleiōn kai manthanontōn* 'expert

---

53   In these phrases the words *yĕdê* and *yad* are construct forms (respectively dual and singular) of the word *yād* 'hand'.

and learner'. Although the Levites had to learn the cultic musical repertory and the traditions associated with its performance, there is nothing in the passages quoted above to suggest that the learning was institutionalized or even formal. A passage from *mishnah Roš Haššanah* 4:8, while not specifically about learning music for Temple use, gives an insight into how such matters were taught:

> [*m. Roš Haš.* 4:8] They do not keep children from sounding the *shofar*. But they work with them until they learn how to do it.

The absence of firm evidence for an institutionalized system of training for Levitical cultic musicians, whether at the Temple or in the Levitical villages, does not of course mean that one did not exist. But when what is known about the Levites' duties at the Temple is viewed in the context of the Levitical way of life, the impression that emerges is that the Levites learned the traditions of their cultic service through a combination of example, direct experience and informal teaching. They were brought up surrounded by the traditions; formal learning would have been unnecessary.

The Musical Instruments: Additional Remarks

In addition to what has been written here and in Chapter 3 about the musical instruments used at the Second Temple, some observations about the three types of wind instrument (horns, trumpets and pipes) are pertinent.

Mishnah Roš Haššanah 3:3–4 says that the shofar used for signalling at New Year was made from the horn of the wild goat (*yāʿēl* 'antelope, chamois, wild goat'),[54] 'It is straight [*pāšûṭ* "ordinary, normal"]. Its mouth is overlaid with gold', but on days of fasting the shofars were made of rams' horns (*zĕkārîm*, literally: 'males'), which are 'curved [*kĕpûpîn*]' and had similar silver overlay. The first of these statements is contradicted in the succeeding paragraph, *mishnah Roš Haššanah* 3:5b, by a pronouncement of Rabbi Judah ben Ilai (active *c.*140–165 CE) which begins by saying that at New Year rams' horns are used. The pronouncement then continues with the new information that at the Jubilee Year wild goats' horns were used.

Metal trumpets in addition to horns were employed for signalling at both New Year and on days of fasting, their role being inferior to that of horns at New Year (trumpets blew a short note, whereas horns blew a long one), but superior on days of fasting (trumpets blew a long note, horns a short one) (*m. Roš Haš.* 3:3b, 4). Since *mishnah Roš Haššanah* 3:5 opens with the statement that the 'proclamation [*latĕqiyāʿh* "(shofar) flourish"] of the year of Jubilee' is like that at

---

[54] Identification of the animal is problematical; suggestions include (in addition to the present 'wild goat') antelope, chamois, ibex and mountain goat. The animal is mentioned in the Hebrew Bible at 1 Sam. 24:3; Ps. 104:18; Job 39:1.

New Year, it is to be inferred that at a Jubilee the horns – wild goats' horns – had the superior role (they blew a long note) and the metal trumpets the inferior one.

Mishnah *Kelim* 11:7 has been taken to imply that each type of horn could have detachable metal mouthpieces and bells.[55] In the light of *mishnah Roš Haššanah* 3:3–4, quoted above, it seems more likely that the references to metal parts mean parts overlaid with metal, and that it was the metal overlay that was detachable not the actual mouthpieces and bells.

Mishnah *Roš Haššanah* 4:9 prescribes how the horns are to be played:

> [*m. Roš Haš.* 4:9] A. The proper way of blowing the *shofar* is to sound three sets of three each.
> B. The length of the sustained blast is three times the length of the quavering blast.
> C. The length of the quavering blast is three times the length of an alarm blast.

The Hebrew, however, does not have 'the shofar' nor 'the length of'. A literal rendering of those sentences is as follows:

> A. The manner of blowings is three [flourishes] thrice.
> B. Long flourishes [are] three quavering flourishes.
> C. A quavering flourish [is] three alarm flourishes.

Example 4.1   Shofar Call: Alarm Flourish

The three-flourish set (which occurs three times in succession) is long–quavering–long: *těqî'â-těrû'â-těqî'â*.[56] The sound of the music hinges on the sound of the 'alarm flourish' (*yabbābâ*), which is uncertain. There is a general consensus

---

[55]   *MAI*, p. 370.

[56]   Thus at *m. Pesaḥ.* 5:5 (at the slaughtering of the Passover offering, when the first group of people had entered the Temple court and the gates were closed), *m. Sukkah* 4:5 (when willow branches were placed against the altar at the Festival of Booths), *m. Sukkah* 5:4 (at cockcrow on the morning after the popular festivities in the Court of Women at the close of the first day of the festival of Booths) and *m. Tamid* 7:3 (during the rite of the daily sacrifice of burnt offering). At the last two references the descriptions are of the playing of metal trumpets, so that the 'manner of blowings' described in the quotation above may be taken to apply to these as well as to the animal-horn instruments.

among the received traditions of shofar calls that a loud call of this type consisted of an iambic rising fifth (Example 4.1).

If this were so, the quavering flourish (*těrû'â*) would have been a succession of three iambic rising fifths.[57] The 'long' flourish was 'three quavering flourishes', which would have resulted in a succession of nine rising iambic fifths (hence 'prolonged' or 'long'). One 'set' of flourishes would thus have consisted of: nine rising iambic fifths, three rising iambic fifths, nine rising iambic fifths. The set would have been blown three times.

Modern traditions differ somewhat from these reconstructions,[58] particularly with regard to the *těrû'â*, which is now usually rendered as 12 rapid notes all at the same pitch (a 'quavering' blast) followed by a long note a fifth above to conclude (in some traditions the long note is followed by a slurred fall to a short unaccented note at the starting pitch), as in Example 4.2.

Example 4.2   Shofar Call: *těrû'â*, Modern Form

Source: Adapted from Paul Fiebig (trans. and ed.), *Die Mischna: Rosch ha-schana, Text, Übersetzung und ausfürliche Erklärung* (Giessen, 1914), p. 104.

Rapid notes all at the same pitch would satisfy the traditional understanding of *těrû'â* as a 'quavering' blast (a tremolo on one note). In terms of the Mishnah's prescriptions at *Roš Haššanah* 4:9 the *těqî'â* should then consist of 36 rapid notes all at the same pitch (perhaps with a concluding rising fifth), and the *yabbābâ* of four rapid notes all at the same pitch (perhaps also with a concluding rising fifth). However, the *těqî'â* of modern Jewry is not a prolonged tremolo on one note. In the absence of fuller information in the Mishnah, it is impossible to say to what extent modern shofar calls reflect what a first- or second-century CE Jew would understand from the prescriptions in *mishnah Roš Haššanah* 4:9.

In Chapter 2, observations were made about the shape and sound quality of the metal trumpets used at the First Temple. A passage in Josephus, *Jewish Antiquities*, book 3, 12:6, describing the '*asōsra*' (a Greek phonetic rendering of the Hebrew word *ḥăṣōṣěrâ*), shows that these also hold good for the cultic metal trumpets used at the postexilic Temple. Josephus says that the *asōsra* was just under a cubit (44.4 cm, approximately 17.5 inches) in length, a little thicker

---

[57]   The Gemara of the Talmud seems to regard the *těqî'â* as a sustained note: see Blackman, *Mishnayoth*, at *Roš Haš.* 4.9, asterisked note.

[58]   See the examples of modern shofar calls given in Paul Fiebig (trans. and ed.), *Die Mischna: Rosch ha-schana, Text, Übersetzung und ausfürliche Erklärung* (Giessen, 1914), pp. 104–5; *MAI*, pp. 353–9. Some calls in the Sephardic tradition range over an octave.

round than a pipe, and that it ended in a bell, like an ordinary trumpet. Two such instruments were used in sacred rituals, when sacrifices were brought to the altar, as well as on Sabbaths and the remaining festival days.

It was noted in Chapter 3 that according to *mishnah 'Arakin* 2:3, the pipe (*ḥālîl*) was played before the altar on 12 days of the year. That *mishnah* goes on to say that the pipers 'did not play on a pipe [or "mouthpiece"] of bronze but on a pipe made of a reed, because its [the reed pipe's] sound is sweet. And one ended [the playing] with one reed only, because it ends well'. This witnesses to the operation of aesthetic considerations and confirms that it was normal for more than one pipe to be played on such occasions. In what way the close with only one pipe 'ends well' is not explained.

A Temple Orchestra?

The idea that the Levite musicians constituted a Temple 'orchestra' belongs with the notion that they were 'professional' Temple musicians. It received strong support from Alfred Sendrey who, in his book *Music in Ancient Israel*, not only referred to the Temple orchestra many times in passing but also devoted a whole section to what he called 'the orchestra'.[59] He wrote of the 'composition of the orchestra', the 'family of wood-winds', 'singing and its orchestral background', 'orchestral performance', 'good orchestral sound', the 'artistic accomplishments' of the Levite musicians and the 'multitude of artists' who would perform on the special platform erected in the Temple. He claimed that 'levitical musicians who were particularly gifted, received a special education that would help them to distinguish themselves ... as composers, rehearsers, and conductors'. Thus Sendrey used the modern professional symphony orchestra and its ethos as an analogy of the musical establishment at the Temple. He is by no means the only writer to have done this, but no other writer has applied the analogy with such unremitting comprehensiveness.

From what has been written about music at the Temple so far in this and the two preceding chapters it should be abundantly clear that the analogy is fallacious: not only is it wildly anachronistic, but it is also contextually inappropriate and based on factual inaccuracies. The Levite musicians were not paid professionals in the modern sense. Heredity, not personal choice, determined which Levites would be Temple musicians. There is no evidence that Levites underwent any institutional education to prepare them for musical service at the Temple; they learned about the traditions of the cult and its music informally. There is also no evidence that especially gifted Levite musicians received special training.

The music of the cult was traditional. Part of this tradition was that certain instruments had special cultic functions. The tradition also prescribed which

---

[59]   *MAI*, pp. 433–40.

types of instrument, and in some cases how many of them, were to be used at the various rites. Aesthetic considerations were no doubt present, but these were secondary to the proper conduct of worship as prescribed by tradition. There is no evidence that features such as 'good orchestral sound' and 'artistic quality' (both of which Sendrey names as characteristics of the music) had any relevance to cultic music although there is no reason to doubt that the Levite musicians were skilled. The music was intrinsic to worship of the Deity; it was never the sole vehicle of worship, nor was it intended for the enjoyment of an audience.

There is also no evidence for the existence of 'conductors' who rehearsed and directed the musicians in subjective interpretation of the music as a modern orchestral conductor would. The various individuals described as being 'in charge of' or 'over' the Levitical song and musicians at sacrifices were most likely responsible as much for the physical guidance of the musicians in the Temple courts as for the specifically musical aspects of the service.

Finally, it may be pointed out that worship of the Deity at the Temple in Jerusalem was unique in Israel and Judah. Although it may have been imitated at places in Israel during the period of the divided monarchy, and at the temple in Leontopolis in Egypt during the last hundred years of the Second Temple period (see below), any such imitations would have been few and short-lived. In no sense is the orchestra an appropriate analogy of the musical establishment at the Jerusalem Temple.

Excursus: Music at Other Pre- and Postexilic Cultic Centres

In Israel and Judah

In the introduction to Chapter 2 it was stated that the Jerusalem Temple was not the only place of cultic worship in Israel and Judah in ancient times. The Hebrew Bible provides evidence of musical activity at two of the additional cultic places, ostensibly very early in the pre-exilic period. In 1 Kings 1:38–40 the anointing of Solomon as king at Gihon is related in the following terms:

> [1 Kgs 1:38] Then the priest Zadok, and the prophet Nathan, and Benaiah son of Jehoiada, went down with the Cherethites and the Pelethites. They had Solomon ride on King David's mule and they led him to Gihon. [39] The priest Zadok took the horn of oil from the Tent and anointed Solomon. They sounded [*wayyitqĕ'û*] the horn [*baššôpār*] and all the people shouted, 'Long live King Solomon!' [40] All the people then marched up behind him, playing on flutes [*baḥălilîm* 'pipes'] and making merry till the earth was split open by the uproar.

A passage in 1 Chronicles implies that there was cultic music at Gibeon in the time of David:

[1 Chr. 16:39] also [David left] Zadok the priest and his fellow priests before the Tabernacle of the Lord at the high place[60] which was in Gibeon; [40] to sacrifice burnt offerings ... [41] With them were Heman and Jeduthun, and the other selected men designated by name to give praise to the Lord ... [42] Heman and Jeduthun had with them trumpets [ḥăṣōṣĕrôt] and cymbals [ûmĕṣiltayim] to sound, and instruments for the songs of God [ûkĕlê šîr hā'ĕlōhîm].[61]

This passage should not be regarded as literal history, but it could be based on traditions that go back to the use of cultic music at Gibeon.

In the Ancient Near East Outside Israel and Judah

Early sources show that the peoples whose territories bordered on Israel and Judah possessed highly developed religious cultures even from long before there was any historical record of Israel. When musical practices at Israelite and Judaean cultic places on the one hand, and non-Hebrew Near-Eastern cultic places on the other are compared, they can be seen to have several significant features in common. This phenomenon is probably not the result of a line of influence, but a natural consequence of the common cultural background of ancient Israel and Judah and their neighbours.

Some idea of the ways in which music was employed in the cults of peoples outside Israel and Judah may be gained from documents that deal with rites at Akkadian (Mesopotamian) and Hittite (Anatolian) temples, and which collectively are representative of a period stretching roughly from the early centuries of the First Temple to Hellenistic times.

Information about music at Akkadian temples shows that priests and singers worked together in performing the traditional rites, that there was a 'kettle drum' of bronze in the Temple, which was beaten by a priest, and that singers sang hymns and lamentations. Song to the gods Ea, Shamash and Marduk was accompanied on the 'ḥalḥallatu-instrument'.[62]

With regard to Hittite temples, relevant information occurs in an order for the celebration of the festival of the warrior-god. The celebration involves various temple personnel and the king and queen. Three pertinent passages mention various liturgical groups who sing and play instruments.[63] There are 'singers' and 'liturgists' and 'psalmodists' who also sing. The liturgists sing 'psalmodies'. Beside the king stand entertainers who dance and play 'tambourines'. Before and behind the king stand 'worshippers of statues' who play three musical instruments: the *arkammi*, the *galgalturi* and the *ḥuḥupal*.

---

[60]   See Chapter 2, n. 5.

[61]   'for the songs of God': thus the JPS *Tanakh* follows the MT. The NRSV has 'for sacred song'.

[62]   *ANET*, pp. 332–42.

[63]   Ibid., pp. 358–61.

The identity of the instruments is uncertain. The *arkammi* was probably a kind of drum, and the *galgalturi* were probably paired cymbals. The *ḫuḫupal* was probably also a drum, but perhaps small and cylindrical, capable of being held in one hand. It may have been fairly short, have had a membrane at one end only, and have been played by being tapped lightly with the fingers of the player's other hand.[64]

Daniel 3 and Music in Babylonian Worship

The third chapter of the book of Daniel (which falls within a section written probably in the fourth or third century BCE) contains a story set in Babylonia during the time of the exile. The story is written in Aramaic and relates that Nebuchadnezzar, king of Babylon, had a large gold statue of himself erected on the plain of Dura. Worshipping the statue was to be a test of loyalty to Nebuchadnezzar for all residents irrespective of their nationality or language (Dan. 3:4). People who refused to worship the statue were to be thrown into a 'burning fiery furnace'. Accordingly, all the people in Babylonia (including the Jews who were in exile there) were instructed that when they heard the sound of the 'horn, pipe, zither, lyre, psaltery, bagpipe, and all other types of instruments' they had to fall down and worship the golden statue (Dan. 3:5, 7, 10, 15).[65] The story goes on to relate that three heroic Jews refused to worship, and were consequently thrown into the furnace. Nevertheless their faith that their God, the God of Israel, would save them was unswerving, and indeed they emerged from the ordeal unscathed. Nebuchadnezzar was so impressed that he granted religious freedom to the Jews in Babylonia.

Whether the story originated in any actual historical persecution of the Jews in Babylonia during the exile is unknown. The fourfold statement of the instructions and list of musical instruments, the miraculous preservation of the three Jews through their faith in God and Nebuchadnezzar's softening as a result give it the character of an edifying folk-tale.

The story contributes nothing new or important to our knowledge of music in Babylonian worship. The practice of 'falling down' in worship (whether bowing down or making prostration) at the sound of musical instruments was not unique to Babylonia in the Near East in antiquity; and the list of musical instruments that the narrative says were played on the occasion is probably nothing more than an archaizing fiction that makes use partly of the names of real instruments and partly of words that sound like the names of instruments.

---

[64]   H.G. Güterbock, 'Reflections on the Musical Instruments arkammi, galgalturi and ḫuḫupal in Hittite', in Theo P.J. van den Hout and Johan de Roos (eds), *Studio Historiae Ardens; Ancient Near Eastern Studies: Presented to Philo Houwink ten Cate on his 65th Birthday* (Leiden and Istanbul, 1995), pp. 57–72.

[65]   'and all other types of instruments': the Aramaic does not have 'other'.

In fact, the names have generated musicological interest out of all proportion to their musical significance.[66]

The names of the instruments as they occur in the lists in Daniel 3:5, 7, 10 and 15 are unique in ancient Hebrew and Aramaic literature. In order of presentation they are: (*a*) *qarnāʾ*; (*b*) *mašrôqîtāʾ* (*-rō-* in 3:10); (*c*) *qayṭĕrôs* (*-rōs* in 3:7, 10, 15); (*d*) *sabĕkāʾ* (*ś-* in 3:7, 10, 15); (*e*) *pĕsantērîn* (*-ṭ-* in 3:7; *p-* in 3:10); and (*f*) *sûmpōnĕyâ* (omitted in 3:7; *syypō-* in 3:10 with *wĕ* prefixed; *wĕ* prefixed in 3:15). Each occurrence of the list concludes with the formula *wĕkōl zĕnê zĕmārāʾ* 'and all sorts of instruments'.

Name (*a*) is the Aramaic equivalent of the Hebrew *qeren* 'horn [of an animal]';[67] and according to Joachim Braun name (*b*) is a Hebrew word from the root *ŚRQ* meaning 'to whistle, to hiss', and may therefore signify some kind of pipe.[68] The remaining names seem to be transliterated approximations of the names of Greek instruments: name (*c*) may have been suggested by the Greek *kithara* (a lyre), name (*d*) by the Greek *sambukē* (a small harp), name (*e*) by the Greek *psaltērion* (possibly a psaltery or a harp held horizontally and beaten with sticks), and name (*f*) by the Greek *sumphonia* (perhaps signifying bagpipes) or *tumpanon* (a drum). Thus the lists use a mixture of Aramaic, Hebrew and Greek-sounding unique names. Name (*f*) is not consistently applied or spelled, and most of the remaining names exhibit variations in orthography. This state of affairs suggests that the narrative tradition of Daniel 3 was ignorant of the types of instrument used in Babylonian worship at the time of the exile. If it was not, why did it not list them with either their Babylonian names or the Aramaic names of familiar equivalents? Evidently the accurate identification of the instruments was not important for the story. What was important, it seems, was to give the impression that the instruments were archaic, foreign and exotic. The list of instruments, with its frequent repetition, seems to be first and foremost a narrative device, rather than an inventory of instruments used in Babylonian worship.

The Jewish Temple at Leontopolis in Egypt

For the sake of completeness, mention may be made of the Jewish temple at Leontopolis in Egypt.[69] This was built in about 160 BCE by Onias IV (a son of the then High Priest in Jerusalem, Onias III) who had come to Egypt in *c.*164 BCE. Seeing that he was never likely to be High Priest in Jerusalem, Onias IV asked the King of Egypt, Ptolemy VI Philometor, to be allowed to build a temple in Egypt like the one in Jerusalem. Ptolemy gave him the site of a ruined pagan temple

---

[66]   See *MAI/P*, pp. 32–5.

[67]   Context determines whether *qarnāʾ/qeren* means a horn for musical use.

[68]   *MAI/P*, p. 33.

[69]   Josephus, *Josephus, The Jewish War* (trans. H.StJ. Thackeray, London, 1927, 1928), book 7, 10:2–4; Josephus, *Jewish Antiquities* (trans. H.StJ. Thackeray et al., London 1930–65), book 13, 3:1–3; *m. Menaḥ.* 13:10; Schürer/Vermes et al., *History*, vol. 3/1, pp. 145–7.

at Leontopolis, in the *nomos* of Heliopolis, on which to built his Jewish temple. Ptolemy also gave Onias a small portion of Egypt so that he could both provide the necessary sacrifices and collect revenue from the inhabitants in order to finance a priesthood. Levites were found to serve the priests. The same sacrifices were offered, and the same festivals and days of distinction observed, as at the Temple in Jerusalem. According to Josephus, Onias IV's temple was not as large or as well appointed as the Jerusalem Temple, although its altar was similar. It was built 'like a tower' 90 feet (27 metres) high; its immediately surrounding area was encompassed by a wall of mud bricks pierced by stone gateways.

The Jewish temple at Leontopolis was in operation from *c.*160 BCE until it was closed down by the Romans in 73 CE. It never had any official status within Jewry; the Jerusalem Temple remained the one official cultic and national centre of Judaism. The fact that there was cultic worship at the Leontopolis temple, and that it was like that at the Jerusalem Temple, implies that there would have been cultic music like that at the Jerusalem Temple; but none of the extant sources says anything about it.

Musical Considerations

While there is no known musical notation extant from Hebrew culture in the period of the First and Second Temples, there are musical documents extant from the adjacent Babylonian and Hurrian civilizations that may have some bearing on cultic and perhaps other music in ancient Israel and Judah.

The most significant documents range from the eighteenth to at least the fourth century BCE, and emanate from a wide geographical area extending from Mesopotamia in the east to Ugarit on the Mediterranean coast of Syria in the west.[70] These form a group which makes use of a nomenclature for the strings of the seven-stringed Babylonian lyre. Close investigation of the documents has shown that the names of the strings also stand for systems or patterns of tuning. Thus there were seven different systems of tuning. Each one required the strings to be tuned in a different order, but in each case the tuning was by intervals of a fourth or a fifth. Instruments so tuned had an overall compass of a ninth. A scalic tonal hierarchy did not apply, however; what seems to have been significant was the note group or set of characteristic musical possibilities produced by each of the seven tunings. The precise pitch of notes and their intervallic relationship cannot be determined in modern terms; the above use of the terms 'ninth', 'fourth' and 'fifth' should be regarded as schematic.

The tuning system was in use for a long time and over a wide area, which suggests that it was normative for ancient Near-Eastern musical culture. This is not to say that there would not have been local or periodic variations

---

[70]   M.L. West, 'The Babylonian Musical Notation and the Hurrian Melodic Texts', *M&L*, 75/2 (1994): 161–71.

or additions, but it is quite possible that ancient Israelite lyre players were acquainted with it and used it. It is tempting to see what have been thought to be the names of melodies in the superscriptions to some of the psalms in the book of Psalms as the names of particular tunings for the plucked-string instruments used in conjunction with those psalms, and thus, by association, for the psalms themselves. It is noteworthy too that the Babylonian documents name a total of seven tunings, a number that would correspond to the requirements of a weekly cycle of cultic music. The possibility exists that the words in the LXX and the Mishnah which allocate the seven proper psalms to respective days of the week in the Jerusalem Temple, also originally identified the tunings used for the psalms of the respective days. Thus, hypothetically, the lyres playing with the Psalm for the first day used tuning system 1, those playing with the Psalm for the second day used tuning system 2, and so on.

Musical notation is found on fragments of tablets from Ugarit dating probably from 1250–1200 BCE.[71] The notation is linked with hymnic poetic texts which are normally written above it, separated from it by a single or double horizontal line. There is therefore no guide as to how the text fitted the notes; syllable counts differ considerably from the numbers of notes. The music is related to the seven tuning systems described above, but seems to presuppose the existence of two further systems. Transcription is controversial. Five suggestions for transcription have been made to date, the latest of which is by M.L. West. West's transcription of Hurrian hymn h.6 is reproduced as Example 4.3. Its rhythmic values and tempo are unknown; its pitch relationships are relative; vertical lines drawn through the staves mark the linear distribution of the music on the tablet.

It is likely that the music in Example 4.3 is merely a melodic framework that would have been filled out by players and singers according to traditions now lost. Without knowing more about the Hurrian hymns, it is impossible to say how they fit into the broader picture of cultic music in the ancient Near East.

The vast majority of items likely to have been sung at the Jerusalem Temple are poetic. It is therefore legitimate to ask whether a consideration of the rhythm and meter of ancient Hebrew poetry can help to give some idea of how the cultic music sounded. The answer must in the end be negative, but this requires some explanation.

Problems lie in two areas: disagreement about Hebrew prosody, and ignorance about how music was matched to texts.[72] With regard to prosody, there is uncertainty as to which elements in some words count as syllables and whether all the theoretically possible syllables were always or only sometimes vocalized, and if the latter, according to what criteria. In addition, scholars are

---

[71]   West, 'The Babylonian Musical Notation', pp. 171–9. There are approximately 36 items extant. The texts are designated 'h' (Hurrian); small fragments are designated 'RS. 19.164' followed by one or two italic lower-case letters. See ibid., p. 171 and n. 23 there.

[72]   These are discussed in S.E. Gillingham, *The Poems and Psalms of the Hebrew Bible* (Oxford, 1994), pp. 51–68.

Example 4.3   Hurrian Hymn (h.6), Melodic Line

Source: Reprinted from M.L. West, 'The Babylonian Musical Notation and the Hurrian Melodic Texts', *M&L*, 75 (1994): 177. By permission of Oxford University Press.

in disagreement as to whether accentuation was qualitative or quantitative. Without a fairly clear idea of the syllable count or the place and nature of the stresses, there is little likelihood of being able to arrive at even an approximation of the rhythm of a text.

There is also the strong possibility that special forms of pronunciation were used for sung texts. Elision of syllables and the pronunciation of otherwise silent letters are common features of song in most cultures, but these are not obvious from the written word. There is no reason to doubt that ancient Hebrew song exhibited similar features, but as yet there is insufficient knowledge about its traditions to give clear pointers to the relationship between written text and sung performance.[73]

As if this were not enough, there is the purely musical problem that even if accurate textual rhythm and meter could be established, knowledge about the degree to which the tradition included syllabic and melismatic song is lacking. Folk music tends to be predominantly syllabic, and in so far as the cultic music of the Temple existed entirely in an oral tradition, it existed under the same conditions as folk music. Yet there is no certainty that the music for something so specialized as the religious cult had not developed a style of its own different from that of the folk music in use away from the Temple. The features generally typical of folk music may not be typical of the cultic music of the Temple.

---

[73]   This could be the case even as late as the Middle Ages. A rule from the medieval work *Diqduqe ha-te'amim*, which is concerned primarily with musical aspects of Masoretic pointing, has been summarized as follows: 'a shewa in the middle of a word has no fixed status. It may be vocal or silent in identical circumstances, and its articulation will depend on melody and accent, not upon historical development or specific morphological considerations': Nahum M. Waldman, *The Recent Study of Hebrew: A Survey of the Literature with Selected Bibliography* (Cincinnati OH and Winona Lake IN, 1989), p. 140, citing Aron Dotan, *Sefer diqduqe ha-te'amim le-Rabbi Aharon Ben-Moshe Ben-Asher*, 3 vols (Jerusalem, 1967), vol. 1, p. 34.

Concluding Remarks

Ancient Jewish cultic music was valid only in connection with the cult, and the cult was valid only at the Temple in Jerusalem. When Jerusalem fell to the Romans in 70 CE, and the Temple destroyed, the cult ceased, and with it cultic music. Hope that the city and the Temple would be rebuilt and cultic worship restored nevertheless persisted, as is witnessed by the Mishnah (*m. 'Abot* 5:20; *m. Tamid* 7:3, end), and persists still among the devout. It may have been this hope that inspired the compilers of the Mishnah to include in its tractates details of the measurements and most important rites of the Temple.

To what extent the cultic musical traditions were preserved in subsequent years is not known; it is possible that Levitical musicians kept their traditions alive. But when the Bar Kokhba revolt failed in 135 CE after three and a half years of bitter fighting, and the Roman emperor Hadrian began to rebuild Jerusalem as a Roman colony, complete with a temple to Jupiter on the site of the former Jewish Temple, and to expel Jews and repopulate the city with Gentiles, it must have been clear that there was no longer any chance of rebuilding the Jewish Temple and restoring the sacrificial cult within the foreseeable future. Any initial impetus there may have been to preserve the cultic musical traditions would inevitably have dwindled as successive generations grew up without the cult. By the beginning of the third century CE, if not earlier, the musical traditions of the Jerusalem Temple would probably have perished irrevocably.

Chapter 5

Music in Ancient Judaism Elsewhere than at the Temple, 1: In Religious Devotion and Worship

Music was an important element in a wide variety of spheres of Jewish life in addition to worship at the Jerusalem Temple. This chapter surveys music in religious devotion and worship in private homes and households, among associates, in sectarian communities and in the synagogue.

In Private Homes and Households

There is evidence of song in domestic contexts on two types of religious occasion: informal and formal. To the informal type belong those intimate hours when parents would discharge their duty as religious teachers of their children. In Judaism, the religious instruction of children was traditionally a parental duty as was shown in Chapter 4 in connection with the quotation of 4 Maccabees 18:15–19, a passage about a father who sang psalms and other biblical material to his children. The singing of lyrical material from the Hebrew Scriptures may be considered to have been a normal part of the less formal side of religious life in the home.

To the formal type of religious occasion belongs the annual domestic Passover meal. While the Jerusalem Temple still stood, the Passover ritual had two consecutive parts the first of which consisted, as has been noted in Chapter 4, of the sacrifice of the Passover lambs in the Temple. The second part consisted of the cooking of the sacrificial meat and the eating of it together with unleavened bread and bitter herbs, which took place in 'households': family groups or similar-sized social groups. All this was to fulfil the Divine commands issued on the occasion of the institution of the Passover as related in Exodus 12:1–47, especially verses 8–14. In the early Second-Temple period the Passover was probably eaten within the Temple precincts. Deuteronomy 16:7 says that the Passover sacrifice is to be cooked and eaten 'at the place that the Lord your God will choose'; this follows directly on from the stipulation in the preceding two verses that the Passover sacrifice may not be offered in just any town (16:5), but only 'at the place that the Lord your God will choose as a dwelling for his name' (16:6), in other words, at Zion, the Temple in Jerusalem. In addition, 2 Chronicles 30:17–19 and 35:10–19 give the strong impression that the Passover was eaten in the Temple precincts. By the end of the Second-Temple period, however, it had become usual for the households to assemble in rooms in private dwellings in Jerusalem, each household in its respective room, to roast and eat the Passover.[1] When or why this change of venue came about is not clear, but it could have been introduced as a solution to the problem of overcrowding that would have arisen sooner or later as the number of Passover pilgrims increased during the Second-Temple period.[2]

Perhaps both the Temple precincts and private dwellings in Jerusalem were used for the Passover meal at some stage in the earlier Second-Temple period. In the Hebrew Bible both the Temple and private dwellings are referred to by the word *bayit*, 'house', the Temple being the house where the Deity was deemed to live. The Torah's prescription that the Passover 'shall be eaten in one house [*bĕbayit*]; you [the Israelites] shall not take any of the animal outside the house [*habbayit*]' (Exod. 12:46) can thus be interpreted as ratifying both the dwelling places of mortals and the dwelling place of God.

The earliest substantial description of the domestic Passover meal occurs in the Mishnah, *Pesaḥim* 10, reflecting the customs of the late Second-Temple period. During the meal blessings and prayers were offered by the head of the household (the senior adult male present), and explanations of the meaning of the occasion and of the symbolism of the foods given. The recitation of the Hallel (*'et-hahallēl*) was obligatory at the meal – at any rate at First Passover (*m. Pesaḥ.* 9:3). The following information is provided about its performance.

1. It was introduced by the liturgical formula:
    [*m. Pesaḥ.* 10:5 end] He brought us forth from slavery to freedom, anguish to joy, mourning to festival, darkness to great light, subjugation to redemption, so we should say ['recite' in the Mishnah] before him, Hallelujah [*halălûyāh*].
2. It was recited in two sections. The division could fall after Psalm 113 or after Psalm 114, depending on which of two first-century CE rabbinic schools was accepted as the authority: that of Shammai or that of Hillel (*m. Pesaḥ.* 10:6).
3. The head of the household completed (that is, recited the second section of) the Hallel.
4. On completing the Hallel the head of the household recited the grace of song (*birkat haššîr*) (*m. Pesaḥ.* 10:7).

This information is sufficient to give a general picture of what the performance was like. There are several points to note. To begin with, although the Mishnah uses 'say' and 'recite' in connection with performance of the Hallel, this does

[1]   *m. Pesaḥ.* 7:13; 8:1, 4; compare Exod. 12:4, 8–10.
[2]   See Joachim Jeremias, *Jerusalem in the Time of Jesus*, trans. F.H. and C.H. Cave (London, 1969), pp. 60–62, 77–84.

not necessarily mean that the Hallel was 'spoken'. The form of the utterance or performance would have been determined by tradition. In the case of the domestic Passover Hallel the tradition may be inferred to have been one of sung performance since the 'grace of song' was recited after it (4 above).

Second, at the end of the liturgical introduction to the Hallel the household is invited to recite *halălûyāh* (point 1 above). Herbert Danby and Philip Blackman have assumed that '*halălûyāh*' here means the Hallel; in his translation of this passage Danby writes 'the Hallelujah' and provides a footnote to explain that this should be taken to mean the Hallel psalms.[3] However, the Hebrew at this place does not prefix the word *halălûyāh* with the definite article; the likelihood is that the word *halălûyāh* in the source text means just that – the actual word 'hallelujah'.

The presence of 'hallelujah' at the head of a psalm normally indicates that the word is to be used as a response during the recital of the psalm, and not only as an opening acclamation. In the text of the Hallel the word 'hallelujah' precedes each of the six psalms except Psalm 115. The absence of 'hallelujah' before Psalm 115 in the MT is most likely because Psalms 114 and 115 were originally one psalm. They are presented as one psalm in the LXX tradition. The form of the LXX text of the Hallel may reflect the form of the Hebrew text in the late Second-Temple period.[4] 'Hallelujah' was thus the response to be used during the singing of all the Hallel psalms. At the end of his liturgical introduction to the Hallel, therefore, the head of the household invited all the members of the household to sing the text that was to be their response during the psalms, namely 'hallelujah'. It is probable that when the head of the household pronounced the word 'hallelujah', he did so in the manner in which the household was to sing it as a response.

Third, the psalm verses would have been sung by the head of the household. This is inferred from the wording of *mishnah Pesaḥim* 10:1–6 and from the statement in *mishnah Pesaḥim* 10:7 that 'he [the head of the household] completes the *Hallel* ['*et-hahallēl*]' (3 above).

There are further points of detail to note about the second section of the Hallel. As is implied in the Mishnah, this would have begun with either Psalm 114 ('When Israel went forth from Egypt') or Psalm 115 ('Not to us, O Lord, not to us') depending on the rabbinic authority (Shammai or Hillel) accepted for the pattern of utterance. In the MT, Psalm 115 is not preceded by the word 'hallelujah': it begins straight away with its poetic psalm text – which the head of the household, if following the school of Hillel, would have taken up to complete the Hallel. Psalm 114 on the other hand is preceded by 'hallelujah'. Among Jews following the school of Shammai, the second section of the Hallel would have

---

[3]   Danby, *Mishnah*, p. 151, n. 2.

[4]   The division of the Hallel in the LXX compared with the MT is as follows: MT Ps. 113 = LXX Ps. 112; MT Pss 114+115 = LXX Ps. 113; MT Ps. 116:1–9 = LXX Ps. 114; MT Ps. 116:10–19 = LXX Ps. 115; MT Ps. 117 = LXX Ps. 116; MT Ps. 118 = LXX Ps. 117. The standard English translations follow MT divisions.

begun with the head of the household announcing the response 'hallelujah', and the remainder of the household repeating it, in the same manner as has been proposed above for the beginning of the Hallel.

To sum up: the text of *mishnah Pesaḥim* 10 suggests that in the late Second-Temple period the domestic Passover Hallel was sung responsively as follows:

First section:
Head of household invites household to sing the response 'hallelujah'
Household sings the response 'hallelujah'
Head of household sings psalm verses
Household responds with 'hallelujah' at intervals as psalm(s^a) is (are^a) sung

Second section:
($^{b-}$Head of household announces the response 'hallelujah'
Household sings the response 'hallelujah' [*and then*]$^{-b}$)
$^{c-}$Head of household sings the psalms that complete the Hallel
Household responds with 'hallelujah' at intervals as the psalms are sung^{-c}

Notes:
^{a} Alternatives consequent on following the school of Shammai as opposed to the school of Hillel.
$^{b-b}$ Form of the beginning of the second section consequent on following the school of Shammai.
$^{c-c}$ Form of the beginning of the second section consequent on following the school of Hillel.

This reconstruction cannot be very wide of the mark since an almost identical form was used in the synagogue in the mid-second century CE. The evidence for this comes from the Tosefta, *Soṭah* 6:3 (see also *m. Soṭah* 5:4), where Rabbi Eleazar ben Rabbi Yosé the Galilean, who was active between *c.*140 and 165 CE, is reported as saying in connection with the Song of the Sea (Exod. 15:1–18) that Moses and the Israelites performed it 'like an adult who proclaims the Hallel in synagogue-worship, responding to him with the foregoing [opening] phrase'.[5] The Rabbi then gives an illustrative example presented here schematically:

Moses: material A (the 'foregoing phrase')
Israelites: material A
Moses: material B
Israelites: material A
Moses: material C
Israelites: material A

5   Jacob Neusner (trans. and ed.), *The Tosefta Translated from the Hebrew With a New Introduction*, 2 vols (Peabody MA, 2002), p. 855.

Thus in reciting the Hallel in the synagogue, the congregation responded to an adult leader with 'material A', the 'foregoing phrase', namely 'hallelujah'. This was most likely a standard pattern for rendering the Hallel away from the Temple.

The extent to which the Hallel of the households exhibited features in common with the Levitical rendering of the Hallel in the Temple is an open question. There would of course have been a considerable outward contrast between the singing of the disciplined choir of adult male Levites and that of a mixed household of adults and children. Nevertheless, it is probably safe to assume that a responsive form of performance was common, but no doubt executed with much less sophistication by households than by Levites. Whether there were common musical elements is not known, but it is reasonable to suppose there were, given that the Passover pilgrims would hear the Levites recite (sing) the Hallel.

Among Associates

There is only one group of associates for which there is evidence of musical activity in ancient Judaism: Jesus of Nazareth and his immediate disciples.[6] Sources witness to two occasions on which there was song and perhaps also pipe playing among them. One is the solemn religious meal known as the Last Supper. According to two parallel New Testament accounts (Matt. 26:20–30; Mark 14:17–26), the meal concluded with the singing of a 'hymn'. This is expressed in the Greek by the participial phrase *kai humnēsantes*, literally 'and having hymned' (Matt. 26:30; Mark 14:26). There is no information about the identity of the hymn or the form of the singing, but since it is likely that the Last Supper was a Passover meal,[7] the hymn was probably the Hallel or the latter portion of it. The REB at this point actually translates: 'after singing the Passover hymn', although this introduces a gloss unwarranted by the Greek text.

The second occasion is a legendary one narrated in the apocryphal *Acts of John*, chapters 94–96.[8] Here Jesus of Nazareth and his disciples dance a ring dance to a hymn sung by Jesus; the disciples respond 'Amen' to Jesus at frequent

---

[6]   Jesus and his disciples became known in some circles as the Nazoreans, the Nazarenes or the Nazoraeans: see NT Acts 24:5; *The Gospel of Philip*, verse 47 (*NTA*, vol. 1, pp. 193–4). The terms were subsequently extended to cover Syrian Christianized Jews (*NTA*, vol. 1, pp. 139–40, 143). Further on the Nazarenes/Nazoraeans, see: Petri Luomanen, 'Ebionites and Nazarenes', in Matt Jackson-McCabe (ed.), *Jewish Christianity Reconsidered: Rethinking Ancient Groups and Texts* (Minneapolis MN, 2007), pp. 81–118, esp. pp. 81–5, 102–17; Wolfram Kinzig, 'The Nazoraeans', in Oskar Skarsaune and Reidar Hvalvik (eds), *Jewish Believers in Jesus: The Early Centuries* (Peabody MA, 2007), pp. 463–87.

[7]   Or at least a meal of Passover character. See Joachim Jeremias, *The Eucharistic Words of Jesus*, trans. N. Perrin (London, 1966), pp. 36, 41–62.

[8]   A detailed introduction to, and annotated English translation of the *Acts of John* are available in *NTA*, vol. 2, pp. 152–212.

intervals as he sings. The episode is introduced by the words, 'Before he [Jesus] was arrested ... he assembled us all [the disciples] and said, "Before I am delivered unto them [the Jews], let us sing a hymn to the Father, and so go to meet what lies before (us)." So he told us to form a circle, holding one another's hands, and himself stood in the middle and said, "Answer Amen to me." So he began to sing a hymn and to say ...'.[9] The text of the hymn is given. It begins:

> [*Acts John* 94] 'Glory be to thee, Father.'
> And we circled round him and answered him, 'Amen.'
> 'Glory be to thee, Logos:
> Glory be to thee, Grace.' – 'Amen.'
> 'Glory be to thee, Spirit:
> Glory be to thee, Holy One:
> Glory be to thy Glory.' – 'Amen.' (*NTA*, vol. 2, p. 182)

A little later, it has the following:

> [*Acts John* 95] 'Grace dances.
> I will pipe,
> Dance, all of you.' – 'Amen.'
> 'I will mourn,
> Beat you all your breasts.' – 'Amen.'
> '(The) one Ogdoad
> sings praises with us.' – 'Amen.' (*NTA*, vol. 2, p. 182)

The phrase 'I will pipe' could mean that a pipe was played to accompany the dance; but on balance it seems more likely to be a metaphor for 'I will sing'.[10]

Although the *Acts of John* itself is a late work, dating probably from the first half of the third century CE, the hymn is considered to be among a quantity of pre-existent material interpolated into the narrative.[11] How old the hymn text might be, and when it might have become associated with Jesus of Nazareth and his disciples (if indeed this happened before the composition of the *Acts of John*), are unknown. Nevertheless, ring-dances are ancient traditional elements in Near-Eastern culture, and while the present episode is merely a legendary event in an apocryphal book, there is no reason to doubt that its basic elements – a ring-dance with responsive song (and perhaps pipe playing) – are drawn from real life. It is not beyond the bounds of possibility that Jesus of Nazareth and his disciples would have performed such a dance.

---

[9]   *Acts John* 94; *NTA*, vol. 2, p. 181.

[10]   Compare the metaphor 'the pipe of my lips' in *The Community Rule* from Qumran, quoted below.

[11]   *NTA*, vol. 2, pp. 164, 167.

In Sectarian Communities

Song was an important element in the religious life of two sectarian communities: the Therapeutai and the Qumran Community. Both flourished during the late Second-Temple period.

The Therapeutai

The Therapeutai are known only from the account of them by Philo of Alexandria in his work *On the Contemplative Life*,[12] and from Eusebius's later reference to this in his *Ecclesiastical History*. Philo's account is particularly valuable because it is contemporary.[13] He says that communities of Therapeutai were to be found in several places, especially in Upper Egypt. The sectarians shunned towns and cities and settled in rural areas where they adopted a semi-anchoritic lifestyle. They lived in celibacy, abstained from bodily pleasures, drank no wine and ate no meat. The community described by Philo was located in Upper Egypt. It included women (mostly elderly and unmarried) as well as men. Its members lived in individual dwellings set at a distance from each other. There they spent most of their time, devoting themselves to prayer, contemplation and study of the Scriptures.

On the eve of every fiftieth day (or, as some understand the text, on the eve of the Festival of Pentecost – the Jewish Festival of Weeks[14]), they assembled in the nearby communal building for a religious festival. This was celebrated with a solemn communal meal followed by a night-long vigil. Philo's account of the meal and its festive sequel (*On the Contemplative Life* 10 (80)) is famous for the details it provides about the musical practices of the Therapeutai. The meal is preceded first by a discourse on some passage of scripture, delivered by the community's president. Then the president stands and

> sings a hymn [*humnon adei*] composed as an address to God, either a new one of his own composition or an old one by poets of an earlier day who have left behind them hymns in many measures and melodies, hexameters [or verses] and iambics, lyrics suitable for processions [*prosodiōn humnōn*] or in libations and at the altars, or for the chorus whilst standing or dancing [*stasimōn chorikōn strophais*], with careful metrical arrangements to fit the various evolutions. After him all the others take their turn as they are arranged and in the proper order while all the rest listen in complete silence except when they have to chant [*adein* 'sing'] the closing lines or refrains [*akroteleutia kai ephumnia*], for then they all lift up their voices, men and women alike. (*Philo*, vol. 9, pp. 162–3)

---

[12] Text in *Philo*, ed. F.H. Colson, 10 vols and 2 supplementary vols (London, 1941, 1985), vol. 9. Later extracts from *Philo* are from the same edition.

[13] On Philo's account of the Therapeutai, see Schürer/Vermes et al., *History*, vol. 2, pp. 591–3, where appropriate references are given.

[14] Ibid., p. 592.

When this is finished, food is brought and the meal eaten. Then, continues Philo, after the meal,

> [Philo, *On the Contemplative Life* 11 (83–9] they hold the sacred vigil which is conducted in the following way. They rise up all together and standing in the middle of the refectory form themselves first into two choirs [*choroi*], one of men and one of women, the leader and precentor [*exarchos*] chosen for each being the most honoured amongst them and also the most musical [or 'the best singer'] [*emmelesatos*]. Then they sing hymns [*adousi ... humnous*] to God composed of many measures and set to many melodies, sometimes chanting together [*sunēchountes*], sometimes taking up the harmony antiphonally [*antiphōnois harmoniais*], hands and feet keeping time in accompaniment, and rapt with enthusiasm reproduce sometimes the lyrics of the procession [*prosodia*], sometimes of the halt and of the wheeling and counter-wheeling of a choric dance [*choreia*]. Then when each choir has separately [*hekateros*] done its own part in the feast ... they mix and both together become a single choir [*choros heis*], a copy of the choir set up of old beside the Red Sea ... [in which] the men [were] led by the prophet Moses and the women by the prophetess Miriam.
>
> ...
>
> It is on this model above all that the choir of the Therapeutae of either sex, note [*melesin*] in response to [*antēchois* 'sounding against'] note and voice [*antiphōnois* responding] to voice, the treble [*oxus*] of the women blending with the bass [*barun ēchon* 'bass voices'] of the men, create an harmonious concert [*enarmonion sumphōnian*], music [*mousikēn*] in the truest sense ... Thus they continue till dawn .... (*Philo*, vol. 9, pp. 164–7)

Philo wrote for an audience of Jews and non-Jews, as is evident from the fact that he explains both the Greek choric dance and 'the choir set up of old beside the Red Sea' (a reference to Exod. 15:1–21, the Song of the Sea). Even though the terminology he uses is that of the ancient Greek religious cults, most of the religious objects, institutions and ritual elements he mentions (altars, choirs, libations and processions[15]) had their counterparts in Jewish worship at the Temple in Jerusalem. One ritual element that did not is the choric dance (*choreia*). This belonged not only to public religious festivals at Greek temples, but also to Greek secular entertainments, public and private. In early antiquity it was performed by any of three possible choral groups: men, boys, females (usually girls); in later antiquity by mixed groups as well (men and boys or men and women). Its performance involved bodily movements such as nodding the head, gesticulating, tapping the feet and turning on the spot in addition to choral

---

[15]   On the ancient Greek procession (*prosodion*), see M.L. West, *Ancient Greek Music* (Oxford, 1992), p. 15; Thomas J. Mathiesen, 'Prosodion', *New Grove/2*, vol. 20, pp. 433–4.

singing or chanting.[16] There is no evidence that choral song in Jewish cultic worship at the Jerusalem Temple, or religious song among the Jews generally, was performed in this way. The use of the choric dance by the Therapeutai in an overtly religious context must be regarded as somewhat unusual in ancient Judaism, although it may have been fairly widespread among the Hellenized Jews of Egypt.

There are several points to note about the singing. First, the complete absence of any reference to musical instruments in connection with the singing suggests that it was without instrumental accompaniment. This is perhaps not surprising given the retiring nature of the Therapeutai and the private circumstance of their religious celebrations. The ancient Greek processions and choric dances, however, were often accompanied by the *aulos*, and processions at the Jerusalem Temple included the playing of musical instruments, as did the liturgical choral song of the Levites.

Second, women took an equal part with men. Philo stresses this as an aspect of the singing both before and after the communal meal. Before the meal 'men and women alike' raised their voices to sing the refrains. Philo does not make clear, however, whether women as well as men were included among the 'all' who took their turn as soloists after the President had sung. He does say that 'all the others' took their turn to sing, which taken at its face value implies the women as well as the men. On the other hand, the fact that he does not specify the gender of the soloists, but specifies that men and women sang the refrains, casts doubt on whether the women sang as soloists. After the meal the men and the women formed their respective choirs which sang both separately and together.

Philo's stance with regard to men and women singing together in a religious context is somewhat defensive. This is evident not only from the lengths to which he goes to explain the biblical precedent for the phenomenon (namely Exod. 15:1-21) but also from his encomium (in the last paragraph quoted above) of the cooperation between male and female Therapeutai. Mixed song under such circumstances as these was probably not widely condoned in Jewish circles, perhaps especially not among devout Jews, and Philo may have wanted to emphasize its scriptural precedent and its philosophical and social good, in order to neutralize any prejudice against the Therapeutai this aspect of his account might otherwise engender. A passage in the Babylonian Talmud, *Sotah* 48a, although ostensibly later than Philo, reflects what may have been the prevalent attitude among orthodox Jews: 'When men sing and

---

[16]   On the ancient Greek choruses and their singing and dancing, see West, *Ancient Greek Music*, pp. 14-21, esp. pp. 17, 20, also 40-41; Walter Blankenburg (extrapolated), 'Chor und Chormusik: 1. Christliche Antike und Mittelalter', in *MGG*, Sachteil [Subject Reference], vol. 2 (1995), p. 767; compare James G. Smith, 'Chorus: Antiquity and the Middle Ages', *New Grove/2*, vol. 5, pp. 767-9.

women join in it is licentiousness; when women sing and men join in it is like fire in tow'.[17]

Third, several forms of singing are in evidence. Before the meal there was responsive singing between each member who sang solo and 'all the rest' who sang the refrains. The formal result would have been very similar to the way in which the Hallel was sung in the synagogue or at the domestic Passover meal, as described above. It is not clear from Philo's account whether corporate responses were also made to the President's singing. This interpretation is possible although a reading of the passage as it stands gives the impression that the President's hymn was sung as a plain solo, and that it was the subsequent singing by the rest of the company that was responsive.

After the meal, the two choirs that were formed sang 'together', 'antiphonally' and 'separately'. The singing described as 'sometimes ... together' and 'sometimes ... antiphonally' should probably be understood as referring to each choir individually, 'together' here meaning 'undivided' or 'whole' as opposed to 'antiphonally' with its implication of division (for alternation in the singing). This makes sense of the ensuing section which places the single mixed choir in apposition to 'each choir ... separately'. The singing during the vigil thus consisted of separate male and female plain choral song, choral antiphony and mixed plain choral song.

Fourth, the musical quality of the performance was important: the leader of each choir was chosen for his or her proven musical skills. Other than this, however, Philo says nothing on the topic. The last paragraph in the above quotation shows that the performance impressed Philo; but one should be wary of attributing this to its musical qualities alone. The 'harmonious concert' could be intended to refer to the cooperation of men and women rather than to the musical ensemble, and 'music' (*mousikēn*) could be intended to be understood in its more literal sense of 'of the muses' – that is, inspired and inspiring. Nevertheless, the likelihood that ambiguous terms were deliberately used for heightened literary effect cannot be ruled out in this context, in which case it could justifiably inferred that the performance was as favourably impressive as a musical event as it was as a religious and social one.

Finally, it is appropriate to say something about Philo's view of the choir at the Red Sea[18] as implied by his comparison with it of the mixed choir of the Therapeutai. He says that the men's and women's choirs of the Therapeutai combined to form a single mixed choir, 'a copy of the choir set up of old beside the Red Sea ... [in which] the men [were] led by the prophet Moses and the women by the prophetess Miriam'. The text of the relevant passage from the Hebrew Bible, Exodus 15:1–21, says nothing about Moses, the Israelites, Miriam and the women who were with her singing together as a single mixed group. It is likely that

---

[17]   Translation: I. Epstein (trans. and ed.), *The Babylonian Talmud Translated Into English with Notes, Glossary and Indices*, 35 vols (London, 1935–52).

[18]   See Exod. 14:10–15:21 and Chapter 4 herein.

Philo's implied view reflects a prevalent popular tradition stemming perhaps from mixed singing in non-sacrificial cultic festivities of the kind described in Chapter 4.

The Qumran Community

The Qumran Community was a grouping of Jewish sectarians which became established at Qumran on the north-western shore of the Dead Sea around the middle of the second century BCE.[19] Its members lived as coenobites in voluntary separation from the world. The sect had many features in common with the contemporary Essenes. The Qumran sectarians are now generally regarded as Essenes although unequivocal evidence for this is lacking. It is also possible that the Therapeutai were Essenes and that the three groups – Therapeutai, Essenes and Qumran sectarians – belonged to one sectarian movement.[20] The sect also had 'lay' members who lived and worked in towns and villages.

The Qumran sectarians regarded themselves as representing the 'true' historical Israel, in direct opposition to the prevalent religious and national regime which they considered to be unlawful. They devoted themselves to studying the Torah and to strict observance of the festivals of the Law of Moses. Their ideal was that their life should be an unbroken act of worship of God.

They followed a solar calendar of 364 days of exactly 52 weeks, which was probably the calendar of the ancient biblical priestly codes. It is common to the Book of Jubilees and 1 Enoch. It is at variance with the lunar calendar followed by the rest of Palestinian Judaism at that time; consequently the Community's religious festivals fell on different days from those of Judaism at large.

As with the Therapeutai and the Essenes, worship in the Community was not sacrificial although the lay members living outside Qumran offered sacrifices in the Jerusalem Temple, like other Jews. Also in common with the Therapeutai and the Essenes, the Qumran sectarians attached great importance to the Festival of Weeks (the Festival of Pentecost) which was observed among them as a Covenant Renewal festival. Otherwise, prayer twice daily, at the times of the perpetual sacrifices at the Temple, was an essential feature of their religious life.

At Qumran, the members of the sect practised common ownership of wealth and property; elsewhere, the lay members practised common charity. Life in the Community was strictly regulated by both the prescriptions in the Torah and the statutes and rules of the Community itself.

There are no contemporary accounts or descriptions of musical activity at Qumran. Nor do any of the contemporary writings about the Essenes, some of which may apply to the Qumran Community, contain references to music.

---

[19]   Background from Schürer/Vermes et al., *History*, vol. 2, pp. 575–83, and *CDSSE*, pp. 26–66.

[20]   On the Therapeutai in relation to the Qumran community and the Essenes, see Schürer/Vermes et al., *History*, vol. 2, pp. 593–7.

Nevertheless, the Qumran sectarian literature among the Dead Sea Scrolls contains, as well as a number of passages designated 'song', several references to song and singing and to musical instruments and the playing of them. These throw considerable light on the significance of song and instruments for the members of the Community.

Three passages from the Qumranic literary sources may be considered to begin with. The first two are from the extended poetic conclusion to the document *The Community Rule* (1QS), column X:

> I will sing with knowledge and all my music
> shall be for the glory of God.
> (My) lyre (and) my harp shall sound
> for His holy order
> and I will tune the pipe of my lips
> to His right measure. (*CDSSE*, p. 112)[21]

and a little later:

> I will open my mouth
> in songs of thanksgiving. (*CDSSE*, p. 114)

Geza Vermes thinks the *Community Rule* was intended for the use of the teachers and leaders of the Community, and sees the closing poetical section as, among other things, a tract outlining the main religious duties of the Community's Master and his disciples.[22] The passages could therefore refer concretely to singing as one of the duties of the sectarians. This is supported by the text of the last two lines of the first passage. The metaphor there expresses the idea that the hymnodist will make sure his utterance is theologically sound; then, by characterising his mouth ('my lips') as a 'pipe', he conveys the idea of musical utterance. Since the author's basic idea could have been expressed perfectly clearly without his introducing a specifically musical element, the inference must be that his use of 'pipe' is deliberate. The passage may thus be justifiably interpreted as expressing an intention to sing.

The third passage is from the 25 or so *Thanksgiving Hymns*[23] or *Hodayot* (1QH). It occurs in column XI, in Hymn number 21:

---

[21] In his translations in *CDSSE*, Geza Vermes uses square brackets to enclose 'hypothetical but likely reconstructions', and rounded brackets to enclose 'glosses necessary for fluency' (p. 93). These are retained in the translations from *CDSSE* quoted here.

[22] *CDSSE*, p. 97.

[23] I follow Vermes's numbering in *CDSSE*. The precise number of individual hymns is difficult to determine (see *DSSE*, p. 189; compare *CDSSE*, p. 243).

> I will sing Thy mercies,
> and on Thy might will I meditate all day long. (*CDSSE*, p. 288)

In the first line, 'sing' could be either a poetical way of expressing 'celebrate' or 'make known', or a straightforward announcement of the intention to sing. There seems to be no firm support for either possibility. Vermes's view that the hymns were probably used at the Community's festival of the Renewal of the Covenant at Pentecost,[24] taken together with Sigmund Mowinckel's that the singing of the Therapeutai is a probable example of what the Qumran sectarians' singing was like,[25] suggests that the Qumran hymns were sung in the manner of the Therapeutai at their Pentecost festival. Unfortunately, the two views are unproven hypotheses, and they therefore cannot quite add up to the coherent picture that would be so satisfying to see.

Ostensibly more certain indications of actual musical activity are the passages designated 'song'. Foremost among these are the 13 *Songs of the Sabbath Sacrifice*.[26] Each of the songs is furnished with a superscription of which that to the first is typical: '[To the Master. Song of the holocaust of the] first [Sabba]th, on the fourth of the first month'.[27] The Masada fragments from Cave 4[28] contain similarly worded superscriptional formulae, as do the *Songs of the Sage*[29] (although these latter do not belong to songs for the Sabbath burnt offering): 'For the Master. [First] Song', and '[For the Master]. Second [S]ong to frighten those who terrify him'.[30] Furthermore, the texts of several of these songs, as well as the text of the poem *Bless, My Soul*,[31] suggest the corporate singing of the congregation during worship. It could be, therefore, that at least the *Songs of the Sabbath Sacrifice* contains material which was sung in worship at Qumran. A difficulty arises here on account of the fact that the sectarians' worship was not sacrificial. It may be resolved by supposing that at Qumran the songs could have been sung at the times of the Sabbath burnt offerings in the Temple. Nevertheless, the *Songs of the Sabbath Sacrifice* are conceived as angelic songs in the worship of the heavenly Temple, and it is therefore possible that they were not envisaged as being sung by mortals.

The position with regard to the references to musical instruments is much less uncertain. With only one possible exception, instruments are treated as symbols or metaphors. The metaphor 'the pipe of my lips' in column X of *The Rule of the Congregation* (document 1QS) has already been discussed. Two lines earlier, that

---

[24] *CDSSE*, p. 244 (there called *Songs for the Holocaust of the Sabbath*).

[25] *PsIW*, vol. 2, p. 122.

[26] Documents 4Q400–407, 11Q5–6.

[27] *CDSSE*, p. 322.

[28] Documents 4Q402, 403 and 405.

[29] Documents 4Q510–511.

[30] Both are from *CDSSE*, p. 421.

[31] *Barkhi Nafshi*[a] (document 4Q434), fragment 1.

passage has: '(My) lyre (and) my harp shall sound for His holy order'.[32] In view of the subsequent metaphorical use of 'pipe', the 'lyre' and 'harp' are probably also poetical figures here, although, given the way the text is worded, there can be no absolute certainty that the passage does not reflect their actual use.

The remaining references, however, leave no doubt that the named instruments are symbols. In the *Thanksgiving Hymns* (document 1QH), column V, in Hymn 14, the hymnodist says:

> They sound my censure upon a harp
> and their murmuring and storming upon a zither. (*CDSSE*, p. 269)

And in column XI, in Hymn number 22:

> I will groan with the zither of lamentation
> ...
> Then I will play on the zither of deliverance
> and the harp of joy,
> [on the tabors of prayer] and the pipe of praise
> without end. (*CDSSE*, p. 289)

Examples of instrument symbolism characterize parts of *The War Scroll* (document 1QM) and related documents such as *The War Scroll from Cave 4*.[33] The *War Scroll* is ostensibly a collection of instructions for military battle. But the Qumran sectarians were pacifists and did not engage in warfare. The *War Scroll* is in fact a theological work, a metaphor of the eternal war of Good against Evil, of Light against Darkness. The instrument symbolism it contains is concerned mostly with metal trumpets and (to a much lesser extent) shofars, which are portrayed as being used in war. In *The War Scroll*, column III, the metal trumpets are given titles such as 'trumpets of Massacre', 'trumpets of Ambush', 'trumpets of Pursuit', 'trumpets of Retreat' and 'trumpets of Return',[34] to which 'trumpets of Summons', 'trumpets of Reminder' and 'trumpets of Alarm' are added in column VII.[35] Eric Werner thought the titles of the trumpets probably referred to the positions of the trumpets on the battlefield.[36] On balance, however, it seems more likely that they indicate the meaning of various calls.

It is probable that what is written about the trumpets and their use in the metaphorical battle reflects something of the way in which trumpets were actually used in military battles in the late Second-Temple period. This matter will be considered in more detail in Chapter 6 in the discussion of music in war.

---

[32] *CDSSE*, p. 112.

[33] Document 4Q493=M^c.

[34] *CDSSE*, p. 166.

[35] Ibid., p. 171.

[36] Eric Werner, *The Sacred Bridge*, 2 vols (New York, 1959, 1984), vol. 2, pp. 36–8.

In the present context it is sufficient to note the frequent mention of trumpets in a theological context in documents from Qumran.

It has been remarked by several commentators that the instruments mentioned in the sectarian literature among the Dead Sea Scrolls are the same as those named in the Hebrew Bible, especially in the book of Psalms. They are, furthermore, instruments that were important in the cult in the Davidic tradition of worship at the Temple. This aspect of the literature illustrates the sectarians' traditional and conservative historical and theological perspective, and increases the likelihood that the references to musical instruments are symbolical rather than related to any actual musical activity in the Community.

In the Synagogue

It is not until the first century CE that reliable evidence about the ancient synagogue as a religious institution begins to appear.[37] The origin and early development of the synagogue are obscure, but by the mid-first century synagogues had become common in Israel/Palestine, the Mediterranean Diaspora and the Balkans. Sources from the early first century CE show that the main religious purpose of the synagogue was the Sabbath instruction of the faithful through scriptural exposition and exegesis.[38] There seems to have been no fixed liturgy for the proceedings and no fixed scriptural passages for reading except that they were taken from the Torah and the Prophets.

After the destruction of the Temple the situation became more developed.[39] In some places there were assemblies on Mondays and Thursdays in addition to Sabbaths (*m. Meg.* 1:3; 4:1) and their content is generally fuller and more regulated than before (*m. Meg.* 3:4–4:10). The Mishnah gives instructions about the readings from the Torah and the Prophets, which are often referred to together, suggesting paired readings. There are lists of passages which may and may not be read, and stipulations as to who may read. Recitation of the Shema and various blessings became normal (*m. Roš Haš.* 4:5; *m. Taʿan.* 2:2–3; *m. Soṭah* 5:4). Among the blessings was the Priestly Blessing (Num. 6:24–26), which had

---

[37]   For comprehensive background, see: Jacob Neusner et al. (eds), *The Encyclopaedia of Judaism*, 3 vols (Leiden, 2000), vol. 3, pp. 1374–83 (with plans and photographs between pp. 1376 and 1377); Lee I. Levine, *The Ancient Synagogue: The First Thousand Years*, 2nd edn (New Haven CT, and London, 2005).

[38]   Philo of Alexandria, *That Every Good Person is Free* 12 (81–2), in *Philo*, ed. Colson, vol. 9, pp. 56–9; Philo, *Hypothetica* 7:13, in ibid., vol. 9, pp. 430–33; NT: Luke 4:16–29 (in Nazareth in Galilee), Acts 13:15 (in Pisidian Antioch).

[39]   Compare Theodor Karp, 'Interpreting Silence: Liturgy, Singing, and Psalmody in the Early Synagogue', *Rivista internazionale di musica sacra*, 20/1 (1999): 60, referring to the Theodotus inscription of the first century CE, and quoting from Th. Reinach, 'L'inscription de Theodotus', *Revue des études juives*, 71 (1920): 46–56.

formerly been part of the Temple liturgy (*m. Ber.* 5:4; *m. Meg.* 4:3, 5–7, 10). The
Eighteen Benedictions might also be included (*m. Ber.* 4:7; *m. Ta'an.* 2:1–3). *Mishnah
Megillah* 2:5 and *mishnah Roš Haššanah* 4:7 suggest that the Hallel was proclaimed
on festival days, as it had been in the Temple. But uniformity of practice was not
expected – the proceedings should follow local custom (*m. Sukkah* 3:11; *m. Meg.*
4:1). Thus by the end of the second century, religious observances had become
more than gatherings for religious instruction. While instruction remained
central, the addition of prayers, blessings and festal psalms had transformed what
took place at religious assembly at the synagogue into something approaching
a liturgy of worship.

Beyond the time of the Mishnah there was increasing liturgical elaboration.
From about the fifth or sixth century, the use of freely composed (non-biblical)
liturgical hymns, *pîyûṭṭîm*, became common.[40] Paragraphs 18–20 of the eighth-
century extracanonical talmudic tractate *Soperim* permit recitation of the
daily proper psalms from the earlier Temple liturgy, perhaps in response to an
increasingly widespread but hitherto unofficial practice.

Despite the elaboration of the liturgy and the gradual inclusion of an
increasing number of elements which had formerly belonged to the Temple
liturgy, the synagogue had no sacrificial cult. This is of fundamental significance
for synagogue music.[41] It explains why in Jewish literature from antiquity there
is no specific mention of *šîr* 'song' or of instruments other than the shofar in
connection with religious assemblies in the ancient synagogue. In Jewish sacred
literature of the late Second-Temple period, *šîr* is a technical term for cultic song;
thus a *šîr* and its concomitant instrumental music were exclusive to the Temple.[42]
The Hallel, however, was not exclusive to the Temple cult, and could be recited
in non-cultic settings. Indeed, in Chronicles, Ezra–Nehemiah and early rabbinic
literature the Hallel is never referred to by the term *šîr*, but by its collective
name Hallel, irrespective of where the Hallel was employed. This statement is
apparently contradicted in *mishnah Pesaḥim* 10:7 which says that at the end of the
domestic Passover meal the leader of the proceedings completes the Hallel and
recites over it the grace of song, the *birkat haššîr* (literally: 'blessing of [*or* "over"]
song'). Here '*šîr*' seems to refer back to the Hallel, thereby implying that the
Hallel was a *šîr*. In this instance, however, '*šîr*' is no more than part of the name

[40]   On the *pîyûṭṭîm*, see, for example, Edwin Seroussi, 'Poetry, Piyyutim', *New Grove/2*,
vol. 13, pp. 49–51.

[41]   On music in the ancient synagogue, see: James W. McKinnon, 'The Exclusion
of Musical Instruments from the Ancient Synagogue', *PRMA*, 106 (1979–80): 77–87; J.A.
Smith, 'The Ancient Synagogue, the Early Church and Singing', *M&L*, 65 (1984): 1–16;
McKinnon, 'On the Question of Psalmody in the Ancient Synagogue', *EMH*, 6 (1986): 159–
91; Karp, 'Interpreting Silence': 47–109; Smith, 'The Ancient Synagogue and its Music: A
Reconsideration in the Light of Ideas Presented by Theodor Karp', *Rivista internazionale di
musica sacra*, 24/2 (2003): 17–38.

[42]   Detailed argument in Smith, 'The Ancient Synagogue and its Music': 32–5.

which identifies the grace, and as such carries no implication about the status of the material sung immediately before. Recitation of the *birkat haššîr* after the completion of the Hallel cannot be taken to imply that the Hallel was regarded as a *šîr* in the sense of a song exclusive to the cultic rites at the Temple.[43]

The shofar too was not exclusive to the Temple cult and could be blown in non-cultic religious contexts. According to the Mishnah, the shofar, besides being used generally for signalling, was blown in the synagogue in connection with the liturgies at New Year and Purim (*m. Roš Haš.* 4:5; *m. Meg.* 2:5).

The absence of references to *šîr* should not be taken to imply that the assemblies were without melodic, or at least semi-musical, vocal utterance. The Scripture readings and the Hallel would have been recited in cantillation, the traditional form of chanting used for sacred texts.[44] The Masoretes placed ekphonetic signs, *ṭěʿāmîm*, above and below the written text to indicate how it was to be punctuated and chanted. The Masoretic system is complex and probably superseded older, perhaps simpler, systems from Babylon and Palestine. The purpose of cantillation was twofold: to carry the text clearly when it was read in assemblies,[45] and to set sacred text apart from ordinary speech.

In addition to the supposition of cantillation, the reference to a *psalmōdos* in a Jewish epitaph of the third to fourth century CE, inscribed in a catacomb beneath the Villa Torlonia in Rome,[46] and the reference to a *psalmo[logos?]*[47] in a Roman-period Jewish inscription on a marble block excavated from the city of Aphrodisias in Caria in south-western Asia Minor,[48] imply song in the synagogue.[49] The Greek terms apply to leaders of the liturgical items in which the congregation participated. Although they cannot be taken as explicit references

---

[43]   Smith, 'The Ancient Synagogue and its Music': 34 and n. 64 there. Of further interest in this connection is the observation that none of the Hallel psalms contains the word *šîr*, neither does the Great Hallel (Ps. 136) which *mishnah Taʿanit* 3:9 reports was sung in thanksgiving by an assembly of Jews in Lydda (herein Chapter 6, at n. 28).

[44]   On cantillation, see Karp, 'Interpreting Silence': 84–7; Daniel S. Katz, 'Biblische Kantillation und Musik der Synagoge: Ein Rückblick auf die ältesten Quellen', *Musiktheorie*, 15 (2000): 57–78; Geoffrey Chew, 'Cantillation', *New Grove/2*, vol. 5, p. 57; Gudrun Engberg, 'Ekphonetic Notation, 2: Hebrew', *New Grove/2*, vol. 8, p. 48; Eliyahu Schleifer, 'Biblical Cantillation', *New Grove/2*, vol. 13, pp. 41–7.

[45]   Katz, 'Biblische Kantillation': 57: 'Beim Singen ist die Stimme des Vorbeters besser zu hören, besonders wenn die Lesung, wie oft in Altertum, im Freien stattfindet' (The voice of the reader is easier to hear when his words are sung, especially when the reading takes place out of doors, as was often the case in antiquity).

[46]   Schürer/Vermes et al., *History*, vol. 3/1, pp. 80–81.

[47]   The end of this word is obliterated in the source. The conjectural completion given here in square brackets is from ibid., p. 26.

[48]   Ibid., pp. 25–6.

[49]   On these two references, see also the discussion (with background) in Christopher Page, *The Christian West and its Singers: The First Thousand Years* (New Haven CT, and London, 2010), pp. 42–3.

to the recitation of psalms,[50] they imply that liturgical song – probably as cantillation – was a significant element in worship in the Greco-Roman Diaspora. Three later passages, from the Babylonian Talmud (*b. Ber.* 6a; *b. Ta'an.* 16a; *b. Meg.* 32a), confirm the continued importance of the musical rendition of scriptural and other elements of the liturgy in late antiquity.

---

[50]   Compare Schürer/Vermes et al., *History*, vol. 3/1, p. 81.

Chapter 6
Music in Ancient Judaism Elsewhere than at the Temple, 2: Outside Religious Devotion and Worship

The contexts of the music to be discussed in the present chapter fall outside those of religious observance. However, they should not on that account be thought of as being without sanctity. For devout Jews, whether in antiquity or later times, the whole of life is sacred, a Divine gift, to be enjoyed and used according to the Deity's will. In joy it is natural for the devout to praise and give thanks to the Deity; in sorrow and distress it is natural for them to appeal to the Deity for comfort and help. It is therefore hardly possible to make a distinction between sacred and secular; even activities which superficially might seem to be profane, such as carousing, prostitution and war, cannot automatically be assumed to be so.[1] While the contexts of the music to be discussed in the following pages might not fall within religious devotion and worship, they do not necessarily lack a religious dimension.

In Sorrow and Distress

Sorrow and distress were expressed in a variety of ways in ancient Near-Eastern culture: by beating the breast, tearing the clothes, wearing sackcloth, baring one shoulder, heaping ashes or dust on the head, uttering dirges, wailing and making lamentation. It is the last three that are of interest here since they are musical, or at least semi-musical forms of expression. In ancient Hebrew they are conveyed by the two nouns *nĕhî* (also *nehî*) and *qînâ* and their respective verb forms *nāhâ* and *qîn*. The *qînâ* was a formal expression of deep sorrow in poetry and song. Its rendition was entrusted to singers versed in the special features of the style. The *nĕhî*, on the other hand, was a more popular and spontaneous expression of grief, perhaps in wordless ululation. It may nevertheless be regarded as a type of song, as is shown in *mishnah Moʿed Qaṭan* 3:9 where the word is implicitly equated with *ʿinûy*, which is defined as 'when all sing together'. The same paragraph in the Mishnah goes on to say that the *qînâ* is performed responsively between a leader and a group:

---

[1]   For Noah's accidental drunkenness used as the basis of an aetiology of the Semites' subjection of Canaan, see Gen. 9:18–27.

[*m. Moʿed Qaṭ.* 3:9] What is a wail [ʾ*innûy*]? When all sing [ʾ*ônôt* (from ʾ*ānâ*)] together. What is a dirge [*qînâ*]? When one starts and then all join in with her, as it is said, *Teach your daughters wailing* [nehî], *and everyone her neighbor a dirge* [*qînâ*] (Jer. 9:19(20)).[2]

The Hebrew words *nĕhî* and *qînâ* are rarely rendered consistently in translations. In the Greek of the LXX the one word *thrēnos* with its verb form *thrēneō* is the usual equivalent of both *nĕhî* and *qînâ* and their respective verb forms in the Hebrew of the MT. Exceptions, such as in LXX Jeremiah 9:19(20) where *thrēnos* is the translation of the MT *qînâ*, but *oiktos* ('expression of grief or pity') is the translation of the MT *nĕhî*, are rare. But the LXX occasionally employs *thrēnos/thrēneō* where the MT parallel has a term other than *nĕhî* or *qînâ*. At Judges 11:40, for example, the LXX has *thrēnein* (from *thrēneō*) where the MT has *lĕtannôt* (from *tānâ* 'commemorate, recount'); and at Joel 1:8 the LXX has *thrēnēson* (also from *thrēneō*) where the MT has ʾ*ĕlî* (from ʾ*ālâ* 'weep, mourn'). The LXX therefore cannot be relied on to translate the Hebrew consistently where terms for the expression of grief and sorrow are concerned.

In English translations the Hebrew terms *nĕhî* and *qînâ* and their respective verb forms are normally rendered 'wail' (noun and verb) and 'lament' (noun and verb) respectively. Nevertheless it is sometimes the case that they are rendered freely and indiscriminately as 'dirge, lament, mourn, wail' treated as more or less interchangeable general terms. Inconsistency in English translations of *nĕhî* and *qînâ* in Jeremiah 9:19(20) has already been noted in Chapter 1. Such freedom is not confined to translations of biblical material. Danby's translation of the passage from *mishnah Moʿed Qaṭan* 3:9, given above in Neusner's translation, has 'lamentation' for ʾ*inûy* and *nehî*, and 'wailing' for *qînâ*, against Neusner's 'wail/wailing' and 'dirge' respectively.

English translations of the Hebrew Bible sometimes use the terms 'lament' and 'wail' to render words other than *nĕhî* and *qînâ*; therefore the English words cannot be relied on always to mean musical expressions of sorrow. In the quotations in the following section, the pertinent Hebrew and Greek terms are supplied for clarification.

At Obsequies

Ancient Jewish customs concerned with death and mourning are most comprehensively catalogued in the Mishnah. Their basic elements are very ancient, as is evident from several pre-echoes in early biblical narratives. They are briefly described below.[3]

---

[2] The quotation from Jer. 9:19(20) is as given in Neusner, *Mishnah*.

[3] The following description is based on NT Matt. 9:23; 11:17; Mark 5:38; Luke 7:12–14; 7:32; 8:52; John 19:40; *m. Ber.* 2:6–7; 3:1, 2; 8:6; *m. Ter.* 10:11; *m. Maʿaś. Š.* 5:12; *m. Šabb.* 23:4–5;

On the occurrence of a death, the closest adult male relative of the deceased had financial and practical responsibility for the funeral. In the case of a married woman who died, her husband assumed these responsibilities, even if her father were still living. Burial had to take place within three days of death for sanitary reasons. During this period the male mourners (only near relatives were regarded as mourners) were forbidden to work. When the family of the deceased was informed of the death, the close relatives assembled at the house of the deceased. Here they prepared the body for burial. This involved washing the body, anointing it, and wrapping it in cloths. While this was in progress, the mourners expressed their sorrow by tearing their clothes, uncovering one shoulder, and weeping. Pipers (Hebrew: *ḥălîlîm*; Greek: *aulētas*, from *aulētēs*, a male *aulos*-player) and professional female mourners – the so-called 'wailing women' or 'keening women' (Hebrew: *qônĕnôt*) – were hired;[4] they played 'dirges' and made wailing (*nĕhî/nāhâ*) respectively. The 'wailing women' may also have clapped their hands as a sign of mourning.

When the body was ready for burial it was placed on a bier and carried in solemn procession to its place of burial. The funeral procession included the deceased's near relatives (some of whom carried the bier), the hired pipers, and the wailing women. The pipers played and the wailing women clapped their hands as the funeral procession moved forward. Seven times on the way from the house of the deceased to the place of burial the procession halted, the bier was put down, and the wailing women uttered a lamentation over the deceased.

After the burial the mourners returned to the house of the deceased but without lamentations, hand clapping, or piping. They were received by their friends and neighbours who stood in rows outside the house and offered condolence. They then went into the house and ate the funeral meal.

The paragraphs above provide a general description of what would normally have taken place. Precisely when, how and to what degree these things were done was governed by a complex set of rules designed to ensure that the sanctity of special days (such as Sabbaths, New Moon days, and the mid-festival days of Passover and Booths) was preserved. There were also regulations governing the conduct of the high priest and the king should any of their close relatives die (*m. Sanh.* 2:1, 3); otherwise there was no basic difference between the funeral of an ordinary person and a person of rank and importance.

Nevertheless, funerals of the prominent and wealthy were generally more opulent than those of ordinary people. One way in which this is evident is in the use of especially composed laments. The biblical tradition knows of three occasions on which unique *qînôt* 'laments' were sung: the death of Saul and Jonathan in battle (2 Sam. 1:1–27), the death of Abner (2 Sam. 3:30–35) and the

---

m. Pesaḥ. 8:6, 8; *m. Ta'an.* 4:7; *m. Meg.* 3:3; 4:3; *m. Mo'ed Qaṭ.* 1:5–6; 2:1; 3:5; 3:7–9; *m. Ḥag.* 2:4; *m. Ketub.* 2:10; 4:4; *m. B. Bat.* 6:1, 7; *m. Sanh.* 2:1, 3; 6:6; *m. 'Ohal.* 18:4.

[4]   Rabbi Judah is reported in *m. Ketub.* 4:4 as saying, 'Even the poorest man in Israel should not hire fewer than two pipes and one professional wailing woman'.

death of Josiah (2 Chr. 35:20–25).[5] It seems that some of the laments which the tradition associates with these occasions became part of (or were drawn from) a national repertory of cultic laments in Israel and Judah. In the biblical account of the first two of these occasions the texts of the respective laments are provided; in the account of the third, laments are referred to but not quoted.

The narrative in which David's lament over Saul and Jonathan occurs (2 Sam. 1:19–27) is highly stylized; although the lament is attributed to David, he may not have composed it. It could have been written by the editors of the biblical book in which it occurs, or it could originally have been an independent poem which was adapted and interpolated in the biblical narrative. The lament is introduced by the words:

> [2 Sam. 1:17] And David intoned this dirge over Saul and his son Jonathan –
> [18] He ordered the Judites to be taught [The Song of the] Bow. It is recorded
> in the Book of Jashar.

A more literal rendering of the opening of verse 17 makes it clear that the ensuing poem is a *qînâ*: 'Then lamented [*wayĕqōnēn*] David this lamentation [*'et-haqqînâ hazz'ōt*]'. The meaning of verse 18, however, is uncertain and much disputed.[6] As was stated in Chapter 5, it suggests that the lament was disseminated throughout Judah and committed to writing in the Book of Jashar, so that it became a national cultic lament.[7] The Book of Jashar (*sēper hayyāšār*) is also referred to at Joshua 10:13 but is otherwise unknown. The word *hayyāšār* means 'the upright'; but the LXX equivalent of the book's title is *bibliō tēs ōdēs* 'The Book of the Song' (LXX 3 Kingdoms 8:53[a]). Perhaps the Book of Jashar was a book of war songs, as a note to Joshua 10:13 in the JPS *Tanakh* suggests.[8]

The biblical account of the death and burial of Abner, Saul's cousin and military captain (1 Sam. 14:50), not only gives the text of a unique lament (attributed to David) but also mentions the tearing of clothes and alludes to the funeral procession and the funeral meal:

---

[5]   Neither David's poignant expression of grief over the death of his son Absalom (2 Sam. 19(18):1(33)) nor the customary annual four-day commemoration of the death of Jephthah's daughter by the 'maidens of Israel' (Judg. 11:39–40) is given a musical context in the Hebrew Bible. While the JPS *Tanakh* says that the maidens of Israel 'chant dirges' for the daughter of Jephthah, and the NRSV says that they would go out to 'lament' her (Judg. 11:40), the Hebrew says that they 'commemorate' her (*lĕtannôt*, from *tānâ* 'commemorate, recount'); the LXX has *thrēnein*; the Vulgate has *plangant* (from *plangere* 'to beat the breast' as a sign of grief).

[6]   J.P. Fokkelman, *Narrative Art and Poetry in the Book of Samuel* (Assen/Maastricht, 1986), pp. 649–51.

[7]   J.L. Mays, 'The David of the Psalms', *Interpretation*, 40 (1986): 148.

[8]   The LXX version of Josh. 10:13 does not mention a book.

[2 Sam. 3:30] Now Joab and his brother Abishai had killed Abner because he had killed their brother Asahel during the battle at Gibeon. – [31] David then ordered Joab and all the troops with him to rend their clothes, gird on sackcloth, and make lamentation (*wĕsipdû*)[9] before Abner; and King David himself walked behind the bier. [32] And so they buried Abner at Hebron; the king wept aloud by Abner's grave, and all the troops wept. [33] And the king intoned this dirge over Abner [literally: 'And the king lamented (*wayĕqōnēn*) over Abner and said (*wayy'ōmar*)'],
'Should Abner have died the death of a churl?
[34] Your hands were not bound,
Your feet were not put in fetters;
But you fell as one falls
Before treacherous men!'
And all the troops continued to weep over him. [35] All the troops came to urge David to eat something while it was still day; but David swore, 'May God do thus to me and more if I eat bread or anything else before sundown.'

The death and burial of king Josiah was another occasion of public mourning, apparently generating unique laments which were sung at his death, and which subsequently became part of a known repertory of laments, as is related in 2 Chronicles 35:23–25:

[2 Chr. 35:23] Archers shot King Josiah [on the plain of Megiddo], and the king said to his servants, 'Get me away from here, for I am badly wounded'.
[24] His servants carried him out of his chariot and put him in the wagon of his second-in-command, and conveyed him to Jerusalem. There he died, and was buried in the grave of his fathers, and all Judah and all Jerusalem went into mourning over Josiah. [25] [So] Jeremiah composed laments [*wayĕqōnēn*] for Josiah which all the singers, male [*haššārîm*] and female [*wĕhaššārôt*], recited in their laments [*bĕqînôtêhem*] for Josiah, as is done to this day; they became customary in Israel and were incorporated into the laments [*haqqînôt*].[10]

The attribution of the laments to Jeremiah (they are not quoted in the biblical text) may be honorific in order to ratify them for use as cultic laments in the Chronicler's own day, long after the time of Josiah (the phrase 'as is done to this day' in verse 25 implies that the Chronicler was writing some considerable time after the events he describes).

The use of unique laments is a prominent feature of similar accounts in post-biblical literature. Substantial sections of the populace, as well as professional

---

[9] 'and make lamentation': the Hebrew word is from *sāpad*, 'beat the breast, mourn, weep'; the NRSV has 'mourn'.

[10] In the LXX version of the last clause of this quotation the Greek says that these laments 'were written (*gegraptai*) among the laments (*thrēnōn*)'.

mourners, were apparently sometimes involved in uttering them. Pseudo-Philo, in his *Liber antiquitatum biblicarum* (a work dating probably from the early first century CE),[11] gives fancifully expanded and embellished versions of the deaths of Joshua (*Lib. ant. bib.* 24:1–6) and Deborah (*Lib. ant. bib.* 33:1–6) which contain descriptions of public mourning at which special laments (the texts of which are supplied) were sung. In the Bible the death of Joshua is narrated as a simple fact followed by notices of his age and where he was buried (Josh. 24:29–30). Pseudo-Philo's expanded version stretches over six long verses and concludes with the text of the 'great lamentation' (*trenum*)[12] which he implies was uttered by 'all Israel' over Joshua.[13]

Deborah's death is not reported in the Bible (Judg. 5:1–31), but Pseudo-Philo says that she was mourned for 70 days by the people (*et planxerunt eam populi septuaginta diebus*). He goes on to give the text of the 'lamentation' (*trenum*) with which he says they mourned her.[14]

Pseudo-Philo's version of the death of Jephthah's daughter is similarly embellished compared with the biblical account in Judges 11:39–40, but does not mention a unique lament. It adds to the biblical statement that 'After two months' time, she returned to her father, and he did to her as he had vowed' (Judg. 11:39a) a notice to the effect that the whole of Israel made a lamentation for her.[15]

Whether Pseudo-Philo's accounts reflect what was common practice at the time when the *Liber antiquitatum biblicarum* was written, or whether his stories of unique lamentations and the mass singing of them were no more than idealized archaizing, is uncertain.

A literary allusion to the custom of making lamentation for the dead while the bier was carried to the place of burial is to be found in a passage from the *Testament of Job*, a pseudepigraphical work thought to have been written during the first century BCE or the first century CE.[16] The pertinent passage (*T. Job* 52:12–53:14) is a free amplification of the LXX version of the death and burial of Job. It relates that when Job died, as his body was carried to the tomb 'his three daughters went ahead ... singing hymns [*humnois*] to God' (52:12), and that his

---

[11]   Text: *SC*, nos 229–230. On Pseudo-Philo and the *Liber antiquitatum biblicarum*, see *OTP*, vol. 2, pp. 279–303; Schürer/Vermes et al., *History*, vol. 3/1, pp. 325–31.

[12]   The Latin in this and the subsequent paragraph is from *SC*, no. 229, p. 256. Latin '*trenum*' is cognate with Greek '*thrēnos*'.

[13]   Pseudo-Philo, *Lib. ant. bib.* 24:6; *OTP*, vol. 2, p. 334.

[14]   Pseudo-Philo, *Lib. ant. bib.* 33:6; *OTP*, vol. 2, p. 348.

[15]   Pseudo-Philo, *Lib. ant. bib.* 40:8; *OTP*, vol. 2, p 354.

[16]   Greek text (basically 'P', namely the eleventh-century Paris BN gr 2658, folios 72ʳ–97ʳ) in S. Brock (ed.), 'Testamentum Iobi', bound with J.-C. Picard (ed.), 'Apocalypsis Baruchi graece', in *Pseudepigrapha Veteris Testamenti graece*, vol. 2 (Leiden, 1967) (see under *Testament of Job* in the Bibliography). Introduction and annotated English translation by R.P. Spittler in *OTP*, vol. 1, pp. 829–68. On dating, see *OTP*, vol. 1, p. 833.

brother Nereus and others in the cortège wept and said, 'Woe to us today! A double woe! Gone today is the strength of the helpless! ...' (53:2–3).[17]

In the Face of Calamity

The characteristic expressions of sorrow and distress, including wailing, pipe playing and uttering laments, were also provoked by national, local and personal calamities. Laments over the nation are represented by the great laments in the biblical books of the Prophets. The biblical prophets frequently inveighed against what they saw as the moral laxity of Israel and warned of dire consequences unless the nation repented and mended its ways. They envisaged these consequences in terms of violent disaster. To drive their message home they deliberately employed ideas, images and vocabulary associated with the sorrow that surrounds death. Amos's words at the opening of the fifth chapter of the biblical book attributed to him are typical:

> [Amos 5:1] Hear this word which I intone [Hebrew: 'take up']
> As a dirge [*qînâ*] over you, O House of Israel.

So begins the lament: 'Fallen, not to rise again, Is Maiden Israel' (Amos 5:2). It concludes:

> [Amos 5:16b–17] In every square there shall be lamenting [*mispēd* 'mourning, weeping'],
> In every street cries of 'Ah, woe!'
> And the farm hand shall be
> Called to mourn [*'ēbel*, 'the mourning ceremony']
> And those skilled in wailing [*nehî*] to lament [*mispēd* 'mourn'];
> For there shall be lamenting [*mispēd* 'mourning']. In every vineyard, too,
> When I pass through your midst
> – said the Lord.

Similarly Jeremiah, during a tirade against Israel's apostasy and moral dereliction, calls for the 'dirge-singers' (-*qônĕnôt* 'keening women') to come and 'quickly start a wailing [*nehî*] for us' (Jer. 9:16(17)–17(18)) because 'the sound of wailing [*nĕhî*] is heard from Zion' (9:18a(19a)); and Ezekiel is commanded by God to 'intone a dirge [*qînâ*] over the princes of Israel' (Ezek. 19:1) because of their transgressions. The text of Ezekiel's lament evidently became widely known: it has a subscription which reads, 'This is a dirge [*qînâ*], and it has become a [familiar] dirge [*qînâ*]' (Ezek. 19:14e).

Enemy nations could also be the subject of prophetic laments. In oracles against proud Moab, Isaiah says that his heart moans for Moab 'like a lyre' (Isa.

---

[17]   *OTP*, vol. 1, p. 868.

16:11), and Jeremiah that his heart moans for Moab 'like a pipe' (Jer. 48:36). There are several more examples in the books of the Latter and Minor Prophets. In Ezekiel 27:2 God commands Ezekiel to 'intone a dirge [qînâ] over Tyre', and in Ezekiel 32:2 to 'intone a dirge [qînâ] over Pharaoh, king of Egypt'. A note at the end of the text of the latter lament adds, 'This is a dirge [qînâ], and it shall be intoned [wĕqônĕnût]; The women of the nations shall intone [tĕqônēnnâ] it, They shall intone [tĕqônēnnâ] it over Egypt and all her multitude' (Ezek. 32:16).

Many of these laments were probably purely literary compositions, or if they were actually delivered as lamentations, they were probably delivered on one occasion only. The fact that one or two of them are mentioned specifically as having become known laments suggests that the others had not.

The five laments which respectively constitute the five chapters of the biblical book of Lamentations are poetic expressions of deep sorrow over the destruction of Jerusalem. Like the prophetic laments discussed and referred to above they are stylized literary compositions.[18] Their author is unknown, and it is not certain whether they were actually uttered. In the LXX version of Lamentations, the first lamentation (the first chapter of the book) carries a superscription saying it was uttered by Jeremiah immediately after the destruction of Jerusalem and the exile of the Jews, but this is probably a popular tradition from the time when the Greek translation was made; it has no historical reliability. (Some translators have even regarded the whole book as the work of Jeremiah: see, for example, the title of the book in the KJV and RSV.) Nevertheless the fact that in the Bible these five laments are collected together may mean that they originally comprised a repertory, or part of a repertory, of cultic laments sung on occasions of national mourning or at times of national penitence such as the Day of Atonement. Lamentation over the destruction of cities or nations was by no means uncommon in the ancient Near East. There is extant a long lamentation over the destruction of Ur, which has been dated to the second millennium BCE.[19]

Ancient literature contains several illustrations of lamenting and wailing by the distressed themselves (as opposed to prophets of disaster and observers of disaster), sorrowing in their plight. The highly charged communal lament that constitutes the fifth chapter of the book of Lamentations is a case in point, although whether this was actually uttered as a lament in antiquity is not known. Further, in 3 Maccabees 4:2 it is related that when the Jews learned of the intention of Ptolemy IV Philopator (221–204 BCE) to deport them to Alexandria and put them to death, they broke into 'incessant mourning, lamentation and tearful cries' (3 Macc. 4:2), and newlyweds exchanged lamentation (thrēnos) for joy (4:6, 8). On a more personal level, in Judges 11:37, Jephthah's daughter, when she learned that she would have to be put to death, asked for a stay of execution so that she could

---

[18]   Each of the first four laments (Lam. 1–4) is an alphabetical acrostic, and the last (Lam. 5), though not apparently an acrostic, has 22 verses, the same as the number of letters in the Hebrew alphabet.

[19]   ANET, p. 455.

go into the mountains with her female companions and mourn her fate. The narrative in the Hebrew Bible gives no indication of the form of the mourning, but in Pseudo-Philo's fictional expansion of the episode it consists of a lamentation which Jephthah's daughter uttered over herself.[20] This cannot be relied upon to have literal historical value, but it may reflect something of traditional practice in antiquity.

Of similar standing is a passage from the *Protevangelium of James*, an apocryphal Christian gospel that originated probably in the second half of the second century CE.[21] Although this is a Christian work it is concerned entirely with Jews. At the beginning of the work it is related that Joachim, a wealthy and devout Jew, and his devout wife Anna were desolate because they were childless. Joachim withdrew in sorrow to the wilderness where he fasted for forty days and nights. In the meantime Anna, forsaken by her husband, and childless, 'uttered a twofold lamentation [*thrēnous ethrēnei*][22] and gave voice to a twofold bewailing [*kopetous ekopteto*]: "I will bewail [*kopsomai*] my widowhood, and bewail [*kopsomai*] my childlessness".'[23]

Distress was all the greater when taunts were heaped in mockery and derision on individuals or groups overtaken by misfortune. The purpose of taunting was to humiliate the subject, no matter how accidental the misfortunes may have been. Taunting was often expressed in taunt songs. Thus, for example, Job and the author of Psalm 69 bemoan their reduced status in the following words: 'Now I am the butt of their gibes [*nĕgînātām* "taunt songs"]; I have become a byword to them' (Job 30:9) and, 'Those who sit in the gate talk about me; I am the taunt [*ûnĕgînôt*] of drunkards' (Ps. 69:13(12)).[24]

A taunt could also be delivered as an oracle in advance of actual misfortune, thereby operating as a particularly potent warning. This was the case, for example, when the prophet Micah, predicting that God's wrath will descend on sinful Israel, announced:

[Mic. 2:4] In that day,
One shall recite a poem about you [Israel],
And utter a bitter lament,[25]

---

[20]   Pseudo-Philo, *Lib. ant. bib.* 40:5; *OTP.* vol. 2, p. 354.

[21]   Greek text with French translation in Emil de Strycker, 'La forme la plus ancienne du Protévangile de Jacques. Recherches sur le Papyrus Bodmer 5 avec une édition du texte grec et une traduction annotée', *Subsidia Hagiographica*, 33 (1961) (see under *Protevangelium of James* in the Bibliography). Introduction and annotated English translation in *NTA*, vol. 1, pp. 421–39.

[22]   Greek from de Strycker, 'La forme la plus ancienne', p. 68.

[23]   *Prot. Jas.* 2:1: *NTA*, vol. 1, p. 426.

[24]   Compare the LXX version (LXX Ps. 68: 12): 'They that sit in the gate talked against me, and they that drank wine sang (*epsallon*) against me'.

[25]   'And utter a bitter lament': the Hebrew has *wĕnāhâ nĕhî nihĕyâ* 'and wail a wailing wail'.

And shall say: 'My people's portion changes hands;
How it slips away from me!
Our field is allotted to a rebel.
We are utterly ravaged'.

In Joy and Pleasure, 1: Public

In the ancient literary sources, song and the sound of musical instruments are frequently associated with the expression of joy, pleasure and prosperity. A corollary of this is that the concept of song and instrumental music are also frequently used as metaphors for happiness. Three passages may be quoted by way of illustration. The first is from Second Isaiah's oracle about God's promises to the faithful:

> [Isa. 51:3c] Gladness and joy shall abide there [in Zion],
> Thanksgiving and the sound of music [*wĕqôl zimĕrâ*]'.

The second and third make their point by means of negative metaphors. First Isaiah expresses the consequences of all the world's people rejecting God's teaching as follows:

> [Isa. 24: 8] Stilled is the merriment of timbrels [*tuppîm* 'hand drums'],
> Ended the clamour of revellers,
> Stilled the merriment of lyres [*kinnôr*].
> [9a] They [the inhabitants of the earth] drink their wine without song [*baššîr lōʾ*].

And in a lamentation for the destruction of Jerusalem, the author of Lamentations 5 expresses the aftermath of the destruction of Jerusalem in these terms:

> [Lam. 5:14] The old men are gone from the gate,
> The young men from their music [*minnĕgînātām*].
> [15] Gone is the joy of our hearts;
> Our dancing is turned into mourning.

In these last two quotations dancing, singing and the music of instruments are metaphors for carefree well-being; their cessation implies desolation.

Sudden or unexpected changes for the better in the nation or the local community often gave rise to the public expression of joy and gladness through music; playing and singing was a natural way for people to celebrate their good fortune. Two passages from First Isaiah look forward optimistically to a time when the fortunes of the nation (or Zion or the Temple) will be restored and the people will celebrate with music. In the first of these the Prophet sees this time as one of general rejoicing, a time when he would be able with good grounds to urge people to celebrate: 'Hymn [*zammĕrû* "make music to"] the Lord, For He has done gloriously' (Isa. 12:5a). In the second he confidently predicts: 'In that day, this song shall be sung in the land of Judah' (Isa. 26:1a).

The music of voices, hand drums and lyres belonged not only to the home and the street but also to the religious cult. The references to music in passages quoted above may therefore have carried additional implications with regard to the cult: the normal use of cultic music would have implied normality in the covenantal relationship between the Deity and the faithful, whereas the cessation of cultic music would have implied a breach in that relationship.

All the above passages from Isaiah and Lamentations are somewhat idealistic. More concrete examples of public musical expressions of joy and happiness are provided by passages in 3 Maccabees and certain of the writings of Philo of Alexandria. In 3 Maccabees it is related that when at some time near the end of the third century BCE Ptolemy IV Philopator's hostile attitude towards the Jewish nation suddenly softened, his persecution of Jews came to an abrupt end. Jews who had been taken prisoner and deported to Alexandria to be put to death were set free and allowed to return to their homes. At intervals on their homeward journey they celebrated their freedom in festive assemblies at which there was singing, as reported in 3 Maccabees 6–7. Verse 32 of 3 Maccabees 6 says that the Jews 'stopped their chanting of dirges [*thrēnōn*] and took up the song [*ōdēn*] of their ancestors', and verse 35 that they 'passed the time in feasting to the accompaniment of joyous thanksgiving and psalms [*psalmois*].' The singing seems to have taken place during a 'banquet of deliverance' (6:31) at which there was also choral dancing (*chorous* 'choruses' at 6:32; *choron* 'choral group' at 6:35). Verse 16 of 3 Maccabees 7 refers in addition to thanksgiving in *pammelesin humnois* 'melodious songs' among the freed Jews. Idealism is not absent from the story of the Jews in 3 Maccabees, of course, but it does not seem to extend to the actual nature and performance of the singing, in contrast to the passages from Isaiah quoted earlier. The passages quoted here from 3 Maccabees probably provide a reliable picture of the typical use of song in joyous public celebrations among Jews in the early Hellenistic period.

Nearly 250 years later, Philo of Alexandria provided a more historically straightforward account of Jewish song in similar circumstances in the Roman period.[26] For some time the Jews of Alexandria had suffered oppression at the hands of the then Roman governor of Egypt, A. Avillius Flaccus. But it seems that Flaccus had been acting without imperial approval. In 38 CE the Roman authorities arrested him and removed him from his post. When the Jews in Alexandria heard that Flaccus had been arrested and taken into custody, they 'sang hymns [*humnoun*] and led songs of triumph [*paianas*] to God', and throughout the night they 'continued to sing hymns [*humnois*] and songs [*ōdais*] of praise'.[27]

---

[26]   Philo, *Against Flaccus*.

[27]   Philo, *Against Flaccus*, in *Philo*, ed. F.H. Colson, 10 vols and 2 supp. vols (London, 1941, 1985), vol. 9, pp. 368, 369.

Still later, the Mishnah, *Ta'anit* 3:9, reports an episode which occurred in Lud [Lydda] when the Jews of that city 'assembled at twilight and proclaimed [*wĕqārĕ'û*] the Great Hallel [Ps. 136]'[28] in thanksgiving for the end of a period of drought.

The singing reported in 3 Maccabees 6–7, by Philo and in the Mishnah had a sacred character: it was part of the Jews' praise and thanksgiving to God for deliverance from suffering. The '*ōdēn* of their ancestors' of 3 Maccabees 6:32, and the '*psalmois*' of 3 Maccabees 6:35 may therefore imply biblical lyrical material, perhaps canonical psalms or poetic passages from elsewhere in the Scriptures. Similar material should probably be understood by the '*paianas* to God' and the '*humnois*' and '*ōdais*' in the passage from Philo.

In Joy and Pleasure, 2: Private and Personal

At Weddings

It is debatable whether weddings in ancient Judaism can be considered private events. In a village all the inhabitants would be present at a wedding, probably most of them would be relatives; in a town all the inhabitants of the immediate district would be present in addition to the families of the bride and groom. However, in so far as a wedding was first and foremost a family event, it was a private one.

Ancient sources contain many references to weddings but few to music in connection with them. A stock phrase, occurring four times in the book of Jeremiah (Jer. 7:34; 16:9; 25:10; 33:11a) refers to what might be singing by the bride and bridegroom at weddings. The Hebrew is an isometric rhyming couplet: *qôl śāśôn wĕqôl śimḥâ | qôl ḥātān wĕqôl kallâ* (literally: 'the sound of mirth and the sound of gladness | the voice of the bridegroom and the voice of the bride'),[29] features suggestive of a popular rhyme. It is possible that the couplet alludes to a custom that required the bride and bridegroom to sing a wedding song. There is no early mention of such a custom, but 3 Maccabees 4:6 mentions a 'wedding song' *humenaiōn*, associating it with brides.

The text of a wedding song (although a somewhat unusual one) is extant in *Joseph and Aseneth*, a pseudepigraphical romance dating probably from the period between the beginning of the first century BCE and the middle of the first century CE.[30] The work is a free expansion of Genesis 41:45 and 41:50–52.[31] It relates that Aseneth, the beautiful daughter of an Egyptian pagan priest, is given by the Pharaoh to Joseph, a Hebrew, to be his wife (Gen. 41:45). She is strongly attracted to Joseph, but pride and arrogance make her resistant to marriage with someone

---

[28]   Hebrew: Blackman, *Mishnayoth*.
[29]   Hebrew *qôl* = 'sound, voice'.
[30]   Introduction and annotated English translation by C. Burchard in *OTP*, vol. 2, pp. 177–247.
[31]   In these two places and at Gen. 46:20 Aseneth's name is spelled *'āsĕnat* 'Asenath'.

of foreign culture and religion. Her attitude gradually changes, however, and she comes to accept Joseph as her husband and to embrace Judaism. The first half of the romance concludes with Pharaoh solemnizing the marriage and giving a wedding feast, and Aseneth uttering a long wedding 'song' (*Jos. Asen.* 21:11–21). Her 'song' is a confession to God; she acknowledges her former paganism, pride and arrogance as sinful, and that it was Joseph who enabled her to see the error of her ways. In one of the 14 extant manuscripts of Latin versions of *Joseph and Aseneth* (all of which date from *c.*1200 CE[32]), Aseneth's song is introduced by the words: 'And it happened after this [the wedding] that Joseph entered to the song of confession which Aseneth sang to the Lord the Most High after she gave birth to Effraim and Menasse.'[33]

The First book of Maccabees 9:39b mentions drums (and implies additional but unspecified instruments) in the wedding procession of a bridegroom: 'and the bridegroom came out with his friends and his brothers to meet them [the bride and her large escort] with tambourines [*tumpanōn* "drums"][34] and musicians [*mousikōn*]'. Otherwise, two passages in the Mishnah, *Soṭah* 9, imply that singing was usual at nuptial meals, and that the drum was associated with wedding celebrations: 'When the Sanhedrin was cancelled [when the Temple was destroyed in 70 CE], singing at wedding feasts was cancelled' (*m. Soṭah* 9:11), and, 'In the war against Vespasian [Roman Emperor 69–79 CE] they decreed against the wearing of wreaths by bridegrooms and against the wedding drum' (*m. Soṭah* 9:14).

In the Mishnah, *Baba Meṣiʿa* 6:1, there is a passing reference to hiring 'pipers [*ḥalîlîm*][35] for a bride'. Since this occurs in conjunction with a reference to hiring pipers for a corpse (that is, for a funeral procession) it is perhaps an allusion to a custom according to which pipes were played during bridal processions. A passage in the early third century CE apocryphon the *Acts of Thomas* relates that at a wedding banquet given by the king of Andrapolis for his daughter, a Hebrew 'flute-girl' went among the guests and played for them (*Acts Thom.* 1:4–8). The passage also contains the text of a wedding hymn purportedly sung (in Hebrew) by Thomas (*Acts Thom.* 1:6–7).[36]

Over Unborn Children and Infants

When a male child was born, or when its birth was imminent, one of his parents customarily made a special utterance over the child. In the Hebrew Bible special utterances over infants usually occur as short orations placed on the lips of mothers in connection with the naming of their offspring (Gen.

---

[32]   *OTP*, vol. 2, p. 179.

[33]   *Joseph and Aseneth* 21:9 as given in University Library, Uppsala, MS C 37 (also designated MS 436: see *OTP*, vol. 2, p. 179). Translation from *OTP*, vol. 2, p. 236, note s.

[34]   The NRSV has 'tambourines'. Probably hand drums are meant.

[35]   Neusner, *Mishnah*, understands 'pipes' here.

[36]   The passage is available in English translation in *NTA*, vol. 2, pp. 340–2.

30:6–24). The orations are mostly aetiologies for the meanings of the children's names.[37] In 1 Samuel 2 there is an extended utterance by Hannah over her child Samuel (1 Sam. 2:1–10, the 'song' of Hannah). According to the narrative in the first two chapters of 1 Samuel, Hannah made this utterance when she delivered the infant Samuel to the temple at Shiloh for his future upbringing in the service of God.

There are also similar more or less extended utterances over unborn children and infants in the New Testament. Luke 1:46–55 is a special utterance attributed to Mary (some sources attribute it to Elizabeth) in anticipation of the birth of a child. It is probably modelled on Hannah's utterance in 1 Samuel 2. Luke 1:68–79 is uttered by a man, Zechariah, on the birth of his son John; Luke 2:29–32 is a short utterance over the infant Jesus by the prophet Simeon. Luke 2:38 reports that an utterance was delivered by the aged prophetess Anna (Hanna in the Greek) over the infant Jesus, but does not give its text.

To what extent such utterances were actually delivered, and delivered as song, in antiquity (as opposed to their existing solely as literary compositions) is not known; song is not mentioned in connection with any of the utterances cited above. However, there is late evidence to suggest that such utterances were delivered as song. The opening portion of the *Protevangelium of James* tells that a devout Jewish married couple, Joachim and Anna, were in sorrow because they were childless. Anna, after lamenting her plight, set aside her sorrow and implored God to grant her a child. Her prayer was answered and she gave birth to a daughter whom she named Mary (*Prot. Jas.* 4:1–5:2). The narrative goes on to relate that on Mary's first birthday

> [*Prot. Jas.* 6:2] Joachim made a great feast, and invited the chief priests and the priests and the scribes and the elders and the whole people of Israel. And Joachim brought the child [Mary] to the priests, and they blessed her ... And they brought her to the chief priests, and they blessed her ... And her mother carried her into the sanctuary of her bedchamber and gave her suck. And Anna sang this song [*asma*] to the Lord God:
> 'I will sing [*aisō*] a {holy} song [*ōdēn*] to the Lord my God,
> for he has visited me and taken away from me the reproach of my enemies.
> And the Lord gave me the fruit of righteousness, unique and manifold before him.
> Who will proclaim to the sons of Reubel [Reuben] that Anna gives suck?
> {Hearken, hearken, you twelve tribes of Israel: Anna gives suck.}'[38] (*NTA*, vol. 1, p. 428)

---

[37] Dan (Gen. 30:6), Naphtali (Gen. 30:7–8), Gad (Gen. 30:10–11), Asher (Gen. 30:12–13), Issachar (Gen. 30:17–18), Zebulun (Gen. 30:19–20), Joseph (Gen. 30:22–24). It is noteworthy that the birth of Leah's daughter Dinah, announced at Gen. 30:21, attracts neither comment nor special utterance.

[38] Greek from de Strycker, 'La forme la plus ancienne', p. 94 (in that edition the chapter and verse reference for the present quotation is 6:3). Braces enclose textual variants.

Anna's song is a set piece exhibiting features that give it the appearance of belonging to Jewish tradition: it is a special utterance over an infant, and it is composed almost entirely of allusions to and quotations from the Hebrew Bible.[39] It is introduced by a formula that announces sung performance, and its text contains a direct reference to singing – features characteristic of ancient Jewish cultic songs.

Yet the song is not entirely in keeping with Jewish tradition. In Jewish tradition the known special utterances over infants are reserved for male offspring, whereas Anna's song is uttered over a daughter; in addition, the way in which the text is composed of short quotations from and allusions to disparate parts of the Bible, is uncharacteristic of such utterances, including those of similar length to, and longer than, Anna's song. The reason why Anna's song exhibits features which are not part of Jewish tradition lies no doubt in the Christian origin of the work where the text of the song appears. It is possible that Anna's song had special doctrinal and cultural significance for the eastern Christianized Jews among whom the *Protevangelium of James* first circulated, especially the Ebionites for whom devotion to Mary was important from early on.[40] Nevertheless, while Anna's song may not harmonize completely with Jewish tradition, and notwithstanding the legendary nature of its narrative context, there seems no reason to doubt that the story of Mary's first birthday reflects an actual and prevalent Jewish tradition as far as the sung delivery of special utterances over infants is concerned.

In Love

It would be surprising if music were not in evidence during amorous encounters, but the sources provide surprisingly little specific information on the matter. In Isaiah 5:1 the prophet begs leave to 'sing' (*'āšîrâ*) for his beloved a 'love song' (*šîrat dôdî*) about the latter's 'vineyard' ('vineyard' is frequently used as a metaphor for 'lover' in ancient Israelite love poetry). The text can be read as a love poem purely and simply, as a legal parable or as an oracle of judgement. It provides very little concrete circumstantial or musical information except to show that even so long ago as the early First-Temple period love songs could be objective as well as subjective.

---

[39]   Hebrew Bible allusions and quotations (as well as New Testament parallels) are identified in *NTA*, vol. 1, p. 437, nn. 22–25. In addition it may be pointed out that the first line of the song, which receives no comment in *NTA*, echoes passages such as Exod. 15:1b, Judg. 5:3b and Judith 16:13a.

[40]   See *NTA*, vol. 1, p. 425. Further on the Ebionites, see: Petri Luomanen, 'Ebionites and Nazarenes', in Matt Jackson-McCabe (ed.), *Jewish Christianity Reconsidered: Rethinking Ancient Groups and Texts* (Minneapolis MN, 2007), pp. 81–118, esp. pp. 81–102; Oskar Skarsaune, 'The Ebionites', in Oskar Skarsaune and Reidar Hvalvik (eds), *Jewish Believers in Jesus: The Early Centuries* (Peabody MA, 2007), pp. 419–62.

In Ezekiel 33:32, a passage which has been quoted earlier in another context, Ezekiel is warned by God that his prophecies will go unheeded by the self-centred, disobedient Israelites: he will be treated like a singer of love songs:

> [Ezek. 33:32] To them you are just a singer [*kĕšîr* (possibly an error for *kĕšār*)] of bawdy songs ['*ăgābîm* 'love songs'], who has a sweet voice [*qôl*] and plays [*nagên*] skilfully; they hear your words but will not obey them.

The content of love songs was evidently somewhat frivolous. A singer of love songs could accompany himself on an instrument, probably a *kinnôr* judging from the earlier-mentioned association of the verb *nāgan* with that instrument, as he sang. The above quotation gives the impression that the type of 'singer of love songs' envisaged is not an ardent lover serenading his beloved, but rather a popular entertainer.

At Banquets and Other Festivities

There is ample evidence of music – vocal and instrumental – in use at private festivities. Music at banquets was much prized by the author of Sirach:

> [Sir. 32:5] A ruby seal in a setting of gold
> is a concert of music [*sunkrima mousikōn*] at a banquet of wine. [6] A seal of emerald in a rich setting of gold
> is the melody of music [*melos mousikōn*] with good wine.

He even went so far as to commend the memory of the reforming king Josiah in terms of the gastronomic and musical delights of a banquet:

> [Sir. 49:1b] His [Josiah's] memory [so the Hebrew; Greek: 'it'] is as sweet as honey to every mouth, and like music [Hebrew *mizmôr*; Greek *mousika*] at a banquet of wine.

Occasionally he waxes philosophical about the frivolity of such pleasures, but not to the extent of denying them:

> [Sir. 40:20] Wine and music [*mousika*] gladden the heart,
> but the love of friends [so the Greek; Hebrew: 'wisdom'] is better than either.
> [21] The flute [*aulos* 'pipe'] and the harp [*psaltērion*] make sweet melody [*melē*],
> but a pleasant voice is better than either.

Indeed, enjoyment should not be interrupted, as is made clear in the following passage from a section about proper conduct at banquets:

> [Sir. 32:3] Speak, you who are older, for it is your right,
> but with accurate knowledge, and do not interrupt the music [*mousika*].

Music at banquets and other festivities did not normally consist solely of singing and the playing of instruments; there was always some necessary extra-musical element present. The cultivation of music as liberal art, a discrete aural experience, as in ancient Greek culture, was something foreign to ancient Israelite/Jewish culture (for example, the ancient Israelites and Jews did not indulge in musical competitions like their Greek contemporaries). Music was thus one element among others which traditionally belonged together in particular settings. It is true that several passages in Sirach indicate that the music was important at banquets. But the Greek *mousikē* used in Sirach (the Hebrew Ben Sira text from Masada has *mizmôr*),[41] and translated 'music' in NRSV, would have meant a combination of several or all of the arts over which the Muses were deemed to preside, especially song, instrumental music and dance. What a garrulous senior citizen was cautioned against interrupting, in the last quotation above, could perhaps be more appropriately translated 'the entertainment' or 'the show'. This is not to deny that music as an aural experience was important at banquets, but to emphasize that 'music' in such contexts would have connoted more than a satisfying composition of pleasing sounds alone.

By way of illustration of the last point, two passages from the NT may be cited. In the parable of the prodigal son (Luke 15:11–32), it is related that the prodigal's father held a feast to celebrate his son's return. Meanwhile, the prodigal's elder brother was out in the fields, unaware of what was happening; 'and when he came and approached the house, he heard music [*sumphōnias*] and dancing [*chorōn*]' (Luke 15:25). And in Matthew 11:17 and its parallel at Luke 7:32, domestic festivity is probably the origin of the imagery in the first part of the children's teasing song, 'We piped for you and you would not dance. We wept and wailed, and you would not mourn' (NEB). In addition, it is difficult to imagine the daughter of Herodias dancing her beguiling solo dance before Herod and his guests at his birthday celebrations (Matt. 14:6–7) without instrumental accompaniment.

The penultimate quotation above is one of several passages in the sources to specify the instruments used. The earliest such passage seems to be Genesis 31:27 where Laban tells Jacob that if circumstances had been different he would have sent Jacob on his way 'with festive [*běśimḥâ* "festivity"] music [*ûběširîm* "and songs"], with timbrel [*bětōp*] and lyre [*ûběkinnôr*]'.

Three further early passages also witness to the use of specific types of instrument, in addition to song, on such occasions. The first is from First Isaiah:

> [Isa. 5:11] Ah, Those who chase liquor
> From early in the morning,
> And till late in the evening

---

[41]   See Yigael Yadin, *The Ben Sira Scroll from Masada* (Jerusalem, 1965).

Are inflamed by wine!
Who, at their banquets,
Have lyre [*kinnôr*] and lute [*wānebel*],
Timbrel [*tôp*], flute [*ḥālîl*], and wine;
But who never give a thought
To the plan of the Lord ...

The second is Isaiah 24:8–9, which is from a section of First Isaiah written probably in the early sixth century, and which has already been quoted above in a different context (see the beginning of the section 'In Joy and Pleasure, 1: Public'). The third is from Job 21:12 where the author of the book has his hero complain, 'They [the wicked] sing to the music of timbrel [*tôp* "hand drum"] and lute [*kinnôr* "lyre"], And revel to the tune [*lĕqôl* "to the sound"] of the pipe ['*ûgāb*]' (Job 21:12). The '*ûgāb* may have been an end-blown flute or set of pan-pipes associated with pagan orgiastic rituals, and chosen deliberately in order to throw Job's plight into high relief.

The performers of the music at banquets and other festivities were the troupes of male and female singers and musicians who were part of the trappings of wealthy households (see Chapter 2, text between nn. 33 and 34; Chapter 3, 'The Role of Women'). It is possible that the Song of Songs is a collection of songs such singers would have performed at banquets and other private festive gatherings.

Music at less dignified social occasions is referred to at two places in the Babylonian Talmud. These are very late references, but for the record they are quoted below. One occurs at the end of paragraph 48a of the tractate *Soṭah*:

> [*b. Soṭah* 48a (end)] When *there is song in the house there is destruction on its threshold. When men sing and women join in it is licentiousness; when women sing and men join in it is like fire in tow ... abolish the latter before the former. Whoever drinks to the accompaniment of the four musical instruments brings five punishments to the world.*

The 'four musical instruments' are not identified in the text. In the light of what is known about the instruments used at banquets, however, it is a reasonable conjecture that the four instruments were the *kinnôr*, *nēbel*, *ḥālîl* and *tôp*.

The other reference occurs in paragraph 7a of the tractate *Giṭṭin*:

> [*b. Giṭ.* 7a] An inquiry was once addressed to Mar 'Ukba: Where does Scripture tell us that it is forbidden [in these times] to sing [at carousals]? He sent back [the following quotation] written on lines: *Rejoice not, O Israel, unto exultation like the peoples, for thou hast gone astray from thy God* [Hosea 9:1]. Should he not rather have sent the following: *They shall not drink wine with music, strong drink shall be bitter to them that drink it* [Isaiah 24:9 (read 24:8)]? – From this verse I

should conclude that only musical instruments are forbidden, but not song; this I learn [from the other (subsequent) verse].[42]

It is noteworthy that the types of musical instrument played at banquets and other entertainments are identical in name with several of the cultic instruments. There was probably no material difference between cultic and non-cultic instruments. What distinguished them was the sanctity which accrued to cultic instruments by virtue of their particular circumstances of use. This may be illustrated by a remark in *mishnah Kelim* 15:6 about the suitability or otherwise of *nĕbālîm* ('harps' in the following translation) for use in non-cultic and cultic contexts: 'Harps for {*nibĕlê*} singing {by ordinary people} are unclean, and {*or* "but"} harps of {*wĕnibĕlê*} the sons of Levi are clean'. Here 'unclean' and 'clean' characterize instruments for secular and sacred use respectively.

In sacred writings, music in the service of the wealthy tends to receive mention primarily in connection with occasions of social revelry such as those mentioned above. But in wealthy households, and especially royal ones, it was often the case that music was more or less permanently available for the delectation of residents and guests. Thus to be attended by music in one's home was a sign of gracious living as may be illustrated, for example, by this verse from the pre-exilic Psalm 45:

[Ps. 45:9(8)] All your [the King's] robes [are fragrant] with myrrh and aloes and cassia; from ivoried palaces lutes [*minnî* (rather: *minnîm*) 'stringed instruments'] entertain you.[43]

In Prostitution

At Isaiah 23:16 there is a short poem about a forgotten prostitute who is trying to remind people of her existence. She is unnamed and addressed in the second person. The poem, referred to in 23:15 as the 'song of the prostitute' (*šîrat hazzônâ*), occurs near the end of the oracle about Tyre which comprises Isaiah 23, and is a metaphorically expressed prophecy of the fate the city of Tyre will have to endure for 70 years. It provides some basic and straightforward musical information:

[Isa. 23:16][44] Take a lyre [*qĕḥî kinnôr*], go about the city, you forgotten prostitute [*zônâ niškāḥâ*]!

---

[42]　Translation from I. Epstein (trans. and ed.), *The Babylonian Talmud Translated Into English with Notes, Glossary and Indices*, 35 vols (London, 1935–52). Square brackets enclose the translator's interpolations and annotations.

[43]　'stringed instruments': so the NRSV.

[44]　The following is a composite translation from the JPS *Tanakh* and the NRSV.

Sweetly play [*hêṭîbî nagēn*], sing many songs [*harbî-šîr*], that you may be remembered.

While the poem is an element in the rhetoric of the prophetic oracle, there seems little doubt that the picture of the prostitute going about the city playing her lyre and singing her songs is drawn from real life. The context and purpose of the poem suggest that an ordinary worldly or secular prostitute is meant rather than a cult prostitute. The poem and the words that introduce it use *zônâ* (from *zānâ*) for prostitute. This word properly signified a secular prostitute as opposed to *qādēš* and *qĕdēšâ* which properly signified respectively a male and a female cult prostitute. These words are frequently used interchangeably in the Hebrew Bible, however, therefore the vocabulary alone is not decisive.[45] The quotation again illustrates the association of the verb *nāgan* with playing the *kinnôr*.

In Intimate Domestic Contexts

Sources reveal two groups of occasions in particular on which music was employed in intimate domestic settings. One of these is concerned with the boy David playing an instrument to soothe king Saul when an 'evil spirit' came over him. In 1 Samuel 16, the biblical narrative relates that Saul's courtiers, seeing their king's changes of mood, suggested to him:

> [1 Sam. 16:16] 'Let our lord give the order [and] the courtiers in attendance on you will look for someone who is skilled [*yōdē'a*] at playing [*měnagēn*] the lyre [*bakinnôr*]; whenever the evil spirit of God comes over you, he will play it [*wěnigēn běyādô*] and you will feel better.' [17] So Saul said to his courtiers, 'Find someone who can play [*lěnagēn*] well [*mêṭîb*] and bring him to me.' [18] One of the attendants spoke up, 'I have observed a son of Jesse the Bethlehemite who is skilled [*yōdē'a*] in music [*nagēn*]'.

The son of Jesse in question, David, was procured, and

> [1 Sam. 16:23] Whenever the [evil] spirit of God came upon Saul, David would take the lyre ['*et-hakkinnôr*] and play it [*wěnigēn běyādô*]; Saul would find relief and feel better, and the evil spirit would leave him.

The narrative later says that David played (*měnagēn běyādô*) daily for Saul (1 Sam. 18:10).

---

[45]   See, for example, Athalya Brenner, *The Israelite Woman* (Sheffield, 1985, repr. 1989), pp. 78–9.

The narrative shows that the soothing property of the sound of music played on the *kinnôr* was something that was generally accepted. The language of the episode shows furthermore that this power is unlocked when an instrument is played by a 'skilled' (*yōdēʿa*, from *yādaʿ*) musician. More than merely technical competence should be read into the word here translated 'skilled'. The word carries the sense of both technical skill in itself and sensitivity to the situation in which the music is used. The KJV at 1 Samuel 16:16 and 18 uses 'cunning' where the JPS *Tanakh* and NRSV have 'skilled'. 'Cunning' in its positive sense of 'ingenuity' is probably the better adjective because it gives the necessary nuance of responding with appropriate imagination and skill to the circumstances of the moment.

The interpretation of *bĕyādô* (literally: 'with his hand'), used in 16:16 and 16:23 to qualify *wĕnigēn*, is problematic. It could be understood as simply a poetic amplifier (it is translated in full at both places in KJV, but only at 16:23 in NRSV). But it could also have a technical sense, for example to distinguish or clarify a particular playing technique ('with the hand' as opposed to 'with a plectrum'). Its frequent use in conjunction with *nāgan* suggests that the two terms together were an idiom having to do with the playing of plucked-string instruments.

The second group of occasions is concerned with music performed by the patriarch Job and others at his residence. The source is the *Testament of Job*. The narrative of the five verses that constitute the work's fourteenth chapter exemplifies Job's charity, piety and humanity. At the same time it provides musical information:

> [*Test. Job* 14:1] And I used to have six psalms and a ten-stringed *lyre* [*kithara*]. [2] I would rouse myself daily after the feeding of the widows, take the lyre [*kitharan*], and play [*epsallon*] for them [*autois*]. And they [*autai*] would chant hymns [*humnoun*]. [3] And with the psaltery [*psaltēr*] I would remind them of God so that they might glorify the Lord. [4] If my maidservants ever began murmuring, I would take up the psaltery [*psaltēr*] and strum as payment in return. [5] And thus I would make them stop murmuring in contempt. (*OTP*, vol. 1, p. 844)

Verses 1–2 show Job playing a 'lyre', and the widows (for whom Job had provided a meal) singing hymns. It is impossible to know from the Greek text in which the *Testament of Job* has been handed down whether readers should understand that Job accompanied the widows' singing or that he played and then afterwards the widows sang.[46] In verse 3 the instrument is changed in order to make the widows think of God: the psaltery was the instrument of psalms. In verses 4 and 5 the narrative says that Job's playing the psaltery had a soothing effect on his contemptuous maidservants. The effect of the playing of the psaltery is similar to

---

[46] See David Halperin, 'Music in the Testament of Job', *Yuval*, 5 (1986): 356–64, and the open correspondence between Halperin and myself in *M&L*, 76 (1995): 480–81.

that of the playing of the *kinnôr* as related in 1 Samuel 16:23 (quoted above) and witnesses to the prevalence of the traditional belief in music's apotropaic power.

The usual caveats must apply when weighing the historicity of these passages. Nevertheless, while the story of Saul and David is mythical, and the episodes in the *Testament of Job* are fiction based on legend, the background details are likely to be appropriate to the times and situations in which they were composed. It is therefore likely that the passages faithfully reflect at least the fact of the domestic use of plucked-string instruments in early pre-exilic and late postexilic times.

At Work

The Hebrew Scriptures witness to only one work-song as a sung item. This is the so-called Song of the Well in Numbers 21:17–18 which, as has been mentioned earlier, is one of the oldest items of Hebrew poetry in the Bible. According to its literary context it was sung by the thirsty Israelites on the miraculous provision of water for them in the wilderness. Although the song is about a well, and may be a work-song for well diggers, there is nothing in its text that binds it to this event alone, and the song is clearly an interpolation. It is introduced into its literary context by a standard preamble: 'Then Israel sang [*yāšîr*] this song [*'et-haššîrâ hazz'ōt*]' (Num. 21:17a). The text of the song follows immediately:

> [Num. 21:17b] Spring up, O well – sing to it [*'ĕnû-loh* 'respond to it'] –
> [18] The well which the chieftains dug,
> Which the nobles of the people started
> With maces, with their own staffs.

An essential feature of a song used to accompany repetitive manual labouring tasks is a recurring pattern of strongly stressed rhythms. This feature is also present in the Song of the Well, in its last three lines (Num. 21:18), each of which has the stress pattern ˘ | – ˘ ˘ | – ˘ ˘ | – | thus:

> *(italic type indicates stressed syllables)*

> Bĕ'*ēr* ḥăpārûhā *śā*rîm
> *kā*rûhā nĕ*dî*bê hā'*ām*
> bimḥōqēq bĕ*miš*'ănō*tām*

The opening line of the song (Num. 21:17b, 'Spring up, O well – sing to it') lacks this pattern of stresses. Perhaps it was sung by a leader or 'caller', to whom the team of diggers responded with the rest of the song as they dug. In support of this point, it may be noted that *'ĕnû-* in verse 17b is a second person plural imperative; it more usually means 'respond' than 'sing'.

In War

When the ancient Israelites and Judaeans went into battle, they did so in the firm belief that they were engaging in a holy undertaking, a sacred act. This belief they held in common with most ancient peoples, but for the Israelites it was strengthened by their conviction that they were a people chosen by their Deity to receive special favour. Because of their special relationship with their Deity, the Israelites regarded any assault on themselves as an indirect assault on God, which it was their religious duty to repel. Before engaging in battle, they prayed to their Deity for victory; during battle they fought believing that their Deity would assist them by fighting with them; and after battle they either celebrated victory in thanksgiving to their Deity, or bewailed their defeat as divine punishment for earlier wrongdoing.

During Preparations for Battle

Before a battle could be fought, warriors had to be assembled. For emperors, kings, princes and other rulers who had armies, this was simply a matter of issuing the appropriate command. Others, however, had to gather a fighting force. This was accomplished through the sounding of the shofar, as is illustrated by two passages in Judges. The first concerns Ehud's gathering an Israelite army to fight the Moabites:

> [Judg. 3:27] When he [Ehud] got there [to Seirah], he had the ram's horn sounded [*wayyitĕqaʿ baššôpār*] through the hill country of Ephraim, and all the Israelites descended with him from the hill country; and he took the lead.

The second concerns Gideon's assembly of a fighting force to do battle for the Israelites against the Midianites:

> [Judg. 6:34] The spirit of the Lord enveloped Gideon; he sounded the horn [*wayyitĕqaʿ baššôpār*], and the Abiezrites rallied behind him.

When troops went off to battle they had with them priests and metal trumpets which the priests would blow:

> [Num. 31:6] Moses dispatched them [Israelite warriors] on the campaign [against Midian], a thousand from each tribe, with Phinehas son of Eleazar serving as a priest on the campaign, equipped with the sacred utensils and the trumpets [*waḥăṣōṣĕrôt*] for sounding the blasts [*hatĕrûʿâ*].

Song in praise of God was also important as the troops marched out to war:

> [2 Chr. 20:21] After taking counsel with the people, he [Jehoshaphat] stationed singers [*mĕšōrărîm*] to the Lord extolling the One majestic in holiness as they

went forth ahead of the vanguard, saying, 'Praise the Lord, for His steadfast love is eternal.'

A later source, 1 Maccabees 4, shows Judas Maccabaeus praying before his battle with the army of Lysias, asking God to grant him success (1 Macc. 4:30–33). The prayer concludes with a plea to God to use the faithful Judaean warriors as instruments of victory, so that all who worship God will be able to offer praise 'with hymns' (*en humnois*).

The preparations for the battle of Jericho (Josh. 6:1–27) were different from any of those described above. According to the narrative in Joshua 6:3–20, they consisted of ritual circumambulations of the city by Joshua's troops accompanied by the Ark of the Covenant and seven priests playing seven horns. There was one circumambulation each day for six days. On the seventh day there were seven circumambulations during the last of which there were shouts as well as horn blasts. As the sound of the horn blasts and shouting rose, the walls of Jericho collapsed and the city lay open for the troops to enter and capture it. It is possible that the events of this preparatory part of the battle reflect actual rituals that preceded assaults on clearly defined and contained areas, such as cities and enemy encampments, in very ancient times. The absence of the name of any specific city in both the Divine instructions for the ritual (Josh. 6:3–5) and the narrative of their implementation (Josh. 6:6–16) supports this idea.

There are several points of musical interest in the narrative of the battle of Jericho. To begin with, although priests are present, they blow horns, not metal trumpets. Second, the narrative uses two words for 'horn': most frequently *šôpār* (shofar), but on one occasion (Josh. 6:5) *qeren*. The latter is the generic word for the horn of an animal. In the present passage the context shows that *qeren* is to be understood as a horn for musical use; it should be regarded as synonymous with *šôpār*.[47] Third, and most important, the words for 'horn' are qualified by one or another form of the word *yôbēl*.[48] '*Yôbēl*' can mean 'cry of joy' or 'shout of joy', but most usually it means 'Jubilee', the Jubilee Year. Thus in Joshua 6:4, 8, 13, the horns are referred to as *šôpĕrôt hayyôbĕlîm* 'shofars of [or "for"] the jubilees', in Joshua 6:5 as *qeren hayyôbēl* 'horn of jubilee', and in Joshua 6:6 as *šôpĕrôt yôbĕlîm* 'jubilee shofars'. Curiously, however, English versions of Joshua 6 usually translate these phrases 'rams' horns' (for example, the JPS *Tanakh* and NRSV). It is not altogether clear in these cases whether 'rams' horns' is meant to be equivalent to the whole phrase *šôpĕrôt (hay)yôbĕlîm*, whether it is meant as a translation of *šôpār* alone (ignoring *yôbēl*) or whether

---

[47]   In the Hebrew Bible the word *qeren* is used to mean a musical instrument at only five places: the present one (Josh. 6:5) and Dan. 3:5, 7, 10, 15. In the Daniel references the word is given in its Aramaic form, *qarnāʾ* (see Chapter 4, at n. 67).

[48]   The instances in Josh. 6 where horns are mentioned without immediate qualification should be understood as referring back to previous mentions where the qualification is present.

'ram' is intended as a translation of *yôbēl*, which Joachim Braun proposes.[49] The last alternative must be dismissed, however, since on the one hand ancient Hebrew has a word for 'ram' meaning a male sheep: *'ayil*; and on the other hand there is no logical or etymological reason why *yôbēl* should mean a ram in addition to its other meanings.[50] The likelihood is that *yôbēl* means something different from 'ram' when used in conjunction with a word for a musical horn. Alfred Sendrey tried to show that it implies a horn with a large detachable metal bell, which produced a louder sound than other types of horn,[51] but the sources he adduced in the Bible and the Mishnah (principally *m. Kelim* 11:7) do not support his arguments.

The significance of '*yôbēl*' as used in Joshua 6:2–20 becomes clearer when the word is considered in the light of a passage in *mishnah Roš Haššanah* 3:5. This has been referred to already in Chapter 4.[52] It states, 'At New Year they blew those [shofars] of rams, but at the Jubilee [*ûbayyôbēl*] those of wild goats [*yě'ēlîm*].' The tradition of the Jubilee Year was already ancient by the time the Mishnah was compiled: its Divine institution is related in the Torah (Lev. 25:8–17). Whether the tradition of the use of wild goats' horns at Jubilees is equally ancient is impossible to say. But there is a strong likelihood that it was in place by the time the book of Joshua received its final form in the late pre-exilic period. Assuming this to be the case, the word *yôbēl* used in Joshua 6 to qualify 'horns' would imply wild goats' horns rather than rams' horns.

Alternatively, it is possible that at some stage during the transmission of Joshua 6 the word *yôbēl* 'jubilee' was mistakenly written instead of *yā'ēl* 'wild goat', and the mistake became permanent. In other words, the word that qualified *qeren* and *šôpār* in Joshua 6 was originally *yā'ēl*. This scenario is not improbable given that when transmitted orally the words are very similar in their respective plural forms (*yôbēlîm; yě'ēlîm*) as well as in their singular ones. It may be added that if the tradition of using wild goats' horns at Jubilees (as illustrated in the Mishnah passage above) were already in place at the time when the hypothetical mistake was made, the two words would have been all the easier to confuse. While the traditional exegesis of the story of the battle of Jericho may require the priests to blow rams' horns, the language of the narrative suggests that wild goats' horns are meant.

---

[49]   Joachim Braun proposes the translation 'horn of a ram' for the phrase *qeren hayyôbēl* in Josh. 6:5, and goes on to state that *yôbēl* means 'ram' as well as 'jubilee' (*MAI/P*, p. 25).

[50]   In support of his contention that *yôbēl* means 'ram', Joachim Braun adduces the root form YBL, meaning '[to] lead, conduct; leader of the flock' (*MAI/P*, p. 25). But this is too distant from 'ram' to carry any weight. In any case, root forms are notoriously unreliable as bases for the definition of words.

[51]   *MAI*, pp. 369–71.

[52]   Chapter 4, in the section 'The Musical Instruments: Additional Remarks'.

On the Battlefield

Traditions in the Torah contain Divine prescriptions about the use of metal trumpets in battle. In Numbers 10:9 the Deity tells Moses:

> [Num. 10:9] When you are at war in your land against an aggressor who attacks you, you shall sound short blasts on the trumpets [*baḥăṣōṣĕrôt*], that you may be remembered before the Lord your God and be delivered from your enemies.

Later in the same chapter, the narrative quotes a text which, though associated with the Ark of the Covenant, could possibly have been a battle song or a battle shout:

> [Num. 10:35] When the Ark was to set out, Moses would say: 'Advance, O Lord!
> May Your enemies be scattered,
> And may Your foes flee before You!'

Trumpet blasts and a battle shout are referred to in the Chronicler's narrative of the battle between the forces of Abijah, king of Judah, and Jeroboam, king of Israel. The following quotation takes up the narrative at the end of a long warning to Jeroboam from Abijah not to engage in battle:

> [2 Chr. 13:12] 'See, God is with us [Abijah and the Judahites] as our chief, and His priests have the trumpets for sounding blasts against you. O children of Israel, do not fight the LORD God of your fathers, because you will not succeed.' [13] Jeroboam, however, had directed the ambush to go around and come from the rear, thus the main body was in front of Judah, while the ambush was behind them. [14] When Judah turned round and saw that the fighting was before and behind them, they cried out to the LORD, and the priests blew trumpets. [15] The men of Judah raised a shout; and when the men of Judah raised a shout, God routed Jeroboam and all Israel before Abijah and Judah.

According to the Chronicler's narrative of the battle between the troops of Jehoshaphat, king of Judah, and enemy warriors, battle shouts and hymns served to provide cover:

> [2 Chr. 20:22] As they [the troops of Jehoshaphat] began their joyous shouts [*bĕrinnâ*] and hymns [*ûtĕhillâ* 'and praises'], the LORD set ambushes for the men of Amon, Moab, and the hill country of Seir, who were marching against Judah, and they were routed.

The 'hymns' may have been psalm verses containing the words 'Praise the Lord, for His steadfast love is eternal,' given that this text is quoted in the preceding verse (2 Chr. 20:21) as being sung by musicians as they marched before the troops going to war.

Trumpet calls, battle cries and hymns were also features of battles in the Hellenistic period. In 1 Maccabees 4:13–14 it is related that 'the men with Judas blew their trumpets [*esalpisan*] and engaged in battle'; and in 2 Maccabees 12:37 that Judas Maccabaeus, using the language of his ancestors (Hebrew), 'raised the battle-cry, with hymns [*meth' humnōn*]; then he charged against Gorgias's troops when they were least expecting it, and put them to flight.'

These features were common in the Near East at the time, as is shown by reports that enemies also made use of them. At 1 Maccabees 6:33, for example, the narrative says that the king of Syria (either the 11- or 12-year-old Antiochus V Eupator, or his regent Lysias) 'took his army by a forced march along the road to Beth-zechariah, and his troops made ready for battle and sounded their trumpets [*kai esalpisan tais salpinxin*].' And 2 Maccabees 15:25 says that Nicanor and his troops (enemies of Judah) advanced against the army of Judas Maccabaeus 'with trumpets [*meta salpingōn*] and battle-songs [*kai paianōn*].'

Among the documents of the Qumran community, the *War Scroll* includes detailed instructions as to how the metaphorical war of Good against Evil is to be waged.[53] In keeping with the metaphorical nature of the document, the instructions give a compressed, stylized and idealistic picture of battle, and the features of the warfare are basically the same as those in the battle narratives of the Torah and the Former Prophets in the Hebrew Bible. It must be doubted whether this picture reflects anything of actual warfare in the period when the Qumran community flourished, even when allowances are made for the character of the work. Nevertheless, the use of trumpet calls to direct the warriors[54] would have been a standard feature of formal warfare throughout antiquity and indeed until relatively modern times.

At Victory Celebrations

The sources show that victory could be celebrated in several ways, and that music – song and the playing of hand drums – and dancing were normal components of the celebrations. The music of the victors consisted of song in thanksgiving to the Deity (who was perceived as having granted the victory). In some instances this is placed on the lips of a leader alone, in others on the lips of all the victors together. Sometimes the idea of 'victors' is hyperbolically expanded to include all who would benefit from the victory, for example 'the Israelites' or 'all the people'.

The archetypal victory song in Jewish scriptural tradition is the Song of the Sea, the song which, according to Exodus 15:1–18, Moses and the Israelites

---

[53]   *CDSSE*, pp. 170–1.

[54]   See Chapter 5, at nn. 34–36, for a discussion of the significance of the trumpets mentioned in the *War Scroll* of the Qumran community.

sang to the Deity after their deliverance from the Egyptian enemy at the Sea of Reeds. As has been noted in an earlier chapter, the song is introduced by a preamble which announces sung performance and names the singers ('Then Moses and the Israelites sang this song to the LORD', Exod. 15:1), and then opens with two clauses which continue the idea of singing, ascribing the victory to the Deity: 'I will sing to the LORD, for He has triumphed gloriously; Horse and driver He has hurled into the sea' (Exod. 15:1b–c). The song as it is preserved occupies 18 verses in the MT of the Hebrew Bible, but the possibility exists that originally it consisted of only the two clauses just quoted.[55]

Joshua 10:12 quotes what may be the text of a short victory song uttered by Joshua himself when the Israelite army under his leadership defeated the Amorites:

[Josh. 10:12b] Joshua addressed the LORD; he said in the presence of the Israelites:
[12c] 'Stand still, O sun, at Gibeon,
O moon, in the Valley of Aijalon!'
[13] And the sun stood still
And the moon halted,
While a nation wreaked judgment on its foes
– as is written in the book of Jashar.

The remark with which this quotation closes suggests that the text of Joshua's song is to be found in the 'book of Jashar' which, as has been noted near the beginning of this chapter, may have been a collection of war songs. The narrative of the episode then concludes with a confirmation of Divine intervention on behalf of the Israelites: 'Thus the sun halted in midheaven, and did not press on to set, for a whole day; for the LORD fought for Israel' (Josh. 10:13–14).

Similarly, when Judas Maccabaeus and his army returned from their victory over Gentile forces under Gorgias, 'they sang hymns [*humnoun*] and praises to Heaven – "For he is good, for his mercy endures for ever"' (1 Macc. 4:24);[56] and again, when Judas Maccabaeus and his army had defeated the Ammonite army, 'with hymns [*meth' humnōn*] and thanksgivings they blessed the Lord who shows great kindness to Israel and gives them the victory' (2 Macc. 10:38).

As well as the victors themselves, women might provide music at victory celebrations, singing, dancing and playing percussion instruments. The traditional Jewish scriptural archetype is again to be found in the narrative of the Israelites' escape from their Egyptian enemies at the Sea of Reeds, in this

---

[55] For example, S.E. Gillingham, *The Poems and Psalms of the Hebrew Bible* (Oxford, 1994), pp. 118, 145.

[56] It is possible, however, that in this instance the tag 'for he is good, for his mercy endures for ever' is a literary device and not a quotation of the text that was used as a victory song on the occasion named.

case in the so-called Song of Miriam at Exodus 15:21. The song and its preamble
are as follows:

> [Exod. 15:20] Then Miriam the prophetess, Aaron's sister, took a timbrel [*tōp*]
> in her hand, and all the women went out after her in dance [*ûbimĕḥōlōt*] with
> timbrels [*bĕtuppîm*].[57] [21] And Miriam chanted [*watta'an*] for them:
> Sing [*šîrû*] to the LORD, for He has triumphed gloriously;
> Horse and driver He has hurled into the sea.

The text of Miriam's song is almost identical with the first two clauses of the Song
of the Sea. The only difference is the form of the verb that is the initial word. In the
Song of the Sea this is first person singular ('I will sing', or 'let me sing') whereas in
Miriam's Song it is second person plural imperative. The gender of the imperative
is masculine which implies that the addressees are either males or a mixed group.
The imperative could be understood as a rhetorical exclamation or as an outburst
of charismatic enthusiasm,[58] but it is perhaps most naturally regarded as an actual
exhortation to all present to sing. The close similarity of Miriam's Song and the
opening of the Song of the Sea, and the fact that in Exodus 15 Miriam's Song is
placed after the Song of the Sea may have caused some Bible translators to regard
Miriam's Song as a refrain. But as has been pointed out in Chapter 1, this has no
support in either the Hebrew of the MT or the Greek of the LXX.

The basic features of Miriam's Song illustrated above (singing, dancing and
the playing of percussion instruments) are also evident in biblical narratives of
women welcoming home victorious troops. According to 1 Samuel 18:6–7,

> [1 Sam. 18:6] When the [Israelite troops] came home [and] David returned from
> killing the Philistine, the women of all the towns of Israel came out singing
> [*lāšîr*] and dancing [*wĕhammĕḥōlôt*] to greet King Saul with timbrels [*bĕtuppîm*],
> shouting [*bĕśimḥâ* 'with joy, with merrymaking'] and sistrums [*ûbĕšālišîm*].[59]
> [7] The women sang[60] [*watta'ăneynâ*] as they danced [*hamĕśaḥăqôt*], and they
> chanted:[61]

---

[57]   'in dance with timbrels': alternatively 'with hand drums and with dancing' for
greater precision and to preserve the word order of the Hebrew (compare the NRSV, which
preserves the word order of the Hebrew but has 'with tambourines' for '*bĕtuppim*').

[58]   *PsIW*, vol. 2, pp. 92–3.

[59]   'the women ... King Saul': the meaning of the Hebrew is uncertain; the LXX has
'the dancing women came out to meet David from all the towns of Israel,' but makes no
reference to 'hand drums', 'shouting' or 'sistrums'. The Hebrew form of the word translated
'singing' (literally: 'with song') is that given in the MT as the marginal reading; the running
text has *lāšiwr* which may be the result of miscopying לשיר (*lšyr*) as לשור (*lšwr*).

[60]   'sang': alternatively 'chanted, responded, answered [one another]'; see the section
above headed 'At Work'.

[61]   The NRSV translation of 1 Sam. 18:7a is probably closer to the sense of the Hebrew:
'And the women sang to one another as they made merry'.

'Saul has slain his thousands;
David, his tens of thousands!'

To the hand drums and dancing that belong with Miriam's Song, this narrative adds shouting (or the sound of merrymaking) and the playing of sistrums. The episode is mentioned on two later occasions in 1 Samuel, on each occasion with reference to David: 'That's the one of whom they sing [*ya'ănû*] as they dance [*bammĕḥōlôt*] [saying (*lē'mōr*)]: Saul has slain ...' (1 Sam. 21:12(11)), and 'he is the David of whom they sang [*ya'ănû-lô*] as they danced [*bammĕḥōlôt*] [saying (*lē'mōr*)]: Saul has slain ...' (1 Sam. 29:5). On each of these occasions the phraseology and vocabulary (which are almost identical) are very much simpler than those of the original at 1 Samuel 18:6–7; they provide clear pointers to the way the somewhat difficult Hebrew of the original should be understood.

According to Judges 11:34a, 'When Jephthah arrived at his home in Mizpah, there was his daughter coming out to meet him, with timbrel [*bĕtuppîm* "with hand drums"] and dance [*ûbimĕḥōlôt*]!' The fact that the nouns 'hand drum' and 'dance' are plural in the Hebrew is probably an indication that several people are to be envisaged as being involved in the welcome, not Jephthah's daughter alone. Although singing is not specifically mentioned, the passages quoted previously show that song normally belonged to such occasions; it should therefore not be automatically excluded here. In support of song on this occasion, the LXX uses the word *chorois* 'choruses' for 'dance', a word that normally implies song as well as dance.

A natural consequence of attributing victory to the Deity was not only that the Deity should be honoured in victory songs, but also that he should be thanked in worship at the Temple. None of the victory celebrations discussed above is reported as concluding in this way. The narrative of the celebration of the dedication of the rebuilt altar of the Temple in 1 Maccabees 4, however, may provide an indirect example. The complete story is related in 1 Maccabees 4:30–58. Summarized, its pertinent points are that, following the military victory of Judas Maccabaeus over enemies who had profaned the Temple and destroyed the altar, the work of restoration could begin. A new altar was built, the Temple was purified and worship was restored. These events were celebrated in 164 BCE with eight days of sacrificial worship at the Temple, in deep and joyous gratitude to the Deity. The reason for the celebration at the Temple was thus threefold: the dedication of the new altar, the restoration of worship at the Temple, and the military victory that had made these possible.

Finally in this section, mention may be made of the celebrations that followed the victory of the Israelites, led by Judith, over the Assyrians, as narrated in the fictional book of Judith in the LXX. The basic details of the celebrations, together with pertinent quotations and background information, have already been presented in Chapter 4. Here, however, it is interesting to note that the celebrations (related in Judith 15:12–16:20) contain all the features mentioned above as being typical of victory celebrations. To begin with, some of the women of Israel performed a dance in Judith's honour (15:12); then Judith 'went before all the people in the dance [*en choreia*; 15:13], leading all the women, while the men of Israel followed, bearing their arms and wearing garlands and singing hymns [*kai humnoun*]' (15:13). Next, the victor herself and 'all the people' sang a long victory psalm (*psalmon*) addressed to God to whom the victory is attributed through the agency of Judith: 'the Lord Almighty has foiled them [the enemy] by the hand of a woman' (16:5). The song begins with a call to play on (hand-?)drums and to sing and play cymbals: 'Begin to my God with drums [*en tumpanois*], sing [*asate*] to my Lord with cymbals [*en kumbalois*]' (16:1). The celebrations conclude with the whole company going to the Temple to offer appropriate sacrifices as tokens of thanks for deliverance from the enemy (16:18). In Chapter 4 it was noted that the victory song in Judith 16 is written in imitation of victory songs of the past, but in view of what has been said here it is evident that not only the song itself, but also its surrounding narrative about the victory celebrations owes a considerable debt to earlier narratives of such occasions.

Chapter 7
Music in Early Christianity, 1: The First to the Early Third Centuries

Christianity arose among Jews in Judaea in the 30s and 40s of the first century of the Common Era in the wake of the ministry of Jesus of Nazareth. The 'Christianized Jews' or 'Jewish Christians',[1] although they added a Christian dimension to their Jewish system of belief, nevertheless followed a lifestyle which for the most part differed little from accepted Jewish norms. They attended the Temple and gathered at the synagogues. Like the contemporary Essenes and Therapeutai, they lived in common fellowship, held material goods and financial resources in common, rejected bodily pleasures and freely accepted men and women together in chaste fellowship.[2] Indeed, Christianity was initially regarded as a movement or sect within Judaism (NT Acts 24:5; 28:22). Unlike the Essenes and the Therapeutai, however, the earliest Christians did not live communally although there is evidence to suggest that some members of the Qumran community were sympathetic to Christianity.[3]

Christianity was a missionary religion; within a remarkably short time after its inception it had spread far beyond Judaea. Since the majority of the earliest Christians were Jews, it was natural that the new religion should be proclaimed first in places where there were Jewish communities. By the time of the destruction of the Jerusalem Temple in 70 CE, Christianity had become established in all the larger Jewish communities in the homeland and the Diaspora. Not all the early missionary targets were Jewish, however. The first six chapters of the Acts of the Apostles show that several Hellenistic communities were evangelized, and a narrative from later in Acts shows Paul of Tarsus putting up a heated defence of

---

[1]   On the nomenclature, see Matt Jackson-McCabe, 'What's in a Name? The Problem of "Jewish Christianity"', in *Jewish Christianity Reconsidered: Rethinking Ancient Groups and Texts*, ed. Matt Jackson-McCabe (Minneapolis MN, 2007), pp. 7–38; Oskar Skarsaune, 'Jewish Believers in Jesus in Antiquity – Problems of Definition', in *Jewish Believers in Jesus*, ed. Oskar Skarsaune and Reidar Hvalvik (Peabody MA, 2nd pr., corrected, 2007), pp. 3–21; James Carleton Paget, 'The Definition of the Terms *Jewish Christian* and *Jewish Christianity* in the History of Research', in ibid., pp. 22–52.

[2]   References to the relevant NT and early extrabiblical Christian sources are provided in J.A. Smith, 'The Ancient Synagogue, The Early Church and Singing', *M&L*, 65/1 (1984): 12–13.

[3]   Carsten Peter Thiede, *The Earliest Gospel Manuscript? The Qumran Papyrus 7Q5 and its Significance for New Testament Studies* (Exeter, 1992).

168   *Music in Ancient Judaism and Early Christianity*

Christianity against Greeks at the Areopagos in Athens, although his first visit when he arrived in the city was to its Jewish community (Acts 17:15–34).

Specifically Christian gatherings took place typically in the private houses of adherents strategically chosen from among well-respected wealthy local citizens.[4] The houses became local centres for Christian communities. The New Testament provides evidence of the existence of such 'house churches' in Colossae (Philem. verses 1–2), Ephesus (1 Cor. 16:19), Jerusalem (Acts 1:13–14; 2:46–47; 5:42b; 12:12), Laodicea (Col. 4:15), Rome (Rom. 16:3–5) and Troas (Acts 20:7–11) in the first century. The domestic intimacy which characterized many of the Christian gatherings reported in later literature, combined with archaeological evidence of a house in Dura-Europos in eastern Syria converted into a Christian church in c.232, suggests that private houses continued to be used for local Christian gatherings until well into the third century.[5]

The majority of gatherings known from the sources included a meal as well as various religious exercises.[6] There are also reports of occasions of individual or corporate devotion where no meal is mentioned, including a small number of gatherings that lasted into or throughout the night.[7]

Christianity differs from Judaism in significant respects in addition to those of religious belief. Being Jewish was (and is) a matter of heredity and nationhood as well as belief. The Jews of antiquity, bound together by their ethnic, historical, national and religious ties, constituted a strong political, religious and social entity recognized throughout the known world. Being Christian, on the other hand, was (and is) a matter of religious conviction alone. Christianity is defined neither by blood ties nor by national or ethnic identity. In the early centuries of the movement Christians had no social or political status. Christianity was a new religion that had continually to define and redefine its doctrinal, ethical and moral stance as it became increasingly independent of Judaism. Christianity's religious, social and, eventually, political development, is described in the sources

---

[4]   Christopher Page, *The Christian West and its Singers: The First Thousand Years* (New Haven CT and London, 2010), pp. 29–52.

[5]   Background and detailed references in J.A. Smith, 'The Ancient Synagogue, The Early Church and Singing': 13.

[6]   Acts 2:42, 46b; 20:7, 11; 1 Cor. 10:16–21; 11:20–34; *Didache* 9; Pliny the Younger, *Letters*, book 10, 96:7; Ignatius, *To the Smyrnaeans* 8:2; Justin Martyr, *First Apology* 65, 67; *Acts of Paul* 9; Tertullian, *Apology* 39; Tertullian, *On the Soldier's Crown* 3. Primary sources for this and other early literature cited in this chapter are listed in the Bibliography. Note that an edition of the Greek text of the *Didache*, with introduction and parallel English translation, is available in *The Apostolic Fathers*, ed. and trans. Bart D. Ehrman (Cambridge MA, 2003), vol. 1, pp. 403–43. An English translation of the *Acts of Paul*, with introduction and notes, is available in *NTA*, vol. 2, pp. 213–70.

[7]   No meals: for example, Acts 16:19–26 (nocturnal); Acts 20:7–11 (nocturnal); Jas. 5:13; Pliny the Younger, *Letters*, book 10, 96:7, beginning; Tertullian, *To His Wife* 2:8; *Acts of Paul* 9, end (nocturnal, after a meal).

that chart its progress as it emerged from the sphere of its parent culture into the wider world. Embedded in those sources are numerous scattered and often incidental references to music.

The Sources: General Remarks

The principal sources of information about Christian music in the first four centuries CE have been described in general terms in Chapter 1. The sources pertinent to the period covered by the present chapter are literary and mostly relate to religious contexts. There is very little information about the music of Christians in secular contexts or in war. However, a work addressed to new Christian converts, *The Instructor* (*Paedagogus*) by Clement of Alexandria (*c*.150– *c*.215), written probably a little before the beginning of the third century, contains a chapter entitled 'How to Conduct Oneself at Banquets' (see below), which includes incidental remarks about the use of instruments in war. Those remarks are all concerned with non-Christian groups, and their references to instruments are negative because Christians are pacifists. While they say what Christians should not do, they do not say what Christians of the time actually did. This is typical of many of the references to musical instruments and also of some of the references to song. In fact, early literary sources contain no concrete references to the playing of musical instruments by Christians until well into the Middle Ages. Nevertheless, the early sources make frequent mention of musical instruments.

Early Christian Attitudes to Musical Instruments

References to musical instruments in early Christian literature are of two main types: figurative and concrete. Figurative references occur most frequently in exegetical, homiletic and instructional writings. They usually form part of the pedagogic method a given writer uses to expound Scripture or impart instruction, and they therefore almost always use instrument imagery in a positive way. Concrete references may be positive or negative depending on the relationship of the writer to the instruments in question.

The earliest extant references to musical instruments in Christian literature are found in the New Testament in 1 Corinthians, a letter written by Paul of Tarsus to the Christian community in Corinth in the mid 50s of the first century CE. There are two references. One occurs as a metaphor embedded in a longer passage of instruction:

> [1 Cor. 13:1] If I speak with the tongues of mortals and of angels, but do not have love, I am a noisy gong or a clanging cymbal.

Here the gong (*chalkos*, literally: 'copper, bronze') and the cymbal (*kumbalon*), which are tuneless noisemakers, are used as metaphors for a loveless person. It is possible that Paul had the cymbals of the Jerusalem Temple in mind: the word he uses to allude to the gong is the same as that used in the LXX version of 1 Chronicles 15:19 to name the material of which the cymbals played by Levites at the Temple were made. His audience, which was predominantly Jewish, would have been familiar with these. But it would also have been familiar with similar instruments used in pagan worship in Greek culture.

The other reference occurs as a simile in an extended passage calling for intelligibility in worship:

> [1 Cor. 14:6] Now, brothers and sisters, if I [Paul] come to you [the assembled Corinthian Christians] speaking in tongues, how will I benefit you unless I speak to you in some revelation or knowledge or prophecy or teaching? [7] It is the same way with lifeless instruments that produce sound, such as the flute [*aulos* 'pipe'] or the harp [*kithara* 'lyre']. If they do not give distinct notes, how will anyone know what is being played? [8] and if the bugle [*salpinx* 'horn, trumpet'] gives an indistinct sound, who will get ready for battle? [9] So with yourselves: if in a tongue you utter speech that is not intelligible, how will anyone know what is being said?

The simile draws on the readers' expected familiarity with wind and plucked-string instruments in contemporary life.

Possibly the earliest references to musical instruments from outside the New Testament are to be found in two of the 42 pseudepigraphical religious poems known as the *Odes of Solomon*. These *Odes* are of uncertain date and provenance. They are possibly contemporary with the latest of the New Testament literature, or a little later, and are thought to stem from Jewish–Christian milieux in Israel/Palestine or Syria, although they are reckoned to be genuinely Christian compositions.[8] The pertinent references are concerned with the *kithara* 'lyre' (but translated 'harp' in the two passages below):

> [*Odes Sol.* 14:7] Teach me the odes [*or* 'songs'] of your truth,
> that I may produce fruits in you.
> [8] And open to me the harp [*kithara*] of your Holy Spirit,
> so that with every note I may praise you, O Lord. (*OTP*, vol. 2, p. 748)
> [*Odes Sol.* 26:2] And I will recite his holy ode [*or* 'song'],
> because my heart is with him.
> [3] For his harp [*kithara*] is in my hand,
> and the odes [*or* 'songs'] of his rest shall not be silent. (*OTP*, vol. 2, p. 758)

---

8 *OTP*, vol. 2, pp. 725–34; Schürer/Vermes et al., *History*, vol. 3/2, pp. 787–9.

It is tempting to see the reference to the '*kithara* ... in my hand' in the latter passage as implying that the poet played the instrument while he sang the odes. But the former passage shows that the *kithara* is a metaphor for the Holy Spirit. The latter passage extends the metaphor by saying that the *kithara* is 'in [the poet's] hand'; in other words, the Holy Spirit (traditionally seen in Christianity as a medium of the Deity's creative energy) is available to the poet to use in his praise of the Lord. The sense of the beginning of the last verse quoted above should probably be something along the lines of: 'For the Holy Spirit is mine'.[9]

At some time towards the end of the first decade of the second century, Ignatius (*c*.35–*c*.107), bishop of Syrian Antioch, was arrested by the Romans for professing Christianity, and was sentenced to death by wild animals in the amphitheatre in Rome. On his journey from Antioch to his martyrdom Ignatius wrote pastoral letters to the principal Christian communities in Asia Minor as well as one to the Christian community in Rome and one to his colleague Polycarp, bishop of Smyrna. Musical references occur in four of the seven genuine Ignatian letters: those to the Ephesians, the Magnesians, the Romans and the Philadelphians.[10] In two places Ignatius uses the image of a lyre with tuned strings as a simile for unanimity. In *To the Ephesians* 4:1 he says that the Ephesian Christians are 'attuned' (*sunērmostai*) to their bishop as are the 'strings to the lyre' (*chordai kithara*); and similarly in *To the Philadelphians* 1:2 he writes that the bishop of Philadelphia is 'attuned [*suneuruthmistai*] to the commandments [of God] like a lyre [*kithara*] to the strings [*chordais*]'. These poetic expressions do not have to imply that the lyre was played at Christian gatherings in these places. Ignatius is using images he knows are familiar to his readers, images they had carried with them from the pagan rites of Greco-Roman religious culture.

Pseudo-Justin, in his *Hortatory Address to the Greeks*, written at around the middle of the second century, illustrates by means of a simile how Divine revelation operated through the prophets: he writes of God 'coming down from heaven like a plectrum and using ... just men as an instrument like the cithara or lyre'.[11]

The references to instruments cited so far have been figurative. There are also several concrete references, even though some occur as poetry. Among them is a passage from towards the end of the second century, which contrasts the styles of Christian and non-Christian worship in Rome at that time through

---

[9]   Compare the translation of *Odes Sol.* 14:7–8 and 26:1–3 in *MECL*, pp. 23–24, nos. 34, 36.

[10]   The three remaining genuine letters of Ignatius of Antioch are those to the Trallians, the Smyrnaeans, and Polycarp. Eight additional letters ascribed to him are late fourth-century forgeries. For a comprehensive survey of the historical, textual and theological background to the Ignatian letters, and an edition of their Greek text with parallel English translation, see Bart D. Ehrman, trans. and ed., *The Apostolic Fathers*, 2 vols (Cambridge MA: 2003), vol. 1, pp. 203–321.

[11]   *MECL*, p. 21, no. 28.

the medium of a rhetorical device which says how the Christians did not behave, and lists the instruments they did not play. The pertinent passage occurs in book 8 of the *Sibylline Oracles*, which falls within a substantial Christian section of this otherwise Jewish work, and which was written in Rome in about 180 CE or a little earlier:[12]

> [*Sib. Or.*, book 8, line 113] They [the Christians] pour no blood on altars in sacrificial libations,
> The tympanum sounds not nor does the cymbal,
> [115] Nor does the much pierced aulos with its frenzied voice,
> Nor the syrinx, bearing the likeness of a crooked serpent,
> Nor the trumpet, barbarous sounding herald of wars;
> Neither are there drunkards in lawless carousals or in dances,
> Nor the sound of the cithara, nor a wicked contrivance [a wooden clapper?];
> [120] Nor is there strife, nor manifold wrath, nor a sword
> Among the dead, but a new era for all. (*MECL*, p. 26, no. 39)

Inevitably, the use of this literary device makes for uncertainty about how the passage should be interpreted. Are readers intended to infer that no musical instruments had a place in Christian worship? In view of the apparent comprehensiveness of the list of instruments not played by Christians, the answer should probably be yes.

Other important concrete references to instruments occur in Clement of Alexandria's *The Instructor*. The following appears among the instructions given there in Chapter 4 of book 2 as to how Christians should conduct themselves at banquets:

> [Clement of Alexandria, *The Instructor*, book 2, 4] Let carousing be absent from our [the Christians'] rational enjoyment, and also foolish vigils which revel in drunkenness ... Let lust, intoxication and irrational passions be far removed from our native choir ... The irregular movements of auloi, psalteries, choruses, dances, Egyptian clappers (κροτάλοις[13]) and other such playthings become altogether indecent and uncouth, especially when joined by beating cymbals and tympana and accompanied by the noisy instruments of deception. Such a symposium, it seems to me, becomes nothing but a theatre of drunkenness ... Let the syrinx be assigned to shepherds and the aulos to superstitious men who are obsessed by idolatry. In truth these instruments are to be banished from the sober symposium; they are less suitable for men than for beasts and the bestial portion of mankind. For we are told that deer are lured by the syrinx and led by its melody into the traps when stalked by huntsmen. And when

---

[12]   *OTP*, vol. 2, pp. 415–29.
[13]   Transliteration: *krotalois*.

mares are being foaled, a sort of nuptial song is played on the aulos; musicians have called it the *hypothoron*. (MECL, p. 32, no. 51)

Christians should not play these instruments because of the instruments' associations with superstition and licentious living.

A few lines later, Clement elaborates on the same theme and in doing so includes remarks about the association of musical instruments with war, pointing out that Christians, being pacifists, have no use for such instruments:

[Clement of Alexandria, *The Instructor*, book 2, 4] For man, in truth, is an instrument of peace, while others, if one investigates them, he will find to be instruments of aggression, either inflaming the passions, enkindling lust, or stirring up wrath. The Etruscans, certainly, make use of the trumpet in their wars, the Arcadians the syrinx, the Sicilians the pektis, the Cretans the lyre, the Lacedaemonians the aulos, the Thracians the horn (κέρατι[14]), the Egyptians the tympanum and the Arabians the cymbal. We [Christians], however, make use of but one instrument, the word of peace alone by which we honour God, and no longer the ancient psaltery, nor the trumpet, the tympanum and the aulos, as was the custom among those expert in war and those scornful of the fear of God who employed string instruments in their festive gatherings, as if to arouse their remissness of spirit through such rhythms. But let our geniality in drinking be twofold according to the Law: for if you love the Lord your God and then your neighbour, you should be genial first to God in thanksgiving and psalmody and secondly to your neighbour in dignified friendship. (MECL, p. 33, no. 53)

Clement of Alexandria was not alone in expressing a hostile attitude to the use of musical instruments by Christians. Many of the church fathers inveighed against instruments at one time or another, presumably to warn their readers that because of the dubious associations the instruments had, playing them would both bring Christianity into bad repute and lead to the moral degeneration and spiritual perdition of adherents. Hostile references were to become noticeably more frequent with the passage of time.

A passage containing several examples of allegory and metaphor, occurring between the last two quoted, sums up not only Clement of Alexandria's, but the whole of orthodox early Christianity's attitude to musical instruments (Clement's quotations are from Psalm 150):

[Clement of Alexandria, *The Instructor*, book 2, 4] The Spirit, distinguishing the divine liturgy from this sort of revelry [the carousals referred to in the passage quoted earlier], sings: 'Praise him with the sound of the trumpet',

---

[14]   Transliteration: *kerati*.

and indeed he will raise the dead with the sound of the trumpet.[15] 'Praise him on the psaltery', for the tongue is the psaltery of the Lord. 'And praise him on the cithara', let the cithara be taken to mean the mouth, played by the Spirit as if by a plectrum. 'Praise him with tympanum and chorus' refers to the Church meditating on the resurrection of the flesh in the surrounding membrane. 'Praise him on strings and the instruments' refers to our body as an instrument and its sinews as strings from which it derives its harmonious tension, and when strummed by the Spirit gives off human notes. 'Praise him on the clangourous cymbals' speaks of the tongue as the cymbal of the mouth which sounds as the lips are moved. (*MECL*, pp. 32–3, no. 52)

The early Christian attitude to musical instruments thus seems to have been that the characteristics of the biblical instruments could be used allegorically and metaphorically in exegesis, homily and moral instruction, for purposes of edification. However, Christians should not play the instruments because in the contemporary world such instruments were associated with paganism, moral degeneration and war. For these reasons, it seems, early Christian music was entirely vocal.

Early Christian Song in its Setting

The First and Early Second Centuries

The New Testament provides the earliest evidence of singing by Christians. It contains six pertinent references, one of which is direct, the remainder of which are either prescriptive or idealistic. The direct reference occurs in Acts 16:25 in the account of an episode in which the two early Christian missionaries Paul and Silas were involved. The immediately preceding narrative relates that they were in Macedonian Philippi where their missionary activities had begun to stir up the people (they were Jews in a Roman colony). They were charged with disturbing the peace, flogged and put in prison. The narrative continues:

> [Acts 16:25] And about midnight [when] Paul and Silas [were] praying [*proseuchomenoi*] in a hymn [*humnoun*] to God, the prisoners listened to them.[16]

Some translations have the two missionaries singing 'psalms', but the Greek does not specify what type of religious text was sung.

---

[15]   In his *Exhortation to the Heathen*, 11. 6:3, Clement of Alexandria allegorizes the trumpet in a Christian context thus: 'The trumpet of Christ is his Gospel: he has blown it and we have heard' (*MECL*, p. 31, no. 49).

[16]   My translation.

The remaining references occur in letters. First, from the earlier of the two letters to the Corinthians, are two passages from a section pleading for intelligibility of utterance in worship so that worship can be edifying:

[1 Cor. 14:15] What should I do then? I will pray with the spirit, but I will pray with the mind also; I will sing praise [*psalō*] with the spirit, but I will sing praise [*psalō*] with the mind also.

And:

[1 Cor. 14:26] What should be done then, my friends [*adelphoi* 'brothers']? When you come together, each one has a hymn [*psalmon*], a lesson, a revelation, a tongue, or an interpretation. Let all things be done for building up.

Probably the two most famous New Testament passages about music among the early Christians are Ephesians 5:19 and Colossians 3:16. The first of these is quoted here with its surrounding verses:

[Eph 5:18] Do not get drunk with wine, for that is debauchery; but be filled with the Spirit, [19] as you sing [*lalountes* 'uttering'] psalms [*psalmois*] and hymns [*humnois*] and spiritual [*pneumatikais*][17] songs [*ōdais*] among yourselves, singing [*adontes*] and making melody [*psallontes* 'praising'] to the Lord in your hearts, [20] giving thanks to God the Father at all times and for everything in the name of our Lord Jesus Christ.

The second has:

[Col. 3:16] Let the word of Christ[18] dwell in you abundantly, in all wisdom teaching and admonishing each other, in psalms [*psalmois*], hymns [*humnois*] [and] spiritual [*pneumatikais*] songs [*ōdais*] with grace singing [*adontes*] in your hearts to God.[19]

Finally, the author of the Letter of James offers the following advice to his readers:

[Jas. 5:13] Are any among you suffering? They should pray. Are any cheerful? They should sing songs of praise [*psalletō*].

---

[17] The word *pneumatikais* 'spiritual' is not present in the earliest extant MS (a papyrus of *c.*200 CE), nor in a number of other important early MSS, but it is present in the majority of sources: see Nestle–Aland.

[18] 'of Christ': other ancient MSS have 'of God' or 'of the Lord' (NRSV margin).

[19] My translation.

Outside the New Testament, the earliest references to Christian song date from around the beginning of the second century. There are four references in the *Odes of Solomon*. These, though direct, are somewhat idealistic in character. *Ode* 7:22–23 refers to 'the Singers' who 'offer their songs' to the 'grace of the Lord', suggesting that singers could constitute a discrete group – a choir – within the worshipping community.[20] If this is indeed a reference to a choir, it is the earliest known reference to choral song (as opposed to collective singing) in a Christian context. General collective song is implied in *Ode* 41:1–2.[21] A reference to 'the composition of his [God's] odes' in *Ode* 36:2[22] is noteworthy for its apparent implication that the *Odes of Solomon* (or at any rate some of the items in the extant collection) were newly composed. The 'composition of his odes' probably refers to the texts; the music is likely to have consisted of pre-existent melodic formulas.

Solo song is implied in *Ode* 16:1–2 where the poet says his task is 'the psalm of the Lord' and that because of his love for the Lord he will 'sing unto him'.[23]

There is one further reference to song in the *Odes of Solomon*, but it is more poetic or symbolic than concrete. It occurs at *Odes of Solomon* 24:1–2 in the personification of a dove in an allusion to Jesus' baptism: 'The dove fluttered over the head of our Lord Messiah, because he was her Head. And she sang over him, and her voice was heard'.[24]

In five places in his genuine letters, Ignatius of Antioch uses images drawn from vocal music. In *To the Magnesians* 1:2, in a veiled reference to his captivity and imminent death, he writes: 'by the bonds I bear I sing [*adō*] the praises of the churches'. This is the closest Ignatius comes to a direct statement about the use of music. Otherwise he uses the images of the chorus and unison song as metaphors of unanimity. In *To the Ephesians* 4:1, in the continuation of a passage referred to above,[25] he says that 'Jesus Christ is sung [*adetai*] in your [the Ephesians'] harmony [*homonoia*] and symphonic [*sumphōnō*] love,' and he goes on to encourage the Ephesians in the following terms:

> [Ign. *Eph.* 4:2] And each of you should join the chorus [*choros*], that by being symphonic in your harmony, taking up God's pitch [*chrōma theou*][26] in unison [*en henotēti*], you may sing [*adēte*] in one voice … (in *The Apostolic Fathers*, trans. Ehrman, vol. 1, pp. 222, 223)

In *To the Ephesians* 5:1 Ignatius writes that he counts the Ephesians fortunate because they are 'mingled together with him [their bishop] as the church is

---

[20]   *OTP*, vol. 2, p. 741.

[21]   Ibid., p. 769.

[22]   Ibid., p. 765.

[23]   Ibid., p. 749.

[24]   Ibid., p. 757.

[25]   See text following n. 10.

[26]   *MECL*, p. 19, no. 21, has 'godly strain'.

mingled with Jesus Christ and Jesus Christ with the Father, so that all things may be symphonic [*sumphōna*] in unison [*en henotēti*]'. Later in the same letter he refers to the stars, the sun and the moon forming 'a chorus [*choros*] to that star [Jesus]' (19:2), and in *To the Romans* 2:2 he begs his readers: 'grant me nothing more than to be poured out as a libation to God while there is still an altar at hand, that by becoming a chorus [*choros*] in love [*agapē*], you may sing forth [*asēte*] to the Father in Jesus Christ'. To what extent these metaphors reflect actual musical practice among Christians in Asia Minor at that time is difficult to know. It is highly likely that there was corporate song at their gatherings, but whether it would have been performed by a specially trained choir or by all the assembled people together is not known. Judging from the metaphors, Ignatius has the whole assembled company in mind; but there is always the possibility that the metaphors are not based on the current practice in worship.

From slightly later, a letter of Pliny the Younger to the Roman Emperor Trajan provides a description of early Christian song in Asia Minor. Pliny's letter dates from 111–112 CE when he was governor of the provinces of Bithynia and Pontus. It contains his report of a statement made by certain Christians of Bithynia who were questioned about their religious customs. The pertinent passage reads:

> [Pliny the Younger, *Letters*, book 10, 96:7] They [the interrogated Bithynian Christians] affirmed, however, that this was the extent of their fault or error, that they were wont to assemble on a set day before dawn and to sing a hymn among themselves (*carmenque ... dicere secum invicem*) to the Christ, as to a god, and that they pledged themselves by vow not to [commit] some crime, but that they would commit neither fraud, nor theft, nor adultery, nor betray their word, nor deny a trust when summoned; after which it was their custom to separate and to come together again later to take food – ordinary and harmless food, however. (*MECL*, p. 27, no. 41)

The word '*carmen*' is a generic term for 'song'; and the phrase '*carmen dicere*' means 'to utter a song'. The phrase '*secum invicem*' has sometimes in the past been regarded as signifying antiphonal song, or at least, and more judiciously, some sort of alternation in the singing.[27] But this is to read more into the Latin than it warrants. According to the lexicons '*invicem*' means 'by turns' or 'in turn', and while Pliny's Bithynian Christians might well have sung responsively, '*secum invicem*' conveys nothing more explicit than 'in turn among themselves'.

[27] Antiphony: for example, Gustav Reese, *Music in the Middle Ages* (New York, 1940), p. 60; Paul Henry Lang, *Music in Western Civilisation* (New York, 1941), p. 43; Henry Bettenson (ed.), *Documents of the Christian Church*, 2nd edn (London, 1963, repr. 1967), p. 4; Craig A. Evans, 'The Life and Teaching of Jesus and the Rise of Christianity', in J.W. Rogerson and Judith M. Lieu (eds), *The Oxford Handbook of Biblical Studies* (New York, 2006), p. 314. Alternation: for example, Betty Radice (trans.), *The Letters of the Younger Pliny* (Harmondsworth, 1963), p. 294.

Nevertheless, the report in Pliny the Younger's letter provides an indication of the place of singing in the order of worship. It also shows that all the assembled Christians participated in the singing.

The Later Second and Early Third Centuries

As the second century progresses there emerge more passages which show in varying degrees of detail how and for what purpose song was used in worship. A passage in the first *Apology* of Justin Martyr (*c.*100–165), written probably in Rome in about 150 CE, contrasts Christian worship with pagan worship and earlier Jewish worship at the Temple, saying that Christian worship consists not in 'the consumption by fire of those things created by him [God] for our nourishment', but in 'the use of them by ourselves and those in need, while in gratitude to him we offer solemn prayers and hymns for his creation and for all things leading to good health'.[28]

Approximately a decade later, a passage in the *Discourse to the Greeks* by Tatian (flourished *c.*160) expresses a personal aversion to the Greek chorus, particularly when the motions of the conductor are intrusive and distracting. The passage is one of the few in the early Christian period to make its point by means of negative comments about song. Tatian writes: 'I do not wish to gape at many singers nor do I care to look benignly upon a man who is nodding and motioning in an unnatural way'.[29] The quotation seems to imply that Christian song was not rendered in that manner.

Later in the century, a similarly informative contrast as that in the first chapter of Justin Martyr's first *Apology* is made in book 8 of the *Sibylline Oracles*:

> [*Sib. Or.*, book 8, line 487] Never may we [Christians] approach the temple sanctuaries,
> Nor pour libations to images, nor honour them with vows,
> Nor with the delightful fragrances of flowers, nor the glow
> [490] Of torches, nor yet adorn them with votive offerings;
> Nor send up flames with incense smoke at the altar;
> Nor pour the blood of slain sheep upon the libations of sacrificial bulls,
> Glad to pay ransom as appeasement for earthly deliverance;
> Nor with reeking smoke from the flesh devouring fire,
> [495] And foul vapours pollute the bright light of the ether.
> But rejoicing with pure heart and cheerful spirit,
> With abundant love and generous hands,
> With propitiary psalms and chants beseeming God,
> we are called upon to hymn thee, immortal and faithful
> [500] God, creator of all and understanding all. (*MECL*, p. 26, no. 40)

---

[28]   Justin, *First Apology*, 1:13; *MECL*, p. 20, no. 24.
[29]   Tatian, *Discourse to the Greeks* 22; *MECL*, p. 22, no. 30.

Here, readers are reminded in poetic terms that Christianity is a non-sacrificial religion; they learn that among Christians 'psalms and chants' are propitiatory, and that to hymn God is regarded as a Divine command.

During the period from the end of the second century to the early decades of the third, sources begin to give a much clearer picture of how singing fitted into Christian worship. The picture is especially clear with regard to two types of gathering: the *agapē* and the Eucharist. An *agapē* was a 'love feast' (*agapē* means 'sibling love'), a social gathering of the local Christian community at which there was a simple meal of bread and wine. It was a Christian form of banquet and was in part a commemoration of the last meal eaten by Jesus and his disciples together, the Last Supper.[30] In contrast to the banquets of contemporary secular society and pagan religions, the food and drink were consumed only in moderate quantities, and the participants conducted themselves with sobriety and in a spirit of mutual respect. The proceedings seem often to have concluded with a form of communal religious devotion. The earliest description of what seems to be an *agapē* with singing occurs in chapter 9 of the apocryphal *Acts of Paul*, a work dating from the end of second century CE.[31] This relates that on the day before Paul's departure from Corinth on his journey to Rome, the local Christian community was gathered together. A woman named Myrta became possessed by the Spirit of God, and she began to speak. Then the Spirit left her and she was quiet. The narrative continues:

> [*Acts Paul* 9] And immediately, when the Spirit that was in Myrta was at peace, each one took of the bread and feasted according to custom ... amid the singing of psalms of David and of hymns. (*NTA*, vol. 2, p. 258)

The narrative is notable for its specific mention of the singing of psalms of David at a Christian gathering – the earliest such mention to have been preserved.

Another significant passage from around the same time occurs in chapter 39 of Tertullian's *Apology*.[32] The passage comes at the end of a description of an *agapē*, and describes how the *agapē* concludes:

> [Tertullian, *Apol.* 39:18] After the washing of hands [after the meal] and the lighting of lamps (*lumina*), each is urged to come into the middle and sing to God, either from the sacred scriptures or from his own invention (*de proprio ingenio*). In this way is the manner of his drinking tested. Similarly the banquet (*conuiuium*) is brought to a close with prayer. (*MECL*, p. 43, no. 74)

Here the type of singing is not specified, but singing 'from the sacred scriptures' most likely implies psalms from the book of Psalms as well as, possibly, other

---

[30]   The NT Last Supper narrative occurs at Matt. 26:20–30 and parallels.

[31]   *NTA*, vol. 2, p. 22.

[32]   Tertullian (*c.*160–*c.*220) spent all his life in the city of Carthage in North Africa.

lyrical Old Testament texts such as the Song of the Sea. It is also possible that the phrase 'the sacred scriptures' included the New Testament, in which case the lyrical texts in Luke 1 and 2 and the exclamations in Revelation would be obvious candidates. The singing of original material is also permitted (compare *Odes Sol.* 36:2; 41:16). The circumstances bear a strong resemblance to those of the pre-dinner singing of the Therapeutai, where the president 'sings a hymn ... to God, either a new one of his own composition or an old one by poets of an earlier day,' and then all the others who are present follow suit in turn (Philo, *On the Contemplative Life*, 10 (80); herein Chapter 5).

There is a further illuminating description of the conclusion of an *agapē* in the *Apostolic Tradition* (to the extent that the description may be considered relevant to the late second or early third century):[33]

> [*Apos. Trad.* 25] And let them arise therefore after supper and pray; let the boys sing psalms, the virgins also. And afterwards let the deacon, as he takes the mingled chalice [cup] of oblation, say a psalm from those in which Alleluia is written. And afterwards, if the presbyter so orders, again from these psalms. And after the bishop has offered the chalice, let him say a psalm from those appropriate to the chalice – always one with Alleluia, which all say. When they recite the psalms, let all say Alleluia, which means, 'We praise him who is God; glory and praise to him who created the entire world through his work alone.' And when the psalm is finished let him bless the chalice and give of its fragments to all the faithful.[34] (*MECL*, p. 47, no. 89)

This passage shows not only what was sung and when, but also how the singing was performed. The boys and the girls (the 'virgins') would probably have sung in separate groups. The deacon alone sang one or more psalms 'from those in which Alleluia is written'. The passage insists that 'Alleluia' was to be sung by all; the manner of performance was thus broadly similar to that of the Hallel at the Jewish domestic Passover meal as reported in contemporaneous Jewish sources (see Chapter 5). It is possible that 'a psalm from those in which Alleluia is written' implies one of the Hallel psalms. The identity of 'a psalm from those appropriate to the chalice – always one with Alleluia' is less certain. Only Psalm 116 of the Hallel contains wording that could be considered appropriate to the chalice and at the same time has 'Alleluia' (Ps. 116:13: 'I raise the cup of deliverance and invoke the name of the LORD'). The free application of an 'Alleluia' refrain to a psalm otherwise without this word, but which speaks of God's provision of sustenance for humankind, may also have been a possibility.

---

[33]   On the *Apos. Trad.*, see Chapter 1, text between nn. 51 and 53.

[34]   The text of *Apos. Trad.* 25 is known only from a version in Ethiopic, which has been translated from a lost Arabic version which in turn may have been translated from a Greek original: see Geoffrey J. Cuming, *Hippolytus: A Text for Students*, 2nd edn (Bramcote, 1987), p. 24.

Compared with the portion of the *agapē* described by Tertullian in chapter 39 of his *Apology*, the proceedings are noticeably more formal. Clergy have a predominant role, the sung material is confined to items from Scripture (there is no opening for singing own compositions), and although there is apparently some room for choice, it is limited to items from the book of Psalms – possibly even to items from the Hallel. The differences may reflect variations of practice between Eastern and Western (in this case North African) Christianity.

Lastly, Tertullian again, in his *On the Soul* (written probably between 208 and 212 CE), provides an insight into the place of singing at the Eucharist. The pertinent passage is concerned with the first part of the Eucharistic rite, the Liturgy of the Word (which precedes the distribution of the bread and wine of Communion), and with a woman who demonstrates extraordinary gifts. Tertullian writes:

> [Tertullian, *On the Soul* 9:4] There is among us today a sister favoured with gifts of revelation which she experiences through an ecstasy of the spirit during the Sunday liturgy. She converses with angels, at one time even with the Lord [Jesus]; she sees and hears mysteries, reads the hearts of people and applies remedies to those who need them. The material for her visions is supplied as the scriptures are read (*leguntur*), psalms (*psalmi*) are sung (*canuntur*), the homily delivered and prayers are offered. (*MECL*, 45, no. 82)

The salient part of this quotation is the last sentence. The phrase '[as the] psalms are sung', used in contrast to 'as the scriptures are read', leaves little doubt that some form of more or less musical utterance is to be understood here. And given that the main elements in the later, standardized form of the Liturgy of the Word in Western Christendom were Scripture reading with the interspersed singing of biblical psalms, and homily, in that order, it is reasonable to suppose that the *psalmi* were psalms from the Psalter. However, this has not been the opinion of all recent commentators. Tertullian was a Montanist, and this fact led James McKinnon to express serious doubts about two aspects of this passage. One is its relevance to mainstream Christianity: Montanism, with its strong emphasis on the ecstatic utterance of personal spiritual revelation, was regarded as a heretical doctrine. The other is the nature of the 'psalms' it says were sung: they may have been non-biblical, freely composed inspired utterances.[35]

James McKinnon considered this passage in his search for the origin of the Christian practice of singing a Gradual psalm. In the developed form of the Christian Eucharist, the Gradual psalm is a biblical psalm sung between Scripture readings during the Liturgy of the Word. McKinnon's doubts about the passage caused him to reject it as evidence for the existence of the Gradual in the Christian Church already at the beginning of the third century, a position

---

[35] James W. McKinnon, 'The Fourth-Century Origin of the Gradual', *EMH*, 7 (1987): 96–7.

to which Paul Bradshaw subsequently added his support.[36] Nevertheless, recent studies have shown that by the time of Tertullian, Montanism was not as extreme – particularly in the West – as it had been in its early days in Asia Minor in the mid-second century.[37] In this light, there seems no need for McKinnon to have been sceptical about *On the Soul* 9:4 as a witness to early Christian practice. While the evidence the passage provides has, admittedly, no contemporary corroboration, it does emanate from an important centre for non-Roman Latin Christianity. It shows the presence of sung 'psalms' in close liturgical proximity to Scripture readings during the Liturgy of the Word of the Eucharist. Furthermore, the form of the verbs which Tertullian uses for utterance of the liturgical items he lists ('are read ... are sung') implies that what he describes was customary in the church in Carthage, and not an isolated occurrence. Whatever the 'psalms' may have been (and given the new light provided by recent research there is no need to be coy about the likelihood that they were biblical psalms), their listing immediately after the Scripture readings in Tertullian's description suggests an embryo Gradual, perhaps in multiple form since readings and psalms are referred to in the plural.

What Did the Earliest Christians Sing?

The question of what the earliest Christians sang in their religious observances is best approached by considering the terminology employed for items which may have been sung and the religious poetic texts which arguably may have been sung in contexts of devotion and worship.

Terminology

Early Christian writings make frequent use of the Greek terms *psalmos*, *humnos* and *ōdē*, and their Latin equivalents *psalmus*, *hymnus* and *carmen* to refer to items uttered in devotion and worship. In Christian literature of the first and early second centuries these terms appear typically without explanation and without informative contexts. In these circumstances they elude individual definition and therefore cannot be differentiated. It is indeed by no means certain that Christians of the time made more than nominal distinctions between them: the presence of *psalmos*, *humnos* and *ōdē* together in Ephesians 5:19 and Colossians 3:16 suggests that they could be used as more or less interchangeable general terms. Unqualified references to 'psalms', 'hymns'

[36] Paul F. Bradshaw, *The Search for the Origins of Christian Worship: Sources and Methods for the Study of Early Liturgy*, 2nd edn (New York and London, 2002), p. 123.

[37] See, for example, Christine Trevett, 'Montanism', in Philip F. Esler (ed.), *The Early Christian World*, 2 vols (London and New York, 2000), pp. 929–51; Antti Marjonen and Petri Luomanen (eds), *A Companion to Second-Century Christian 'Heretics'* (Leiden, 2005).

and 'songs' can therefore be understood only in the general sense of religious poetic texts susceptible of being sung.[38]

From the later second century onwards, an increasing number of sources provide fuller information about what was sung. This is clearly illustrated by the quotations from Christian literature of this period presented and discussed above. The *Acts of Paul*, for example, refers specifically to 'the singing of psalms of David', Tertullian reports the singing of what were probably biblical psalms in the liturgy of the Carthaginian church, and the *Apostolic Tradition* refers to 'psalms ... in which Alleluia is written', which leaves no doubt that biblical psalms are meant, perhaps the Hallel. Nevertheless, the caveat about unqualified references to 'psalms', 'hymns' and 'songs' still applies at this time, as it does throughout the remainder of antiquity.

Religious Poetic Material in Early Christian Literature

The earliest examples of religious poetry in Christian literature are to be found in the New Testament. They may be regarded as consisting of four main types:

1. Direct quotations (sometimes composite) from Jewish Scripture (generally in the LXX version).
2. Altered quotations from Jewish Scripture, the alterations sometimes providing a Christian slant to the texts.
3. Material dependent on Jewish models, and often containing allusions to Jewish biblical or post-biblical literature, and
4. Christian material without any obvious Jewish dependence.

Insofar as all poetic material from Mediterranean and Near-Eastern cultures in antiquity was susceptible of being sung, the question here is whether any of the poetic material in the New Testament is likely to have been used in early Christian worship up to and including the time when each of the pertinent New Testament books was composed. The answer will depend to a large extent on the nature of the poetic material and on how this material is used in the New Testament.

Poetic material is used in three main ways in the New Testament: as an element in theological discourse, as an element intrinsic to narrative and as an element occurring in conjunction with narrative but extrinsic to it. The first involves mainly material of type 1 of the four types listed above, drawn mostly from the Prophets and Psalms. It normally occurs as proof texts, as precepts for right conduct or as bases for exegesis. The quotations are often short and sometimes fragmentary since New Testament authors quote only the minimum

---

[38]   See John Arthur Smith, 'First-Century Christian Singing and its Relationship to Contemporary Jewish Religious Song', *M&L*, 75 (1994): 1–15, for a detailed examination of the use of these terms in early Christian literature.

of text necessary to support their points. Longer and sometimes self-contained passages are also to be found, although passages as long as the quotations from Joel 3:1–5a in Acts 2:17–21, and from Psalm 16:8–11 in Acts 2:25–28, are exceptional. This intellectualized use of poetic material from the Jewish Scriptures militates against the idea that the New Testament authors were quoting material that was familiar from its use in Christian worship. Material from the Jewish scriptural tradition would have been familiar, of course, but from the Temple, the synagogues and private devotion among Jews rather than from Christian gatherings.

Two items of type 4 of those listed above are also used in theological discourse. One is the inspiring command and promise in the New Testament, Ephesians 5:14b: 'Sleeper, awake! Rise from the dead, and Christ will shine on you.' The other is the summary of belief at 1 Timothy 3:16b: 'He [God] was revealed in flesh, vindicated in spirit, seen by angels, proclaimed among Gentiles, believed in throughout the world, taken up in glory.' These two short passages are noteworthy for being Christian in content (although with echoes of Isaiah 26:19 and 60:1 in the former), self-contained and capable of standing alone, independent of the literary contexts in which they appear. These features are consistent with the idea that the passages could have been imported into the letters from Christian worship, whether worship in Ephesus (the destination of both letters)[39] or in some other place known to the correspondents.

The second mode of use, in which poetic material is intrinsic to narrative, involves mainly material of types 1 and 2 of those listed above. Such material often occurs as acclamations such as, for example, 'Glory to God in the highest heaven, and on earth peace among those whom he favours!' (Luke 2:14) uttered by angels in the narrative of the birth of Jesus, and 'Hosanna to the son of David! Blessed is the one who comes in the name of the Lord!' (Matt. 21:9b), which, according to the New Testament narrative of Jesus' entry into Jerusalem (Matt. 21:6–10), was shouted by the people who went ahead of him. The latter narrative has parallels in Mark 11:7–11 and Luke 19:35–38, which also contain the acclamation but in partly different versions:

> [Mark 11:9b] Hosanna! Blessed is the one who comes in the name of the Lord!
> [10a] Blessed is the coming kingdom of our ancestor David! Hosanna in the highest heaven!
> [Luke 19:38] Blessed is the king who comes in the name of the Lord! Peace in heaven, and glory in the highest heaven!

As may be seen from these quotations, all three versions have the clauses 'blessed is [...] who comes in the name of the Lord' in common. This is a Jewish acclamation taken from Psalm 117(118):26. The exclamation 'hosanna!'

---

[39]   The Ephesian destination of 1 Tim. is implied by 1 Tim. 1:3 where the correspondent, Paul, writes, 'I urge you [Timothy, the addressee of the letter] ... to remain in Ephesus'.

which opens the passages quoted from Matthew and Mark, is a direct Greek transcription (*ōsanna*) of the Hebrew *hôšî'â nā'* in Psalm 118:25.[40]

Also pertinent are the many acclamations in the New Testament book of Revelation. In their narrative contexts they are uttered by heavenly beings in visions of heaven experienced and related by John, the author of the book. The following is a small selection of fairly typical examples:

[Rev. 4:8b] Holy, holy, holy, the Lord God the Almighty, who was and is and is to come.

[Rev. 5:9b] You are worthy to take the scroll and to open its seals, for you were slaughtered and by your blood you ransomed for God saints from every tribe and language and people and nation; [10] you have made them to be a kingdom and priests serving our God, and they will reign on earth.

[Rev. 7:10] Salvation belongs to our God who is seated on the throne, and to the Lamb!

[Rev. 15:3b] Great and amazing are your deeds, Lord God the Almighty! Just and true are your ways, King of the nations! [4] Lord, who will not fear and glorify your name? For you alone are holy. All nations will come and worship before you, for your judgements have been revealed.

Before discussing the acclamations, consideration may be given to the third mode of use, namely that in which poetic material, though occurring in conjunction with narrative is extrinsic to it. This involves exclusively material of type 3 of the four types listed above. The material occurs as set pieces that do not in themselves further the narrative but instead provide theological comment upon it. In its literary context it is put into the mouths of worthy and respected Jewish individuals. It comprises some of the earliest and best-known religious poetry associated with Christianity although none of it actually mentions Jesus or manifests especially Christian themes. The pertinent items are Mary's (or, according to some early manuscripts, Elizabeth's) hymn of praise, 'My soul magnifies the Lord' (Luke 1:46–55), Zechariah's prophecy, 'Blessed be the Lord God of Israel' (Luke 1:68–79), and Simeon's oracle, 'Master, now you are dismissing your servant in peace' (Luke 2:29–32).

Some of the acclamations, and all the set pieces, came to have a fixed place in Christian worship as time went on. Whether they were included in the Christian Scriptures because they were already familiar from use in Christian worship is difficult to determine. The set pieces in Luke 1 and 2, the angelic acclamation of praise in Luke 2, and the acclamations in Revelation are heavily dependent on the Jewish Scriptures.[41] Their presence in the Christian Scriptures suggests that they

---

[40]   At the corresponding place in the LXX (LXX Ps. 117:25) the Greek phrase *sōson dē* 'save now' is a translation of the Hebrew *hôšî'â nā'* in MT Ps. 118:25.

[41]   For quotations from and allusions to Jewish sacred literature in these items, see the marginal apparatus at the respective places in Nestle-Aland. For fuller details, see

are products of Jewish Christianity, if not of Judaism itself. But it is not known whether they were composed especially for the New Testament books in which they appear, or whether they pre-date them, and if they pre-date them, by how long. It is possible that they were used in Christian worship among Jewish Christians prior to their appearance in Luke and Revelation, but this is speculation.

Alternatively, those acclamations and set pieces may have been purely literary compositions unconnected with either song or worship. This reservation applies particularly to the acclamations in the book of Revelation. They occur within the author's descriptions of the fantastic visions of heavenly worship he experienced while he was 'in the spirit' (*en pneumati*, Rev. 1:10; 4:2), that is to say in an ecstatic state or a state of trance, and it is therefore possible that they do not reflect anything at all of actual contemporary Christian worship. The visions contain frequent allusions to features of worship at the Jerusalem Temple, but these are little more than exotic colouring: the Temple had been laid in ruins long before Revelation was written.

In addition to the points made above, it may be noted that two of the acclamations in Revelation are introduced by preambles that announce sung performance. The preamble to Revelation 5:9b–10 (quoted above) has: 'And they sing [*kai adousin*] a new song [*ōdēn kainēn*], saying [*legontes*]' (5:9a), and the preamble to Revelation 15:3b–4 (quoted above) has: 'And they sing [*kai adousin* or *adontas*] the song [*tēn ōdēn*] of Moses, the servant of God, and the song [*kai tēn ōdēn*] of the lamb, saying [*legontes*]' (15:3a). These are the only instances in the New Testament of given texts being mentioned as sung. Elsewhere where singing or song is mentioned, no song texts are supplied, as, for example, in the letters and in Revelation 14:3 where a song is referred to but not quoted: 'And they sing [*kai adousin*] a new song [*ōdēn kainēn*] before the throne'.

Since the acclamations in the book of Revelation were conceived while their author was 'in the spirit', it is tempting to see them – especially the two mentioned as being sung – as examples of the 'spiritual [*pneumatikais*] songs' enjoined on the Ephesians and Colossians, and implicitly on the Corinthians (1 Cor. 14:15, 26). The attractiveness of the idea is enhanced by the fact that the island of Patmos, where the author of Revelation says he received his visions and wrote his apocalypse (Rev. 1:9, 17–19), lies in the same geographical region (western Asia Minor), and was then in the same Roman province (Asia), as Ephesus and Colossae. However, there is nothing in the New Testament that either states or implies a material connection between the 'spiritual songs' of Ephesians and Colossians and the 'in the spirit' acclamations of Revelation. Furthermore, the intellectual coupling of the acclamations in Revelation with the songs in Ephesians and Colossians on account of the respective use of the terms '*en pneumati*' and '*pneumatikais*' is problematic. The Greek phrase *en pneumati* is an idiomatic expression meaning 'in the spirit, in a trance, in a state of ecstasy', whereas *pneumatikais* is a common adjective meaning 'spiritual, of the spirit' or 'religious'. In the book of Revelation,

Smith, 'First-Century Christian Singing': 11.

the former is used to describe its author's state of mind when he experienced visions, but in Ephesians and Colossians the latter expression is used to describe or characterize songs. The two usages have nothing to do with each other; it is a mere coincidence that *pneumati* and *pneumatikais* are derived from the same basic word *pneuma* 'breath, spirit'. It is therefore probably unwarranted to think of the acclamations in Revelation as possible examples of the spiritual songs referred to in Ephesians and Colossians.

The conclusion is that many of the poetic passages in the New Testament could have been quoted from their use in Christian worship. The most likely candidates are the short Christian hymns at Ephesians 5:14b and 1 Timothy 3:16b, the set pieces in Luke 1 and 2, the angelic acclamation of praise in Luke 2, and the acclamations in Revelation. Of course, there can be no certainty that the remaining material quoted on the preceding pages was *not* used in early Christian worship, although it seems unlikely that the poetic passages drawn from the Jewish Scriptures and used to support theological arguments would have been used in that context.

Looking beyond the New Testament, it is possible that Anna's song over her infant daughter Mary, as given in the *Protevangelium of James* 6:2[42] was used in worship among Ebionite Christians. It exhibits features similar to some of those in Mary's hymn in Luke 1:46–55 in the New Testament, but here too, there is neither clue nor concrete information about its possible use in Christian worship.

The position is different where the *Odes of Solomon* (see above) are concerned. Passages such as, 'Let the Singers sing the grace of the Lord Most High, and let them offer their songs,' in *Odes of Solomon* 7:22, and, 'his children shall be acknowledged by him, therefore let us sing by his love,' in *Odes of Solomon* 41:2, suggest that sacred song occurred in the setting of corporate worship. And the passages, '[the Spirit of the Lord] caused me to stand on my feet in the Lord's high place, before his perfection and his glory, where I continued praising (him) by the composition of his odes,' in *Odes of Solomon* 36:2, and, 'A new chant [is] for the Lord from them that love him,' in *Odes of Solomon* 41:16, suggest that new sacred songs ('odes'), such as the ones before the reader, were composed for use in corporate worship. If it is legitimate to link these two ideas, the *Odes of Solomon* contains material which by its wording and context suggests that the *Odes* themselves – or at least some of them – were newly composed sacred songs intended for singing in Christian worship.

---

[42] See Chapter 6.

Chapter 8

Music in Early Christianity, 2: The Later Third and the Fourth Centuries

The third and fourth centuries were a time of rapid expansion for the church. The spread of Christianity into all the lands round the Mediterranean and northward and eastward, brought with it both a large increase in the material wealth of local Christian communities and a gradually more pressing need for an overall form of government. The form of government which evolved was synodical. This required bishops to convene in council to discuss matters of current importance in Christendom, and from the discussions to make decisions on church doctrine, legislation, policy and practice. The decisions were formulated as canons which were then binding on all the Christian communities in the jurisdictions of the attendant bishops. The most important early councils of the Christian church were the First Council of Nicaea (the present city of İznik in Turkey) in 325 and the First Council of Constantinople in 381. Through the canons issued by these and other councils, doctrinal orthodoxy and norms of church practice were established over a wide geographical area.

Some of the conciliar decisions impinged on the music of the church. Four of the so-called Canons of Laodicea, which may have resulted partly from the deliberations of the Council (or Synod) of Laodicea (held in Phrygia Pacatiana in Asia Minor in c.364) and partly from those of another contemporary council,[1] provide relevant illustration. Canon 15 forbids anyone except the properly appointed singers to sing in the church; Canon 17 stipulates that in public services in church psalms are not to be sung consecutively without a break: a reading must intervene between them; Canon 23 says that the readers and singers have no right to wear a stole or to read or sing wearing one; and Canon 59 forbids the reading in church of privately composed psalms or of any material outside the canonical Old and New Testaments.

---

[1]   In addition to having an uncertain origin, the Canons may be no more than headings with brief annotations. For an edition of the Canons of Laodicea, see Périclès-Pierre Joannou, *Fonti*, Fasicolo IX, *Discipline générale antique (IVe-IXe s.)*, vol. 1/2: *Les canons des Synodes Particuliers* (Grottaferrata, Rome, 1962), pp. 130–55 (see under 'Canons of Laodicea' in the Bibliography). See also *The Oxford Dictionary of the Christian Church*, ed. F.L. Cross and A.E. Livingstone (New York, 1997), s.v. 'Canons of Laodicea'.

The third and fourth centuries also saw the rise of Christian monasticism.[2] This movement, in which men and women chose to withdraw from the ordinary world and live as ascetics, devoting themselves to prayer, contemplation and meditation, stood in marked contrast to the material advancement of the church at large.

Early Christian monasticism was basically of three types: anchoritic, in which anchorites or hermits lived alone in small, isolated, single-room dwellings called cells; coenobitic, in which many religious lived together in a house – monastery or convent – where each coenobite had his or her own room or cell; and a hybrid type in which anchorites lived in cells loosely grouped into a 'village' (sometimes called a 'laura'), and came together for collective devotions once or twice a week. Monasticism developed first in the lands around the eastern end of the Mediterranean. Desert areas were the most sought-after since the majority of religious withdrew from the world at large not only by shutting themselves out of it but also by physically distancing themselves from it. The warmth of a desert climate allowed people to live with only the bare minimum of material possessions. Nevertheless, urban monasticism became increasingly common. The greatest concentration of monastic communities was in the Nile delta of Lower Egypt and along the western bank of the Nile in Upper Egypt. By the end of the fourth century monasticism had become established in the West as well as the East, and in cities as well as in deserted areas away from them. Western monasticism was, however, primarily urban.

Despite the occasionally violent persecution of Christians, the faith survived and the number of its adherents increased rapidly. With this came a gradually more clearly evident number of divergent shades of belief. It was during this period that the large heretical movements, such as Arianism and Montanism, flourished, and gnostic cults became widespread.

Private Devotion and Music

From the earliest days of Christianity, prayer was an important element in the religious life of believers. For the Christians who were Jewish by upbringing, this was natural. Devout Jews would recite the Shema in the morning and the evening, and the Eighteen Benedictions (in full or shortened form) in the morning, the middle of the day and the evening.[3] In the New Testament, Acts 3:1 refers to 'the hour of prayer, three o'clock in the afternoon [the ninth hour of the day]', and Acts 10:30 reports a Jewish proselyte as saying, 'at this very hour, at three o'clock, I was praying in my house ...'. In addition, prayer before, during and after meals,

[2]   For detailed background and discussion, see Joseph Dyer, 'The Desert, the City and Psalmody in the Late Fourth Century', in Sean Gallagher, James Haar et al. (eds), *Western Plainchant in the First Millennium: Studies in the Medieval Liturgy and its Music* (Aldershot, 2003), pp. 11–43.
[3]   See the discussions in *m. Ber.* 1:1–4:3.

over produce, and on beginning and completing daily tasks was customary.[4] These prayers might have been recited privately or in the company of others.

In the Old Testament, the book of Psalms contains occasional references to prayer or praying, which also influenced the times and nature of Christian private devotion. Prayer is mentioned as occurring 'day and night' (Ps. 1:2), 'at daybreak' (Ps. 5:4), 'by/at night' (Pss 22:3(2); 42:9(8)), 'at midnight' (Ps. 119:62), 'before dawn' (Ps. 119:147), 'seven times a day' (Ps. 119:164), and as 'an offering of incense ... as an evening sacrifice' (Ps. 141:2). The book of Daniel relates that its eponymous hero, exiled in Persia, 'went to his house ... and three times a day he knelt down, prayed, and made confession to his God, as he had always done' (Dan. 6:11; JPS *Tanakh*).

Among the earliest Christians, prayer took place ideally in solitude[5] or in small groups,[6] and constantly.[7] The times of prayer were most usually in the morning and at night.[8] Prayer might consist of religious song, supplication and thanksgiving,[9] and it was not exclusive to men (Acts 1:14).

It is reasonable to assume that these features continued to be present in the private devotional life of Christians after the New Testament period. Nevertheless it is not until the beginning of the third century that concrete information on this point emerges. The earliest is provided by Tertullian who lived and worked all his life in Carthage, the centre of Latin-speaking North Africa. In Chapter 25 of his book *On Prayer* (written *c.*200),[10] Tertullian recommends five times of prayer each day: at the third, sixth and ninth hours, and at dawn and dusk.[11] In Chapter 27 of the same book he witnesses to psalms as accepted elements of ordinary prayer:

> The more exacting in their prayer are accustomed to add to their prayers an Alleluia and that sort of psalm in which those present respond with the closing verses (*clausulis respondeant*). (*MECL*, p. 44, no. 78)

This would allow for the possibility of responsive performance if more than one person were present. Perhaps it was just such a possibility that influenced Tertullian to express his ideal of the Christian married couple in these metaphorical terms: 'Psalms and hymns sound between the two of them (*sonant inter duos psalmi et hymni*), and they challenge each other to see who better sings

---

4   See the discussions in *m. Ber.* 4:2, 6:1–9:4.

5   Matt. 4:1–11; 6:6; 14:23; 26:36–44; Mark 1:35; Luke 6:12; 9:18 11:1.

6   Luke 9:28; Acts 1:14; 16:25.

7   Luke 18:1; Acts 1:14; Eph. 6:18; 1 Thess. 7:17.

8   Acts 16:25; 1 Tim. 5:5.

9   Acts 16:25; Eph. 6:18; Phil. 4:4–6.

10   Primary sources for this and other early literature cited in this chapter are listed in the Bibliography.

11   Robert Taft, *The Liturgy of the Hours in East and West*, 2nd rev. edn (Collegeville MN, 1993), pp. 17–18.

to the Lord'.[12] It is doubtful whether any distinction should be drawn between the *psalmi* and *hymni*: the terms are probably used here in a general sense. But this passage, taken together with the above inset quotation from *On Prayer* 27, leaves little doubt that psalms from the book of Psalms were a normal concomitant of daily prayer among Latin-speaking Christians of North Africa around the beginning of the third century.

The same times of prayer plus one more, at night, are recommended by Cyprian, an admirer of Tertullian and bishop of Carthage from 248 until his death in 258. In chapters 34–36 of *On the Lord's Prayer* (written *c.*250) he advocates prayer at the third, sixth and ninth hours, noting that prayer at these times was an ancient and obligatory practice (chapter 34). He goes on to say that devout Christians of his own day must pray additionally in the morning and the evening (chapter 35). He concludes (chapter 36) by recommending prayer at night also, supporting this by referring to the example of the Prophetess Anna who 'never left the temple but worshipped there with fasting and prayer night and day' (Luke 2:37).[13]

Origen (died *c.*254), representing Alexandrian and Israelite/Palestinian Christianity, regards three periods of daily prayer as a minimum, and recommends four (in the morning, in the middle of the day, in the evening and in the night) but without specifying times.[14] Two of his supporting Bible references imply the sixth hour (the middle of the day) and midnight, but it is possible that Alexandrian and Palestinian Christians did not observe fixed times of prayer.[15]

A strenuous regime of seven times of daily prayer is recommended in chapter 41 of the *Apostolic Tradition*. The third, sixth and ninth hours are specified; the remaining times are approximated: on rising in the morning, before sleeping at night, 'about midnight' and at cockcrow (before dawn). Nothing is said about the substance of prayer.[16]

In addition to prayer hours as such there were two eventide occasions at which devotion in the form of religious song was either customary or deemed desirable. One was the evening meal, at which Cyprian in *To Donatus* advocates the singing of a psalm (unspecified).[17] The other was the lighting of the lamps indoors as darkness encroached. According to Basil of Caesarea (*c.*330–379), who spent most of his working life in Cappadocia, and the last eight or so years of it as bishop of Caesarea, this latter occasion was customarily accompanied by a ritual of 'thanksgiving for the light' in pious households in Eastern Christendom. In his treatise *On the Holy Spirit* 29:73 he implies that the text

---

[12]   Tertullian, *To his Wife* [written *c.*203], book 2, 8:9; *MECL*, p. 44, no. 80.

[13]   Taft, *Hours*, pp. 19–21.

[14]   Origen, *On Prayer*; Taft, *Hours*, p. 16.

[15]   Taft, *Hours*, pp. 14 (on Clement of Alexandria), 17.

[16]   J. Cuming, *Hippolytus: A Text for Students, with Introduction, Translation, Commentary and Notes*, 2nd edn (Bramcote, 1987), pp. 29–31. See Cuming's notes on pp. 29–31.

[17]   Cyprian, *To Donatus* 16; *MECL*, p. 49, no. 94.

of the thanksgiving was the hymn *Phōs hilaron* ('Hail gladdening light') or the hymn *Doxa en hupsistois theō* ('Glory to God in the highest').[18]

From the details noted above it is clear that the times of private prayer were not uniform in all parts of Christendom. There was, however, a general preference for three times: in the morning, in the middle of the day and in the evening. These were the core times of prayer. Various additional times were observed at each end of the day, both very early (at cockcrow; at dawn; on rising from sleep) and very late (at dusk; before going to sleep; in the night).

Tertullian is the only one of the authors cited above who mentions the use of psalmody at the prayer hours. However, it would be strange if the use of psalms at times of prayer were limited to North-African Christianity, and in fact there is evidence to suggest that it was not. Origen, in chapter 12 of *On Prayer* (referred to above), supports his recommendation of prayer in the morning by quoting Psalm 5:4(3): 'O LORD, in the morning you hear my voice; in the morning I plead my case to you, and watch'; he supports his recommendation of prayer in the evening by quoting from Psalm 140(141):2b: 'the lifting up of my hands as an evening sacrifice'; and he supports his recommendation of prayer at midnight with a reference to the New Testament episode of Paul and Silas praying in a 'hymn' at midnight in prison (Acts 16:25) and by quoting Psalm 118(119):62: 'At midnight I rise to praise you, because of your righteous ordinances'.[19] It is clear that the quoted verses make the pertinent psalms (or portion of a psalm in the case of the long Psalm 118(119)) appropriate for use at the respective hours of prayer. Origen may have been quoting from psalms already in use at prayer hours in parts of Eastern Christendom. This is speculation, but at the same time it is noteworthy that Psalm 140(141) was to become the characteristic psalm of the evening Office in the urban churches throughout Christendom by the last decades of the fourth century.

Prayerful devotion was thus evident not only at the ordained times of prayer but also in connection with domestic activities such as eating the evening meal and lighting the lamps at nightfall. Psalms and occasional hymns were significant elements of prayer.

Early Christian Monasticism and Music

The Monastic Regime

The monastic regime consisted of religious devotion at set times, 'hours', interspersed with periods of manual labour during the day and sleep at night.[20]

---

[18]   See Taft, *Hours*, pp. 36–8.

[19]   See Taft, *Hours*, p. 16.

[20]   Parts of this section rely heavily on relevant material in Taft, *Hours*, pp. 31–145, and Dyer, 'The Desert, the City and Psalmody', pp. 11–43. Detailed references are given

The daily course of monastic hours came to be known as the Office, and each individual hour as an 'office'. The number and times of the hours which constituted the Office varied from place to place, but there were basic common times, principally in the morning and evening, and also in many cases at the third, sixth and ninth hours – times at which devout non-monastic Christians would also normally have prayed.

The style of the anchoritic regime in the Egyptian desert may be appreciated from the following anecdote in chapter 22 of Palladius's *Lausiac History* about Antony the Great (251–356), one of the most influential of the early Christian ascetics, and popularly regarded as the founder of anchorite monasticism in Egypt. It tells of how Antony instructed an old man who visited him and expressed a keen interest to join him in the ascetic life:

> Again Antony arose and said twelve prayers and chanted twelve psalms. He lay down for his brief first sleep and arose once more in the middle of the night to chant psalms until it was day. As he saw the old man eagerly following him in this regimen, he said to him: 'If you can do this every day, then remain with me.' (*MECL*, p. 60, no. 118)

An anecdote about another (but unnamed) anchorite of the period says:

> [*Sayings of the Fathers*, Anonymous Sayings, 229] Some brethren went from their monastery into the desert to visit an anchorite. He received them with joy, and according to the custom of the hermits, seeing that they were weary, he prepared a table before the usual hour, offered them whatever he had, and provided rest for them. And late in the day they recited the twelve psalms, and did likewise throughout the night. (*MECL*, p. 63, no. 128)

While the regime of the anchorites was austere, that of their community-dwelling brothers and sisters was more varied. One of the earliest systems of coenobite monasticism was established in Upper Egypt by Pachomius (died *c.*345 in Tabennisi, Egypt).[21] According to Jerome's preface to his translation of the monastic *Rule of Pachomius*, a Pachomian monastery consisted typically of 30 to 40 houses with about 40 monks in each house. There were two offices daily: on waking at dawn and in the evening before retiring to bed. Originally these were held in plenum, but in later times the evening office was held collectively in each house simultaneously. Night vigils extending throughout the night were held from time to time privately by individual monks in their cells, but in plenum on

---

where appropriate. See also Peter Jeffery, 'Monastic Reading and the Emerging Roman Chant Repertory', in Gallagher, Haar et al. (eds), *Western Plainchant in the First Millennium*, pp. 45–50.

[21] The standard work on Pachomian monasticism is Armand Veilleux, *Pachomian Koinonia*, 3 vols (Kalamazoo MI, 1980, 1981, 1982).

the eve of Easter and at the obsequies of fellow monks. On Sundays there was an office in plenum called 'Psalms' followed by a Eucharist.

According to the *Institutes* of John Cassian (*c.*360–433), who lived for a time in Scetis (possibly between 380 and 399) and visited the nearby monasteries at Nitria and Kellia, the monasteries of Lower Egypt also had two collective[22] offices each day: at cockcrow in the early hours of the morning and in the evening. The remaining offices were performed by each monk privately except on Saturdays and Sundays when there was a collective office at the third hour, which included a Eucharist. The offices are termed 'synaxes'.[23]

Athanasius (*c.*298–373) gives the following general description of Egyptian desert monasticism: 'So there were monasteries in the mountains, like tabernacles, filled with saintly choirs reciting psalms, devoutly reading, fasting, praying, rejoicing in the hope of things to come, and labouring to give alms, while maintaining love and harmony among themselves.'[24] The reality was less idyllic. Rule 9 of Jerome's translation of the *Rule of Pachomius* states, 'During the day, when the trumpet[?] had rung for the sinaxis [*sic*], the one who gets there after the first prayer will be lectured by his superior with a reprimand and will stay standing in the refectory'; and Rule 13 states, 'If the weekly person in charge of officiating [in] the choir or [at] the altar forgets or hesitates when reciting something, he will get the correction that negligence and forgetfulness deserve'.[25] The slightly later *Regulations of Horsiesios* say that the Pachomian monks who failed to hold their private vigil at night had to rise early and recite five to ten psalms alone in their cells prior to the office in common in the morning.[26]

With regard to urban monasticism in the East, John Cassian describes the daily Office in Bethlehem as he knew it at the time of his short stay there from *c.*382 or 383. It consisted of seven offices: at cockcrow, sunrise, the third, sixth and ninth hours, evening and bedtime.[27] According to John Chrysostom, this was also the scheme of the Office in Syrian Antioch and the surrounding area before the end of the fourth century.[28] A sevenfold Office was also observed in Cappadocia in the time of Basil the Great, as is apparent from the version of his monastic rules known as the *Longer Rules* 37:2–5. This had offices at the third, sixth and ninth hours, in the early morning, the evening, before retiring to bed and in the middle of the night. Egeria, in her account of her travels, describes a fivefold

---

[22]   Taft, *Hours*, p. 60, uses the word 'public' for these offices, but this is misleading since the monasteries in question were built in areas populated only by religious.

[23]   Taft, *Hours*, pp. 59–60.

[24]   Athanasius, *Life of St Anthony*; MECL, p. 55, no. 105.

[25]   English: *The Rule of Pachomius*, Part 1, trans. Esmeralda Ramirez de Jennings, ed. Daniel R. Jennings, in Patristics in English Homepage: <http://www.seanmultimedia. com/Pie_Pachomius_Rule_1.html> [accessed 10 January 2010].

[26]   See Taft, *Hours*, p. 66 and n. 22 there.

[27]   John Cassian, *Institutes*, books 3 & 4. See also Taft, *Hours*, pp. 77–80.

[28]   John Chrysostom, *Homily 68(69) on Matt. 3*. John Chrysostom, *Homily 14 on 1 Tim. 4*.

daily weekday Office in Jerusalem at the time of her stay there (c.384).[29] She lists the offices as Vigil, Matins, Sixth hour, Ninth hour and *Lychnicon* (Lucernare, Vespers). On Sundays the pattern was amplified by the insertion of an office at cock-crow between the night vigil and Morning Hymns.[30]

Urban monasteries in the West in the late fourth century apparently observed a sevenfold Office similar to that of their Eastern counterparts. This was the case in Latin-speaking North Africa, as is shown in the second chapter of the anonymous *Ordo monasterii*, written in Latin in North Africa in about 395 and attributed to Alypius of Thegaste.[31] The source describes the hours of Matins, Terce (third hour), Sext (sixth hour), None (ninth hour), Lucernarium (Vespers), Before Sleep, and Nocturnal Prayers. This was also the case in southern Gaul: John Cassian's *Institutes*, referred to above, provides evidence that the southern Gallican Office was similar to the Office of Bethlehem and consisted of the hours of Nocturns (very early in the morning, before daylight), Sunrise, Terce, Sext, None, and Eleventh hour (Vespers). To these six a Vigil was added on Friday night.

The Cathedral Office

It was often the case that an urban monastery or convent was associated with the main local church. Where the main church was the seat of the local bishop, the church was referred to as the 'cathedral' church. In such cases the resident monks or nuns provided the 'staff' of the church (under the direct authority of the bishop), looking after its administration and its physical and financial well-being as well as having responsibility for conducting the prayer hours and the celebration of the Eucharist. It was from the resident monks and nuns that the cathedral's readers, cantors and choral singers were drawn, and it was the resident monks who provided any ordained clergy that might be required in addition to the bishop for the performance of services outside the Office.

Church buildings were then, as now, public places of worship; this had a bearing on the form and content of the Office observed by the monks and

---

[29]   Egeria, *Travels*, pp. 142–4. Subsequent references to and quotations from the English translation of the text of Egeria's *Itinerarium/Peregrinatio* are to chapter and verse in John Wilkinson's edition (Oxford, 1999, 2006); subsequent references to other aspects of that edition are by page number and signalled '*Egeria's Travels*, ed. Wilkinson'. Interpolations of the Latin text in subsequent quotations from Egeria follow Louis Duchesne, *Origines du culte chrétien* (Paris, 1889), trans. M.L. McClure, as *Christian Worship: Its Origin and Evolution*, 5th edn (London, 1919, repr. 1931), pp. 492–523.

[30]   Egeria, *Travels*, 24:9.

[31]   Robert Taft says that although the attribution is uncertain, the document emanates from Latin-speaking North Africa towards the end of the fourth century, and that there is general agreement that it originated in the 'time and milieu of St Augustine' (Taft, *Hours*, p. 94, n. 1). St Augustine (Augustine of Hippo) lived from 354 to 430.

nuns. It was normal for two of the hours to be observed as public offices: one in the morning and one in the evening. Devout Christian citizens were expected to attend the morning office before embarking on their day's work, and the evening office when the day's work was over. These two offices were normally of a more popular nature than the remaining offices which the monks and nuns observed privately in their own building. In some places and at certain times there were cathedral vigils during or throughout the night which were attended by the monks and nuns and the general Christian populace. Such was the case, for example, in Alexandria during the patriarchate of Athanasius (328–339, 346–373),[32] in Constantinople during the episcopate of John Chrysostom (397–404),[33] and in Jerusalem during the episcopate of Cyril (350–386).[34]

Available information about the cathedral Office in the West in the latter half of the fourth century is principally concerned with Milan and Rome, but it is not as plentiful as for the cathedral Office in the East.[35] There is also a small amount of data about Latin-speaking North Africa and Gaul.[36] In Milan during the time of the episcopate of Ambrose (374–397) there were public offices in the early morning (Matins) and in the evening (Vespers), as Ambrose himself relates.[37] Similarly in Rome there were public offices at dawn and in the evening at lamp lighting time: in a letter giving spiritual advice to the daughter of a lady of Rome, Jerome (who was in Rome from 382 to 385) refers to prayer hours at night, in the morning, at the third, sixth and ninth hours, and in the evening.[38] However, this may be a reference to hours of private prayer rather than to a monastic Office.[39] Evidence for the existence of public offices in the early morning and in the evening in North Africa and Gaul at this time is supplied by Augustine of Hippo (354–430) and Hilary of Poitiers (c.300–367) respectively.[40] Thus the cathedral Office, as it became known, was different from the 'pure' monastic Office (as Robert Taft calls it) observed by monks and nuns whose monasteries or convents were not attached to a cathedral church.[41]

The main elements of the religious exercises of the monastics, irrespective of whether their houses were rural or urban or associated with a cathedral

---

[32]   Athanasius, *History of the Arians* 81. Athanasius, *Apology for his Flight* 24. Athanasius' patriarchate was interrupted several times by major conflicts, some of them resulting in his temporary exile.

[33]   Sozomen, *History of the Church*, book 8, 7–8. See Taft, *Hours*, p. 48.

[34]   Egeria, *Travels*, 24:8. Cyril of Jerusalem lived from c.315 to 386.

[35]   Taft, *Hours*, pp. 141–4.

[36]   Ibid., pp. 144–5.

[37]   Ambrose, *Exposition of Psalm 118*, Sermon 7:30, 32. Taft, *Hours*, p. 142.

[38]   Jerome, *Letter 107, to Laeta* 9.

[39]   Taft, *Hours*, pp. 143–4.

[40]   Augustine, *Confessions*, book 5, 9. Hilary of Poitiers, *Tract on Psalm 64*, 2, verse 2. Both are quoted in Taft, *Hours*, pp. 144, 145.

[41]   Taft, *Hours*, p. 65.

church, were Scripture reading, free prayer (in some instances silent as well as aloud), psalms, and sometimes also hymns and biblical canticles. Psalmody and hymnody were the most prominent musical genres in the monastic devotions.

The Place and Form of Psalms, Psalmody and Hymnody

Several of the earliest extant documents concerned with monasticism show that from at least the beginning of the fourth century the recitation of psalms of the Psalter – usually several at a time, in order – was the main vehicle of devotion for all religious. The expectation that members of monastic communities would know most of the Psalter, if not all of it, by heart is implicit in many early accounts of monasticism. In the Pachomian monasteries and convents, knowledge of at least the Psalter and the New Testament from memory was a requirement of continued membership: Precept 140 from the *Rule of Pachomius* says, 'And there shall be absolutely no one in the monastery who does not learn to read and retain something from the Scriptures, at least the New Testament and the Psalter.'[42] The appeal of psalms for devotional purposes was manifold, as Jerome noted at length.[43] It is axiomatic that since the Psalms are scriptural, they are theologically orthodox as a matter of course. This was especially important in an age when heresy was so rife, and some of its adherents so influential, that it posed a threat to the stability of the church.

Hymns and canticles were popular elements that belonged almost exclusively to the public morning and evening hours of the cathedral Office. Canticles (Greek: *ōdai*; Latin: *odae*) are the poetic portions of the Bible outside the book of Psalms. The early manuscripts of the LXX contain a collection of 13 (14) canticles[44] which were probably used in the offices of the Greek-speaking Eastern church. These and their Latin versions probably constituted the entire repertory of canticles of the Eastern and Western branches of the church in the second half of the fourth century.

By 'hymn' in the context of the monastic Office is meant the regularly strophic, isosyllabic Christian poetry of the type written by Hilary of Poitiers, Ephrem the Syrian (*c*.306–373) and Ambrose of Milan (*c*.340–397). The hymns of these writers may well have come into being as a means of re-affirming orthodox doctrine in the face of heretical influences. Hilary of Poitiers said that one of the functions of hymnody is to 'put the enemy to flight';[45] Ephrem the Syrian is said to have begun to write hymns in order to counteract heretical doctrines embodied in the popular hymns of Bardaisan (*c*.154–222) and his son Harmonius, both of whom

---

[42]   *MECL*, pp. 57–8, no. 112.

[43]   Jerome, *Letter 51, to Paula and Eustochium, On the Virtue of the Psalms*.

[44]   See the LXX, ed. Rahlfs, vol. 2, pp. 164–83.

[45]   Hilary of Poitiers, *Homily on Psalm 65*, 4; English trans. in *NPNF/2*, vol. 9, Introduction and nn. 132–4.

were Syrian gnostics;[46] and Ambrose of Milan acknowledged the popular appeal of his own hymns when he wrote that the Arians claimed 'the people have been led astray [from Arianism] by the strains of my hymns'.[47] In his *Confessions*, book 9, 7:15, Augustine of Hippo refers to the introduction of hymns in Milan in the following terms:[48]

> At that time [when Ambrose and the church in Milan were under pressure from powerful Arians to surrender the Milanese basilica to them] the custom began [*institutum est*] that hymns and psalms be sung [*hymni et psalmi ut canerentur*] after the manner of the eastern regions [*secundum morem orientalium partium*] lest the people be worn out with the tedium of sorrow. The practice has been retained from that time until today and imitated by many, indeed, by almost all your congregations throughout the rest of the world. (*MECL*, p. 154, no. 351)

The Church historian Sozomen records that in Constantinople John Chrysostom introduced nocturnal and processional hymn singing among the faithful as a means of combating the doctrines of Arianism. The Arians in the city attempted to inculcate their beliefs through *akroteleutia* (literally 'ends of verses', perhaps 'doxologies' or 'responses' or 'refrains') sung at their nocturnal assemblies and while they marched in procession to their places of assembly.[49] It is possible that the Arians' hymns were not in fact hymns in the present sense, but psalms of the Psalter to which were added Arian doxologies; the hymns with which John Chrysostom's followers countered may therefore have been psalms with orthodox doxologies. This would be consistent with the likelihood that they were performed antiphonally.[50]

Robert Taft, drawing on John Cassian's *Institutes*, books 2 and 8, summarizes the monastic morning office in Lower Egypt as follows: 12 psalms in Psalter order were recited by a soloist standing, while the remaining monks sat and listened; the monks responded 'Alleluia' as the twelfth psalm was recited, then the whole psalmody was concluded with the doxology 'Glory to the Father and to the Son and to the Holy Spirit, as it was in the beginning, is now and throughout all ages, amen'; then all stood and made silent prayer with their arms extended; then all prostrated themselves, praying silently as they did so; all stood again and made

---

[46] Sozomen, *History of the Church*, book 3, 16. Briefly on the literary relationship between Ephrem the Syrian and Bardaisan, see, *Ephrem the Syrian: Hymns*, trans. and introd. Kathleen McVey (New York, 1989), p. 26. Several of Ephrem's hymns are specifically against Bardaisan.

[47] Ambrose, *Sermon Against Auxentius on the Giving Up of the Basilicas*, §34; English trans. in NPNF/2, vol. 10, p. 50.

[48] Augustine's *Confessions* were written in 397–398.

[49] Sozomen, *History of the Church*, book 8, 8.

[50] Ibid. Compare Taft, *Hours*, p. 48.

silent prayer; this was followed by a collect prayer read by the presiding monk; finally there were two readings from the Bible.[51]

It was noted earlier that in the monasteries of Lower Egypt there was a collective office at the third hour on Saturdays and Sundays, which included a Eucharist (above, at n. 23). The composition of that office is not known for certain, but according to the *Rule of Pachomius*, in the monasteries of Upper Egypt there was a Sunday office called 'Psalmody', which consisted of the chanting of several psalms responsively as a prelude to the celebration of the Eucharist.[52] The content of the third-hour weekend office in Lower Egypt may have been similar.

With regard to urban monasticism in Lower Egypt, Canon 21 of the *Canons of Hippolytus* (composed *c*.336–340) says, 'Let the priests gather in church every day, and the deacons, subdeacons, readers, and all the people, at cockcrow. They shall do the prayer, the psalms, and the reading of the books and the prayers'.[53] In a passage from his *Apology for His Flight* 24, Athanasius in Alexandria writes of a situation in which he 'urged the deacon to read a psalm and the people to respond "For his mercy endures for ever"' during a nocturnal vigil in his besieged church.[54]

Moving further East, beyond Egypt, the urban daily monastic Office in Bethlehem, and most likely the whole of the rest of Israel/Palestine, was generally as follows:[55]

1. From cockcrow until daybreak 12 psalms were recited as described above with reference to Lower Egypt, followed by Lauds with Psalms 148–150.
2. At sunrise there was morning prayer consisting of Psalms 50(51), 62(63) and 89(90), with prayers.
3. At the third, sixth and ninth hours there were three psalms and three prayers.
4. In the evening there was Vespers, probably with Psalm 140(141) and perhaps an evening hymn.

In Cappadocia the early morning office (Matins) included two *odai* (*Eulogētos ei, kurie ho theos* – the Benedicite – and *Doxa en hupsistois theō* – the Gloria in excelsis Deo) as well as psalmody;[56] the evening office included the hymn *Phōs hilaron*.[57] Basil of Caesarea's *Letter* 207 provides evidence of antiphonal psalmody (that is, a psalm sung by two alternating groups) and responsive psalmody (that is, a psalm

[51] Taft, *Hours*, pp. 58–61.
[52] Ibid., p. 65.
[53] Taft, *Hours*, pp. 34–5.
[54] *MECL*, p. 54, no. 102.
[55] Taft, *Hours*, pp. 77–80.
[56] Anonymous [Athanasius?], *On Virginity*; cited in Taft, *Hours*, p. 89.
[57] Taft, *Hours*, pp. 38–9.

sung by a soloist with a regular collective response) at a nocturnal vigil and its following morning office in the year 375. He implies that the practices he describes are in use throughout Eastern Christendom from Libya to Mesopotamia.[58]

The two daily cathedral offices in Antioch and its environs included Psalm 62(63) in the morning and Psalm 140(141) in the evening.[59] The morning office also included the canticle *Doxa en hupsistois theō*.[60] The Church historian Sozomen, writing of the cathedral Office in Constantinople at the time of John Chrysostom's patriarchate there (397-404), says that the people 'used the morning and night hymns',[61] but it is uncertain whether this is a specific reference to hymns or a loose reference to psalms or canticles. John Chrysostom himself, in *On 1 Corinthians: Homily 36:5-6*, witnesses to a formal style of psalmody and other items in the cathedral liturgy:

> All came together in earlier times and sang psalms in common ... Then the houses themselves were churches, while now the church is a house ... And indeed there must always be but one voice in the church, as there is but one body. Thus the reader alone speaks, and he who holds the episcopacy sits and maintains silence, and the singer sings psalms alone, and, while all respond, the sound issues as if from one mouth, and only he preaches who gives the homily. (*MECL*, p. 86, no. 184)

Representing western Gaul in the West, Hilary of Poitiers remarks, 'The progress of the Church in the delights of morning and evening hymns are a great sign of God's mercy in the Church. The day is begun with God's prayers, the day is ended with God's hymns'.[62] Here too the terminology is ambiguous and there is no way of knowing whether hymns (perhaps of the type he is supposed to have written)[63] or psalms or canticles are meant. Evidence from southern Gaul a little later than the time of Hilary shows that Psalms 62(63) and 118(119):147-148 were recited at the office at sunrise and Psalms 148-150 at Lauds. The 'little hours' of Terce, Sext and None had three psalms each, and it is likely that at the evening office at the eleventh hour (Vespers) Psalm 140(141) was recited.[64]

The *Ordo monasterii* provides evidence of a more sophisticated regime in Latin-speaking North Africa towards the end of the fourth century. At the early

---

[58]   *MECL*, pp. 68-9, no. 139.

[59]   John Chrysostom, *Commentary on Psalm 140*. See also *MECL*, p. 82, no. 171, and *MECL*, p. 110, no. 236, from the *Apostolic Constitutions*, book 2, 59.

[60]   John Chrysostom, *On Matthew*, Homily 68, 3. *MECL*, p. 85, no. 180.

[61]   Sozomen, *History of the Church*, book 8, 7; Taft, *Hours*, p. 48.

[62]   *Tract on Psalm 64*, 12; Taft, *Hours*, p. 145 (where the chapter reference is mistakenly given as '21').

[63]   See the Introduction to the works of Hilary of Poitiers in *NPNF*/2, vol. 9, pp. i–lvii, esp. pp. xlvi–xlviii.

[64]   John Cassian, *Institutes*, book 3. See Taft, *Hours*, pp. 96–100.

morning office Psalms 62(63), 5 and 89(90) were recited. Terce, Sext and None each consisted of one psalm recited responsively, two antiphonal psalms, a reading and a concluding rite. Lucernarium (Vespers) consisted of one psalm recited responsively, four antiphonal psalms, another psalm recited responsively, a reading and a concluding rite. In the night office (Nocturns) the number of psalms varied with the time of year. There were eight or ten or twelve antiphonal psalms, followed by four or five or six psalms recited responsively, followed by two or three readings.[65]

Mention of psalms and other matter recited antiphonally and responsively is also found in connection with the monastic and cathedral rites in the one important metropolitan area not yet considered here, Jerusalem. Jerusalem was a special case among the cities of Christendom both because it was the focal point of the Christian Holy Land as well as the Jewish, and because it had several churches. At the time of Egeria's visit the most important of the churches were those built by Constantine on the hill called Golgotha (the site of the crucifixion of Jesus of Nazareth) where they were grouped as a complex of buildings joined together. The complex comprised, moving from west to east: a circular church called the Anastasis; a colonnaded courtyard before a large mausoleum called the Cross (which contained a relic said to be the cross on which Jesus of Nazareth had been crucified); a small chapel behind the Cross; a large, colonnaded rectangular apsidal church called the Martyrium; and a colonnaded court beyond the east end of the Martyrium.[66]

A feature of the worship in Jerusalem was that it was stational, moving from one church to another during the course of each day. Egeria's *Travels* shows that most of the offices were held in the Anastasis and that the Eucharist was normally held in the Martyrium. Removal from station to station was accomplished in procession, with singing (see below).

Egeria's description of the weekday Office in Jerusalem begins at the point when people assembled in the early morning, long before dawn. She writes:

> [Egeria, *Travels* 24:1] All the doors of the Anastasis are opened before cock-crow each day, and the *'monazontes* and *parthenae'* ['monks and virgins'], as they call them here, come in, and also some lay men and women, at least those who are willing to wake at such an early hour. From then until daybreak they join in singing the refrains to the hymns, psalms and antiphons [*dicuntur ymni et psalmi responduntur similiter et antiphonae*].
>
> There is a prayer between each of the hymns [*ymnos*], since there are two or three presbyters and deacons each day by rota, who are there with the monazontes, and say the prayers between all the hymns and antiphons [*ymnos uel antiphonas*].

[65]   Taft, *Hours*, p. 96.
[66]   See the line drawing of this site in *Egeria's Travels*, ed. Wilkinson, p. 39.

The early morning office followed: 'As soon as dawn comes, they start the Morning Hymns [*matutinos ymnos*]' (*Travels* 24:2).[67] Then followed the hours of Sext and None which were identical to each other in form: 'Again at midday everyone comes into the Anastasis, and says psalms and antiphons [*et dicuntur psalmi et antiphonae*] ... At three o'clock they do once more what they did at midday' (24:3–4).

The evening office was in two parts. The first began with *Lychnicon* (Lucernare, Vespers) at the Anastasis at the tenth hour (four o'clock). Egeria says, 'For some time they have the Lucernare psalms and antiphons [*psalmi lucernares sed et antiphonae*]; then they send for the bishop, who enters and sits in the chief seat. The presbyters also come and sit in their places, and the hymns and antiphons go on [*dicuntur ymni uel antiphonae*]' (*Travels* 24:4). The office proceeded with a commemoration of individuals by name, to which the many small boys who were always present responded '*Kyrie eleison*' as each name was read out (24:5). The first part of the office concluded with the bishop blessing the faithful. For the second part, the bishop was conducted from the Anastasis to the Cross with 'hymns' (*ymnis*). There he prayed aloud and blessed the catechumens and the faithful. This was then repeated in the chapel behind the Cross. The rite lasted until after darkness had fallen (24:7).

The Office on Sundays began in the same manner as that on the other days of the week, with a gathering of religious and laity outside the doors of the Anastasis very early in the morning, before cock-crow. On Sundays the crowd was large. Egeria says, 'Those who are afraid they may not arrive in time for cock-crow come early, and sit waiting there singing hymns and antiphons [*dicuntur ymni nec non et antiphonae*]'; there were prayers between the hymns and antiphons (*Travels* 24:8). At cock-crow the bishop came and all the people were admitted to the Anastasis. Egeria continues: 'a psalm is said by one of the presbyters, with everyone responding [*dicet psalmum ... et respondent omnes*], and it is followed by a prayer; then a psalm is said [*dicit psalmum*] by one of the deacons, and another prayer; then a third psalm [*tertius psalmus*] is said by one of the clergy, a third prayer, and the Commemoration of All' (24:9). After a reading of the resurrection narrative, everyone proceeded to the Cross where there was one psalm and a following prayer. Then the bishop went home to his house and the monks and nuns returned to the Anastasis where psalms and antiphons were said (*psalmi dicuntur et antiphonae*), with prayers interpolated between each psalm and antiphon, until daybreak (24:11–12).

At daybreak the main office of Sunday began in the Martyrium. After sermons from several of the priests and the bishop, the monks led the bishop *cum ymnis* 'with hymns' to the Anastasis. There, after prayers and the episcopal blessing, the office concluded at around the fifth or sixth hour with the dismissal of the people.

---

[67] Wilkinson's capitalization of 'Morning Hymns' is problematical. It is not certain from the Latin that Egeria meant the phrase to be understood as the name of the office.

The evening office of Lucernare (Vespers) was conducted according to the daily pattern (*Travels* 25:1–4).

Egeria makes no mention here of the celebration of the Eucharist on Sundays. Nevertheless, elsewhere, in connection with the main morning service in the Martyrium on Whit Sunday, she refers to the Offering being made (the Eucharist being celebrated) after the sermons by the priests and the bishop, 'in the way which is usual on a Sunday' (*Travels* 43:2), as noted above. More striking is the absence of any information about psalms or hymns in the main Sunday office after the office at cock-crow. Perhaps her remark at 25:4 that Lucernare was conducted 'in the same way as on other days' is to be understood as having not only direct reference to Sunday Lucernare but also indirect reference to the main Sunday morning office.

Egeria nowhere identifies any of the 'psalms', 'hymns' and 'antiphons'. On one occasion she refers to 'the morning hymns [*mautinos ymnos*]' (*Travels* 24:2), and on another to 'the Lucernare psalms [*psalmi lucernares*]' (24:4). The references are made in such a way as to suggest that her readers would have known which hymns and psalms she meant. It is likely that she uses the term 'hymns' in a general sense, meaning in fact psalms (or perhaps psalms and canticles). Since in nearby Bethlehem the morning office included Psalms 148–150 and 50(51), 62(63), and 89(90) (as has been noted above), and Bethlehem lay within the jurisdiction of the bishop of Jerusalem (indeed, there was stational worship at the church there on the festivals of Epiphany and Ascension), it is reasonable to suppose that these were the *matutinos ymnos* used in Jerusalem. Furthermore, Psalms 62(63) and 148–150 were recited at the two morning offices in southern Gaul, and may therefore have been used thus in the region where Egeria had her home. Whatever the Lucernare psalms were, they almost certainly included Psalm 140(141) since this was universal in the evening office in the Eastern church, and probably also (in its Latin version) in the Western church.

A feature of the rites which impressed Egeria was the appropriateness of the 'antiphons', 'hymns' and 'psalms' to the times of day and the occasions on which they were used. She mentions this first in her *Travels* at 25:5 and a further eight times in the course of chapters 29–40.

Egeria mentions several types or forms of psalmody and hymnody. She uses the word *ymni* 'hymns' in a general sense to refer to sacred song; its meaning in each instance therefore has to be deduced from the context. For example, when she mentions hymns, psalms and antiphons together at *Travels* 24:1, in connection with the daily assembly before daybreak, 'hymns' is likely to mean something other than psalms: perhaps biblical canticles or metrical hymns. However, the 'Morning Hymns' of 24:2 were probably morning psalms, as suggested above. But when she writes that the bishop was accompanied from church to church 'with hymns', it is again possible that she means biblical canticles or metrical hymns, rather than psalms, although psalms cannot be ruled out.

Psalmi (literally 'psalms') are likely to have been psalms of the Psalter and nothing more. In *Travels* 24:1 Egeria refers to *psalmi responduntur*. The structure of the Latin sentence in which this phrase occurs shows that a particular style of psalmody is meant: 'psalms to which response is made' or 'responsive psalmody'.[68] This implies psalmody in which the assembled company answered with a recurring short acclamation at intervals as a soloist sang the psalm verses. (Responsive psalmody should not be confused with the later and more complex 'responsorial' psalmody.)

Responsive performance was not confined to psalms. It was noted earlier that during the first part of the evening office there was a commemorative litany with the response '*Kyrie eleison*' uttered by young boys (*Travels* 24:5). In addition, Egeria says that on Palm Sunday there was a procession of all the people from the top of the Mount of Olives, through the city, and so to the Anastasis, and that as they went they sang 'hymns and antiphons, all the time repeating, "Blessed is he that cometh in the name of the Lord [*benedictus qui uenit in nomine Domini*]"' (31:1–4). This may be understood to mean that 'Blessed is he ...' was sung as a response at frequent intervals as the 'hymns and antiphons' were sung.

Antiphonae (literally: 'antiphons') are likely to have been psalms sung antiphonally, that is to say psalms sung by groups in alternation, the groups being more or less balanced in size. But during this period the term was not used consistently. 'Antiphon' could also refer to the textual material that was used as the refrain in responsive performance, and by extension to psalms furnished with antiphons. Judging from the contexts in which Egeria uses the term *antiphonae* it seems unlikely that she would have meant merely the refrain texts themselves; however, she could have meant psalms furnished with antiphons. If she did indeed mean the latter, it is highly likely these would have differed from responsive psalms. Sources from the fifth century onwards show that an antiphon in the sense of a refrain text to a psalm was normally a psalm verse (usually extrapolated from the psalm being sung), or at least a text as long as a psalm verse.[69] In responsive psalmody, on the other hand, the response material was usually a short acclamation such as 'Hallelujah' or 'For his mercy endures for ever'. Short acclamatory phrases were also typical of the responses in other situations where responsive forms were used, as has been shown above. Responsive psalmody was thus popular in style whereas psalmody with antiphons was more learned, better suited to performance by the clergy and monks and nuns than the laity. In antiphonal psalmody in the sense of psalmody with antiphons, the psalm verses could well have been sung by a soloist and the antiphon refrains by the assembled religious together; but it is also possible

---

[68]   There would have been no need for Egeria to specify *responduntur* in the passage from *Travels* 24:1 quoted above, if the *psalmi* had not been of this particular type, since *dicuntur* would have sufficed for both *ymni* and *psalmi*.

[69]   See, for example, the tabular version of a fifth-century Armenian lectionary for Jerusalem, presented with background material and commentary in *Egeria's Travels*, ed. Wilkinson, pp. 175–92: each of the psalm antiphons consists of one or more extrapolated psalm verses.

that the verses could have been sung by groups of religious in alternation, and the antiphons themselves sung by the groups combined. This would make the psalmody antiphonal in the formal as well as the textual sense. Basically, however, it seems that *antiphonae* signified psalms with antiphons (intended for recital by clergy, monks and nuns), as opposed to *psalmi responduntur*, which signified responsive psalms intended for popular participation.

Given that the monastic Office was a daily occurrence, and that there could be as many as seven offices each day, it is understandable that James McKinnon could see the plethora of psalmody in the late fourth-century church as evidence of the operation of a 'psalmodic movement'.[70] However, a more sober view would see the apparent rapid increase in the use of psalmody during this period as a natural consequence of the development of the monastic and cathedral Offices in the benign climate created by the Edict of Milan.

The Early Christian Eucharist and Music

The cathedral Office was different from the 'pure' monastic Office not only in its inclusion of public offices but also in that at some stage in its course a celebration of the Eucharist intervened. The Eucharist was a service, not an office, and unlike the hours of the Office it was not necessarily celebrated daily. However, it was a service that was public, and was most usually celebrated at least on a Sunday (the Lord's Day), but sometimes also on a Saturday (the Sabbath). It was noted above with reference to the Pachomian Office in Upper Egypt that on Sundays the monks came together for an office called 'Psalms' followed by a Eucharist, and with reference to the Office in the monasteries of Lower Egypt, that the monks came together on Saturdays and Sundays for an office that included a Eucharist. In those cases the Eucharist, though collective, was not public in the modern sense since it was open only to the resident monks or nuns. But in the urban cathedrals the Eucharist was open to the Christian public at large as well as the monks and nuns. Egeria, for example, writing of Saturdays in Lent as observed in Jerusalem, says, 'Anyone who wishes may make his Communion [partake of the Eucharist] in the Anastasis on Saturdays' (*Travels* 27:9, end); and writing of the Whit Sunday celebrations in Jerusalem, she says, 'In the morning the people all assemble in their usual way in the Great Church, the Martyrium, and have sermons from the presbyters and then the bishop, and the Offering is duly made [the Eucharist is celebrated] in the way which is usual on a Sunday' (43:2).

Egeria does not say whether the Eucharist at Jerusalem contained any potentially musical items. However, the likelihood is that it did. This is suggested by evidence from the *Apostolic Constitutions*, the church order reflecting the state of Christian liturgy in Syria and the East generally at the beginning of the last

---

[70]   James W. McKinnon, 'Desert Monasticism and the Later Fourth-Century Psalmodic Movement', *M&L*, 75 (1994): 505–21.

quarter of the fourth century. In book 2, 57:5–7, liturgical readers are instructed to conduct the pre-Eucharistic synaxis as follows:

> In the middle [of the eastern end of the church] the reader is to stand on something high (ὑψηλοῦ τινος[71]) and read the books of Moses, of Joshua the son of Nun, of Judges and Kings, of Chronicles and those from after the return [of the Jews from exile], and in addition those of Job, of Solomon and of the sixteen Prophets. [6] After two readings let someone else sing the hymns of David, and let the people respond with verses (ἀκροστίχια[72]). [7] After this let our Acts be read and the epistles of Paul our fellow worker ... and after these let a deacon or priest read the Gospels. (*MECL*, pp. 108–9, no. 233)

It is probable that the 'hymns of David' and the 'verses' with which the people were to respond were psalms with antiphons, since simple acclamations used as response material would not have amounted to 'verses'. The 'people' who made the response were most likely the assembled monks, not the laity in general.

Book 8 of the *Apostolic Constitutions* contains significant prescriptions for the Eucharist itself. Chapter 12:27 prescribes the collective rendering of a version of a short hymn beginning, 'Holy, holy, holy', based on the angelic acclamation in LXX Isaiah 6:3 and NT Revelation 4:8b:

> The Cherubim and six-winged Seraphim, their feet covered with two, their heads with two, and flying with two', saying together with thousand times thousands of archangels and ten-thousand times ten-thousands of angels, without ceasing and in a loud voice; and let all the people say with them, 'Holy, holy, holy, Lord of Sabaoth, heaven and earth are full of his glory; blessed be he for ever; Amen. (*MECL*, p. 109, no. 234)

This hymn, the Trisagion of the Orthodox liturgy, and the forerunner of the Sanctus of the Latin Mass, was already an established item in the Eucharist in the East by the last decades of the fourth century although not so in the West until somewhat later.[73]

Chapters 13–14 of book 8 of the *Apostolic Constitutions* not only prescribe a particular psalm during the distribution of the bread and wine at the Eucharist, but also provide an insight into the place of the canonical singers in the hierarchy of clergy and laity in the institutionalised church:

---

[71]   Transliteration: *hupsēlou tinos.*

[72]   Transliteration: *akrostichia.*

[73]   On the Sanctus see, for example, *MECL*, p. 109, no. 234, headnote; Bryan Spinks, *The Sanctus in the Eucharistic Prayer* (Cambridge, 1991), pp. 1–125; Gabriele Winkler, *Das Sanctus. Über den Ursprung und die Anfänge des Sanctus und sein Fortwirken* (Rome, 2002).

[*Apos. Con.*, book 8, 13:14] And after this let the bishop receive [consume the bread and wine of the Eucharist], then the priests, and the deacons, and the subdeacons, and the readers, and the cantors (ψάλται[74]), and the ascetics; and among the women the deaconesses, and the virgins, and the widows; then the children, and then all the people in good order with reverence and piety and without commotion. [15] And let the bishop give the oblation [distribute the bread and wine of the Eucharist] ... [16] Let the thirty-third psalm be sung while all the rest receive. [17] And when all have received, men and women, let the deacon take what remains and carry it into the sacristies. [14:1] And when the singer (ψάλλοντος[75]) is finished, let the deacon say .... (*MECL*, p. 109, no. 235)

Psalm 33(34) is particularly appropriate at this point in the liturgy on account of the first clause of its ninth (eighth) verse: 'Taste and see that the LORD is good'. The singular form *psallontos* 'singer' in 14:1 in the quotation above implies that this psalm was sung by a soloist, probably one of the canonical singers. Two terms are used in this passage to refer to the singers: *psaltai* (singular: *psaltēs*) and *psallontos*. As James McKinnon has pointed out, the first of these is used several more times in the *Apostolic Constitutions* (at book 8, 28:7–8 and 47:26, for example), but at two places a completely different term, *psaltōdos*, is used (book 2, 28:5; book 6, 17:2).[76] *Psaltēs* and *psaltōdos* seem to be interchangeable special terms referring to a canonical singer, whereas *psallontos* seems to be a general word meaning simply 'the singer' in the sense of 'the person who is singing'.

Musical Aspects of Psalmody and Hymnody

There can be no doubt that psalmody was chanted or sung rather than spoken.[77] While some sources use neutral terms meaning 'utter' to refer to the rendition of psalms, others refer specifically to the singing of them, either directly through the use of verbs meaning 'sing', or indirectly through the mention of 'singers' in relation to the utterance of psalmody or unspecified liturgical texts that would have included psalms.[78]

---

[74] Transliteration: *psaltai*.

[75] Transliteration: *psallontos*.

[76] *MECL*, p. 109, no. 235, headnote.

[77] See Dyer, 'The Desert, the City and Psalmody', pp. 18–21.

[78] For example, John Chrysostom, *On 1 Corinthians*, Homily 36:5–6, quoted above. Also Canons 15 and 23 of the Canons of Laodicea, which refer to 'canonical singers' and 'singers' in church respectively; these would have been singers specially appointed to perform sacred song during worship.

Psalmody

The outward musical form of psalmody is dictated by the literary form of psalms. A psalm text consists of several short, self-contained prose verses, each having a bipartite structure, the two parts separated by a clear caesura. Occasionally a tripartite structure is found, in which case there are two caesuras. The two (or three) parts are often similar in length and related in thought and use of language. But because the text is prose and not regularly metrical, the verses are not of equal length. This naturally generates a musical form consisting of a melodic line punctuated by a medial cadence (or by two cadences where a verse is tripartite) and concluding with a final cadence. This formula is repeated for each psalm verse, the melodic line varying in length from verse to verse. The musical form of psalmody may thus be described as basically unequal-length strophic, each strophe consisting of two (or three) main phrases of more or less equal length.

In antiphonal psalmody, where an antiphon introduced into a psalm consists of a verse derived from within the psalm (as seems to have been typical) or of a verse from another psalm, the antiphon would most likely be sung to the same melody as the psalm verses. An antiphon would function as a refrain only in so far as its text would be repeated regularly.

In reponsive psalmody, where the response material is a short acclamation, however, new elements are introduced in so far as the response is not a psalm verse but a single word or a short phrase set to its own music. The resultant overall musical form would thus be a recurring twofold pattern in which one element is the psalm verse, the other the response.

Occasionally the sources give some indication of the musical style of psalmody. Athanasius, for example, in two passages from his *Letter to Marcellinus on the Interpretation of the Psalms*, chapters 27 and 28, witnesses to a certain mellifluousness in psalmody. In one of these passages he clearly distinguishes the manner of reading the non-poetic parts of the Bible (he regards the prophetic books as non-poetic) from that of reading 'psalms, odes and songs':

> [Athanasius, *Letter to Marcellinus* 27] Some of the simple ones among us, even while believing the texts [of the psalms] to be divinely inspired, still think that the psalms are sung melodiously for the sake of good sound and the pleasure of the ear. This is not so. Scripture has not sought what is sweet and persuasive; rather this was ordained to benefit the soul for every reason, but principally these two. First, because it was proper for Divine Scripture to hymn God not only with continuity but with expanse of voice. Recited with continuity, then, are such words as those of the Law and the Prophets, and all those of history, along with the New Testament; while recited with expanse are those of psalms, odes and songs. (*MECL*, pp. 52–3, no. 98)

In the other passage he appears to distinguish between the musical character of canticles and psalms. However, in view of what he wrote in the passage quoted immediately above, this may be literary parallelism rather than a reflection of the prevalent situation. Nevertheless the musical character of the performance of canticles and psalms is not in doubt:

> [Athanasius, *Letter to Marcellinus* 28] Just as we make known and signify the thoughts of the soul through the words we express, so too the Lord wished the melody of the words to be a sign of the spiritual harmony of the soul, and ordained that the canticles be sung with melody and the psalms read with song. (*MECL*, pp. 53, no. 99)

Athanasius preferred a relatively modest melodic style of psalmody: Augustine of Hippo recalled being frequently told that Athanasius 'required the reader of the psalm to perform it with so little inflection (*flexu*) of voice that it was closer to speaking (*pronuntianti*) than to singing (*canenti*)'.[79]

Towards the end of the fourth century, John Cassian, writing of psalmody in the monasteries of Lower Egypt, says that during the early morning office the chanter chanted psalms, 'verse after verse being evenly enunciated'.[80] In similar vein, Evagrius Ponticus (346–399) advised his readers to 'pray with moderation and calm, and chant psalms with understanding and proper measure (*euruthmōs*) ...'.[81]

There is seldom mention of the musical style of psalmody sung by women. The following is one of the rare instances; it is taken from chapter 90 of the first *Epistle* of Isidore of Pelusium (died *c*.435).[82] The singing seems to have had unfortunate consequences:

> [Isidore of Pelusium, *Epistle* 1. 90] The apostles of the Lord, who wanted to put an end to idle talk in the churches ... wisely permitted women to sing psalms there. But as every divine teaching has been turned to its opposite, so this, too, has become an occasion of sin and laxity for the majority of the people. They do not feel compunction in hearing the divine hymns, but rather misuse the sweetness of melody to arouse passion .... (*MECL*, p. 61, no. 121)

Several authors experienced the sound of psalmody in the monasteries and churches as pleasurable, even moving. Palladius (*c*.364–425), for example, describing the monastery of Nitria in Lower Egypt in the last decade of the fourth century, wrote: 'one who stands there at about the ninth hour can hear the psalmody issuing forth from each cell, so that he imagines himself to be high

---

79   Augustine, *Confessions*, book 10, 33:50; *MECL*, p. 155, no. 352.
80   John Cassian, *Institutes*, book 2, 5; Taft, *Hours*, p. 59.
81   Evagrius Ponticus, *On Prayer* 82; *MECL*, p. 59, no. 115.
82   Pelusium, where Isidore was priest and possibly abbot of the monastery, is near Alexandria: see *MECL*, p. 61.

above in paradise'.[83] Augustine, recalling his time with Ambrose in Milan, wrote in one place: 'How much I wept at your hymns and canticles, deeply moved by the voices of your sweetly singing church'; elsewhere he referred to the 'melody of the sweet songs to which the Davidic Psalter is usually set'.[84] However, these reactions are subjective and therefore of little help in making objective assessments of the music.

Taking stock of the information provided by the sources adduced above, the normal style of utterance for psalmody appears to have been some kind of heightened speech or semi-musical recitative, perhaps in some cases approaching song, or at any rate a distinctly musical rendition, with perhaps occasional instances of ornate ornamentation or lyrical effusion. The same basic melodic formula would have been used for each psalm verse, but the length of the reciting note would have varied from verse to verse in keeping with the varying number of syllables. These features of style and form are precisely what is found in the earliest extant examples of simple psalmody in decipherable musical notation from Eastern and Western Christendom.[85] They were probably fundamental to Christian psalmody from a very early date.

Hymnody

The circumstances in which the early Christian hymns were used, and the formal and literary features of the hymns, provide valuable pointers to the musical style employed when the hymns were sung. The hymns were intended for popular use in public processions and vigils, in the public morning and evening offices at cathedral churches, and in daily prayer and other devotions in the home. They are usually strophic in form, in some cases with refrains. In most cases the language is poetic but simple, sometimes making use of assonance and rhyme. Nevertheless, the details of form and literary style differ considerably.

The Oxyrhynchus hymn and *Phōs hilaron* are the earliest extant Christian hymn texts in Greek independent of the Bible or biblical models, which are reasonably certain to have been used in Christian worship.[86] *Phōs hilaron* consists

---

[83]   Palladius, *Lausiac History*, book 7; *MECL*, p. 59, no. 117. Palladius visited the monasteries of the Egyptian desert during the period from *c*.388 to 400.

[84]   Augustine, *Confessions*, book 9, 6:14; *MECL*, p. 154, no. 351. Augustine, *Confessions*, book 10, 33:50; *MECL*, p. 155, no. 352.

[85]   For Eastern simple psalmody, see the musical examples given by Kenneth Levy in his article 'Byzantine Rite, Music of the', *New Grove*/1, p. 555. For Western simple psalmody, see the transcription of the anonymous *Commemoratio brevis de tonis et psalmis modulendis* in M. Gerbert, *Scriptores ecclesiastici de musica sacra potissimum* (St Blasien: 1784; facsimile edn Milan, 1931), vol. 1, p. 231.

[86]   The few hymns of Clement of Alexandria (*c*.150–*c*.215), which are appended to the end of book 3 of his *The Instructor*, are written in a learned, classical style and are more appropriate to intellectual appreciation than to use in worship.

Table 8.1   Hymn *Phōs hilaron*: Transliterated Greek Text and English Translation

Transliterated Greek text	Translation
phōs hilaron agias doxēs	cheering light of the holy glory
athanatou Patros	of the immortal Father
ouraniou agiou makaros Iēsou Christe	heavenly holy blessed Jesus Christ
elthontes epi tēn ēliou dusin	having come to the setting of the sun
idontes phōs esperinon	having seen the evening light
umnoumen Patera Uion kai	we hymn the Father the Son and
agion Pneuma	the Holy Spirit
Theon	God
axion se en pasi kairois	you are worthy at all times
umneisthai phōnais aisiais	to be hymned with happy voices
Uie Theou zōēn o didous	O Son of God giver of life
dio o kosmos se doxazei	therefore all creation glorifies you

of a single stanza written in unpretentious poetic prose. The ideas are presented in short phrases and left undeveloped (see Table 8.1).[87]

The text of the Oxyrhynchus hymn (see Example 8.1 later in this chapter) is similar in character to that of *Phōs hilaron* in so far as simplicity of language and treatment of ideas is concerned. Otherwise it differs notably from *Phōs hilaron* in that it is metrical. The metre is predominantly anapaestic, but it is not uniformly applied. In addition, the text makes much use of rhyme on the syllable -*ōn*, and the closing lines are notable for the repeated twofold 'Amen'. The use of the first person plural form ('we hymn') suggests collective song. The extant text is a fragment; it is the conclusion of what was originally a longer hymn, but how much longer is not known.

Ephrem the Syrian is reckoned to have written around 1,000 hymns and religious poetical works of which some 400 are extant. He wrote only in Syriac but many of his works were subsequently translated into Armenian, Coptic, Greek, Latin and other languages. There is also a large body of works in Greek falsely attributed to him. Most prominent among his hymns are the *mêmrê* (metrical homilies) and the *madrāšê* (teaching hymns). The *mêmrê* are written in stanzas of two lines, with seven syllables per line (heptosyllabic couplets), and are often long. The *madrāšê* are also written in stanzas of isorhythmic lines, but the number of lines per stanza and the number of syllables per line differ from one *madrāšâ* to another although strict uniformity is observed within any given *madrāšâ*. The extant *madrāšê* exhibit over 50 different metrical patterns. Normally a *madrāšâ* has a refrain (*unîṯâ*), which is sung after each stanza. Traditional melodies (*qālê*) were originally assigned to the *madrāšê*, but none has survived. Andrew Palmer has published a translation of one of Ephrem's Hymns on the Nativity which

---

87   In Table 8.1 the Greek text is from <http://en.wikipedia.org/wiki/Phos_Hilaron> [accessed 26 October 2009]. The English translation is mine.

preserves not only the immediacy of the language and the vividness of the imagery of the original, but also the syllabic scheme.[88] The hymn is a *madrāšâ* of ten stanzas, each stanza consisting of four lines of 12, 8, 8 and 12 syllables respectively. The hymn has a 12-syllable response to be sung after each stanza. In Palmer's translation the syllabic scheme is accentual: iambic hexameter in the first and last lines of each stanza, and iambic tetrameter in the second and third. In the original Syriac, syllable count (quantity) would have had priority over accentual rhythm. Palmer himself describes the metre as 4+4+4 for the first and fourth lines of each stanza, and 4+4 for the second and third.[89] The first stanza and the response are quoted below in Palmer's translation:

[Ephrem the Syrian: *Hymn on the Nativity*, no. 15]:
With You I'll start and so, I trust, with You will end!
I'll open wide: You fill my mouth!
I'll be the earth: You drive the plough!
You sowed Yourself inside my womb: sow now your Voice!
Response after each stanza:
To You, and through You, to your Sire, we offer praise![90]

The Latin hymns of Ambrose of Milan combine isometer and accentual rhythm. Only four hymns are universally acknowledged to be genuine compositions of Ambrose, and all are very similar in form, metrical structure and use of language. The four hymns in question are *Aeterne rerum conditor, Deus creator omnium, Jam surgit hora tertia* and *Veni redemptor genitum*. The characteristics of the Ambrosian hymns may be aptly illustrated by the first-named of these four. It consists of eight stanzas,[91] each of four lines, with each line having eight syllables grouped as four iambic feet. As may be seen in Table 8.2, which quotes the first two stanzas in Latin and English prose translation,[92] the language is simple, restrained and

---

[88]   Andrew Palmer, 'The Influence of Ephraim the Syrian', *Hugoye: Journal of Syriac Studies* [online journal], available at <http://syrcom.cua.edu/Hugoye>, vol. 2, no. 1 (1999), paragraph 40, no. 3 [accessed 11 January 2010]. In *Ephrem the Syrian: Hymns*, trans. and introd. McVey, pp. 145–7, this hymn is designated number 15 of the Hymns on the Nativity. It is superscribed by the instruction, 'The same melody', referring back to the superscription to Hymn no. 5: 'To the melody "Who is able to speak?"' (ibid., p. 106). The Hymns on the Nativity are among the genuine works of Ephrem Syrus: see Sebastian Brock, 'Introduction', in *St. Ephrem the Syrian: Hymns on Paradise* (Crestwood NY, 1990), pp. 230–33, cited in Christine Shepardson, *Anti-Judaism and Christian Orthodoxy: Ephrem's Hymns in Fourth-Century Syria* (Washington DC, 2008), p. 12, n. 35.

[89]   Palmer, 'Influence', paragraph 40, no. 3.

[90]   Ibid.

[91]   In some versions a Trinitarian doxology is added as a ninth stanza.

[92]   In Table 8.2 the Latin text and English prose translation are from <http://medieval.ucdavis.edu/20A/Music.html> [accessed 4 February 2010].

Table 8.2   Hymn *Aeterne rerum conditor,* Stanzas 1 and 2: Latin Text and
              English Translation

Latin text	English prose translation
1. aeterne rerum conditor,	1. Eternal founder of the world,
noctem diemque qui regis	who rules night and day
et temporum das tempora,	and gives changes in due season,
ut alleves fastidium,	to relieve our weariness,
2. praeco diei iam sonat,	2. the herald of the day now sounds out,
noctis profundae pervigil,	ever watchful through the depth of night,
nocturna lux viantibus,	a light in the dark to travellers,
a nocte noctem segregans.	marking off one night-watch from another.

devotional. The natural accentuation of the words fits the iambic metre with only very few exceptions (for example, the last two words at the end of the second line of the first stanza).

The elegant simplicity of Ambrose's hymns was so much admired that it gave rise to a host of imitations in the Latin-speaking Christian world. In the centuries following Ambrose's death, his name became not only an adjective that identified the style (*hymni ambrosiani*), but also a noun for hymns in that style: *ambrosiani*.

The majority of the Greek, Latin and Syriac hymns discussed above were intended for popular use. This usage is reflected not only in their basic form but also in their general simplicity of language and treatment of ideas. Their musical style is likely to have been in keeping with these, and therefore to have been simple both melodically and rhythmically. Rhythmic simplicity is hardly in doubt, at least as far as the early Christian hymns in Greek are concerned. It was normal in classical Greek (non-Christian) hymns that the words should be chosen so that their innate long and short syllables should match the patterns of long and short syllables in the chosen metrical scheme, and furthermore that the music should follow suit, giving long notes to long syllables, and short notes to short ones. Generally, long syllables were set to note values twice as long as those to which short ones were set. This could vary at points of rest such as the ends of lines or ends of stanzas where a long syllable could be set to a note longer than twice the length of a short one.[93] This practice would have produced a syllabic melodic style. A simple, syllabic style of melody, in which long and short notes are for the most part set respectively to long and short syllables in the text, is exactly what is found in the Oxyrhynchus hymn (Example 8.1).[94] Although

[93] See, for example, M.L. West, *Ancient Greek Music* (Oxford, 1992), pp. 130–33.

[94] M.L. West, *Ancient Greek Music*, p. 325, gives the following translation of the words of the hymn: '... Let it be silent, let the luminous stars not shine, let the winds(?) and all the noisy rivers die down; and as we hymn the Father, Son and Holy Spirit, let all the

Example 8.1   The Oxyrhynchus Hymn

(Original a tone higher)

u - ta - nê__ ô__   si ga - tô,   mêd' as - tra pha-es - pho-ra lam - pes - thôn

po- ta - môn__   rho - thi - ôn__ pa - sai;__   hum - noun - tôn   d'hê - môn pa - te - ra

k'yi - on__ k'ha - gi - on__   pneu - ma   pa - sai dy-na-meis   e - pi-phô - noun - tôn

A - mên,__ A - mên,__   kra-tos, ai - nos a - ei__   kai   do - xa the - oi__

dô - tê - ri mo-nôi   pan - tôn__ a - ga - thôn.__   A - mên,__ A - mên.__

Note heads given as × are of uncertain pitch.

The wavy diagonal line in the fifth bar indicates a lacuna.

In the text a circumflex accent marks *êta* and *ômega*.

Note: Reprinted from M.L. West, *Ancient Greek Music* (Oxford: Oxford University Press, 1992), pp. 324–5. By permission of Oxford University Press.

the hymn deviates from the classical norms occasionally,[95] the predominantly anapaestic metre of the text (˘ ˘ ‒) is closely followed in the musical setting. Here the ratio of the duration of long to short notes is 1:2. Sometimes a rest for the combined duration of two short notes precedes a long note.

The Syriac *madrāšê* of Ephrem the Syrian and the Latin Ambrosian hymns are even simpler in style than the Greek hymns examined above, so that a melodically and rhythmically simple musical style may be assumed for these also, even though the musical character of the Eastern and Western melodies is likely to have differed considerably. The strophic form of the *madrāšê* and Ambrosian hymns implies in addition that the melody used for the first stanza

---

powers add "Amen, amen". Empire, praise always, and glory to God, the sole giver of all good things. Amen, amen.'

[95]   West, *Ancient Greek Music*, p. 132, n. 11, explains this by the lateness (in terms of ancient Greek culture) of the composition, by which time there was no longer a general adherence to the classical rules of quantity in poetry.

of a given hymn would have been repeated for each of the subsequent stanzas. The refrains of the *madrāšē* probably used the same melody as the stanzas. All this is conjectural for the fourth century itself, but is the case in the earliest surviving examples with musical notation. Post-fourth-century Greek Christian hymns have a similar strophic form and simple, basically syllabic, musical style, although the music tends to be more ornate than that of the Ambrosian and Ambrosian-style hymns. It is quite possible that among the ancient melodies traditionally associated with the oldest known Greek, Latin and Syriac Christian hymns (many of which are still sung today) are some that date back to the fifth or even the fourth century, and have remained almost unchanged since that time.

Music in the Nag Hammadi Codices

The 52 tractates assembled in 13 codices discovered in Nag Hammadi in Upper Egypt constitute the largest extant corpus of writings representing the beliefs and teachings of a variety of syncretic mystical cults which have hitherto been termed 'gnostic'.[96] In very general terms, the gnostics offered salvation through 'secret' knowledge of the Divine, which only initiates were privileged to receive. This knowledge (*gnōsis*) was imparted through teaching designed to lead initiates to gradually higher planes of spiritual awareness. Asceticism, mystical contemplation, recitation of secret formulas, self-knowledge and the study of gnostic sacred texts were typical means by which increased spiritual awareness could be achieved. Gnostic elements are evident to a greater or lesser extent in all religions in the Near East, Egypt and the Levant, including Judaism, Christianity, Neo-Platonism and the Greek mystery religions, from about the end of the first century CE onwards. In the fourth century gnostic doctrines were made heretical for Christians. Many Christians perceived by their peers to be gnostics were expelled from their towns and villages; writings considered gnostic were ordered to be burnt.

The tractates of the Nag Hammadi codices are Coptic translations of Greek originals some of which probably emanated from elsewhere in the eastern Mediterranean lands than Egypt. The Nag Hammadi codices may be regarded as representative of gnostic thought over a broad geographical area. The literature is varied in genre and scope. It consists mainly of apocalypses, apocryphal Acts, didactic works and pseudepigraphical gospels. Some tractates contain polemical

---

[96]   On the gnostics, see, for example: Elaine Pagels, *The Gnostic Gospels* (Harmondsworth, 1982), pp. 13–32; Oskar Skarsaune, *In the Shadow of the Temple* (Downers Grove Il, 2002), pp. 245–53; Alastair H.B. Logan, *The Gnostics: Identifying an Early Christian Cult* (New York, 2006). On the Nag Hammadi codices, see: James M. Robinson (ed.), *The Nag Hammadi Library in English*, 3rd (rev.) edn (San Francisco, 2000), pp. 1–26; *NHS*, pp. 1–13 (also pp. 803–26 for a substantial bibliography up to 2006 compiled by Brent A. Smith). On the need for redefinition of 'gnostic' and 'gnosticism', see especially: Michael A. Williams, *Rethinking 'Gnosticism': An Argument for Dismantling a Dubious Category* (Princeton NJ, 1996).

narratives, descriptions of visions, dialogues with imaginary heavenly beings and dialogues with mentors or religious teachers. The imagined spiritual world figures prominently, and it is impossible to know whether, or to what extent, the written texts defined the actual daily lives of adherents.

Musical references are relatively few considering the extent of the literature. There are some five references to instruments or instrumental music and approximately twice as many to song or chant. There are also several passages consisting of strings of repeated vowels, which may represent wordless ululation. These are included in the following survey since they could have been susceptible of musical rendition.

Song

References to song constitute the majority of the references to music. Two passages from the *Secret Book of James* (I,2)[97] refer to 'hymns' and 'praises' sung by heavenly beings. However, they give no information about the texts that were sung, nor about the style of the music. One has:

> [*Secr. Bk. Jas.* (I,2 p. 14)] Be attentive to the glory that awaits me, and when you have opened your hearts, listen to the hymns that await me up in heaven. (*NHS*, p. 29)

The other provides slightly more contextual information:

> [*Secr. Bk. Jas.* (I,2 p. 15)] When we passed beyond that place, we sent our minds up further. We saw with our eyes and heard with our ears hymns, angelic praises, and angelic rejoicing. Heavenly majesties were singing hymns, and we rejoiced too. (*NHS*, p. 30)

Two short passages on consecutive pages of the *Tripartite Tractate* (I,5) mention hymning the Deity: '... his great exaltedness can be revealed when they speak about him and see him, gratefully singing hymns to him about his abundant sweetness' (I,5 p. 63; *NHS*, p. 67); and, '... that which they sing as hymns, giving glory' (I,5 p. 64; *NHS*, p. 67). Later in the tractate there is a passage that may allude to the use of song in a liturgical context; this is the closest the Nag Hammadi codices come to concrete musical reference:

> [*Tri. Trac.* (I,5 p. 121)] After having confessed the Lord, having given thought to what is good for the Church, and having sung together with it the hymn of the humble, they will ... partake of the fellowship in hope. (*NHS*, pp. 94–5)

---

[97]   In citations of *NHS* herein, upper-case roman numerals identify codices, italic arabic numbers identify tractates within codices, a lower-case roman 'p.' followed by an arabic number indicates the page number within a codex.

A passage in the *Holy Book of the Great Invisible Spirit* (two copies extant: III,2; IV,2), formerly sometimes referred to as the 'Gospel of the Egyptians', seems to support the apparent allusion to liturgical song in the above quotation. However, the 'spiritual church' referred to on page 55 of codex III,2, could be a mystical concept:

> [*Great. Inv. Spirit* (III,2 p. 55)] The incorruptible spiritual assembly [or 'church' (*ekklēsia*)] expanded within the Four Luminaries of the great living Self-Generated God of truth. They praised, sang, and gave glory with one voice, with one accord .... (*NHS*, p. 260)

In the tractate *On the Origin of the World* (II,5), musical references (to the extent that lamenting and mourning can be regarded as musical) occur within a prophecy of disaster:

> [*Orig. World* (II,5 p. 125)] The archons will lament because of their [fear of] [p. 126] death, the angels will grieve ... and their people will mourn and cry on account of their death. (*NHS*, p. 220)

The most esoteric references to song in the Nag Hammadi codices occur in the tractate called *The Discourse on the Eighth and Ninth* (VI,6). The ordinal numbers in the title refer to ancient beliefs which held that the earth is surrounded by spheres of mystic importance and influence; spheres eight and nine were heavenly spheres. The tractate takes the form of a dialogue between teacher and pupil. In VI,6, page 58, the idea of silent song is presented:

> [*Disc. 8-9* (VI,6 p. 58)] ... all of the eighth, my child, and the souls in it {the eighth sphere}, and the angels, sing a hymn in silence. I, Mind, understand.
> 'How does one sing a hymn through silence?'
> 'Can no one communicate with you?'
> 'I am silent, father. I want to sing a hymn to you while I am silent.'
> 'Then sing it. I am Mind.' (*NHS*, p. 416)

The idea of silent song is taken up again on the next page when the teacher says to his pupil: 'Sing <praise> again, my child, and sing while you are silent' (*Disc. 8-9* [VI,6 p. 59]; *NHS*, p. 417). Later, the teacher relates a vision in which he sees heavenly beings singing a hymn:

> [*Disc. 8-9*, (VI,6 p. 59)] I see the eighth, and the souls in it, and the angels singing a hymn to the ninth and its powers. (*NHS*, p. 417)

Then the teacher instructs his pupil further, returning to the idea of silent, interior song:

[*Disc. 8–9* (VI,6 p. 60)] 'It is fitting to sing [a hymn] to the Father until the day we leave the body.'

'What you sing, father, I also want to sing.'

'I am singing a hymn in myself. While you rest, sing praise. You have found what you seek.'

'But is it right, father, for me to sing praise when my heart is filled?'

'What is right is for you to sing praise to God so that it may be written in this imperishable book.'

'I shall offer up the praise in my heart ... No hidden word can speak of you, lord. My mind wants to sing a hymn to you every day.' (*NHS*, p. 417)

The pupil's reply continues for a further five or so lines. When this is finished, the teacher gives his approval and the pupil offers thanks to the Deity:

[*Disc. 8–9* (VI,6 p. 61)] 'Right, my child.'

'O grace! After this, I thank you by singing a hymn to you. You gave me life when you made me wise. I praise you. I invoke your name hidden in me,

A

Ō EE

Ō ĒĒĒ

ŌŌŌ III

ŌŌŌŌ OOOOO

ŌŌŌŌŌ UUUUUU

ŌŌŌŌŌŌ ŌŌŌŌŌ

ŌŌŌŌŌŌŌ ŌŌŌŌ

You exist with spirit.

I sing to you with godliness.' (*NHS*, p. 417–18)

It is possible that the passage from 'O grace!' to the end of the quotation is the pupil's hymn.

A remarkable feature of the passage is the succession of vowels towards the end of the above quotation. Similar passages occur in the same tractate[98] and in the *Holy Book of the Great Invisible Spirit*.[99] Shorter examples of the phenomenon occur in the tractates *Zostrianos*,[100] *Allogenes the Stranger*[101] and *Three Forms of First Thought* (otherwise known as *Trimorphic Protennoia*).[102] They seem to be vocalizations on the vowels of various names and other words, such as Jesus, Yesseus Mazareus Yessedekeus, Zoxathazo, phoē, and zoē. How they were rendered is a mystery. Whether each vowel sound was sustained, or whether it was reiterated for the

---

[98]   Codex VI, p. 56.

[99]   Codex III, p. 44; Codex IV, p. 60.

[100] Codex VIII, pp. 52 and 127.

[101] Codex XI, p. 53.

[102] Codex XIII, p. 38.

number of times it was written, is not known. The vowels may possibly have been sung on a quiet monotone. It is also possible that 'overtone singing' or 'throat singing', an ancient style of religious chant practised by Buddhist monks in Mongolia, Tibet, southern Russia (especially Tuva) and northern India (regions from which gnostic ideas spread to the Near East in late antiquity), may give a clue as to how the strings of vowels were uttered.[103] Overtone singing consists principally of singing low monotones while changing the shape of the mouth cavity to form vowels, thereby creating various overtones above the monotones. But there is no concrete evidence of a connection between central Asian chant and the strings of vowels in gnostic literature.

Musical Instruments

The instruments referred to in the Nag Hammadi codices are those already familiar from the Old Testament. Their names are Coptic transliterations of their Greek names as they occur in scriptural literature in Greek. In the *Discourse on the Eighth and Ninth*[104] the relationship between neophyte, teacher and Deity is expressed allegorically in terms of the playing of a plucked-string instrument: 'I am the instrument of your spirit, mind is your plectrum, and your guidance makes music with me' (*NHS*, p. 417). And in *The Second Revelation of James*[105] the '<silencing> of your trumpets, your flutes and your harps' (*NHS*, p. 340) is a metaphor for God's displeasure.

The tractate *On the Origin of the World* (II,5) has at one place:

[*Orig. World* (II,5 p. 105)] At his left the virgin of the holy Spirit sits upon a throne and glorifies him. Seven virgins stand before her, with thirty harps and lyres and [p. 106] trumpets in their hands, and they glorify him [*or* while thirty others, with lyres and harps and trumpets in their hands, glorify him]. (*NHS*, p. 208)

Harps and lyres are also referred to in a passage from *The Nature of the Rulers* (also known as the *Hypostasis of the Archons*) (II,4):

[*Nat. Rulers*, (II,4 p. 95)] When these things happened, he [Sabaoth] made himself a huge four-faced chariot of cherubim, and an infinity of angels as ministers, and harps and lyres .... (*NHS* p. 197)

Trumpets are also referred to twice on their own, in these cases in contexts of conflict. The *Secret Book of James* (I,2) has:

103   On overtone singing, see Mark C. Tongeren, *Overtone Singing: Physics and Metaphysics of Harmonics in East and West*, 2nd rev. edn (Delft, 2006).

104   Codex VI, p. 60.

105   Codex V, p. 60.

[*Secr. Bk. Jas.* (I,2 p. 15, line 9] We heard with our ears and saw with our eyes the noise of wars, a trumpet blast and great turmoil. (*NHS*, p. 30)

The *Tripartite Tractate* (I,5) refers to

[*Tri. Trac.* (I,5 p. 138)] the [sound of a] trumpet, which will announce the great and complete reconciliation from the resplendent East .... (*NHS*, p. 101)

None of these passages can be taken to have any bearing on the actual music of the gnostics: either they are figurative or they relate events that happened (or prophecies of what will happen) in an imaginary supernatural world. A possible exception is the passage from the *Secret Book of James*, which may refer to some actual historical 'great turmoil'. Nevertheless, the writer stands outside the turmoil, observing it, and the passage cannot be taken to imply that gnostics might have played trumpets or used them for signalling in war. The imagery of 'trumpets', 'flutes' and 'harps' in *The Second Revelation of James*[106] is most likely based on the use of such instruments in festal rites at the Jerusalem Temple. The imagery of the plucked-string instruments (and also of the trumpets in *On the Origin of the World*[107]) is clearly also borrowed from the liturgical use of such instruments in the Jerusalem Temple, perhaps influenced by similar imagery in the New Testament book of Revelation and contemporaneous Jewish apocalypses. The image of the trumpet that will 'announce the ... reconciliation from the resplendent East', in the last passage quoted, is perhaps an allusion to the eschatological end time when, according to the Apostle Paul, 'the trumpet will sound, and the dead will be raised imperishable' (1 Cor. 15:52).

---

[106]   Codex V, p. 60.
[107]   Codex II, p. 106.

Chapter 9
Relationships and Influences

The Relationship of Early Christian Chant to Ancient Jewish Sacred Chant

The extent to which the form and content of ancient Jewish worship influenced early Christian worship, and the extent to which Christian worship retained elements of its supposed Jewish liturgical heritage after Christianity became a religion in its own right, are topics that have interested theologians, historians of religion and liturgiologists for many centuries, and especially from the end of the nineteenth century onwards.[1] Since the 1950s, scholarly interest in these topics has increased considerably.[2]

The question of the relationship of Christian liturgical chant to Jewish sacred chant in the early centuries of the Common Era has been debated by musicologists and others since at least the early eighteenth century. The serious historiography of the topic begins with Roger North's *Memoires of Musick*, a handwritten fair copy of which was made in 1728.[3] Since that time the musicological discussion has unfolded in tandem with the gradual deepening of knowledge about Christian and Jewish liturgies in the first three to four centuries CE. But whereas information about liturgical forms and texts in that period is relatively plentiful, information about liturgical music is scant. In view of this situation, it is perhaps inevitable that writers who have discussed this question down through the centuries have

---

[1] For example, Louis Duchesne, *Origines du culte chrétien* (Paris, 1889); W.O.E. Oesterley, *The Jewish Background of the Christian Liturgy* (Oxford, 1925); Oesterley, *A Fresh Approach to the Psalms* (London, 1937), pp. 175–84; Oesterley (ed.), *Judaism and Christianity: The Age of Transition* (London, 1937); H. Loewe (ed.), *The Contact of Pharisaism with Other Cultures* (London, 1937); Erwin I.J. Roenthal (ed.), *Law and Religion* (London, 1938); [the last three works were later reissued in one volume, with a Prolegomenon by Ellis Rivkin, as *Judaism and Christianity*, ed. Ellis Rivkin (New York, 1969)]; Clifford W. Dugmore, *The Influence of the Synagogue upon the Divine Office* (1st edn, London, 1944; 2nd edn [= repr. of 1st edn with Introduction added], London, 1964); Gregory Dix, *The Shape of the Liturgy* (London, 1945).

[2] Paul Bradshaw, 'Jewish Influence on Early Christian Liturgy: A Reappraisal' (International Council of Christians and Jews, 2009), published online at <http://www.jcrelations.net/en/?item=2988>.

[3] Roger North, *Memoires of Musick, being some Historico-critticall Collections of that Subject* [1728]. This work was not published during his lifetime (the first of the editions listed in the Bibliography is its earliest publication) but it was made known by Charles Burney who referred to it eight times in vols 3 and 4 of his *A General History of Music* (1789): see Charles Burney, *A General History of Music*, edited, with critical and historical notes, by Frank Mercer (London, 1935; repr. New York, 1957).

often relied heavily on assumptions to carry their arguments forward. Recently, serious doubts have been raised about the validity of some of the premises on which those assumptions rest.[4]

Four areas are appropriate for consideration: (1) the implications of recent scholarship about the 'parting of the ways' between Judaism and Christianity, (2) the relative chronology of the earliest sources of Jewish and Christian chant, (3) the implications of the introduction of the system of the eight modes into Eastern and Western Christian chant and (4) the Jewish sacred music milieu of the earliest Christians.

The Implications of Recent Scholarship on the 'Parting of the Ways'

According to earlier generations of scholars, by about the time of the Bar Kokhba revolt in 135 CE, antipathy between Jews and Christians had reached a point where mutual toleration was no longer possible, and an irrevocable breach occurred between Christianity and Judaism. This parting of the ways, it was supposed, effectively put interaction between Christians and Jews (such as could have occurred prior to this time) beyond the bounds of possibility.[5] Recent scholarship about the parting of the ways, however, shows that while inevitably there came a time when the doctrinal differences between Judaism and Christianity forced them to separate, at the intellectual level there was continued contact.[6] Although the subsequent relationship between Christians and Jews was complex,[7] the ideological separation of Christianity from Judaism was not an obstacle to the continued exchange of ideas.

For earlier generations of scholars, the second-century breach between Judaism and Christianity marked the end of a period of time during which

---

[4]   On music, see Peter Jeffery, *Re-Envisioning Past Musical Cultures: Ethnomusicology in the Study of Gregorian Chant* (Chicago and London, 1992); on liturgy, see Bradshaw, 'Jewish Influence'. The ideas presented and the perceptive questions raised in these works are basic to the arguments in the present section.

[5]   John Arthur Smith, 'Three Anglican Church Historians on Liturgy and Psalmody in the Ancient Synagogue and the Early Church', in Emma Hornby and David Maw (eds), *Essays on the History of English Music in Honour of John Caldwell: Sources, Style, Performance, Historiography* (Woodbridge, 2010), pp. 307–9. The musicologist Eric Werner associated the parting of the ways with the Council of Nicaea in 325 and regarded the time from the second century onwards as a period of 'incipient separation': Eric Werner, *The Sacred Bridge*, 2 vols (New York, 1959, 1984), vol. 1, pp. 37, 41, 58.

[6]   William Horbury, *Jews and Christians in Contact and Controversy* (Edinburgh, 1998); Adam H. Becker and Annette Yoshiko Reed (eds), *The Ways That Never Parted: Jews and Christians in Late Antiquity and the Early Middle Ages* (Minneapolis MN, 2007).

[7]   See esp. Paula Fredriksen, 'What "Parting of the Ways"?' in Becker and Reed (eds), *The Ways That Never Parted*, pp. 35–63; Annette Yoshiko Reed, '"Jewish Christianity" after the "Parting of the Ways": Approaches to Historiography and Self-Definition in the Pseudo-Clementines', in ibid., pp. 189–231.

Christians could freely adopt synagogue chant for use in their worship. With this obstacle now removed, the musical relationship between the two religions must be seen in a new light: musical interaction can no longer be regarded as occurring only up until the early decades of the second century CE. The way is thus open to consider the possibility of musical interaction throughout late antiquity and the Middle Ages; it is by no means unlikely that in some localities Christians were influenced by the melodic idioms of Jewish chant during those periods.[8] It is possible that the few instances of close melodic similarity between Jewish and medieval Christian chant, which some scholars claim to have found (see below), are the result not of the Christian preservation of Jewish musical traditions from before the parting of the ways, but of musical interaction at a much later date.

The Relative Chronology of the Earliest Examples of Jewish and Christian Chant

Serious chronological and musical issues arise when the earliest extant items of Christian chant are considered in relation to the earliest extant items of Jewish chant (to some of which certain medieval Christian chants have been found to be similar). The salient point here is that for Jewish chant the earliest extant written examples are not medieval (except for one item), but much later, whereas for Christian chant the earliest extant examples are well and truly medieval, the earliest manuscripts dating from around the middle of the ninth century.

Jewish chant   The earliest extant example of Jewish sacred music in readable music notation is a manuscript of a *pîyût* (a liturgical hymn with a free text) written down and perhaps composed by Obadiah the Proselyte probably in the early twelfth century.[9] Beyond this isolated item, the earliest written sources date from the sixteenth and seventeenth centuries and exemplify German traditions.[10] The earliest of these is a table song for domestic use at meals; the remainder are biblical chants with the *ṭĕ'āmîm* (the Masoretic accents) written out in notation. For the rest of the Jewish synagogue chant tradition, the most comprehensive source is Abraham Z. Idelsohn's ten-volume *Thesaurus of Hebrew-Oriental Melodies* published in German between 1914 and 1932.[11] Idelsohn assembled the material

---

[8]   For a detailed study of a situation in which this kind of musical interaction could have taken place, see Thomas H. Connolly, 'Traces of a Jewish–Christian Community at S. Cecilia in Trastevere', *Plainsong and Medieval Music*, 7/1 (April 1998): 1–19.

[9]   Daniel S. Katz, 'Biblische Kantillation und Musik der Synagoge: Ein Rückblick auf die ältesten Quellen', *Musiktheorie*, 15 (2000): 71–4, which includes, as illustrations 3 and 4, photographic reproductions of Obadiah's manuscript; Edwin Seroussi, 'Poetry, Piyyutim', *New Grove/2*, vol. 13, pp. 49–51.

[10]   Katz, 'Biblische Kantillation', pp. 72 (Table 4), 74–7.

[11]   Abraham Z. Idelsohn, *Hebraïsch-orientalischer Melodienschatz*, 10 vols (Jerusalem and Leipzig, 1914–32).

for this work by transcribing phonographic recordings which he made in the field. The material thus collected formed the basis for the early chapters of his book *Jewish Music in its Historical Development* published in 1929,[12] by which time five volumes of his *Thesaurus* had been published.

For Idelsohn the melodies from the Near East, which he designated 'Semitic-Oriental', were significant because they were the most ancient examples of Jewish chant. He regarded those from Jewish communities in Babylonia and Persia as the oldest of all because those communities are the oldest established of all, dating back to around the time of the destruction of the First Temple. The melodies of Yemenite Jews are especially noteworthy since, according to Idelsohn, the Yemenite community remained virtually isolated for 1,300 years, thereby allowing for the possibility that its traditional melodies had been preserved in almost pristine form. Writing of the Near-Eastern Jewish cantillation of the Bible, he said, 'As proof of the antiquity of the traditional tunes in which the Scriptures are chanted, we cite their Oriental origin.'[13]

Idelsohn set great store by the tenacity of the oral tradition among the Near-Eastern peoples. He clearly believed that the melodies as he heard them when he collected them for his *Thesaurus* went back to the time when the ancient Jewish communities became established. However, vocal melodic material is not immutable when transmitted orally, but is susceptible of local variation and to gradual change over time. External influences are probably the most usual causes of change in orally transmitted monophonic chant, but change can also come about without them. Three factors are significant in this respect. One is that the oral tradition is dependent on human beings, and human beings are not disposed towards rigid uniformity in their repeated renderings of items of vocal melody. Another is that the oral tradition of chant is dependent on human beings *alone*, being free of the addition of any mechanical device that might act as a constraint or control, such as a tuned musical instrument played in accompaniment. The third is that the tradition itself may permit a certain amount of melodic freedom. Thus even in Near-Eastern Jewish communities that remained relatively isolated for long periods, such as the community of Yemenite Jews, changes in the melodies of the sacred chants are likely to have occurred over time.

Idelsohn's description of the Semitic-Oriental melodies to which he drew attention[14] is in fact a description of the traditional vocal music of the Arab world, the style of which has been prevalent in the Near East for thousands of years. While most of what Idelsohn said about the general characteristics of Arab music remains valid, newer research has supplemented and refined the picture he presented, especially where intonation and the compositional element

[12]　Abraham Z. Idelsohn, *Jewish Music in its Historical Development* (New York, 1929, repr. 1967).

[13]　Ibid., p. 58.

[14]　Ibid., pp. 24–8.

maqām (which Idelsohn called 'mode') are concerned. The quartertone system of traditional Arab music is not equally tempered,[15] and might more accurately be described as microtonal.[16] Practitioners of traditional Arab music have avoided transcribing their melodies into readable music notation even though the means of transcription have been available for several centuries. They have no doubt done this deliberately so as to allow their orally transmitted music to be open to such variation and change as is deemed natural within the prevalent tradition and culture.

There is no guarantee that the supposedly most ancient Semitic-Oriental melodies had the same form when Idelsohn transcribed them as they did 2,000 years ago. Furthermore, other Jewish sacred chant melodies extant in readable notation, but deemed to be very ancient, may not exhibit the same melodic form as they possessed in antiquity.

Eastern (Byzantine) Christian chant   The earliest traditions of Eastern (Byzantine) Christian chant emanate from the four main early centres of Eastern Christianity: Alexandria, Antioch in Syria, Byzantium (Constantinople) and Jerusalem. Manuscripts of the chant are extant from the eighth to the thirteenth centuries.[17] There are two main styles of chant. One, used for the liturgical reading of Scripture, including the biblical psalms, is a form of liturgical recitative. In the manuscripts this is transmitted in ekphonetic notation, which consists of paired signs placed above the text at the beginning and end of each verbal phrase (some 20 conventional pairings have been identified). The ekphonetic signs therefore indicate at one and the same time the intonation formulas for the readings, and, by virtue of their placement in relation to the phrases of text, how the readings are to be punctuated. The signs provide no clues as to the pitches they represent, and are therefore unreadable as musical notation. They probably functioned as memory aids for the liturgical readers. Manuscripts of Scripture readings with ekphonetic notation are extant from the late eighth to the thirteenth century. Manuscript evidence for the music of the liturgical recitatives other

---

[15]   A tempered octave scale of 24 equal quartertones was introduced into Arabic music in the mid-nineteenth century as a result of the work of Mikha'il Mishaqa (1800–88), but this seems not to have affected the performance of traditional Arabic music nor of Semitic-Oriental synagogue chant. See Shireen Maalouf, 'Mikha'il Mishaqa: Virtual Founder of the Twenty-Four Equal Quartertone Scale', *Journal of the American Oriental Society*, 123/4 (October, 2003): 835–40.

[16]   On traditional Arab music, see Habib Hassan Touma, *The Music of the Arabs*, trans. Laurie Schwartz (Portland OR, 1996); Shireen Maalouf, *History of Arabic Music Theory: Change and Continuity in the Tone Systems, Genres and Scales* (Kaslik, Lebanon, 2002).

[17]   On Byzantine chant, see relevant articles in *MGG*; *New Grove*/1/2; Peter Jeffery (ed.), *The Study of Medieval Chant: Paths and Bridges, East and West: In Honor of Kenneth Levy* (Woodbridge, 2001).

than Scripture readings is late, most likely indicating that this music existed primarily in an oral tradition.

The other style of chant is melodic. Melodic chant is used for the more substantial liturgical texts, and is extant in manuscripts from the tenth century onwards. Its notation consists of neumes organized as a cipher or code, which, given the starting note and the mode (see below), indicates the intervallic relationship of each successive note to its predecessor. Chants written in this 'digital' notation, as Kenneth Levy has called it,[18] can therefore be transcribed into musical notation. During the tenth and eleventh centuries the notation also provided the singers with information about nuances of performance.

Western Christian chant   The earliest extant examples of Western Christian chant with musical notation are to be found in manuscripts that emanate probably from Gaul in around 800 CE.[19] The music is notated in neumes that have various linear shapes arranged all on one level above the lines of text to which they apply. There is no clear indication of the pitches represented by the neumes, and therefore the music cannot be transcribed into readable notation. Some writers believe that the shapes of these neumes result from attempts to represent in written form the hand-movements used by choir leaders when directing their singers, hence this style of neumatic notation is sometimes called 'cheironomic' (literally: 'directed by [movements of] the hand').

The earliest extant examples of musically readable Western Christian chant are found in manuscripts from the ninth century containing respectively the *Commemoratio brevis de tonis et psalmis modulendi*, and the *Musica enchiriadis*. The *Commemoratio brevis* is a combined tonary and short catalogue of the tones of the psalms. The *Musica enchiriadis* contains the earliest written examples of Western polyphony, making use of short melodic formulas for the purpose of illustration. In both cases the music is notated in daseian neumes, symbols used as ciphers for the pitches of notes, thus allowing the pitches to be accurately transcribed. However, these documents are somewhat exceptional since on the one hand they are didactic treatises and therefore not in themselves intended for liturgical use, and on the other hand they pre-date the general availability of Western chant manuscripts with readable notation by some 200 years.

The main body of readable liturgical manuscripts of Western Christian chant is that of the so-called Gregorian repertory, which dates from the tenth to the twelfth centuries. The earliest manuscripts of Ambrosian (Milanese), Beneventan (southern Italian), Mozarabic (Iberian) and Old Roman chant – additional important Western chant repertories closely related to, but different from Gregorian chant – date from the eleventh and twelfth centuries. Although

---

[18]   Kenneth Levy, 'Byzantine Chant', *New Grove*/1, vol. 3, p. 554.

[19]   On Western Christian chant, see relevant articles in *MGG*; *New Grove*/1/2; Willi Apel, *Gregorian Chant* (London, n.d. [1958]); David Hiley, *Western Plainchant: A Handbook* (Oxford, 1993); Jeffery, *The Study of Medieval Chant*.

the musical notation of a small number of items in these repertories is given in daseian neumes, in the vast majority of manuscripts the notation is written in diastematic (or 'heightened') neumes – neumes placed on the page at varying levels 'above' each of the lines of text, hence 'heightened'.

Implications of the Introduction of the Modal System

The eight modes is a compositional system for Eastern and Western Christian chant of the Middle Ages. It defines the limits of musical operation within generally an octave range and other musical features such as predominating notes and concluding notes. It was applied uniformly throughout the Byzantine church. In the West it was applied later than in the East and not with equal stringency in all regions.

In the Eastern (Byzantine) tradition the modal system is referred to as the *octōēchoi*, 'the eight modes', and is known from at least the eighth century.[20] The most comprehensive ancient sources of modal chants are the *Heirmologion* (a book of *kontakia* – hymns), and the two Byzantine service books, the *Oktōēchos* ('book of the eight modes') and the *Paraklētikē* ('book of intercessional services'). The contents of the *Heirmologion* are arranged in order of mode. The *Oktōēchos* contains eight complete Sunday services, one in each of the eight modes in order (the four authentic, then the four plagal), one service to be used on each successive Sunday. The *Paraklētikē* contains the weekday services for eight weeks, also arranged in modal order, one mode per week. The resultant eight-week cycle of services begins at Easter and is repeated throughout the year.

In the Western tradition, which probably derived its modal theory from the Eastern Church, the system of eight modes was applied first and foremost to the chant used in the monasteries and churches in the areas within the jurisdiction of the Frankish king Charlemagne in the early ninth century. It was this version of the chant repertory, emanating from the choirs and scriptoria of Frankia, that came to be regarded as the exemplar of the eight church modes of Western modal theory and the archetype of 'Gregorian' chant. At the same time some smaller, localized repertories of Western Christian chant, which do not exhibit the same conformity to modal theory, continued in use for a brief period in Rome (Old Roman chant), Milan (Milanese, or Ambrosian, chant), on the Iberian peninsula (Old Spanish, or Mozarabic chant) and in southern Italy (Beneventan chant). Even in the Gregorian repertory itself several individual chants and classes of chant are noted for their non-conformity to modal theory.

An important aspect of the introduction of modality, however, is that in both Eastern and Western traditions it was imposed on existing chant repertories.

---

[20]   See Levy, 'Byzantine Chant'; Peter Jeffery, 'The Earliest Octōēchoi', in Jeffery (ed.), *The Study of Medieval Chant*, pp. 147–209; Peter Jeffery, 'The Sunday Office of Seventh-Century Jerusalem in the Georgian Chantbook (Iadgari): A Preliminary Report', *Studia Liturgica*, 21 (1991): 52–75.

Exactly how this was effected is not known. It is likely that while some of the existing chant melodies would have had to be altered to conform to modal requirements, a certain number of the remaining extant chants would have been newly composed. How extensive these processes might have been is impossible to say with certainty. It is therefore impossible to know which chants might exhibit the melodic form they possessed before the introduction of modality.[21]

The Jewish Sacred Music Milieu of the Earliest Christians

Since the earliest Christian believers were Jews or Gentile adherents of Judaism, many of whom continued to live and worship as Jews, it is reasonable to assume that when they assembled as 'Christianized' Jews they employed the chants familiar to them from the synagogue. The question is, what were those chants? From the brief glimpses of Sabbath assemblies afforded by the descriptions in Philo of Alexandria's *That Every Good Person is Free* 12 and *Hypothetica* 7:12–13, and by the narratives in the New Testament books of Luke 4:16–29 and Acts 13:15, it seems that around the middle of the first century CE the proceedings consisted of little more than Scripture reading and exegesis, 'except when it [was] the practice to add something to signify approval of what [was] read'[22] – perhaps by the interjection of 'amen'. There is no mention of hymns or psalms. Only after the destruction of the Temple, and then not until around the beginning of the second century, is there concrete evidence that psalms – the Hallel – were recited at the assemblies. This does not preclude the possibility that psalms other than the Hallel were recited occasionally, but it does mean that there are no grounds for believing that their number was large. It also means that there are no grounds for believing that the recitation of psalms was a fixed and discrete liturgical item of the kind which certain Anglican liturgists read back into first-century synagogue worship from later Christian practice.[23] The synagogue chants with which the earliest Christians would have been familiar are likely to have been those to which the Scriptures, and later the Hallel, were cantillated.

However, material presented in chapters 5 and 6 shows that in ancient Judaism there was sacred song on a wide variety of types of occasion in addition to the regular assemblies at the synagogue. This serves to suggest that there was an equally wide variety of styles of song on such occasions and therefore that it was not only 'chant' in the sense of semi-musical utterance that was employed in religious contexts. While the formal reading of Scripture would have occurred as cantillation, the proclamation of festal psalms, the utterance of lamentations, the performance of ring-dances and the singing of thanksgiving hymns or psalms or songs would have evinced several different musical styles. This was the Jewish

21   Jeffery, *Re-Envisioning*, p. 107.
22   Philo of Alexandria, *Hypothetica* 7:13, in *Philo*, ed. F.H. Colson, 10 vols and 2 supp. vols (London, 1941, 1985), vol. 9, pp. 432, 433.
23   Smith, 'Three Anglican Church Historians', pp. 298–310, esp. pp. 305–7.

sacred music environment of the earliest Christian believers. Whether later Christianity might have preserved anything of this early musical heritage, and whether it is possible to discover, are questions that must be approached in the light of the discussions above.

Comments

The essential point which emerges from the second and third discussions above is that there are breaks in the chain of musical historical evidence. With regard to Jewish chant the Near-Eastern Jewish examples regarded by Idelsohn as the most ancient have been subject to the vicissitudes of oral transmission; it is naive to assume that their melodic form could have remained unaltered for over 2,000 years. With regard to Christian music, the processes surrounding the imposition of modality have effectively compromised the pre-modal melodic heritage of Christian chant, thereby depriving us of reliable pointers to its likely musical state prior to about the seventh or eighth century in the case of Eastern chant and the ninth century in the case of Western.

In the context of the possibility of continuing musical interaction between Jews and Christians in late antiquity and the Middle Ages it may be pointed out that the many comparisons between Semitic-Oriental chant and Eastern and Western Christian chant presented by Idelsohn in his copious musical examples in chapters 2–5 of his *Jewish Music* rarely show any close melodic similarity. Such points of similarity as do occur are of so general a nature that they could have arisen accidentally. Apparently more promising points of similarity occur in the comparative examples of simple chants.[24] Eric Werner has claimed to find a Yemenite chant resembling the Gregorian *tonus peregrinus* and sung to the same text.[25] But Werner's scholarship in this instance is highly suspect.[26] In any case, the *tonus peregrinus* has been, and is still the subject of much discussion but little agreement;[27] it would therefore be unwise to set any great store by Werner's claims. It is worth bearing in mind that the delivery of a simple recitation in psalmodic style does not allow for a great deal of variety of approach. There must be melodic formulas for opening and closing each verse, there must be a reciting note to carry most of the text of each verse, and it would be natural for there to be some small deviation from the reciting note to mark a medial caesura. Nothing more complex is required, and it would therefore not be

---

[24] For example, Idelsohn, *Jewish Music*, pp. 63–4, Table X, nos. 6, 9, 18.

[25] Werner, *The Sacred Bridge*, vol. 1, p. 466.

[26] See Peter Jeffery, 'Werner's *The Sacred Bridge*, Volume 2: A Review Essay', *Jewish Quarterly Review*, 77 (1987): 283–98.

[27] On the historiography of the *tonus peregrinus*, see Mattias Olof Lundberg, 'Historiographical Problems of the *Tonus Peregrinus*', *Min-Ad: Israel Studies in Musicology Online*, 2004, vol. 3 [online journal] at <http://www.biu.ac.il/hu/mu/min-ad04> [accessed 14 March 2008].

surprising if several close similarities of melody occurred across cultural and
religious boundaries.

The somewhat negative picture that has emerged so far is enhanced by three
factors which point to a measure of disparity between the Jewish and Christian
chant traditions. One is that the modes of medieval Christian chant do not have
a Semitic origin. This was shown to be the case in Eastern Christian chant by
Aelred Cody in 1982 in the course of his study of the early history of the modes
in Syria.[28] Since modality in Western Christian chant was strongly influenced
by, if not adopted wholesale from, the practice of Eastern Christendom, the
same must apply by association to Western Christian chant, as Peter Jeffery has
pointed out.[29]

This explains a second factor, namely that modality in medieval Christian
chant is not like *maqām* in traditional Near-Eastern vocal music.[30] There are
superficial similarities (delimitation of range, the presence of predominating and
concluding notes, a generally motivic style), but the differences are of greater
significance. In traditional Near-Eastern vocal music there are literally dozens of
maqāmāt,[31] the style is motivic, free improvisation is an important element, and
the musical idiom is microtonal. It is true that Byzantine chant makes use of a
number of standard melodic formulas, or motives, and that in Western Christian
chant the use of centonized motives is a feature of certain classes of chant in
certain modes, but these nowhere approach the motivic richness of traditional
Arab music, nor are they built around the division of the overall range into tri-,
tetra- and pentachords, as would be the case in traditional Arab music.

The third factor is that while both Christian and Jewish traditions of sacred
chant make use of neumatic notation in some form, the Christian differs from
the Jewish in several respects. Daniel Katz gives a table listing eight points of
comparison between the Christian neumes and the Jewish *ṭěʿāmîm*.[32] There is
only one point on which he registers agreement: the notation does not supply
the musical rhythm, it must be supplied by the singer according to the rhythm
of the verbal text (point 5 in Katz's table). The most significant difference is that
whereas in the Jewish tradition the *ṭěʿāmîm* are applied to the whole Tanakh,
in the Christian tradition neumes are not applied to the text of the Bible but
only to material used liturgically; in the Jewish tradition, liturgical material not

[28]　Aelred Cody, 'The Early History of the Octoechos in Syria', in *East of Byzantium:
Syria and Armenia in the Formative Period*, ed. Nina Garsoïan et al. (Washington DC, 1982),
pp. 89–113.
[29]　Jeffery, 'The Earliest Octōēchoi', p. 178 and n. 105 there.
[30]　But see Jeffery, *Re-Envisioning*, pp. 105–6: identification of the *octōēchoi* with certain
maqāmāt in West Syrian (Jacobite) and Byzantine-Melkite Christian chant.
[31]　There are nine traditional families of *maqāmāt* consisting of from two to seven
maqāmāt each. About 100 *maqāmāt* are in use today.
[32]　Katz, 'Biblische Kantillation', p. 63 (Table 2: Comparison of *ṭěʿāmîm* and neumes).

from the Tanakh does not have *ṭĕ'āmîm*.[33] The *ṭĕ'āmîm* are therefore not primarily liturgical neumes.[34]

Several recent books claim to find historical continuity between liturgy and ritual in Judaism and early Christianity.[35] However, their conclusions are not altogether reliable. This has been pointed out in an article by Paul Bradshaw.[36] The position is that the presence in early Christian sources of liturgical texts or descriptions of liturgical actions exhibiting strong similarity to those of ancient Judaism cannot automatically be regarded as evidence of continuity from one into the other. A case in point is the Christian Sanctus. This item first appears in Christian sources in the fourth century; by this time it had been present in Jewish liturgy for several centuries. But the current thinking is that the Sanctus was probably not a continuation from Judaism, but more likely a fourth-century Christian import.[37] Nor in such matters should it be 'automatically assume[d] that the traffic was all one-way'.[38] Bradshaw is sophisticated about the questions that should be asked and the caveats that should be applied in the face of apparently similar liturgical material in Jewish and early Christian sources. His point is that continuity has to be demonstrated historically, and this is impossible to do.

Bradshaw's article is concerned with liturgy. Further dimensions enter the arena when music is added. A liturgical text is not its music. Even though a text

---

[33]   In the Jewish tradition, *ṭĕ'āmîm* are applied also to the text of the Mishnah and Talmuds, whereas in the Christian tradition neumes are not applied to any of the works of the Church Fathers. Katz may be wrong in point 6 in his comparative table (as n. 32) where he says that neumes embody only the melody. The neumes, especially the earlier types (non-diastematic and diastematic), probably embody interpretive instructions as well as melodic reminders.

[34]   Even Eastern and Western Christian chant were perceived as belonging to two different musical cultures in the early Middle Ages, an apt illustration of which is provided by Kenneth Levy, 'Gregorian Chant and the Romans', *Journal of the American Musicological Society*, 56 (2003): 5–41, collected in Thomas Forrest Kelly (ed.), *Chant and its Origins* (Farnham, 2009), pp. 427–63. On p. 438 of that collection Levy relates and comments on an anecdote in Notker Balbulus's *Vita Caroli*. He writes, 'While at Aachen, probably in 802, Charlemagne hears a visiting Greek choir perform the antiphons of the *Veterem hominem* series for the Epiphany octave in their original Byzantine versions. The emperor calls for an accurate Latin translation, and the results appear in the GREG [Gregorian] antiphoners of the tenth through the twelfth centuries, in which the Greek texts have been changed into Latin, and the BYZ [Byzantine] music has been turned into GREG [Gregorian] melodic style.'

[35]   For example, Margaret Barker, *The Great High Priest: The Temple Roots of Christian Liturgy* (London, 2003); Stephane Verhelst, *Les traditions judéo-chrétiennes dans la liturgie de Jérusalem*, Studies in Liturgy, vol. 18 (Louvain, 2003); Margaret Barker, *Temple Themes in Christian Worship* (London, 2008).

[36]   Paul Bradshaw, 'Jewish Influence', at n. 41.

[37]   Ibid., between nn. 32 and 33.

[38]   Ibid., after n. 36.

may exist in similar form in both religions, there is no guarantee that it would have been chanted to the same music in both of them, nor that it would have been chanted to the same music in all places in either one of them. To prove musical continuity between Judaism and early Christianity is not possible given the present state of knowledge.

Ultimately it must be conceded that there is simply insufficient reliable information available at present to permit more than general and inconclusive observations about the relationship between ancient Jewish and early Christian chant in the first four centuries of the Common Era.

The Earliest Christian Chant

The large amount of attention given by many earlier writers to questions about the relationship between Jewish and Christian chant has tended to obscure the fact that there were influences on Christian chant from quarters other than Judaism. These are sometimes difficult to identify and quantify, but their existence cannot be doubted.

One feature of early Christianity which provides valuable clues, if not concrete information, about its wider musical aspects is its diversity. Christopher Page paints a vivid picture of this diversity.[39] It was evident not only in the widespread geographical locations and the multifaceted cultural and social milieux in which Christianity became established, but also in the variety of forms of worship in early Christianity, and in the kaleidoscopic variety of shades of belief that underpinned them. Irenaeus (early second century to late second or early third century), bishop of Lyon, and Hippolytus of Rome (*c.*170–*c.*236), wrote of some 24 and some 50 different forms of Christianity respectively that were current in their day. Exactly what all this might have meant in terms of music is impossible to know for certain, but it is highly likely that something of this diversity was reflected in musical types and styles.

Positive musical proof of this is not forthcoming generally, but the literature of late antiquity that is concerned with Christianity in the first four centuries or so provides several hints about the existence of varieties of musical style employed in Christian contexts. The following details may be noted. In three of his genuine letters, Ignatius of Antioch (*c.*35–*c.*107) employs metaphors which make use of imagery drawn from the performance of vocal music in Hellenistic culture (see Chapter 7 in this volume), and of musical terminology from the same environment. Nevertheless the contexts of his remarks are Christian worship and ethics. The possibility exists therefore that the Christians for whom he wrote were accustomed to employing music and styles of musical performance from the ambient Greek culture in their specifically Christian gatherings and

---

[39]   Christopher Page, *The Christian West and its Singers: The First Thousand Years* (New Haven and London, 2010), pp. 29–116.

worship. That Christians in predominantly Hellenistic environments did make use of native Greek musical styles in their religious song is shown by the music of the Oxyrhynchus hymn, the melodic and rhythmic style of which resembles that of several Greek hymns, such as Mesomedes' hymns to the Sun and to Nemesis, as well as other Greek vocal and instrumental pieces.[40]

The style of psalmody seems to have varied from place to place. It was noted in Chapter 8 that Athanasius of Alexandria was said to have required a minimally melodic style of psalm recitation, from which it may be inferred that such a style was not in use generally. Augustine of Hippo's reference to the 'melody of the sweet songs to which the Davidic Psalter is usually set', and to his being moved by Ambrose of Milan's 'sweetly singing church' (also noted in Chapter 8), lend support to the inference despite the disparities of place and time.[41]

A comparison of the literary styles of Ephrem the Syrian and Ambrose of Milan suggests that the respective hymnographic output of these two men would have been sung in two very different musical styles. There is no proof of this from antiquity, but the traditional styles of the music in use today (Gregorian hymnody and Syriac hymnody) are indeed very different. The existence of a specifically Western style of Christian hymnodic vocal music in western Gaul in the fourth century is implied not only by the comparison of Syriac and Latin hymnography, but also by a remark about Hilary of Poitiers (c.300–368) made by Jerome (347–420) in the Preface to his *Commentary on the Letter to the Galatians*, book 2. This says that when Hilary tried to introduce hymnody into the West after his return from his sojourn and exile in the East, he found the Gauls incapable of learning to sing sacred song. The point here is not that the Gauls could not sing (they presumably sang their Office), but that they were resistant to learning something new – perhaps hymn melodies in Eastern style.

Certain of the Nag Hammadi codices contain hints of a Middle-Eastern – perhaps even western Asian – vocal musical style. The strings of repeated vowels found in tractates such as the *Discourse on the Eighth and Ninth* (see Chapter 8) suggest vocalization on a monotone or with limited variation in pitch. Here too there is no musical proof from antiquity, but it is noteworthy that similar features are present in the traditional religious music of non-Christian monks in certain areas of Tibet, southern Russia and north India. These are regions whence, in the first century CE, gnostic influence began to extend westwards to the lands bordering the eastern half of the Mediterranean.

The material presented in the foregoing paragraphs suggests that three basic styles of Christian vocal music were prevalent in the period up to the end of the

---

[40]   See M.L. West, *Ancient Greek Music* (Oxford, 1992), pp. 283–326 ('Transcriptions'), esp. pp. 304–5 (no. 18), pp. 306–8 (no. 19), pp. 311–13 (no. 30), pp. 316–19 (nos. 34, 40, 41).

[41]   The disparity of place represents also a difference of cultural setting, namely between Greek-speaking Eastern and Latin-speaking Western Christendom. As regards time, some eleven years separate the death of Athanasius and the beginning of Augustine's four years in Milan.

fourth century: Middle-Eastern/western Asian (gnostic), Near-Eastern (Greek and Syriac) and Western. Although the styles are listed here according to their regional provenance, this should not be thought of as delimiting their actual areas of use (Greek styles, for example, are likely to have been predominantly Eastern, but nevertheless in use in parts of the West). Even before late antiquity the peoples of the lands bordering the Mediterranean were typically multi-ethnic and bi- or multilingual. The larger towns and cities were just as cosmopolitan as modern capitals, with Rome and Jerusalem probably the most cosmopolitan of all.[42] It is conceivable that in any given urban area there would have been a mixture of musical styles among Christians, reflecting the ethnic background of individual communities, perhaps in some cases also reflecting a variety of ethnic backgrounds within one and the same worshipping community. While the very earliest Christians no doubt simply continued to use their customary Jewish musical traditions in worship (as indeed Jewish Christians in subsequent centuries would have done), when Christianity spread into cultural environments outside those of Homeland and Diaspora Judaism, it seems highly likely that Christians in those wider spheres would have made use of the musical traditions of the local ambient religious cultures.

---

[42]   On multiculturalism and multilingualism in the Mediterranean lands in late antiquity, see John F.A. Sawyer, *Sacred Languages and Sacred Texts* (London, 1999), esp. pp. 9–22.

Appendix

Septuagint and Vulgate Concordances for Musical Terms which in the Hebrew Bible are Built on the Root *ZMR*

Ref no.	Hebrew word	Hebrew Bible (MT) reference[1]	Septuagint reference	Greek (LXX) text	Latin (Vulgate) text[2]
1	*wĕzimrāt*	Exod. 15:2	15:2	*kai skepastēs*[3]	*et laus*
2	*'ăzammēr*[4]	Judg. 5:3[5]	5:3	*psalō*	*psallam*
3	*'ăzammēr*	2 Sam. 22:50	22:50	*psalō*[6]	*cantabo*
4	*zĕmirôt*	2 Sam. 23:1	23:1	*psalmoi*	*psalta* (one MS has *psaltes*)
5	*zammĕrû*	Isa. 12:5	12:5	*humnēsate*	*cantate*
6	*zĕmirōt*	Isa. 24:16	23:16	*kitharan ... kitharison*	*cane ... canticum*
7	*zimrâ*	Isa. 51:3	51:3	*phōnēn aineseōs*	*vox laudis*
8	*wĕzimrat*	Amos 5:23	5:23	*psalmon*	*cantica lyrae*
9	*mizmôr*	in the superscriptions of 57 psalms		*psalmos* (etc.)	*psalmus*
10	*wa'ăzammĕrâ*	Ps. 7:18	7:18	*psalō*	*psallam* (G)[7] *cantabo* (H)[8]
11	*'ăzammĕrâ*	Ps. 9:3	9:3	*psalō*	*psallam* (G) *canam* (H)
12	*zammĕrû*	Ps. 9:12	9:12	*psalate*	*psallite* (G) *cantate* (H)
13	*'ăzammērâ*	Ps. 18:50	17:50	*psalō*	*psalmum dicam* (G) *cantabo* (H)
14	*ûnĕzammĕrâ*	Ps. 21:14	20:14	*psaloumen*	*cantab[/v]imus et psallemus* (G+H)
15	*wa'ăzammĕrâ*	Ps. 27:6	26:6	*psalō*	*psalmum dicam* (G) *psallam* (H)
16	*zammĕrû*	Ps. 30:5	29:5	*psalate*	*psallite* (G) *cantate* (H)
17	*yĕzammerĕkā*	Ps. 30:13	29:13	*psalē*	*cantet* (G)

18	*zammĕrû*	Ps. 33:2	32:2	*psalate*	*psallite* (G) *cantate* (H)
19	*zammĕrû* (× 2) *zammĕrû* (× 2)	Ps. 47:7	46:7	*psalate* (× 4)	*psallite* (× 4) (G) *canite* (× 4) (H)
20	*zammĕrû*	Ps. 47:8	46:8	*psalate*	*psallite* (G) *canite* (H)
21	*wa'ăzammērâ*	Ps. 57:8	56:8	*psalō*	*psalmum dicam* (G) *psallam* (H)
22	*'ăzammerĕkā*[9]	Ps. 57:10	56:10	*psalō*	*psalmum dicam* (G) *cantabo* (H)
23	*'ăzammērâ*	Ps. 59:18	58:18	*psalō*	*psallam* (G) *cantabo* (H)
24	*'ăzammĕrâ*	Ps. 61:9	60:9	*psalō*	*psalmum dicam* (G) *canam* (H)
25	*zammĕrû*	Ps. 66:2	65:2	*psalate*	*psalmum dicite* (G) *cantate* (H)
26	*wîzammĕrû ... yĕzammĕrû*	Ps. 66:4	65:4	*psalatōsan* (× 2)	*psallant[/-at] ... psalmum dicant[/-at]* (G) *cantet* (× 2) (H)
27	*zammĕrû*	Ps. 68:5	67:5	*psalate*	*psalmum dicite* (G) *canite/cantate* (H)
28	*zammĕrû*	Ps. 68:33	67:33	*psalate*	*psallite* (G) *canite* (H)
29	*'ăzammĕrâ*	Ps. 71:22	70:22	*psalō*	*psallam tibi in cithara* (G) *cantabo tibi in cithara* (H)
30	*'ăzammĕrâ*	Ps. 71:23	70:23	*psalō*	*cum cantavero tibi* (G+H)
31	*'ăzammĕrâ*	Ps. 75:10	74:10	*psalō*	*cantabo* (G+H)
32	*zimrâ*	Ps. 81:3	80:3	*psalmon*	*psalmum* (G) *carmen* (H)
33	*ûlĕzammēr*	Ps. 92:2	91:2	*psallein*	*psallere* (G+H)
34	*bizmirôt*	Ps. 95:2	94:2	*psalmois*	*psalmis* (G) *canticis* (H)
35	*wĕzammĕrû*	Ps. 98:4	97:4	*psalate*	*psallite* (G) *canite* (H)
36	*zammĕrû*	Ps. 98:5a	97:5a	*psalate*	*psallite* (G) *cantate* (H)
37	*zimrâ*	Ps. 98:5b	97:5b	*psalmou*	*psalmi* (G) *carminis* (H)

38	'ăzammĕrâ	Ps. 101:1	100:2	psalō	(Ps 100:1) psallam (G+H)
39	'ăzammĕrâ	Ps. 104:33	103:33	psalō	psallam (G+H)
40	zammĕrû	Ps. 105:2	104:2	psalate	psallite (G+H)
41	wa'ăzammĕrâ	Ps. 108:2	107:2	psalō	psallam (G+H)
42	wa'ăzammerĕkā	Ps. 108:4	107:4	psalō	psallam (G) cantabo (H)
43	zĕmirôt	Ps. 119:54	118:54	psalta	cantabiles (G) carmina (H)
44	zammĕrû	Ps. 135:3	134:3	psalate	psallite (G) cantate (H)
45	'ăzammĕrekâ	Ps. 138:1	137:1	psalō	psallam (G) cantabo (H)
46	'ăzammĕrâ	Ps. 144:9	143:9	psalō	psallam (G+H)
47	'ăzammĕrâ	Ps. 146:2	145:2	psalō	psallam (G) cantabo (H)
48	zammĕrâ[10]	Ps. 147:1	146:1	aineite	laudate (G+H)
49	zammĕrû	Ps. 147:7	146:7	psalate	psallite (G) canite/cantate (× 2) (H)
50	yĕzammĕrû	Ps. 149:3	149:3	psalatōsan	psalterio psallant (G) cithara can(t)ent (H)
51	zĕmirôt	Job 35:10	35:10	nothing that corresponds	nothing that corresponds
52	hazzāmîr	S. of S. 2:12	2:12	tomēs[11]	putationis
53	zĕmārā'[12]	Dan. 3:5	3:5	mousikōn	musicorum
54	zĕmārā'[12]	Dan. 3:7	3:7	mousikōn	musicorum
55	zĕmārā'[12]	Dan. 3:10	3:10	mousikōn	musicorum
56	zĕmārā'[12]	Dan. 3:15	3:15	mousikōn	musicorum
57	zammārayyā'[12]	Ezra 7:24[13]	7:24	adousin	cantoribus
58	zammĕrû[14]	1 Chr. 16:9	16:9	humnēsate	psallite

Notes

[1] Books are listed in the order of the Hebrew Bible.
[2] Vulgate references are the same as the Septuagint references except at no. 38 (Ps. 101).
[3] See note on wĕzimrāt at Exod. 15:2 in *BHS*.
[4] The clause in which this word occurs is probably an addition.
[5] Within the Song of Deborah (Judg. 5:2–31).
[6] Compare no. 13: LXX Ps. 17:50.

[7] G = *Psalterium Gallicanum*, the 'Gallican' Psalter.

[8] H = *Psalterium iuxta Hebraeos*, the 'Hebrew' Psalter.

[9] The majority of Vulgate (Latin) MSS precede the translation of this word with *et* 'and'; one Hebrew MS prefixes this word with *wa* 'and'.

[10] The MS has *zammĕrû*.

[11] This word means 'cutting' (gerund) or 'pruning' (gerund) or 'picking' (gerund).

[12] Aramaic word.

[13] This verse is in Aramaic; it falls within the Aramaic section Ezra 7:12–26.

[14] Compare no. 40: Ps. 105:2 (= LXX Ps. 104:2).

Bibliography

Manuscripts Cited

Oxford
Oxford, Sackler Library, Papyrology Rooms, Papyrus P. Oxy. XV 1786.
Paris
Paris BN gr 2658, folios 72^r–97^r.
Uppsala
University Library, Uppsala, MS C 37 (also designated MS 436).

Primary Sources: Editions

Alypius of Thegaste (attrib.), *Ordo monasterii*, in D. de Bruyne, 'La première règle de S. Benoît', *Revue bénédictine*, 42 (1930).

Ambrose of Milan, *Exposition of Psalm 118: Expositio de psalmo CXVIII*, ed. Michaela Zelzer, *CSEL*, vol. 62 (1999).

——, *Sermon Against Auxentius on the Giving Up of the Basilicas*, in *Sancti Ambrosi Opera, pars decima, Epistularum liber X*, ed. Michaela Zelzer, *CSEL*, vol. 72 (1983).

Apostolic Constitutions: Les constitutions apostoliques, ed. and trans. Marcel Metzger, *SC*, nos 320 (1985), 329 (1986), 336 (1987).

Apostolic Fathers, Writings: *The Apostolic Fathers*, ed. and trans. Bart D. Ehrman, 2 vols (Cambridge MA: Harvard University Press, LCL, 2003).

Apostolic Tradition (attrib. Hippolytus): *La Tradition Apostolique*, ed. Bernard Botte, *SC*, no. 11 bis (1984).

Athanasius, *Apology for His Flight: Apologia de fuga sua*, ed. Hans-Georg Opitz, *Athanasius Werke*, vol. 2 (Vienna: der Kirchenväterkommission der Preussischen Akademie der Wissenschaften, 1934–1940, 1996–), fascicles 2 (1935) and 3 (1938).

——, *History of the Arians: Historia Arianorum*, ed. Hans-Georg Opitz, *Athanasius Werke*, vol. 2, fascicles 5 (1938) and 6 (1940).

——, *Letter to Marcellinus*, in *PG*, ed. Migne, vol. 27.

——, *Life of St Anthony: Vie d'Antoine, Athanase d'Alexandrie; introduction, texte critique, traduction, notes et index par G.J.M. Bartelink, SC*, no. 400 (1994).

——, [attrib.] *On Virginity* [anonymous, 4th century]: ed. E.F. von der Goltz, *De virginitate. Eine echte Schrift des Athanasius*, Texte und Untersuchungen, vol. 29/2 (Leipzig: J.C. Hinrichs, 1905).

Augustine of Hippo, *Confessions: Augustinus: Confessionum libri XIII*, ed. L. Verheijen, *CCSL*, vol. 27, 2nd edn (1981).

Basil of Caesarea (Basil the Great), Letters: *Saint Basil: The Letters*, trans. Roy J. Deferrari et al., 4 vols (London: Heinemann, LCL, 1961–62).

——, *On the Holy Spirit: Über den Heiligen Geist*, ed. Hermann Josef Sieben, Fontes Christiani, vol. 12 (Freiburg: Herder, 1993).

——, *Rules: Basili Regula a Rufino latine versa*, ed. Klaus Zelzer, *CSEL*, vol. 86 (1986).

Ben-Asher, Aharon Ben-Moshe, *Sefer diqduqe ha-te'amim*: Aron Dotan, *Sefer diqduqe ha-te'amim le-Rabbi Aharon Ben-Moshe Ben-Asher*, 3 vols (Jerusalem: Mugash le-Sinat shel Ha-Universitah Ha-Ivrit, 1967) [in Hebrew].

Ben Sira Scroll: Yigael Yadin, *The Ben Sira Scroll from Masada* (Jerusalem: Israel Exploration Society and the Shrine of the Book, 1965).

Bible, ancient Versions:

——, Hebrew Bible: *Biblia Hebraica Stuttgartensia*, ed. Karl Elliger and Wilhelm Rudolph et al., 2nd edn, with emendations by Wilhelm Rudolph and H.P. Rüger (Stuttgart: Deutsche Bibelgesellschaft Stuttgart, 1983).

——, New Testament: *Novum testamentum graece*, ed. Ebhard Nestle, Kurt Aland et al., 26th edn, 4th rev. pr. (Stuttgart: Deutsche Bibelstiftung, 1981).

——, Septuagint: *Septuaginta. Id est Vetus Testamentum graece iuxta lxx interpretes*, ed. Alfred Rahlfs, 2 vols (Stuttgart: Württembergische Bibelanstalt, 1935).

——, Vulgate: *Biblia Sacra iuxta Vulgatam Versionem*, ed. Bonifatio Fischer, OSB, et al. (Stuttgart: Württembergische Bibelanstalt, 1969, repr. 1995).

Burney, Charles, *A General History of Music*, 4 vols [1782–89], edited, with critical and historical notes, by Frank Mercer (4 vols in 2, London: G.T. Foulis, 1935; repr. New York: Dover, 1957).

Canons of Hippolytus (attrib.): *The Canons of Hippolytus, with a translation by Carol Bebawi*, ed. P.F. Bradshaw (Bramcote: Grove Books, 1987).

Canons of Laodicea: Périclès-Pierre Joannou (ed.), *Fonti*, Fasicolo IX, *Discipline générale antique (IVe-IXe s.)*, vol. 1/2: *Les canons des Synodes Particuliers* (Grottaferrata, Rome: Tipografia Italo-Orientale 'S. Nilo', 1962), pp. 130–55.

Cassian, John, *Institutes: Jean Cassien. Institutions cénobitiques*, ed. Jean-Claude Guy, *SC*, no. 109 (1965).

Chrysostom, John, *Commentary on Psalm 140*, in *PG*, ed. Migne, vol. 55.

——, *Homily 14 on 1 Tim. 4*, in *PG*, ed. Migne, vol. 62.

——, *Homily on Matthew*, in *PG*, ed. Migne, vol. 58.

——, *On 1 Corinthians*, in *PG*, ed. Migne, vol. 61.

Clement of Alexandria, *Exhortation to the Greeks*, in *Clement of Alexandria*, trans. G.W. Butterworth (London: Heinemann, LCL, 1960), pp. 2–263.

——, *The Instructor*, in *Clementis Alexandrini Paedagogus*, ed. Miroslav Marcovich with the collaboration of J.C.M. van Winden (Leiden: Brill, 2002).

Cyprian, *To Donatus: Ad Donatum*, ed. M. Simonetti, in *Sancti Cypriani Episcopi Opera*, *CCSL*, vol. 3/2 (1972).

——, *On the Lord's Prayer: De dominica oratione*, ed. C. Moresch, in *Sancti Cypriani Episcopi Opera*, *CCSL*, vol. 3/2 (1972).

Dead Sea Scrolls (and related matter): see *Discoveries in the Judaean Desert*, various eds (Oxford: Clarendon Press, 1955–).

Egeria, *Itinerarium/Peregrinatio: Itinerarium Egeriae*, ed. Georg Röwekamp and Dietmar Thönnes, Fontes Christiani, vol. 20 (Freiburg: Herder, 1995).

——, Latin text of chs. 24:1 to 49:3 in Louis Duchesne, *Christian Worship: Its Origin and Evolution*, pp. 490–523; English translation in ibid., pp. 541–71. See also Wilkinson, John.

Ephrem the Syrian, *Hymns*: Translation only: Kathleen McVey (trans. and introd.), *Ephrem the Syrian: Hymns* (New York and Mahwah NJ: Paulist Press, 1989). See also: Palmer, Andrew; Shepardson, Christine.

Eusebius, *Ecclesiastical History: The Ecclesiastical History: Eusebius; with an English Translation by Kirsopp Lake*, vols 1–2 (London: Heinemann, LCL, 1965).

Evagrius Ponticus, *On Prayer*, in *PG*, ed. Migne, vol. 40.

Hilary of Poitiers, *Homily on Psalm 65*, in *PL*, ed. Migne, vol. 9.

——, *Tracts on the Psalms: Sancti Hilarii Pictaviensis Episcopi Tractus super Psalmos*, ed. Jean Doignon and R. Demeulenaere, *CCSL*, vols 61, 61A, 61B (1997–2009).

Horsiesios [Orsisius], *Regulations of Horsiesios*, in *Pachomiana Latina: texte latin de S. Jérôme*, ed. Amand Boon and L.Th. Lefort, Bibliothèque de la Revue d'histoire ecclésiastique, vol. 7 (Louvain: Bureaux de la Revue, 1932).

Ignatius of Antioch, *Letters*, in *The Apostolic Fathers*, trans. Bart D. Ehrman, 2 vols (Cambridge MA: Harvard University Press, LCL, 2003).

Isidore of Pelusium, *Epistles: Isidore de Péluse: Lettres,* ed. and trans. Pierre Evieux, *SC*, nos 422, 454 (1997, 2000).

Jerome, *Letters: Hieronymus, epistolae*, ed. I. Hilberg, 2 vols (1910/1918); editio altera supplementis aucta 1996, *CSEL*, vols 54, 55.

——, (trans.), *Rule of Pachomius: La règle de S. Pachôme*, in *Pachomiana Latina*, ed. Amand Boon and L.Th. Lefort (Louvain, 1932) [see under Horsiesios].

Josephus, *The Jewish War* [7 books], trans. H.St.J. Thackeray, vols 2–4 (London: Heinemann, LCL, 1927, 1928).

——, *Jewish Antiquities* [20 books], trans. H.St.J. Thackeray, Ralph Marcus et al., vols 5–13 (London: Heinemann, LCL, 1930–1965).

Justin Martyr, *First Apology: Justin: Apologie pour les chrétiens*, ed. Charles Munier, *SC*, no. 507 (2006).

Mishnah: *The Six Orders of the Mishnah*, ed. Ḥ. Albeck (Tel Aviv and Jerusalem, 1954–1958).

——, *Mishnayoth*, trans. and ed. Philip Blackman, 6 vols (Gateshead: Judaica Press, 2000).

Nag Hammadi codices: *The Facsimile Edition of the Nag Hammadi Codices*, ed. James M. Robinson (Leiden: Brill, 1972).

New Jerusalem Scroll: *The New Jerusalem Scroll from Qumran*, ed. Michael Chyutin, trans. Richard Fiantz (Sheffield: Sheffield Academic Press, 1997).

North, Roger, *Memoires of Musick, being some Historico-critticall Collections of that Subject* [1728]. Repr. As Roger North, *Memoires of Musick: Now Printed from the*

Original MS. and Edited, with Copious Notes by Edward F. Rimbault (London: G. Bell, 1846).

——, *Roger North on Music: Being a Selection from his Essays Written During the Years c. 1695–1728 Transcribed from the Manuscripts and Edited by John Wilson* (London: Novello, 1959), pp. 315–359.

Odes of Solomon: Oden Salomos: Text, Übersetzung, Kommentar, ed. Michael Latke, Novum Testamentum et orbis antiquus, 41, 3 vols (Freiburg: Universitätsverlag; Göttingen: Vandenhoeck & Ruprecht, 1999–2005).

On Virginity: See under Athanasius [attrib.].

Origen, *On Prayer*, in *PG*, ed. Migne, vol. 11.

Pachomius, *Rule*, in *Pachomiana Latina*, ed. Amand Boon and L.Th. Lefort (Louvain: Bureau de la Revue, 1932) [see under Horsiesios].

Palladius, *Lausiac History: Histoire Lausiaque: vies d'ascètes et de pères du désert. Palladius, texte grec, introduction et traduction française par A. Lucot*, Textes et documents pour l'étude historique du christianisme, vol. 15 (Paris: A. Picard, 1912).

Philo of Alexandria, *Philo*, ed. F.H. Colson, 10 vols and 2 supplementary vols (London: Heinemann, LCL, 1941, repr. 1985).

Pliny the Younger, *Pliny, Letters*, trans. Betty Radice, 2 vols (London: Heinemann, LCL, 1969).

Protevangelium of James: Emil de Strycker (ed.), 'La forme la plus ancienne du Protévangile de Jacques: Recherches sur le Papyrus Bodmer 5 avec une édition du texte grec et une traduction annotée', *Subsidia Hagiographica*, vol. 33 (1961).

Psalms of Solomon, in *Septuaginta*, ed. Rahlfs, vol. 2.

Psalms Scroll from Qumran Cave 11: The Psalms Scroll from Qumran Cave 11 (11QPs^a), ed. J.A. Sanders, *Discoveries in the Judaean Desert*, vol. 4 (Oxford: Clarendon Press, 1965, repr. 1998).

Pseudo-Justin, *Hortatory Address to the Greeks*, in *Pseudo-Iustinus: Cohortatio ad Graecos; De monarchia; Oratio ad Graecos*, ed. Miroslav Marcovich, Patristische Texte und Studien, vol. 32 (Berlin: Walter de Gruyter, 1990).

Pseudo-Philo, *Liber antiquitatum biblicarum*, in D.J. Harrington et al. (eds), *Pseudo-Philon: Les Antiquités Bibliques*, *SC*, nos 229–230 (1976).

Sibylline Oracles: Johannes Geffcken (ed.), *Die Oracula Sibyllina*, Die Griechischen Christlichen Schriftsteller der ersten drei Jahrhunderte, vol. 8 (Leipzig, 1902, repr. Amsterdam: A.M. Hakkert, 1967).

Sozomen, *History of the Church: Histoire ecclésiastique*, in *Sozomène*, ed. Joseph Bidez, introd. Bernard Grillet and Guy Sabbah, trans. André-Jean Festugière, annotated by Guy Sabbah, *SC*, nos 306 (1983), 418 (1996), 495 (2005), 516 (2008).

Tatian, *Discourse to the Greeks*, in *Tatiani: Oratio ad Graecos. Theophili Antiocheni: Ad Autolycum*, ed. Miroslav Marcovich, Patristiche Texte und Studien, vols 43–44 (Berlin: Walter de Gruyter, 1995).

Tertullian, *Works*, in *Tertullianus: Opera*, ed. E. Dekkers et al., *CCSL*, vols 1 & 2 (1954).

Testament of Job: 'Testamentum Iobi', ed. S. Brock, bound with 'Apocalypsis Baruchi graece', ed. J.-C. Picard, in *Pseudepigrapha Veteris Testamenti graece*, vol. 2 (Leiden: Brill, 1967).

Tosefta: M.S. Zuckermandel (ed), *Tosefta nach den Erfurter und Wiener Handschriften mit Parallelstellen und Varianten* (Pasewalk and Trier: Meir, 1880).

——, M.S. Zuckermandel (ed.), *Supplement enthaltend Übersicht, Register und Glossar zu Tosefta* (Pasewalk and Trier: Meir, 1882).

Secondary Sources

Alexander, Patrick H., et al. (eds), *The SBL* [Society of Biblical Literature] *Handbook of Style* (Peabody MA: Hendrickson, 1999, 5th printing, 2006).

Apel, Willi, *Gregorian Chant* (London: Burns & Oates, n.d. [1958]).

Barker, Margaret, *The Great High Priest: The Temple Roots of Christian Liturgy* (London: T&T Clark, 2003).

——, *Temple Themes in Christian Worship* (London: T&T Clark, 2008).

Bayer, Bathja, *The Material Relics of Music in Ancient Palestine and its Environs: An Archaeological Inventory*, 2nd edn (Tel-Aviv: Israel Music Institute, 1964).

——, 'The Biblical Nebel', *Yuval*, 1 (1968): 89–131.

——, 'The Titles of the Psalms', *Yuval*, 4 (1982): 29–137.

Becker, Adam H., and Anette Yoshiko Reed (eds), *The Ways That Never Parted: Jews and Christians in Late Antiquity and the Early Middle Ages* (Minneapolis MN: Fortress Press, 2007).

Ben-Dov, Meir, *In the Shadow of the Temple: The Discovery of Ancient Jerusalem* (New York: HarperCollins, 1985).

Bettenson, Henry (ed.), *Documents of the Christian Church*, 2nd edn (London: Oxford University Press, 1963, repr. 1967).

Bible, modern Versions:

——, Tanakh: The Holy Scriptures [the Jewish Bible]. The New JPS Translation According to the Traditional Hebrew Text (Philadelphia PA: Jewish Publication Society, 1985 and 1988).

——, The Holy Bible, Containing the Old and New Testaments Translated Out of the Original Tongues [= King James Version] (1611).

——, The Holy Bible, New International Version (London, Sydney, Auckland, Toronto: Hodder & Stoughton, 1980).

——, The Holy Bible, New Revised Standard Version, Anglicized Edition, with Apocrypha (Oxford: Oxford University Press, 1995).

——, The Holy Bible, Revised Standard Version, Containing the Old and New Testaments With the Apocrypha/Deuterocanonical Books, Expanded Edition (New York and Glasgow: Collins, 1973).

——, The Jerusalem Bible, with Abridged Introductions and Notes (London: Darton, Longman & Todd, 1968).

——, The New English Bible, with the Apocrypha (Oxford University Press and Cambridge University Press, 1970).

——, The New Jerusalem Bible, (London: Darton, Longman & Todd, 1985).

——, The Revised English Bible, with the Apocrypha (Oxford University Press and Cambridge University Press, 1989).

Bienkowski, Piotr, and Alan Millard (eds), *Dictionary of the Ancient Near East* (London: British Museum, 2000).

Blankenburg, Walter (extrapolated), 'Chor und Chormusik: 1. Christliche Antike und Mittelalter', *MGG*, Sachteil, vol. 2 (1995).

Bradshaw, Paul F., *The Search for the Origins of Christian Worship: Sources and Methods for the Study of Early Liturgy*, 2nd edn (New York: Oxford University Press, 2002; London: SPCK, 2002).

——, 'Jewish Influence on Early Christian Liturgy: A Reappraisal' (International Council of Christians and Jews, 2009), at <http://www.jcrelations.net/en/?item=2988>.

Braun, Joachim, *Music in Ancient Israel/Palestine: Archaeological, Written, and Comparative Sources*, trans. Douglas W. Stott (Grand Rapids MI: Eerdmans, 2002).

——, 'Biblical Instruments', *New Grove/2*, vol. 3.

Brenner, Athalya, *The Israelite Woman* (Sheffield: Sheffield Academic Press, 1985, repr. 1989).

Brock, Sebastian, *St. Ephrem the Syrian: Hymns on Paradise* (Crestwood NY: St. Vladimir's Seminary Press, 1990).

Bromiley, Geoffrey W., et al. (eds), *The International Standard Bible Encyclopedia* (Grand Rapids MI: Eerdmans, 1986).

Burkert, Walter, *Greek Religion*, trans. John Raffan (Cambridge MA: Harvard University Press, 1985, 12th repr. 2001).

Burrows, Millar, *The Dead Sea Scrolls of St Mark's Monastery*, 2 vols (New Haven CT: The American School of Oriental Research, 1951), vol. 2/2.

Busink, Th.A., *Der Tempel von Jerusalem*, 2 vols (Leiden: Brill, 1970, 1980).

Butterick, George Arthur, et al. (eds), *The Interpreter's Bible* (Nashville TN: Abingdon Press, 1955).

Calmet, Augustin, *Dictionnaire historique, critique, chronologique, géographique et litteral de la Bible*, 5 vols (Geneva, 1780; English edition: Boston: Crocker & Brewster, 1832).

The Cambridge History of Christianity, vol. 1, ed. Margaret M. Mitchell and Frances M. Young (Cambridge: Cambridge University Press, 2006).

The Cambridge History of Judaism, various eds, 4 vols (Cambridge: Cambridge University Press, 1984, 1989, 2000, 2006).

Cavallo, Guglielmo, and Roger Chartier (eds), *A History of Reading in the West*, trans. Lydia G. Cochrane (Cambridge: Polity, 2003).

Chambers, G.B., *Folksong-Plainsong*, 2nd edn (London: Merlin Press, 1972).

Charles, R.H. (ed.), *The Apocrypha and Pseudepigrapha of the Old Testament*, 2 vols (Oxford: Oxford University Press, 1913).

Charlesworth, James H. (ed.), *The Old Testament Pseudepigrapha*, 2 vols (London: Darton, Longman & Todd and Yale University Press 1983, 1985).

Chew, Geoffrey, 'Cantillation', *New Grove/2*, vol. 5.

Cody, Aelred, 'The Early History of the Octoechos in Syria', in Nina Garsoïan et al. (eds), *East of Byzantium: Syria and Armenia in the Formative Period* (Washington DC: Dumbarton Oaks Publ. Service, 1982), pp. 89–113.

Cohen, Shaye J.D., *From the Maccabees to the Mishnah* (Philadelphia PA: Westminster Press, 1987).

Connolly, Thomas H., 'Traces of a Jewish-Christian Community at S. Cecilia in Trastevere', *Plainsong and Medieval Music*, 7/1 (April 1998): 1–19.

Coogan, Michael D. (ed.), *The Oxford History of the Biblical World* (New York: Oxford University Press/BCA, 1999).

Corpus Christianorum, Series Latina, various eds (Turnhout: Brepols, 1953–).

Corpus Scriptorum Ecclesiasticorum Latinorum, various eds (Vienna: Österreichische Akademie der Wissenschaften, 1864–).

Cross, F.L., and A.E. Livingstone (eds), *The Oxford Dictionary of the Christian Church* (New York: Oxford University Press, 1997).

Cuming, J., *Hippolytus: A Text for Students, with Introduction, Translation, Commentary and Notes*, 2nd edn (Bramcote: Grove Books, 1987).

Dahood, Mitchell, SJ, *Psalms III: 101-150* (New York: Doubleday, 1970).

——, and Tadeusz Penar, 'The Grammar of the Psalter', in Mitchel Dahood, SJ, *Psalms III: 101-150* (New York: Doubleday, 1970), pp. 361-456.

Danby, Herbert (trans. & ed.), *The Mishnah Translated from the Hebrew with Introduction and Brief Explanatory Notes* (Oxford: Oxford University Press, 1933, repr. 1980 from the corrected sheets of the 1st edn).

Davies, Philip, *In Search of 'Ancient Israel'* (Sheffield: Sheffield Academic Press, 1992).

de Vaux, Roland, *Ancient Israel: Its Life and Institutions*, trans. John McHugh, 2nd edn (London: Darton, Longman & Todd, 1965).

Dix, Gregory, [trans. and] ed., *The Apostolic Tradition of St Hippolytus* (London: SPCK, 1937).

——, *The Shape of the Liturgy*, 2nd edn (London: A. & C. Black, 1945).

Duchesne, Louis, *Origines du culte chrétien* (Paris: Thorin, 1889). [English translation by M.L. McClure as *Christian Worship: Its Origin and Evolution*, 5th edn (London: SPCK, 1919, repr. 1931).]

Dugmore, Clifford W., *The Influence of the Synagogue Upon the Divine Office*, 1st edn (London: Oxford University Press, 1944), 2nd edn [reprint of 1st edn with added Introduction] (London: Faith Press, 1964).

Dunn, James D.G., *Unity and Diversity in the New Testament*, 2nd edn (London: SCM Press 1990; Philadelphia PA: Trinity Press International, 1990).

Dyer, Joseph, 'The Desert, the City and Psalmody in the Late Fourth Century', in Sean Gallagher, James Haar, et al. (eds), *Western Plainchant in the First*

Millennium: Studies in the Medieval Liturgy and its Music (Aldershot: Ashgate, 2003), pp. 11–43.

Eissfeldt, Otto, *Einleitung in das Alte Testament*, 3rd (rev.) edn (Tübingen: Mohr, 1964).

Encyclopaedia Judaica (Jerusalem: Keter, 1971).

Engberg, Gudrun, 'Ekphonetic Notation, 2: Hebrew', *New Grove/2*, vol. 8.

Epstein, I. (trans. and ed.), *The Babylonian Talmud Translated into English with Notes, Glossary and Indices*, 35 vols (London: Soncino Press, 1935–52).

Esler, Philip F. (ed.), *The Early Christian World*, 2 vols (London and New York: Routledge, 2000).

Evans, Craig A., 'The Life and Teaching of Jesus and the Rise of Christianity', in J.W. Rogerson and Judith M. Lieu (eds), *The Oxford Handbook of Biblical Studies* (New York, 2006), pp. 301–16.

Fenlon, Iain (ed.), *Early Music History* (Cambridge: Cambridge University Press, 1981–).

Fiebig, Paul (trans. and ed.), *Die Mischna: Rosch ha-schana, Text, Übersetzung und ausfürliche Erklärung* (Giessen: Verlag von Alfred Töpelmann [formerly J. Ricker], 1914).

Finkelstein, Israel, and Neil Asher Silberman, *The Bible Unearthed: Archaeology's New Vision of Ancient Israel and the Origin of its Sacred Texts* (New York: Simon & Schuster, 2002).

Finscher, Ludwig, et al. (eds), *Die Musik in Geschichte und Gegenwart*, 2nd rev. edn, Subject Encyclopedia (10 vols), Biographical Encyclopedia (17 vols) (Basel: Bärenreiter, 1994–).

Fokkelman, J.P., *Narrative Art and Poetry in the Book of Samuel*, Studia Semitica Neerlandica, vol. 23 (Assen/Maastricht, 1986).

Foley, Edward, *Foundations of Christian Music: The Music of Pre-Constantinian Christianity* (Collegeville MN: Liturgical Press, 1996).

Fredriksen, Paula, 'What "Parting of the Ways"?' in Adam H. Becker and Anette Yoshiko Reed (eds), *The Ways That Never Parted* (Minneapolis MN, 2007), pp. 35–63.

Freedman, David Noel, 'The Evolution of Hebrew Orthography', in David Noel Freedman, A. Dean Forbes and Francis I. Andersen (eds), *Studies in Hebrew and Aramaic Orthography* (Winona Lake IN: Eisenbrauns, 1992), pp. 3–15.

——, et al. (eds), *The Anchor Bible Dictionary* (New York: Anchor Bible, 1992).

Freedman, H., and M. Simon (eds), *Midrash Rabbah Exodus*, 3 vols (London: Soncino Press, 1961), vol. 3 (trans S.M. Lehrman).

Fritz, Volkmar, *An Introduction to Biblical Archaeology*, trans. Birgit Mänz-Davies (Sheffield: Sheffield Academic Press, 1994; pbk edn, 1996).

Gallagher, Sean, James Haar, et al. (eds), *Western Plainchant in the First Millennium: Studies in the Medieval Liturgy and its Music* (Aldershot: Ashgate, 2003).

Garsoïan, Nina, et al. (eds), *East of Byzantium: Syria and Armenia in the Formative Period* (Washington DC: Dumbarton Oaks Center for Byzantine Studies, 1982).

Gerbert, Martin (ed.), *De cantu et musica sacra* (St Blasien: 1774, repr. Graz: Akademische Druck und Verlagsanstalt, 1968, facsimile edn).

—— (ed.), *Scriptores ecclesiastici de musica sacra potissimum* (St Blasien: 1784, repr. Graz: Akademische Druck und Verlagsanstalt, 1963).

Gillingham, S.E., *The Poems and Psalms of the Hebrew Bible* (Oxford: Oxford University Press, 1994).

Gordon, Cyrus H., and Gary A. Rendsburg, *The Bible and the Ancient Near East* (New York: Norton, 1997).

Güterbock, H.G., 'Reflections on the Musical Instruments Arkammi, Galgalturi and Huhupal in Hittite', in Theo P.J. van den Hout, Ph.H.J. Houwink ten Cate and Johan de Roos (eds), *Studio Historiae Ardens; Ancient Near Eastern Studies: Presented to Philo Houwink ten Cate on his 65th Birthday* (Leiden: Nederlands Historisch-Archaeologisch Instituut te Istanbul, 1995), pp. 57–72.

Haïk-Vantoura, Suzanne, *The Music of the Bible Revealed: The Deciphering of a Millenary Notation*, ed. John Wheeler, trans. Dennis Weber, 2nd rev. edn (N. Richland Hills TX: Bible Press, 1991).

Halperin, David, 'Music in the Testament of Job', *Yuval*, 5 (1986): 356–64.

Harrington, D.J., 'Pseudo-Philo', in *OTP*, vol. 2, pp. 297–377.

Helyer, Larry R., *Exploring Jewish Literature of the Second Temple Period: A Guide for New Testament Students* (Madison WI: Inter-Varsity Press, 2002).

Hiley, David, *Western Plainchant: A Handbook* (Oxford: Oxford University Press, 1993).

Hoftijzer, J., and K. Jongeling, *Dictionary of the North-West Semitic Inscriptions*, with appendices by R.C. Steiner, A. Mosak Moshavi and B. Porten (Leiden: Brill, 1995).

Horbury, William, *Jews and Christians in Contact and Controversy* (Edinburgh: T&T Clark, 1998).

Hornby, Emma, and David Maw (eds), *Essays on the History of English Music in Honour of John Caldwell: Sources, Style, Performance, Historiography* (Woodbridge: Boydell, 2010).

Idelsohn, Abraham Z., *Hebraïsch-orientalischer Melodienschatz* [*Thesaurus of Hebrew-Oriental Melodies*], 10 vols (Jerusalem and Leipzig: B. Harz, 1914–1932).

——, *Jewish Music in its Historical Development* (New York: Holt, Rinehart & Winston, 1929, repr. Shocken Books, 1967).

——, *Jewish Liturgy and its Development* (New York: Holt, Rinehart & Winston, 1932, repr. Shocken Books, 1975).

Jackson-McCabe, Matt, 'What's in a Name? The Problem of "Jewish Christianity"', in *Jewish Christianity Reconsidered: Rethinking Ancient Groups and Texts*, ed. Matt Jackson McCabe (Minneapolis MN: Fortress Press, 2007), pp. 7–38.

——, (ed.), *Jewish Christianity Reconsidered: Rethinking Ancient Groups and Texts* (Minneapolis MN: Fortress Press, 2007).

Jacob, B., 'Beiträge zu einer Einleitung in die Psalmen', *Zeitschrift für die Alttestamentliche Wissenschaft*, 16 (1896): 129–81.

Jacob, Edmond, *Theology of the Old Testament* (London: Hodder & Stoughton, 1971).

Jeffery, Peter, 'Werner's *The Sacred Bridge*, Volume 2: A Review Essay', *Jewish Quarterly Review*, 77 (1987): 283–98.

——, 'The Sunday Office of Seventh-Century Jerusalem in the Georgian Chantbook (Iadgari): A Preliminary Report', *Studia Liturgica*, 21 (1991): 52–75.

——, *Re-envisioning Past Musical Cultures: Ethnomusicology in the Study of Gregorian Chant* (Chicago and London: University of Chicago Press, 1992).

——, 'The Earliest Octōēchoi', in Peter Jeffery (ed.), *The Study of Medieval Chant: Paths and Bridges, East and West: In Honor of Kenneth Levy* (Woodbridge: Boydell & Brewer, 2001), pp. 147–209.

——, (ed.), *The Study of Medieval Chant: Paths and Bridges, East and West: In Honor of Kenneth Levy* (Woodbridge: Boydell & Brewer, 2001).

——, 'Monastic Reading and the Emerging Roman Chant Repertory', in *Western Plainchant in the First Millennium: Studies in the Medieval Liturgy and its Music*, ed. Sean Gallagher, James Haar et al. (Aldershot, 2003), pp. 45–103.

Jeremias, Joachim, *The Eucharistic Words of Jesus*, trans. N. Perrin (London: SCM Press, 1966).

——, *Jerusalem in the Time of Jesus*, trans. F.H. and C.H. Cave (London: SCM Press, 1969).

Karp, Theodor, 'Interpreting Silence: Liturgy, Singing, and Psalmody in the Early Synagogue', *Rivista internazionale di musica sacra*, 20/1 (1999): 47–109.

Katz, Daniel S., 'Biblische Kantillation und Musik der Synagoge: Ein Rückblick auf die ältesten Quellen', *Musiktheorie*, 15 (2000): 57–78.

Kelly, Thomas Forrest (ed.), *Chant and its Origins* (Farnham: Ashgate, 2009).

Kempinski, Aharon, and Ronny Reich et al. (eds), *The Architecture of Ancient Israel: From the Prehistoric to the Persian Periods* (Jerusalem: Israel Exploration Society, 1992).

Kinzig, Wolfram, 'The Nazoraeans', in Oskar Skarsaune and Reidar Hvalvik (eds), *Jewish Believers in Jesus: The Early Centuries* (Peabody MA: Hendrickson, 2007).

Kirkpatrick, F., *The Book of Psalms*, 2 vols (Cambridge: Cambridge University Press, 1894).

Kleinig, John W., *The Lord's Song: The Basis, Function and Significance of Choral Music in Chronicles* (Sheffield: Sheffield Academic Press, 1993).

Kraus, Hans-Joachim, *Psalmen*, 6th edn, 2 vols (Neukirken-Vluyn: Neukirkener Verlag, 1989).

Lamb, J.A., *The Psalms in Christian Worship* (London: Faith Press, 1962).

Lang, Paul Henry, *Music in Western Civilisation* (New York: Norton, 1941).

Levertoff, Paul, 'Synagogue Worship in the First Century', in W.K. Lowther Clarke and Charles Harris (eds), *Liturgy and Worship* (London: SPCK, 1932), pp. 60–77.

Levi, Peter (trans.), *The Psalms* (Harmondsworth: Penguin Books, 1976).

Levine, Lee I., *The Ancient Synagogue: The First Thousand Years*, 2nd edn (New Haven CT: Yale University Press, 2005).

Levy, Kenneth, 'Byzantine Chant', *New Grove/1*, vol. 3, p. 554.

——, 'Byzantine Rite, Music of the', *New Grove*/1, vol. 3, p. 555.

——, 'Gregorian Chant and the Romans', *Journal of the American Musicological Society*, 56 (2003): 5–41, collected in Thomas Forrest Kelly (ed.), *Chant and its Origins* (Farnham: Ashgate, 2009), pp. 427–63.

Liddell, Henry George, and Robert Scott (rev. Henry Stuart Jones et al.), *A Greek-English Lexicon* (Oxford: Oxford University Press, 1940).

Lindblom, J., *Prophecy in Ancient Israel* (Oxford: Oxford University Press, 1962).

Loewe, H. (ed.), *The Contact of Pharisaism with Other Cultures* (London: Sheldon Press, 1937).

Logan, Alastair H.B., *The Gnostics: Identifying an Early Christian Cult* (New York: T&T Clark, 2006).

Lundberg, Mattias Olof, 'Historiographical Problems of the *Tonus Peregrinus*', *Min-Ad: Israel Studies in Musicology Online*, 2004, vol. 3 [online journal], at <http://www.biu.ac.il/hu/mu/min-ad04>.

Luomanen, Petri, 'Ebionites and Nazarenes', in Matt Jackson-McCabe (ed.), *Jewish Christianity Reconsidered: Rethinking Ancient Groups and Texts* (Minneapolis MN: Fortress Press, 2007).

Maalouf, Shireen, *History of Arabic Music Theory: Change and Continuity in the Tone Systems, Genres and Scales* (Kaslik, Lebanon: Université Saint-Esprit, 2002).

——, 'Mikha'il Mishaqa: Virtual Founder of the Twenty-Four Equal Quartertone Scale', *Journal of the American Oriental Society*, 123/4 (2003): 835–40.

Macy, Laura (ed.), *Grove Music Online*, at <www.oxfordmusiconline.com>.

McGrath, Alister E., *Christian Theology: An Introduction* (Oxford UK and Cambridge MA: Blackwell, 1994).

McKinnon, James W., 'The Exclusion of Musical Instruments from the Ancient Synagogue', *PRMA*, 106 (1979–1980): 77–87.

——, 'On the Question of Psalmody in the Ancient Synagogue', *EMH*, 6 (1986): 159–91.

——, 'The Fourth-Century Origin of the Gradual', *EMH*, 7 (1987): 91–106.

——, (ed.), *Music in Early Christian Literature* (Cambridge: Cambridge University Press, 1987, repr. 1993).

——, 'Desert Monasticism and the Later Fourth-Century Psalmodic Movement', *M&L*, 75 (1994): 505–21.

——, *The Temple, the Church Fathers and Early Western Chant* (Aldershot: Ashgate, 1998).

——, 'The Musical Character of Early Christian Song', *New Grove*/2, vol. 5.

McVey, Kathleen (trans. and introd.), *Ephrem the Syrian: Hymns* (New York and Mahwah NJ: Paulist Press, 1989).

Manguel, Alberto, *A History of Reading* (London and New York: Penguin, 1997).

Marjonen, Antti, and Petri Luomanen (eds), *A Companion to Second-Century Christian 'Heretics'* (Leiden: Brill, 2005).

Martin, Ralph P., 'The Bithynian Christians' *Carmen Christo*', *Texte und Untersuchungen*, 93 (1966): 259–65.

——, *Carmen Christi: Philippians ii. 5-11 in Recent Interpretation and in the Setting of Early Christian Worship* (Cambridge: Cambridge University Press, 1967).

Mathiesen, Thomas J., 'Prosodion', *New Grove/2*, vol. 20.

Mays, J.L., 'The David of the Psalms', *Interpretation*, 40 (1986): 143–55.

Meeks, Wayne A., et al. (eds), *The HarperCollins Study Bible* (New York: HarperCollins, 1993).

Meibom, Marcus (ed.), *Antiquae musicae auctores septem* (Amsterdam, 1652).

Meschonnic, Henri (trans. and ed.), *Gloires: Traduction des psaumes* (Paris: Desclée de Brouwer, 2001).

Metzger, Marcel, *History of the Liturgy: The Major Stages*, trans. Madeleine Beaumont (Collegeville MN: Liturgical Press, 1997).

Meyer, Marvin (ed. and joint trans.), *The Nag Hammadi Scriptures* (New York: HarperOne, 2007).

Meyers, Eric M. (ed.), *The Oxford Encyclopedia of Archaeology in the Near East* (New York: Oxford University Press, 1997).

Migne, J.P. (ed.), *Patrologiae cursus completus, series latina* (221 vols, Paris: Garnier, 1844–1864).

——, (ed.), *Patrologiae cursus completus, series graeca* (166 vols, Paris: Garnier, 1857–1866).

Mishnah. See Blackman, Philip; Danby, Herbert; Neusner, Jacob.

Montagu, Jeremy, *Musical Instruments of the Bible* (Lanham MD: Scarecrow Press, 2002).

Mowinckel, Sigmund, *Offersang og sangoffer: Salmediktningen i Bibelen* (Oslo: Aschehoug [W. Nygaard], 1951). (See also next entry.)

——, *The Psalms in Israel's Worship*, trans. D.R. Ap-Thomas, 2 vols (Oxford: Blackwell, 1962, repr. 1967 with additional notes by Mowinckel) (English translation of preceding item). References are to the 1967 repr.

Music & Letters (Oxford: Oxford University Press, 1920–).

Nag Hammadi Codices. See Meyer, Marvin.

Neusner, Jacob (ed. and joint trans.), *The Mishnah: A New Translation* (New Haven CT: Yale University Press, 1988).

——, (trans. and ed.), *The Talmud of the Land of Israel* [Talmud Yerushalmi (the Jerusalem Talmud)] (Chicago, IL: University of Chicago Press, 1982–86).

——, (trans. and ed.), *The Talmud of the Land of Israel* [Talmud Yerushalmi (the Jerusalem Talmud)]: *An Academic Commentary to the Second, Third, and Fourth Divisions* (Atlanta GA: Scholars Press, 1998).

——, (trans. and ed.), *The Tosefta Translated from the Hebrew With a New Introduction*, 2 vols (Peabody MA: Hendrickson, 2002).

——, Alan J. Avery-Peck and William Scott Green (eds), *The Encyclopaedia of Judaism*, 3 vols (Leiden: Brill, 2000).

——, and William Scott Green (eds), *Dictionary of Judaism in the Biblical Period: 450 BCE to 600 CE*, 2 vols (New York: Macmillan, 1996).

New Grove. See under Sadie, Stanley.

Newsom, Carol (trans. and ed.), *Songs of the Sabbath Sacrifice: A Critical Edition* (Atlanta GA: Harvard University Press, 1985).

New Testament Apocrypha. See Schneemelcher, Wilhelm.

Norton, Gerard J., 'Ancient Versions and Textual Transmission of the Old Testament', in J.W. Rogerson and Judith M. Lieu (eds), *The Oxford Handbook of Biblical Studies* (New York: Oxford University Press, 2006), pp. 224–6.

Oesterley, W.O.E, *The Psalms in the Jewish Church* (London: Skeffington & Son, 1910).

——, *The Jewish Background of the Christian Liturgy* (Oxford: Clarendon Press, 1925).

——, *A Fresh Approach to the Psalms* (London: Ivor Nicholson & Watson, 1937).

——, (ed.), *Judaism and Christianity: The Age of Transition* (London: Sheldon Press, 1937).

Page, Christopher, *The Christian West and its Singers: The First Thousand Years* (New Haven CT and London: Yale University Press, 2010).

Pagels, Elaine, *The Gnostic Gospels* (Harmondsworth: Penguin [Pelican], 1982, repr. 1985).

Paget, James Carleton, 'The Definition of the Terms *Jewish Christian* and *Jewish Christianity* in the History of Research', in *Jewish Believers in Jesus*, ed. Oskar Skarsaune and Reidar Hvalvik (Peabody MA: Hendrickson, 2nd pr., corrected, 2007), pp. 22–52.

Palmer, Andrew, 'The Influence of Ephraim the Syrian', *Hugoye: Journal of Syriac Studies* 2/1 (1999) [online journal] at <http://syrcom.cua.edu/Hugoye>.

Parkes, James, *The Conflict of the Church and the Synagogue* (London: Soncino Press, 1934).

Pazzini, M., 'La trascrizione dell'ebraico nella versione di Teodozione', *Studium biblicum franciscanum Jerusalem*, 41 (1991): 201–22.

Pietersma, Albert, and Benjamin G. Wright (trans. and eds), *A New English Translation of the Septuagint* (New York: Oxford University Press, 2007).

Pliny the Younger, *Letters*. See Radice, Betty.

Pritchard, James B. (ed.), *Ancient Near Eastern Texts Relating to the Old Testament*, 2nd edn (Princeton NJ: Princeton University Press, 1950).

—— (ed.), *The Ancient Near East in Pictures Relating to the Old Testament*, 2nd edn (Princeton NJ: Princeton University Press, 1969).

Proceedings of the Royal Musical Association (London: Royal Musical Association, 1874–1985).

Radice, Betty (trans.), *The Letters of the Younger Pliny* (Harmondsworth: Penguin Books, 1963).

Reed, Annette Yoshiko, '"Jewish Christianity" after the "Parting of the Ways": Approaches to Historiography and Self-Definition in the Pseudo-Clementines', in Adam H. Becker and Anette Yoshiko Reed (eds), *The Ways That Never Parted* (Minneapolis MN, 2007), pp. 189–231.

Reese, Gustav, *Music in the Middle Ages* (New York: Norton, 1940).

Reicke, Bo, *The New Testament Era*, trans. D.E. Green (Minneapolis MN: Fortress Press, 1968).

Reinach, Th., 'L'inscription de Theodotus', *Revue des études juives*, 71 (1920): 46–56.

Ritmeyer, Kathleen, and Leen Ritmeyer, 'Reconstructing Herod's Temple Mount in Jerusalem', *Biblical Archaeological Review*, 15/6 (1989): 23–42.

Rivkin, Ellis (ed.), *Judaism and Christianity* (New York: Ktav, 1969).

Roberts, Alexander, and James Donaldson (eds), *Ante-Nicene Fathers: The Writings of the [Church] Fathers down to AD 325*, 10 vols (Edinburgh: T&T Clark, 1867; additional introductory material and notes provided for the American edition by A. Cleveland Coxe, 1886; repr. Grand Rapids MI: Eerdmans, 2001).

Robinson, James M. (general ed.), *The Nag Hammadi Library in English*, 3rd (rev.) edn (San Francisco CA: HarperCollins, 2000).

Robinson, John A.T., *Redating the New Testament* (London: SCM Press, 1976).

Roenthal, Erwin I.J. (ed.), *Law and Religion* (London: Sheldon Press, 1938).

Rogerson, J.W., and Judith M. Lieu (eds), *The Oxford Handbook of Biblical Studies* (New York: Oxford University Press, 2006).

Sadie, Stanley (ed.), *The New Grove Dictionary of Music and Musicians*, 1st edn, 20 vols (London: Macmillan, 1980).

—— and John Tyrrell (eds), *The New Grove Dictionary of Music and Musicians*, 2nd edn, 29 vols (London: Macmillan, 2001).

Sanders, E.P., *Judaism: Practice and Belief 63 BCE–66 CE* (London: SCM Press, 1992; Philadelphia PA: Trinity Press International, 1992).

Sawyer, John F.A., *Sacred Languages and Sacred Texts* (London: Routledge, 1999).

Schaff, Philip (ed.), *Nicene and Post-Nicene Fathers*, Series 1, 14 vols (Edinburgh: T&T Clark, 1889; repr. Grand Rapids MI: Eerdmans, 2001).

—— and Henry Wace (eds), *Nicene and Post-Nicene Fathers*, Series 2, 14 vols (Edinburgh: T&T Clark, 1890; New York: Christian Literature Publishing Co., 1890).

Schleifer, Eliyahu, 'Biblical Cantillation' (Jewish Music, §III, 2(ii)(b): 'Synagogue Music and its Development'), *New Grove/2*, vol. 13.

Schremer, Adiel, *Brothers Estranged: Heresy, Christianity, and Jewish Identity in Late Antiquity* (Oxford and New York: Oxford University Press, 2010).

Schneemelcher, Wilhelm (ed.), *New Testament Apocrypha* (rev. edn), trans. Robert McLachlan Wilson, 2 vols (Cambridge: James Clarke, 1991 [vol. 1]; Louisville KY: Westminster/John Knox Press, 1992 [vol. 2]).

Schürer, Emil, *The History of the Jewish People in the Age of Jesus Christ*, trans., rev. and ed. Geza Vermes et al., 3 vols (Edinburgh: T&T Clark, 1973 [vol. 1], 1979 [vol. 2], 1986 [vol. 3/1], 1987 [vol. 3/2]).

Seidel, Hans, *Musik in Altisrael: Untersuchungen zur Musikgeschichte und Musikpraxis Altisraels anhand biblischer und ausserbiblischer Texte* (Frankfurt: Peter Lang, 1989).

Sellin, Ernst (rev. George Fohrer), *Einleitung in das Alte Testament* (Heidelberg, 1969).

Sendrey, Alfred (ed.), *Bibliography of Jewish Music* (New York: Columbia University Press, 1951).

——, *Music in Ancient Israel* (New York: Philosophical Library, 1969).

Seroussi, Edwin, 'Poetry, Piyyutim', *New Grove/2*, vol. 13.

Shepardson, Christine, *Anti-Judaism and Christian Orthodoxy: Ephrem's Hymns in Fourth-Century Syria* (Washington DC: Catholic University of America Press, 2008).

Skarsaune, Oskar, *In the Shadow of the Temple* (Downers Grove IL: Inter-Varsity Press, 2002).

——, 'Jewish Believers in Jesus in Antiquity – Problems of Definition', in Oskar Skarsaune and Reidar Hvalvik (eds), *Jewish Believers in Jesus: The Early Centuries* (Peabody MA: Hendrickson, 2007), pp. 3–21.

——, 'The Ebionites', in Oskar Skarsaune and Reidar Hvalvik (eds), *Jewish Believers in Jesus: The Early Centuries* (Peabody MA: Hendrickson, 2007), pp. 419–62.

—— and Reidar Hvalvik (eds), *Jewish Believers in Jesus: The Early Centuries* (Peabody MA: Hendrickson, 2nd pr., corrected, 2007).

Smiraglia, Pasquale, 'Problemi di struttura e cronologia interna nel diario epistolare della pellegrina Egeria', presented at the congress *La città e il libro II*, mounted by the Accademia delle Arti del Disegno, Accademia Colombaria, Florence, 4–7 September 2002, at <http://www.florin.ms/beth.html>.

Smith, James G., 'Chorus: Antiquity and the Middle Ages', *New Grove/2*, vol. 5.

Smith, John Arthur, 'The Ancient Synagogue, The Early Church and Singing', *M&L*, 65 (1984): 1–16.

——, 'Which Psalms Were Sung in the Temple?' *M&L*, 71 (1990): 167–86.

——, 'First-Century Christian Singing and its Relationship to Contemporary Jewish Religious Song', *M&L*, 75 (1994): 1–15.

——, 'Concordances for SingingTerms Common to the Septuagint and the Greek New Testament', *Royal Musical Association Research Chronicle*, 28 (1995 [1996]): 1–19.

——, 'Musical Aspects of Old Testament Canticles in their Biblical Setting', *EMH*, 17 (1998): 221–64.

——, 'The Ancient Synagogue and its Music: A Reconsideration in the Light of Ideas Presented by Theodor Karp', *Rivista internazionale di musica sacra*, 24/2 (2003): 17–38.

——, Review of Braun, *Music in Ancient Israel/Palestine*, in *M&L*, 85 (2004): 95–9.

——, 'Psalm 1', in Laura Macy (ed.), *Grove Music Online* (update April, 2006).

——, 'Three Anglican Church Historians on Liturgy and Psalmody in the Ancient Synagogue and the Early Church', in *Essays on the History of English Music in Honour of John Caldwell: Sources, Style, Performance, Historiography*, ed. Emma Hornby and David Maw (Woodbridge: Boydell, 2010): pp. 298–310.

Smith, William S., *Musical Aspects of the New Testament* (Amsterdam: Uitgeverij W. Ten Have, 1962).

Soggin, J. Alberto, *An Introduction to the History of Israel and Judah*, trans. John Bowden (London: SCM Press, 1993).

Sophocles, E.A., *Greek Lexicon of the Roman and Byzantine Periods (from BC 146 to AD 1100)* (New York, 1900; repr. New York: Georg Olms Verlag, 1992).

Sources chrétiennes, various eds (Paris: Cerf, 1943–).

Spinks, Bryan, *The Sanctus in the Eucharistic Prayer* (Cambridge: Cambridge University Press 1991).

Stacey, W.D., *Prophetic Drama in the Old Testament* (London: Epworth, 1990).

Stapert, Calvin R., *A New Song for an Old World: Musical Thought in the Early Church* (Grand Rapids MI; Cambridge UK: Eerdmans, 2007).

Stern, Ephraim, et al. (eds), *The New Encyclopedia of Archaeological Excavations in the Holy Land*, 4 vols (New York: Carta, 1993).

Sukenik, E.L., *The Dead Sea Scrolls of the Hebrew University* (Jerusalem: Magnes Press, 1954 [Hebrew], 1955 [English]).

Tadmor, H., 'The Chronology of the First Temple Period', in B. Mazar (ed.), *The World History of the Jewish People* (Jerusalem, 1979), vol. 4/1, pp. 44–60, 318–20 [repr. in J. Alberto Soggin, *An Introduction* (London, 1993), pp. 394–409].

Taft, Robert, SJ, *The Byzantine Rite: A Short History* (Collegeville MN: Liturgical Press, 1992).

——, *The Liturgy of the Hours in East and West*, 2nd rev. edn (Collegeville MN: Liturgical Press, 1993).

Talmud Bavli [The Babylonian Talmud]. See: Epstein, I.

Talmud Yerushalmi [The Jerusalem or Palestinian Talmud]. See: Neusner, Jacob.

Thiede, Carsten Peter, *The Earliest Gospel Manuscript? The Qumran Papyrus 7Q5 and its Significance for New Testament Studies* (Exeter: Paternoster Press, 1992).

Tongeren, Mark C., *Overtone Singing: Physics and Metaphysics of Harmonics in East and West*, 2nd rev. edn (Delft: Eburon VB, 2006).

Tosefta. See: Neusner, Jacob; Zuckermandel, M.S.

Touma, Habib Hassan, *The Music of the Arabs*, trans. Laurie Schwartz (Portland OR: Amadeus, 1996).

Trevett, Christine, 'Montanism', in Philip F. Esler (ed.), *The Early Christian World*, 2 vols (London and New York: Routledge, 2000), pp. 929–51.

Veilleux, Armand, *Pachomian Koinonia*, 3 vols (Kalamazoo MI: Cistercian Publications, 1980, 1981, 1982).

Verhelst, Stephane, *Les traditions judéo-chrétiennes dans la liturgie de Jérusalem*, Studies in Liturgy, vol. 18 (Louvain: Peeters, 2003).

Vermes, Geza (trans. and ed.), *The Dead Sea Scrolls in English*, 4th edn (Harmondsworth: Penguin, 1995).

—— (trans. and ed.), *The Complete Dead Sea Scrolls in English* (Harmondsworth: Penguin, 1998).

von Rad, Gerhard, *Old Testament Theology*, trans. D.M.G. Stalker, 2 vols (Edinburgh: Oliver and Boyd, 1965).

Wagner, Peter, *Einführung in die gregorianischen Melodien*, 3 vols (Leipzig: Breitkopf & Härtel, 1895–1911), vol. 1 (1895).

Waldman, Nahum M., *The Recent Study of Hebrew: A Survey of the Literature with Selected Bibliography* (Cincinnati OH: Hebrew Union College Press; Winona Lake IN: Eisenbrauns, 1989).

Watson, Wilfred G.E., *Classical Hebrew Poetry: A Guide to its Techniques* (Sheffield: Sheffield Academic Press, 1984).

Weingreen, Jacob, *A Practical Grammar for Classical Hebrew*, 2nd edn (Oxford: Oxford University Press, 1959).

Weiser, Artur, *Introduction to the Old Testament*, trans. Dorothea M. Barton (London: Darton, Longman & Todd, 1961).

——, *The Psalms*, trans. Herbert Hartwell (London: SCM Press, 1962).

Wellesz, Egon, 'The Earliest Example of Christian Hymnody', *The Classical Quarterly*, 39 (1945): 34–45.

——, 'Early Christian Music', in *The New Oxford History of Music*, 4 vols (London: Oxford University Press, 1954), vol. 2, pp. 1–39.

——, 'Early Christian Music', in *The New Oxford History of Music*, rev. edn, 4 vols (London: Oxford University Press, 1955), vol. 2, pp. 1–34.

——, *A History of Byzantine Music and Hymnography*, 2nd edn (Oxford: Clarendon Press, 1961).

Werner, Eric, 'The Music of Post-Biblical Judaism', in *The New Oxford History of Music*, 4 vols (London: Oxford University Press, 1957), vol. 1, pp. 313–35.

——, *The Sacred Bridge*, 2 vols (New York: Ktav, 1959, 1984).

——, 'Jewish Music, §I, 4: The Instruments of the Temple', *New Grove*/1, vol. 9.

West, M.L., *Ancient Greek Music* (Oxford: Oxford University Press, 1992).

——, 'The Babylonian Musical Notation and the Hurrian Melodic Texts', *M&L*, 75 (1994): 161–79.

Whitelam, Keith, *The Invention of Ancient Israel: The Silencing of Palestinian History* (London: Routledge, 1996).

Wilkinson, John (trans. and ed.), *Egeria's Travels*, 3rd edn (Oxford: Aris & Phillips, 1999, corrected repr. 2006).

Williams, Michael A., *Rethinking 'Gnosticism': An Argument for Dismantling a Dubious Category* (Princeton NJ: Princeton University Press, 1996).

Wilson, Robert R., *Prophecy and Society in Ancient Israel* (Philadelphia PA: Fortress, 1980).

Winkler, Gabriele, *Das Sanctus. Über den Ursprung und die Anfänge des Sanctus und sein Fortwirken*, Orientalia Christiana Analecta, vol. 267 (Rome: Pontificio Istituto Orientale, 2002).

Wulstan, David, 'The Origin of the Modes', in Egon Wellesz and Miloš Velimirović (eds), *Studies in Eastern Chant*, 2 vols (Oxford: Oxford University Press, 1966, 1971), vol. 2, pp. 5–20.

Würthwein, Ernst, *The Text of the Old Testament: An Introduction to the Biblia Hebraica*, 2nd edn, trans. Erroll F. Rhodes (Grand Rapids MI: Eerdmans, 1995).

Wybrew, Hugh, *The Orthodox Liturgy* (Crestwood NY: St Vladimir's Press, 1990, repr. 2003).

Yadin, Yigael (ed.), *Megillat haMiqdash* [The Temple Scroll], 3 vols (Jerusalem: Israel Exploration Society, 1977) [in Hebrew].

—— (trans. and ed.), *The Temple Scroll*, 3 vols (Jerusalem: Israel Exploration Society, 1977–83) [English trans. of preceding item].

Index

CPSIA information can be obtained
at www.ICGtesting.com
Printed in the USA
LVOW13s0550270418
575061LV00002B/12/P

9 781138 273931